INVENTING THE NATION

Series Editor: Keith Robbins

Titles in preparation for the Inventing the Nation series:

Russia   Vera Tolz

Italy   Nick Doumanis

China   Henrietta Harrison

Ireland   R. V. Comerford

Germany   Stefan Berger

France   Tim Baycroft

The United States of America   Richard Carwardine

India and Pakistan

Ian Talbot
Professor of South Asian Studies, Coventry
University

A member of the Hodder Headline Group
LONDON
Co-published in the United States of America by
Oxford University Press Inc., New York

First published in Great Britain in 2000 by
Arnold, a member of the Hodder Headline Group,
338 Euston Road, London NW1 3BH

http://www.arnoldpublishers.com

Co-published in the United States of America by
Oxford University Press Inc.,
198 Madison Avenue, New York, NY10016

British Library Cataloguing in Publication Data
A catalogue record for this book is available from the British Library

Library of Congress Cataloging-in-Publication Data
A catalog record for this book is available from the Library of Congress

ISBN 0 340 70632 5 (hb)
ISBN 0 340 70633 3 (hb)

1 2 3 4 5 6 7 8 9 10

Production Editor: Lauren Mcallister
Production Controller: Fiona Byrne

Typeset in 10/12 Sabon by Saxon Graphics Ltd, Derby
Printed and bound in Great Britain by MPG Books Ltd, Bodmin, Cornwall

What to you think about this book? Or any other Arnold title?
Please send your comments to feedback.arnold@hodder.co.uk

Contents

Maps

General Editor's Preface

The contemporary world is both repelled and attracted by the existence of the nation. Talk of globalisation sometimes presumes that the nation will fade away as organisations and individuals build for themselves new networks which by-pass the commonalities and loyalties expressed in the idea of the nation. Nationalism, too, whenever it is that various writers have supposed it to have 'risen', has been held to have been an unmitigated disaster, at least when it has been accompanied, as it not infrequently has been, by virulent xenophobia and intolerance. In the twentieth century there were significant attempts to restrain or circumvent the influence of nationalism by creating international or supranational structures and agencies.

On the other hand, it is apparent that the nation has not in fact faded away and, despite the surge of new nations, or at least new states, in the second half of that century, there remain across the contemporary world communities which feel themselves to be nations, or are in the process of becoming nations, and who see in the attainment of statehood a legitimate, desirable and beneficial goal. In other contexts, too, old nations reaffirm themselves as necessary carriers of individuality and distinctiveness in a world threatened by homogeneity. It is asserted that the nation remains the essential building block in the structure of the contemporary world. Nationalism need not be vicious. Nations can and do speak peace unto nations.

It becomes clear, however, reading references of 'narrow nationalism' on the one hand or 'national liberation' on the other, that how particular nations come to exist or be defined remains obscure and contentious. This series revisits these issues in the light of extensive debates about national identity which have been conducted over recent decades by historians, anthropologists, political scientists and sociologists in particular. To speak of 'Inventing the Nation' picks up one of the interpretations which has gained favour, or at least excited interest. Influential writers have seen 'invention' taking place in Europe in the 'springtime of the nations' at the dawn of 'modern' history, though their explanations have varied. Others, however, have regarded 'invention' with some suspicion and identify a medieval if not primordial 'nation'. Problems of definition and location clearly abound.

In these circumstances, it is pertinent to revisit the history of particular countries with these concepts and issues firmly in mind, though individual authors are not restricted or restrained in their interpretations by the series title. It is a fortunate circumstance that the first title to be published tackles a history of particular complexity where these issues are concerned: the Indian subcontinent. It is also a history which is of major importance in the contemporary world insofar as the fallout from a failure to resolve or at least accommodate conflicts could now be nuclear. The analysis of the development of particular European nations can even look straightforward when compared with the problem of nation building in the Indian subcontinent before, during and after British rule. European ideas of nationhood were understood and in play but could they be applied (and should they be applied?) in a vast territory with such a plurality of languages, religions and cultures?

In examining these issues, Professor Talbot has boldly not restricted himself to either 'India' or 'Pakistan' or 'Bangladesh'. Rather, he brings together, in comparison and contrast, their diverging and sometimes conflicting but always interlinked interpretations of nation in an environment which can scarcely be said to offer easy answers. The author does not himself invent solutions to these problems but does make admirably clear the problems which have accompanied invention.

Keith Robbins
Vice-Chancellor
University of Wales, Lampeter

Preface

The Indian subcontinent has given birth simultaneously to an immensely complex interplay between national consciousness and local collectivities based on religious and caste identity and to simplistic and stereotypical historical narratives of community consciousness. This study addresses the paradox by first acknowledging that national and community-based collective identities were both modern Indian responses to the material developments and intellectual challenges of the colonial state, although they frequently sought to cloak themselves in the legitimacy of tradition. Second, it recognises that the interaction between community and national identity was supportive as well as conflictive, notwithstanding the apparently divergent ideological positions of secularism and communalism. The concept of communitarian nationalism coined by K. L. Tuteja (1997) is of utility in this respect. As this writer points out, a sense of national subjugation to colonial rule and the need to cooperate against it could coexist with the need to secure community interests, although there was always the danger that, under pressure, it could topple over into outright communalism.

Conflicting visions of 'secular' and 'communitarian' nationalism were intensified by the human tragedies of partition which accompanied the British departure from India. Although India and Pakistan achieved statehood, they remained nations in the making. The second part of this book examines the key institutions and ideas which have influenced the nation-building process in India and Pakistan. It reveals both their achievements and the challenges which arise from historical legacies and the increasing impact of globalisation.

This work has emerged out of a long-standing engagement with the history of the Indian subcontinent. Many friends over the years have encouraged and inspired me. I would especially like to thank Professor

Judith Brown and Professor Gurharpal Singh for their helpful comments when this work was first conceived. Thanks are also due to Christopher Wheeler at Arnold for his forbearance and to the staff of Coventry University library who processed innumerable inter-library loan requests. Especial thanks are due to Professor Francis Robinson and to Lois who were of crucial assistance to me in the early days of my career in South Asian history. Any errors of fact or omissions are my responsibility alone.

Ian Talbot
Coventry, November 1999

Glossary

Adi Granth	sacred scripture of the Sikhs
ahimsa	non-violence
akhand path	unbroken reading of the Adi Granth
amir	commander, chief
amrit	nectar; water used for Sikh initiation
anjuman	association
ashraf	gentlefolk
ashram	caste division
'Bande Mataram'	'Hail to thee mother'
bhadralok	gentlefolk
Bhagavad Gita	The Song of the Lord, part of the Mahabharata which contains Krishna's teaching to Arjun
bhakti	devotional worship
bhangra	originally rural Punjabi music and dance, now popularised in the West
Bharat	India
bindi	red mark on forehead of (mainly Hindu) women signifying that they are married
biraderi	brotherhood, patrilineal kinship group
Brahmin	member of a priestly caste
chakra	wheel
dalit	oppressed, self-designation of Untouchables
darbar	court of a ruler
desh	country

dhoti	loincloth
diwan	chief officer
Durga	the goddess as consort of Shiva
fatwa	ruling by an expert in Muslim religious law
faqir	holy man
fiqh	jurisprudence
ganj	rural market
ghadr	revolution
goonda	hired thug
gurdwara	Sikh temple
hajj	pilgrimage to Mecca
hartal	strike
havan	religious ritual involving prayer and fire
hijrat	Muslim religious flight
Hindutva	Hindu nationalism
holi	spring festival
itihas	history
intifada	uprising
izzat	honour, status
jagirdar	landholder
jai	victory
jati	occupational caste group
jihad	holy war
kafir	unbeliever, non-Muslim
Kali	the mother goddess
karma	actions, behaviour
kar sevaks	temple volunteers (especially those at Ayodhya)
khadi	handspun cloth
Khalifa	Caliph
Khalsa	Sikh brotherhood instituted by Guru Gobind Singh
kisan	peasant
kshatriya	member of warrior and ruler caste
lathi	wooden club
lingam	phallus, symbol of Shiva
Lok Sabha	house of the people; lower house of India's parliament

madrassah	Muslim college
mahant	manager of a religious centre
maharaja	great king
Mahatma	great souled one; title given to M. K. Gandhi
Majha	central Punjab lying between the Beas and Ravi rivers
malik	tribal chief
Malwa	area of Punjab south and south-east of the Sutlej river
maulana	Muslim scholar learned in the Quran
mela	fair
mofussil	rural hinterland
mohajir	Muslim migrant from India to Pakistan
moksha	salvation
mullah	preacher
murid	disciple of a *pir*
pandit	scholar
pir	a Muslim *sufi* saint, spiritual guide
pracharak	preacher (usually refers to fulltime RSS organiser)
pradesh	province
purana	ancient sacred narrative
Ramayana	Hindu epic story of Rama
sabha	council of elders
sadhu	holy man, ascetic
sajjada nashin	custodian of a Sufi shrine
sangam	Tamil association
sangathan	organisation of Hindus
sant	peripatetic Sikh teacher/preacher
Sarbat Khalsa	the entire Khalsa, assembly of Khalsa Sikhs
sati	'true one'; widow sacrificed on husband's funeral pyre
satyagraha	truth-force or soul-force; non-violent struggle
shaka	meeting/organisation for exercise, drill and ideological training
shakti	female power; energy, life-force
shariah, shariat, shari'a	Muslim law
Shiv Sena	Maharashtrian Hindu Party named after the warrior figure Shivaji
shuddhi	purification rite which became a vehicle for conversion to Hinduism
sufi	Muslim mystic

swadeshi	'own country', indigenous
swaraj	independence
takht	throne, temporal authority in Sikhism
'ulama	Muslims learned in Islamic religious sciences
urs	death anniversary of a *sufi* saint
var	heroic song of praise
varna	caste
vedanta	'end of the vedas'; school of Hindu philosophy
vedas	oldest Hindu scriptures
Vishwa Hindu Parishad	Universal Hindu Society
zamindar	landholder

Abbreviations

AIADMK	All-India Anna Dravida Munnetra Kazhagam
AIML	All-India Muslim League
AISSF	All-India Sikh Students Federation
APMSO	All-Pakistan Mohajir Students' Organisation
BJP	Bharatiya Janata Party
CENTO	Central Treaty Organisation
CPI	Communist Party of India
CPM	Communist Party Marxist
DMK	Dravida Munnetra Kazhagam
EBDO	Elective Bodies (Disqualification) Order
IDBP	Industrial Development Bank of Pakistan
ISI	Inter-Services Intelligence Agency (Pakistan)
JI	Jamaat-i-Islami
MQM	Mohajir Quami Mahaz
MQM(A)	Altaf Hussain faction
MQM(H)	Afaq Ahmed faction
OBC	Other Backward Castes
PICIC	Pakistan Industrial and Credit and Investment Corporation
PPP	Pakistan People's Party
RAW	Research and Analysis Wing (Indian Intelligence Agency)
RSS	Rashtriya Swayam Sevak Sangh
SEATO	South-East Asia Treaty Organisation
SGPC	Shiromani Gurdwana Prabandhak Committee
UDF	United Democratic Front
UNPO	Unrepresented Nations and Peoples' Organisation

VHP   Vishwa Hindu Parishad (World Hindu Congress or World Hindu Society)

WAPDA   Water and Power Development Authority

Chronology of events

1857   Civilian and military uprising against the East India Company rule
1875   Foundation of the Arya Samaj; establishment of the Muhammadan Anglo-Oriental College at Aligarh
1882   Dayananda founds first Cow Protection Society
1883   Ilbert Bill controversy
1885   Foundation of the Indian National Congress at Bombay
1892   Indian Council Act
1893   Tilak popularises Ganesh festival in Maharashtra; cow protection riots sweep UP; Swami Vivekananda attends the Parliament of the World's Religions in Chicago.
1895   Tilak revives Shivaji festival
1900   Urdu Protection Society founded in UP
1905   Partition of Bengal leads to the launching of the *swadeshi* movement
1906   Foundation of the All-India Muslim League at Dhaka
1907   Split between extremist and moderate wings of the Congress at Surat session
1909   Morley–Minto constitutional reforms establish separate electorates for Muslims; foundation of the Punjab Hindu Sabha
1911   Partition of Bengal annulled
1914–15 Ghadr movement and Besant and Tilak Home Rule League movements; first session of the All-India Mahasabha held in April 1915
1916   Lucknow Pact between the All-India Muslim League and the Congress allows cooperation between the two organisations in the Khilafat/non-cooperation movements

1919	Montagu–Chelmsford reforms; Jallianwallah Bagh massacre in Amritsar; Gandhi leads Rowlatt non-cooperation movement, his first all-India *satyagraha*
1920	Reorganisation of Congress at Nagpur Session
1920–25	*Gurdwara* reform movement
1921	Moplah uprising
1925	Foundation of the Rashtriya Swayam Sevak Sangh (RSS)
1928	Simon Commission evokes outrage because it has no Indian representation
1929	Call at Lahore annual session of Congress for 'Purna Swaraj'; Jinnah's Fourteen Points and the 'parting of the ways'; formation of the Khudai Khidmatgars
1930	Gandhi's salt *satyagraha*
1932	Communal Award provides separate representation for Sikhs and Untouchables; Gandhi's fast leads to Poona Pact with B. R. Ambedkar
1935	Government of India Act introduces provincial autonomy
1937	Muslim League polls poorly in majority areas in provincial elections; Congress forms governments in seven of the eleven Indian provinces; Muslim League reorganised at Lucknow session
1939	Muslim League celebrates day of deliverance following resignation of Congress ministries in protest against Viceroy Linlithgow's declaration without consultation that India was at war
1940	Passage of Lahore Resolution
1941	Foundation of Jamaat-i-Islami
1942	Cripps Mission and Quit India movement
1945	Collapse of Simla Conference strengthens Jinnah's status
1946	Muslim League electoral breakthrough in majority areas; Cabinet Mission proposal for a federal India; Sikh deputation calls for an independent Punjab; Great Calcutta Killing; Lord Mountbatten sent to India as the final Viceroy
1947	Transfer of power to the Indian and Pakistani Dominions amidst massacres and migrations
1947–50	Integration of Princely States; Naga secessionist movement begins following the rejection of the Naga National Council's demand for independence
1948	Indo-Pakistan war over Kashmir; Gandhi assassinated by a Hindu militant; death of Jinnah; ban on RSS lifted
1950	Indian constitution comes into effect: India is the first republic within the Commonwealth
1951	Dr S. P. Mookerjee, former president of the Hindu Mahasabha, forms the Jana Sangh
1952	Congress election victories establish the pattern of one-party dominance; language riots in East Pakistan

1953	Beginning of the formation of linguistic states in India with the creation of Andhra Pradesh; Akali Dal launches demand for Punjabi Subha
1954	Defeat of Muslim League by United Front in East Pakistan elections; dismissal of United Front government
1956	Pakistan constitution introduces presidential system of government; One Unit System introduced; militant phase of the Naga insurgency begins
1957	Second five-year plan emphasises Indian import-substitution industrialisation
1958	Ayub Khan becomes martial law administrator of Pakistan
1962	New constitution for Pakistan; India's war with China
1963	Indian government creates the state of Nagaland
1964	Nehru dies; Shashtri becomes Prime Minister; foundation of the Vishwa Hindu Parishad by Swami Chinmayananda
1965	Indo-Pakistan war over Kashmir
1966	Death of Shastri at Tashkent; syndicate chooses Indira Gandhi as Indian Prime Minister; Mizo insurgency enters militant phase
1967	Elections mark the end of the Congress system of dominance; the Pakistan People's Party (PPP) founded
1969	Yahya replaces Ayub following widespread agitation
1970	Pakistan's first national elections reveal a pattern of extreme provincialisation of politics
1971	Breakup of Pakistan with the emergence of Bangladesh following Indian military intervention; Indira Gandhi triumphs in parliamentary elections
1972	Pakistan's third constitution introduced; riots following Sind Language Bill
1973	Beginning of tribal insurgency in Balochistan
1974	Akali Dal passes Anandpur Sahib Resolution; India conducts underground nuclear explosion
1975	Proclamation of Indian emergency
1977	Election of first non-Congress government in India; introduction of Zia's martial law in Pakistan
1978	Nirankari-Sikh clash in Amritsar; foundation All-Pakistan Mohajir Students Organisation
1979	Execution of Zulfiqar Ali Bhutto; Tehrik-i-Nifaz-i-Jafria founded by Shias in response to Zia's state-sponsored Islam favouring Sunni *fiqh*
1980	Mrs Gandhi wins seventh parliamentary general election, following the disintegration of the Janata Party; Jana Sangh renamed the Bharatiya Janata Party (BJP)

1981   Rajiv Gandhi becomes the political heir following his brother
        Sanjay's death; Akali Dal launches Dharam Yudh Morcha for
        Punjab autonomy; Mandal Commission report; foundation of the
        Movement for the Restoration of Democracy in Pakistan

1983   Launching of the Movement for the Restoration of Democracy;
        insurgency in Sind

1984   Indian armed forces' action in the Golden Temple at Amritsar; Mrs
        Gandhi's assassination by her Sikh bodyguards; Delhi riots; Rajiv
        Gandhi secures Congress election triumph; formation of the
        Mohajir Qaumi Mahaz (MQM) by Altaf Hussain and cadres of the
        APMSO; VHP calls for the liberation of the Ramjanmabhoomi

1985   Partyless elections in Pakistan strengthen ethnic consciousness;
        Rajiv Gandhi accord with Sant Harchand Singh Longowal;
        Longowal assassinated

1986   Shah Bano case; Babri Masjid Committee formed

1987   MQM triumphs in Karachi elections; Bofors scandal; V. P. Singh
        forms the Janata Dal; Punjab placed under the control of the centre
        as several militant groups campaign for Khalistan

1988   Zia's death and restoration of democracy in Pakistan; Benazir
        Bhutto leads PPP government

1989   National Front wins Indian elections which mark the rise to
        prominence of the BJP, increasing its total from 2 to 85 seats;
        implementation of Mandal Commission report; Ram Shila Pujan
        programme; insurgency begins in Kashmir

1990   L. K. Advani's *rath yatra* (chariot procession); *kar sevaks* killed in
        police action at Ayodhya; armed secessionist movement in Assam;
        Pucca Qila incident in Hyderabad; dismissal of Benazir Bhutto
        government; BJP withdraws support from Janata Dal government

1991   Assassination of Rajiv Gandhi; P. V. Narasimha Rao forms minority
        Congress government; majority BJP government formed in the
        state of UP for the first time

1992   Operation Cleanup; economic liberalisation further encouraged in
        India; destruction of the Babri Masjid by *kar sevaks* leads to serious
        communal rioting; Beant Singh heads Congress ministry in Punjab

1993   Political crisis in Pakistan following the dismissal of Nawaz Sharif
        results in the return to power of Benazir Bhutto after elections;
        Indo-Pakistan Cold War persists

1994–5 Mounting violence in Karachi occasioned in part by MQM
        factionalism; return to 'normalcy' in Indian Punjab

1996   Thirteen-day minority BJP government; Bhutto government
        dismissed in Pakistan, in part because of alleged extra-judicial
        killings in Karachi

1997   Improvement in Indo-Pakistan relations under the Gujral doctrine;
        celebration of fiftieth anniversary of independence; power tussle in
        Pakistan between the government of Nawaz Sharif and the judiciary

1998   Fall of Gujral government; BJP-led government takes office;
        nuclear tests by first India and then Pakistan; growing disquiet in
        Pakistan about the domination of the Punjab in national life – the
        powerbase of Nawaz Sharif
1999   Bus diplomacy; Lahore declaration; fall of Vajpayee BJP-led
        coalition; Indo-Pakistan conflict in Kargil; military coup removes
        Nawaz Sharif from power; National Democratic Alliance led by
        BJP wins Indian general election

Introduction

The television pictures of soldiers scrambling over fences to seize public buildings in Islamabad in the coup of 12 October 1999 once again turned the international spotlight on Pakistan. The internal calm that greeted the army action contrasted with the frenzied media responses in the West. In a series of radio interviews, I was repeatedly asked to comment on the dangers raised by the military intervention; yet for many Pakistanis the attitude was one of relief. We live in a fast-changing world in which instantaneous judgements are called for and in which the emphasis is on the present rather than the past. In another interview earlier in the year, despite being assured by the producer that the theme would be an examination of Pakistan's 52 years of independence, the conversation revolved entirely around the crisis of the moment following the military clashes between India and Pakistan in the Kargil region of Kashmir.

Contemporary developments, whether in the subcontinent or elsewhere, can only be fully understood in their historical context. The emotions aroused by the Kashmir issue must be traced back to the Pakistani sense of injustice in 1947 and to the searing psychological impact of partition violence and migration across much of North India. To understand the 1999 Pakistan coup, we need to move beyond personalities to discuss the role of the army in the nation-building process since independence, and the circumstances in which it has intervened in politics. Similarly, the quiescent responses to the coup arise not just from the unpopularity of the deposed Prime Minister Nawaz Sharif, but also from the army's long-established image in Pakistan and its importance as an employer, educator and development agency.

The Pakistan coup occurred hard on the heels of India's third general election in three years. This brought to office the National Democratic Alliance (NDA) of Atal Bihari Vajpayee, which won 301 of the 543 seats in the Lower House of Parliament. Congress, led by Sonia Gandhi, suffered its third consecutive election defeat. The BJP, the leading component in the NDA, emerged as the single largest party, although it polled 4 per cent less of the vote than Congress, whose share rose to nearly 29 per cent. An immediate journalistic response was to interpret the results as a defeat for the secular Congress by the Hindu nationalist (some termed it fundamentalist) BJP. Again, viewed in a longer historical perspective, the situation is not so clear-cut. The past decade has witnessed increased voter hostility to sitting MPs of all parties. Moreover, it has seen the rise not only of the BJP as the mouthpiece of Hindu nationalism, but of regional and lower-caste and *dalit* (Untouchable) parties. Although the 1999 general elections were cast as a struggle between two national parties with rival visions of India, the outcome hinged on the ability to forge strategic regional alliances and on the anti-incumbency factor. The BJP suffered less than Congress from the latter and was readier to play the coalition game. In order to do so, it had to lay aside some of the most cherished ideals of its hardcore supporters regarding the scrapping of Kashmir's special constitutional status, the temple-building programme at Ayodhya and the imposition of a uniform civil code. In the words of one distinguished scholar, the Hindutva (Hindu nationalist movement), 'arguably the most authoritarian movement ever in power in the country, has come to power at a time when the prospects for actually imposing cultural homogeneity, political unity and uniform governance on the country as a whole never seem bleaker' (Hansen, 1999, p. 237). Nevertheless, BJP-led governments at state level have attempted, with some success, to impose Hindutva values by renaming Muslim provincial cities, ignoring Urdu as a language and altering historical textbooks. The Shiv Sena–BJP government, following the 1995 Maharashtra state elections, disbanded not only the Minorities Commission, but the Srikrishna Commisssion of Inquiry into the horrific Bombay riots of December 1992 and January 1993 in which Shiv Sena had been implicated. The coalition government also cut the grant-in-aid to the Urdu Academy and the metropolis of Bombay was renamed Mumbai.

There are thus no simple answers to such questions as whether Pakistan is governable only by the army, or whether the BJP is capable of reinventing India in its own image. The present and future prospects of the subcontinent are better understood, however, when there is a grasp both of the colonial legacy's impact on governance and identity formation and of the influence upon them of rapid contemporary socio-economic transformation. Can, for example, the influence of the army in Pakistan's politics be explained in part by an inherited viceregal tradition of governance? Is the appeal of the Hindu nationalist movement derived in part from the fears of the middle class anxious to preserve its 'security and respectability' from an 'uncontrollable social world'? (Hansen, 1999, p. 193). This book will attempt to answer such questions. Nevertheless, the task is difficult. Not only are many of the events highly complex and contradictory, but they have been fought over tenaciously by historians.

Colonialist historiography, because of its conservatism and Eurocentricism which denied agency to its 'native' subjects, has been discredited in a liberal post-imperial age. At its crudest, in, for example, accounts of the 1857 'Mutiny', India provided no more than an exotic and dangerous backdrop for the display of British character and virtues. There are faint echoes of this attitude in modern travelogues of the subcontinent of the 'great train journey' genre. They convey the sense that India is exotic, but also reassuringly familiar as a result of the legacies of the Raj, whether it is the taking of afternoon tea, the presence of steam trains, or such Gothic masterpieces as the Victoria Terminus in Bombay, which was inspired by George Gilbert Scott's St Pancras Station.

The state or official history of India and Pakistan cannot be regarded as any less romanticised. The great-man-of-history approach has been perpetuated in many official studies of the roles of Nehru, Gandhi and Jinnah in the freedom struggle. Recent attempts to provide Jinnah with a more realistic human personality, both on celluloid and in print, have evoked immense hostility in Pakistan from the guardians of state history. Equally problematic are community histories, each with their religious, caste or linguistic axes to grind. Flying in the face of the evidence, the refugees from India (*mohajirs*), in order to strengthen their claim to their rights in Pakistan, maintain that two million of their brethren died in the massacres which accompanied the 1947 partition of the subcontinent.

While some writers would accept the idea of India being invented around the 1880s and now being reinvented afresh by the Hindutva movement, others would regard it as a natural 'given' which can be traced to a golden Vedic age in antiquity. Similarly, Pakistan may be variously regarded as a modern invention or as the 'natural' outcome of two separate Hindu and Muslim nations inhabiting the subcontinent from the time of the first invasions of Muhammad Bin Qasim in AD 712. Still another understanding is that Pakistan was contingent upon the intentional and unintentional divide-and-rule policies of the colonial state. Such issues point us to wider debates and understandings of group identities, which in shorthand terms can be called modernist, perennialist and primordialist theories of identity formation.

Those who see the nation as a 'natural order' are regarded as primordialists, whilst those who regard it as a recent construct arising from the socio-economic transformation of the past two centuries are modernists. Perennialists understand nationalism as being rooted in long-standing ethnic allegiances, but do not regard these as immutable. In recent years, modernism's 'meta-narrative' has been increasingly 'deconstructed' by postmodernists who emphasise multiculturalism and fragmentation and see lying beyond the nation state both a new identity politics and a globalised culture.

Despite its critiques, however, the modernist paradigm dominates and is a potent influence on the 'nation-building' activities of many third world states. One of India's greatest twentieth-century figures, Jawaharlal Nehru, who was Prime Minister from independence until his death in 1964, sought to forge a new national unity resting on a modernised relationship between a politicised and socially mobilised citizenry and an intrusive state.

Two important refinements were made to modernist understandings of nationalism during the 1980s. Eric Hobsbawm's work (1983) on the 'invention of tradition' understood nations and nationalism primarily as cultural constructs. They are held together in a time of rapid social change by invented neo-traditional symbols and practices. Nations, despite their claims to antiquity, are modern inventions. This idea of the nation as a construct was further refined by Benedict Anderson's simultaneous publication (Anderson 1983). This maintained that nations were 'imagined communities' made possible by the emergence of 'print capitalism'. The nation is an abstraction because its members will never know each other on a one-to-one basis, but the technology of print communications and the interaction of 'commodity capitalism' provide the necessary conditions for its 'imagining'. Taking his cue from these insights, Sudipta Kaviraj has declared:

> India, the objective reality of today's history, whose objectivity is tangible enough for people to try to preserve, to destroy, to uphold, to construct and to dismember, the reality taken for granted in all attempts in favour and against, is not an object of discovery but of invention. It was historically instituted by the nationalist imagination of the nineteenth century.
>
> Kaviraj (1992, p. 1)

Hobsbawm and Anderson have been criticised for their reductionist Eurocentric approaches. Nevertheless, their works remain influential texts in the general theory of nationalism. This study will shed light on the suitability of their ideas for a non-literate and immensely plural society.

Although early Indian historians such as the Bengali author Kedarnath Datta in his *Bharatbarsher Itihas* (1860) continued to utilise Puranic terminology and traditional mythological periodisation, indigenous historiography increasingly adopted the 'factual' and 'scientific' historical practice of the dominant European culture. This 'new' historiography fed both the streams of a primordialist view of the nation derived from the organicist German understanding of nationalism and French and English positivist, and thus modernist, understandings of historical progress.

Nehru, in his magisterial autobiographical work, *The Discovery of India,* (1946), blended a perennialist and voluntarist understanding, but his actions as Indian Prime Minister epitomised the modernist, 'constructed', understanding of the nation.

Despite the empiricist character of Indian historiography and the reluctance of South Asian scholars to engage in theoretical debate (a notable exception was the 1979 controversy between Brass and Robinson on instrumentalist and primordialist understandings of Islam's role in Muslim separatism), most works have been implicitly influenced by these approaches. Christopher Bayly (1985), for example, in his examination of communalism (the essentialisation and politicisation of religious community) over the *longue durée* of the pre-colonial era reflects a perennialist approach. Mendelsohn and Vicziany's recent study of the Untouchables (1998) blends perennialism and modernism in the judgement that 'the British did not "imagine" the Untouchables into existence. Rather they helped create ... the conditions whereby an Untouchable leadership could attempt to assert an independent political presence united across caste and region for the first time.' (p.18). Official histories of the emergence of Pakistan (Qureshi, 1962; Malik, 1963), on the other hand, are unambiguously cast in primordialist terms with their attachment to the two-nation theory.

Rival accounts which stress the colonial state's role in the emergence of a Muslim political identity are, on the other hand, modernist in their conception. This is most explicit in the linkage of Muslim separatism with Deutsch's social mobilisation arguments and in Paul Brass's (1979) portrayal of the elite construction of the Pakistan demand for and 'instrumentalist' use of Islam for the purposes of political mobilisation. In one sense, of course, Pakistan was 'invented' first as a term and then as a nation carved out of a united India. But such 'invention' only carried power because it drew on the deep-seated cultural values and anxieties of sections of the North Indian Muslim community.

Robin Jeffrey (1986) has explicitly utilised Anderson's modernist concept of 'print capitalism' to explain the emergence of Sikh militancy during the 1980s in the Punjab. The background to the Kashmir *intifada* is seen by Sumit Ganguly (1997) in terms of the increase of political mobilisation arising from the growth of literacy and the resulting expansion of the mass media. A new generation of politically aware Kashmiri youth was not only conscious of political developments elsewhere in India and the wider world, but was less tolerant of the 'local chicanery' that had accompanied the electoral process in the state from its initial polls in 1957. Accounts such as that by Gyanendra Pandey (1989), which link the emergence of a monolithic Hindu identity with the colonial state's classificatory mechanisms and reading of history, are equally explictly modernist in approach.

Sudipta Kaviraj has provided one of the most striking accounts of the imaginary institution of India in the modernist setting of colonial rule. In an echo of the Italian intellectual Gramsci, he links the historicist and anachronistic tendency of much historical 'nationalist' writing precisely to the fact that:

the [Indian] nation is a thing without a past. It is radically modern. It can only look for subterfuges of antiquity. It fears to face and admit its own terrible modernity, because to admit modernity is to make itself vulnerable. As a proposal for modern living, on a scale quite unprecedented ... in a society still knowing only one legitimizing criterion – tradition – it must seek to find past disguises for these wholly modern proposals.

Kaviraj (1992, p.13)

This book, despite its appearance in a series entitled 'Inventing the Nation', does not deal just in the modernist constructionist model, but synthesises elements from all of the above paradigms. If it leans towards any single theoretical model it is that of Anthony Smith's (1998) ethno-symbolism. This acknowledges nationalism as an ideology arising from the challenges of modernisation, but also recognises that it builds on pre-existing shared identities. Crucial to ethno-symbolism, as to this book, is the way in which modern nationalists have not 'invented', but rather rediscovered and reinterpreted the symbols, myths and popular memories of pre-modern identities. Hence the importance this book attaches to history's role in forging modern national and communal attachments.

The theme of the first part of the book is that the 'imagined cultural artefact' of Indian nationalism was in reality a blend of tradition and modernity rather than, as Anderson argues, the replacement of traditional cosmological beliefs and 'hierarchical consciousness' by modern 'bonds of human affection' based on notions of fraternity and equality. Moreover, the emergent national self was not, as Anderson portrays it, self-defining, but was rather accompanied by an overt process of differentiating self from other. This was as much central to 'popular nationalism', with its 'otherising' of Muslim from Hindu, as to the 'official nationalism' which Anderson deprecates in his model. Nationalism in the subcontinent was thus neither an entirely 'new consciousness' as Anderson argues, nor was it constructed solely around notions of self-sacrifice and fraternity, but carried with it rather the seeds of divisions which could culminate in fratricidal conflict.

If Indian nationalism contained within its 'imagined' consciousness elements of traditional values inconsistent with Anderson's modernist assumptions, the supposed 'traditional' identities of religion and ethnicity possessed aspects of modernity that represented a break with the past. An enhanced awareness of belonging to a larger religious or ethnic community, just as to a national one, resulted at the intellectual level from the 'reinvention of tradition' and at the material level from the impact of social mobilisation on localised ascriptive loyalties centred around the family and occupational group. Attachment to a supra-local caste identity, to a sense of regional identity, like for example Bengali (Kaviraj, 1992, p. 23), or to a Hindu identity, was in fact as 'modern' as attachment to Indian nationalism. It reflected a similar indigenous engagement with European ideas. This was reflected in the importance religious reformers attached to monotheism and scripture in the forging of a 'neo-Hindu' identity. This intellectual process has in fact been dubbed by Christophe Jaffrelot 'strategic syncretism' (1995, p. 3).

Religious reformers cloaked this modernist transformation by appeals to the past, especially to the myth of a Vedic golden age. The past to which they turned for justification was, however, a past largely understood through the writings of Western Orientalist scholars. The back-to-basics endeavours of the reformers resulted not in a restoration of tradition, but the construction of a hybrid neo-traditional value system.

If identities based on the 'givens' of religion and ethnicity thus became 'modernised' by the colonial impact, nationalism became 'traditionalised' in order to dig deeper roots in Indian society. If it had remained simply the Western-educated elites' emulation of European beliefs, it would have made no headway. By grounding it in Indian values and culture, opponents of the Raj could communicate to a much wider audience. The increasing Hindu cultural strain within Indian nationalism, however, alienated minority communities. Even amongst Hindus, the heavily Brahminised elements within Indian nationalism proved divisive. This was particularly the case within southern Dravidian India.

Both the fixed view of primordialists and the constructionist outlook of modernisation theories rooted in the European historical experience miss the complexities and subtleties of these processes. An important focus in the second part of the book is the way in which the ambiguous relationship between tradition and modernity in both Indian and Pakistani nationalism has continuously complicated the nation-building process in the post-independence era.

Chapter 1 introduces 'traditional' Indian notions of community and authority and examines the impact upon them of Western technology and 'Orientalist' understandings. It argues that Indian responses to the colonial impact laid the basis for the 'construction' of communal and ethnic as well as of national identities. Indian ideas and new senses of community form the theme of the succeeding chapter. Chapter 3 explores the articulation of community and national identities to wider sections of society. The role of the press, novels and short stories is discussed at the elite level and the role of songs, poetry, rituals and festivals at the popular level. The fourth chapter examines how these ideas were institutionalised by socio-religious movements in the Hindu, Muslim and Sikh communities.

Chapter 5 examines the movement from collective consciousness to political community. The importance of the 'event' as a catalyst for politicisation is brought out by means of a number of case studies. The next chapter examines the emergence of the Congress as a mass movement under Gandhi's leadership and also asks the question why the Muslims alone were able successfully to stake a claim for nationhood beside the

Indian nationalists in 1947. It also considers the importance of partition for future community identity. The remaining chapters consider the processes of nation building and identity politics in the post-independence era. Chapters 7 and 8 focus on ideas, institutions and nation-building strategies in India and Pakistan. The final chapters examine the impact of globalisation and the challenges to Indian and Pakistani national unity in recent years.

|1|

Community, nation and the British Raj

We pigeon holed everyone by caste and if we
could not find a true caste for them, labelled
them with the name of hereditary occupation. We deplore
the caste system and its effect on social and economic
problems, but we are largely responsible for the system
we deplore ... Government's passion for labels and
pigeon holes has led to the crystallization of the caste
system.

Superintendent of Government of India 1921 Census
Operations (cited in Das, 1994, p. 191)

Much recent scholarship has focused on the modernising impact of the Raj. This is seen in terms of ideas, institutions and economic and infrastructural change. The colonial state introduced educated Indians to Western concerns with progress, technological mastery over nature and the ideals of democracy and nationhood. New institutions included not just an intrusive state organised around the principles of bureaucratic rationalism, but representative political bodies at local, district, provincial and eventually national level. At the heart of socio-economic transformation was a communications revolution centred around the improved roads, the introduction of railways and the explosion of printed publications. These developments encouraged a greater movement of goods, ideas and people than ever before.

Many writers attribute a reinforced sense both of 'Indianness' and of caste and religious community to this colonial impact. Some accounts see increased community awareness arising not just from the changes brought by the British, but their uneven spread. There were winners and losers in the scramble to respond to the new environment. Even within localities some communities profited from the British presence, while others saw their fortunes decline. A classic case can be seen in the United Provinces (UP) where the impact of the railways on trade in agricultural and industrial goods in its western region led to the rise of commercial groups whose Hindu revivalist sentiments prompted a Muslim separatist reaction. In eastern UP, however, railways undermined the trade of existing riverine entrepots without encouraging the rise of new trade centres, Gorakhpur excepted (Robinson, 1975, p. 59). A conservative Hindu–Muslim landlord composite culture based on attachment to Urdu thus survived much longer in eastern than western UP.

The bulk of this chapter will focus on the Raj's modernising impact during the closing decades of the nineteenth century. It is nevertheless important at the outset also to consider ways in which British rule may have 'traditionalised' Indian society and to raise the interlinked question of how 'traditional' pre-colonial India was.

British rule and the 'traditionalisation' of Indian society

Explanations for the 'traditionalisation' of Indian society under British rule focus on the limited capacity of the colonial state, its conservative security concerns and its blocking off of earlier processes of political and social change. Such understandings play down the differences between the colonial state of the second part of the nineteenth century and East India Company rule a century earlier. The portrayal of the British Raj as a 'thin' state, adapting itself to native conditions, is diametrically opposed to the dominant image of an intrusive colonial state fracturing society. Nevertheless, it does point up the conservatism of British rule and the important role which was played by native collaborators. Even if one disagrees with the portrayal of the colonial state as playing little more than a night watchman role, the British were always pragmatic rulers, more preoccupied with law and order than with developmentalist concerns. Since independence, the Indian state has engaged in social engineering on a far greater scale than the British ever contemplated. The British presence in India, however, resulted in the unleashing of ideas and patterns of socio-economic change with often unintended consequences. Even a 'thin' colonial state could therefore have ushered in considerable modernisation.

More convincing are arguments which see 'traditionalisation' as the outcome of British attempts to limit the effects of rapid socio-economic change in the cause of political stability. In Oudh and the Punjab primogeniture was introduced to prevent the breakup of large landed estates. In the latter province the British also put up legal barriers, most notably in the 1900 Alienation of Land Act, to the permanent alienation of land from agriculturalists to the moneylenders who were eager to acquire it as values rocketed. In another effort to shore up the rural elites whose loyalty had been crucial at the time of the 1857 revolt, the British also uniquely privileged custom over religious law with respect to personal law. The introduction of the Islamic law would have increased women's rights with regard to divorce and most crucially inheritance (Saiyid, 1998), although at the expense of the breakup of large landholdings. But the British were just as prepared to uphold the status quo in matters of personal law in order to prevent land alienation from 'traditional' powerholders as they were to overturn their free market beliefs. Customary practice was enshrined with the force of the colonial legal system in the Punjab Laws Act of 1872. This measure, along with the later Alienation of Land Act, encouraged the emphasis on tribal as opposed to Islamic identity amongst rural Punjabi Muslims.

Finally there is the argument that the British demilitarisation of Indian society blocked off previous avenues of mobility and therefore ironically contributed to its 'traditionalisation' (Kaviraj, 1997, p. 122). What appeared ancient was in fact a recent social system frozen by the incoming colonial rulers. This understanding leads into a consideration of the nature of pre-colonial Indian society and its sense of identity.

'Traditional India'

Colonial historiography provided the stereotype of a 'changeless' village India before the advent of the British. It is now apparent that Indian society, especially in the wake of the collapse of Mughal authority, was dynamic. This period saw the rise of the Jats to prominence in the Punjab, while in what is now UP armed ascetic Vaishnava and Saiva orders wielded considerable political authority in the confused conditions of eighteenth-century North India. This was an extension of their earlier 'tax-collecting' activities at Hindu pilgrimage sites. Membership of these ascetic orders cut across caste boundaries. Social mobility accompanied the frequent changes in political power. In this analysis British rule brought about, at least in some respects, a 'traditionalisation' as much as a modernisation of Indian society. This resulted, first, from shutting off the avenues of eighteenth-century military mobility, thereby creating a more static village-based society in which both religious and caste identity became more important; second, by ossifying previously fluid and uncodified religious rights and identities. Many of the hierarchies that marked colonial India were thus not steeped in antiquity, but were of modern origin.

Scholarship has also been concerned with the extent to which a sense of 'Indianness' and communal solidarity and conflict pre-dates the colonial era. With regard to the former, some recent research again parts company with the outlook of the Raj. This was exemplified by John Strachey's (1823–1907) famous comment made in 1885 that, 'there is not, and never was an India, nor ever any country of India, possessing according to European ideas, any sort of unity, physical, political, social or religious; no nation, no "people of India" of which we hear so much'. A number of historians, however, have drawn attention to the albeit brief periods of imperial rule from the Guptas (circa AD 320–540) onwards as a factor in shaping supra-local allegiances. They have also pointed to the Hindu scriptures' sacrilisation of Indian geography and to its actualisation through the perambulations of pilgrims and holy men. This practice indicates that Hindu belief and practice were not totally encapsulated in local community situations. The caste system itself is seen as providing trans-local cohesion with its uniform regulations regarding social behaviour. Such regulations were based on the Brahminic vision of a universal moral order. Finally, a sense of Indianness has been linked to the wide geographical spread of both high culture aesthetics and popular myths and customs.

Communal solidarities and conflicts, it has also been argued, possess a pre-colonial history. The works of such writers as C. A. Bayly (1985) and Katherine Prior (1990) question the depiction of eighteenth-century Indian society as small-scale, static and syncretic. They maintain that the regional states of the Sikhs, Marathas and Bhumihar Brahmins of Benares, which succeeded the Mughals, actively patronised religion in their public ceremonial as part of their assertion of independence, while at the local level there was increasing competition between a declining Muslim service gentry and rising Hindu merchant classes. A further feature of the 'pre-history' of communalism was the growth of an elite-level view of an all-India Hindu identity arising from the increased trade, military mobility and pilgrimage of the eighteenth century. Whatever we may think of this argument, it is clear that there were 'existing fault-lines' for the creation of nineteenth-century communal identities. Moreover, the preceding century witnessed much greater social mobility than those studies admit that juxtapose the modern phenomenon of communalism with the small-scale syncretic and sedentary society of pre-colonial India.

It is thus clear that pre-colonial Indian realities do not fit easily either with primordialist portrayals of monolithic communities, or with the modernist vision of a static society dominated by localised and eclectic cultural identities. Normative understandings of social organisation and duties provided by the Hindu and Muslim scriptures did not necessarily reflect the reality of social practice. At the same time, the eighteenth century had witnessed important shifts in power, encouraging more community-mindedness. Finally, pilgrimage and the practice of Hindus marrying outside their natal village ensured that individuals did possess some awareness of a supra-local caste and religious identity.

The colonial impact: institutions

While British rule displayed some similar features to the Mughal Empire and even borrowed institutions such as the *darbar* in attempts to 'traditionalise' itself, the colonial state was far more intrusive. Modern technology had increased its coercive capacity. Troops, for example, could be moved around the country more rapidly than ever before with the introduction of the railways from the early 1860s onwards. By the eve of the First World War, India possessed the fourth largest railway system in the world. The state's ability to transmit information had also been revolutionised. Again, with respect to law and order, reports of unrest could be flashed from one end of the subcontinent to the other by telegram. The advent of the printing press enabled all types of knowledge to be amassed on an unprecedented scale. Indeed, the almost insatiable thirst for knowledge was another characteristic of British rule which marked a break with the past. Especially decisive was the enumeration of population, with the introduction of the decennial census from 1871 onwards. The imperial head count revealed that the Indian population was increasing slowly and stood at around 280 million. Much more important, in an age of the introduction of representative politics, was the information it yielded up regarding the relative local strength of the Hindu, Muslim and Sikh communities.

Ever since the publication in 1978 of Edward Said's seminal study *Orientalism,* some scholars have recognised that European Orientalist knowledge, classification, definition and representation of non-Western societies were more about the power to control than about intellectual curiosity. Orientalism was first premised on the military ability to control the colonised and, second, helped through 'knowledge power' to perpetuate this domination. Such writers as George Stocking (1991) have revealed how ethnography and philology were tools of colonialism.

Immense knowledge of local society was required, not only in the regular round of land revenue settlement, but in such 'sentinel' regions as the Punjab in order to bolster the 'traditional' institution of the tribe, the patrilineal kin-based community. Customary personal law, for example, frequently varied from district to district in the province. 'Orientalist empiricism' attained its intellectual apogee in the 1870s and 1880s with a series of settlement reports, codification of customary law and census reports by such scholar administrators as Septimus Smet Thorburn (1844–1924), Sir Charles Louis Tupper (1848–1910) and Sir Denzil Charles Jelf Ibbetson (1848–1908). Like a later generation of structural–functionalist anthropologists in Africa, they provided the knowledge of social institutions necessary for colonial administration. The politically motivated maintenance of the status quo was not only made possible, however, by the Punjab's 'amateur anthropologists', but was rationalised by their studies, which drew on the evolutionist ideas of Sir Henry Maine (Dewey, 1991, p. 29) with respect to jurisprudence and property rights to argue that India was not yet sufficiently advanced to have Western notions of contract and ethics imposed on it.

The new institution of the census was the crowning glory of the colonial rational bureaucratic state. A decennial census was introduced throughout

India from 1881 onwards. The censuses were not of course about curiosity for its own sake, but in Said's terms formed part of the 'expropriation' of knowledge in order to better sustain the imperial edifice. The censuses profoundly influenced Indian self-perceptions. They were forced to identify themselves with a religious, caste or tribe category. They were also made aware of the numbers of their fellows. This was important with the spread of political representation, for numbers count in a democracy. The essentialisation of community by the census operations is brought out most clearly in the following statement from Denzil Ibbetson who supervised the 1881 enumeration in the Punjab. 'Every native who was unable to define his creed', he declared, 'or described it by any name *other than that of some recognised religion* [emphasis added], was held to be classed as a Hindu' (Census of India Report, 1881, vol 1, p. 19). The multiple identities and fluid boundaries of Punjabi society were to be reduced to religious categories which were easily understandable to British 'outsiders'. Two decades later, the Indian Census Commissioner E. A. Gait expressed similar attitudes when rapping the Bombay census superintendent over the knuckles for using the hybrid term 'Hindu-Muhammadans' for groups who did not fit easily into any category. The persons concerned, Gait opined, should have been assigned to 'the one religion or the other as best he could' (Census of India Report, 1911, I:i, p. 118). Interestingly, while the British in India were essentialising religion for enumeration purposes, it was omitted as a category in the censuses they conducted at home. Whether or not the Indian census was as much a political exercise as a scientific survey, its consequences for self-identity and its politicisation were immense. This can be illustrated with reference to both the Untouchable and Sikh communities.

From the time of the 1871 census onwards, the issues of who were the Untouchables and whether they were separate from or a part of Hindu society exercised enumerators. In a situation where numbers would count in terms of political power, the question of the Untouchables' identity took on an increasing significance. Reformers' attacks on the orthodox exclusion of Untouchables from Hindu temples and even, in parts of South India, from being able to use public roads at all on the grounds of their ritual pollution, were prompted not just by a rising tide of humanitarianism, but by the anxieties arising from the colonial state's possible location of them as a non-Hindu community. Indeed, if it had not been for Gandhi's celebrated 'fast unto death' in September 1932 the Untouchables would have secured separate electorates. Eventually the Untouchable leader Dr B. R. Ambedkar (1891–1956) gave way in the Poona Pact which greatly increased the reservation of seats for Untouchable candidates, although they were to be elected from general, i.e. Hindu, rather than separate electorates.

By this juncture the British census enterprise had established an overarching identity of the 'depressed classes' which for the first time lumped Untouchables from different regions and communities together in a single social category. The process was completed in 1936 when a list of scheduled castes was promulgated. These were eligible for preferential treatment because of their 'depressed' and 'outcaste' situation. Both the ideological identity of the scheduled castes and the principle of affirmative action were to acquire further legal status in the 1950 Indian constitution. The emergence of the scheduled castes/Untouchables ideology in the bureaucratic context of the colonial state has led some scholars to claim that the British invented the Untouchable identity. More accurately, the British may be said to have essentialised into monolithic uniformities clusters of communities which occupied a degraded status in terms of the principle of purity and pollution. The colonial essentialisation of Untouchability was no different from that of caste or religious community. The reality beneath the Untouchable identity was that Chamars (leather workers) from the UP, Mahars (village servants) from Maharashtra, Holeyas (village servants) from Karnataka and Chuhras (sweepers) across India, to name just some of the major Untouchable groups, possessed little in common. Just as traditional occupation (e.g. the Chamar's leather working) led caste Hindus to look down on Untouchables as ritually defiled, so there were levels of degradation within the Untouchable grouping itself. Dietary habits led some Untouchables to regard themselves as 'cleaner' than other communities. The low status, for example, of the third largest Untouchable group in Bihar, the Musahars (landless labourers), was linked with their reputation as rat eaters (Mendelsohn and Vicziany, 1998, p. 246). Untouchable groupings in fact displayed many features of caste Hindu society in terms of a sense of ranking, attachment to endogamy and restrictions on inter-dining. Such divisions in part explain the failure of the great Untouchable leader Dr Ambedkar to establish a strong Untouchable political interest, despite the reservation of seats following the 1932 Poona Pact. Ambedkar's greatest support was always amongst his own Maharashtrian Mahar community.

The colonial state's arrogation of the right to decide who was a member of a communal grouping raised increasing problems of definition with respect to the Sikhs. From the 1868 Punjab census onwards, they were listed as a separate religious group, despite the claims of some Hindu ideologues that they were a reformist group within the Hindu fold. Sikh revivalists' endeavours to reconstitute the Sikh tradition around the 'Khalsa sub-tradition' were undoubtedly spurred on by the fact that until the 1901 census only Khalsa Sikhs were defined as 'Sikhs'. The drive for a Sikh autonomous identity received its fullest rhetorical expression when Khan Singh Nabha produced his famous tract, *Ham Hindu Nahin* ('We Are Not Hindus'). The greatest practical achievement was to secure legislation of a de-Brahminised Sikh marriage ceremony with the passage in October 1909 of the Anand Marriage Act.

Hindu revivalists reacted violently to the suggestion that the 1901 census should both widen the definition of 'Sikhs' and eliminate Untouchables from the Hindu category. The census reports revealed that the Hindu proportion of the Punjab's population was falling, leading some Punjabi Hindus to fear that theirs was a 'dying race'. An important contributory factor was the Muslims' higher birthrate. Hindu authors, however, focused attention on the inroads of Christianity. In all, a forty-fold increase was recorded in the size of the Christian community between the 1881 and 1911 censuses. Arya Samajist Hindu reformers responded with 'strategic syncretism'. They echoed many of the missionaries' criticisms of Hindu social practice: for example, 'idol worship', 'priestly domination' and 'child marriage', in order to strengthen their community from within. Most importantly, as we shall see in a later chapter, they transformed the concept of *shuddhi* (ritual purification) into a weapon of conversion. This was a reconstitution of tradition with a vengeance.

Increased communal competition was also the outcome of another British innovation: the creation of popularly elected political institutions. The colonial state was primarily authoritarian in outlook and for much of its existence did not see its role as encouraging participatory democracy. Good governance was to be secured through the activities of the civil administration. Nevertheless, part of the British rationale for their rule was the tutelage of Indians in the democratic arts which had been perfected in the mother of parliaments. Moreover, the recurring financial crises of the closing decades of the nineteenth century encouraged the establishment of a system of elective local government in order to secure consent for the raising of additional taxes.

There was thus a process of constitutional reform, from the time of the 1861 Indian Councils Act to the 1935 Government of India Act, that devolved more power into Indian hands building upwards from the localities. A number of important consequences were to flow from it. Aside from an intellectual elite, for many involved in politics 'rice and roti' local issues were to take precedence over commitment to ideas. All-India parties like the Congress and the Muslim League thus had to grow by means of accommodating local interests and those who were powerful in these settings. To achieve subcontinental success, whether involved in agitation against the Raj or in vote winning, it was necessary to stitch together alliances and articulate local grievances and concerns alongside national demands. This meant that politicians with a strong regional base could cut a dash in all-India politics. The key to all-India leadership ultimately lay, however, with those who through their moral authority could transcend regional affiliations and link disparate communities together in a common national cause. Gandhi, Nehru and Jinnah, the founder of Pakistan, were to be the supreme examplars of this type of leadership during the colonial era.

Local and provincial government bodies not only provided a vital role in the knitting together of all-India political organisation, they also acted as new 'arenas of conflict' for communal rivalries. These were particularly intense where processes of socio-economic change were unsettling old power arrangements, as in the towns of western UP. From the early 1880s onwards, municipal boards not only possessed tax-raising powers which could be used to reward allies and punish rivals, but considerable powers of patronage in terms of public works contracts. Finally, they gave control over sanitation regulations concerning, for example, butchers' shops and slaughterhouses. These powers were to be used by militant Hindus as soon as they gained the electoral upper hand in such towns as Moradabad, Chandpur and Bijnor in order to further their religious interests by protecting cows (Robinson, 1975, p. 82). Such actions not only offended the Muslims' religious sensibilities, but revealed the perils which they faced as a religious minority.

Indeed, it was in the rough and tumble of UP local government that a sense of a solidified Muslim interest threatened by a Hindu electoral majority first emerged. This feeling was intensified and communicated upwards into provincial and national levels of politics with the passage of time. The British creation of 'new arenas' of community conflict thus formed an important material context for the 'imagination' of community identity by political elites who were responding to the cultural and intellectual impact of colonial rule.

The colonial impact: ideas – perceptions of Indian society

The key British ideas regarding Indian society were a disbelief in a sense of Indian nationalism, with an emphasis instead on the existence of monolithic communities organised on the basis of religion and caste. Such communities were not only seen as coherent but fixed in characteristics. This idea was taken to its logical extreme in the 1872 Criminal Tribes and Castes Act which attached a hereditary criminality to a number of vagrant communities and placed them under close colonial supervision.

Mughal administrative documents also acknowledge caste as a social marker. But this referent is used unsystematically and coexists with occupational status and conceptions of 'honour' and 'respectability'. The British reading of Indian society was to have profound implications, as it not only influenced policy implementation but was internalised by significant groups of their subjects.

The ideology of martial castes provides a good example of both processes at work. The belief that the Muslim Rajputs, Sikh Jats and Hindu Dogras of the Punjab were 'naturally' suited for military service was based on 'empirical' ethnographic research. Recruiting officers produced detailed caste handbooks which provided genealogies and histories of the martial castes and details of their customs and physique all set within a fashionable social Darwinist scientific terminology. Such 'Orientalist empiricism' conveniently rationalised the movement of recruitment from more volatile areas to the politically quiescent rural Punjab.

Indians internalised this ideology and mimicked it, as in the following comment by Sir Umar Hayat Khan, the leading spokesman of the martial caste lobby. 'Everybody could not become a soldier', he declared in a speech to the Council of State in March 1922.

> If a cart horse is put in a race it will not do and similarly if a race horse is put onto a cart, it cannot pull a cart. People in India are like that, especially in the North. If a person is weak he is unable to stand the cold and dies; the theory of the 'survival' of the fittest is correct. There are some places where there are people with limbs like fingers. How on earth can they fight?
>
> Tiwana (1929, p. 105).

The British patronage of the martial castes encouraged the perpetuation of 'loyalist' sentiments in the Punjab until the eve of independence. The last two Muslim Prime Ministers of the undivided province were members of the martial castes, including Umar's son Khizr who was to oppose the Pakistan movement. The existence of the martial caste lobby was to form part of the new Pakistan state's 'democratic deficit' when the resistance of Khizr and his Unionist supporters was finally overcome in 1947.

British ideas of monolithically constituted religious communities were institutionalised with the granting of separate electorates. These were conceded for Muslims in 1909. Their scope was further extended by the 1919 Government of India Act and the 1932 Communal Award. Separate electorates had in fact been introduced piecemeal in a number of North Indian provinces from the 1880s for elections to district and municipal boards, in reponse to the declining Muslim influence on such bodies. Officials argued that, as democratisation proceeded, separate electorates were needed to safeguard the interests of the 'backward' Muslim minority. The debate still rages whether this was part of a Machiavellian divide-and-rule policy or merely reflected a colonial balancing act. While it is facile to argue that the introduction of separate electorates made the creation of Pakistan inevitable, it lent credence to the premise that people following a particular religion naturally shared common interests from which 'others' were excluded. Those seeking political power took their cue and mobilised around the symbols of identity which were recognised by the state.

The other side of the coin of separate electorates and the British attempt to balance community interests was the colonial state's attempt to demonstrate religious neutrality by withdrawing from the patronage of public religious ceremonial. Like separate electorates, this policy had the unintended consequence of sharpening community identity. As Katherine Prior (1990) has revealed, the state's withdrawal created a space for competing groups drawn from the rising Hindu merchant classes to sponsor public ritual to enhance their 'social dignity'. The spread of new Ramlila celebrations in the towns of the United Provinces in the early nineteenth century must be understood in this context. Hindu families were spurred on not only by competition from within their community, but by the need to establish a 'precedent' for their celebrations before the colonial state ossified public religious practice, which it sought to regulate while 'standing above' it. Public ritual, according to Sandria Freitag (1989), helped create a supra-local Hindu community identity. Another consequence was rising tension between 'Hindus' and 'Muslims'.

Explanations for the British understanding of Indian society

Indian nationalist writers traditionally argued that the British, for simple divide-and-rule purposes, constructed notions of a caste-ridden, communally divided society over which they could preside as a unifying factor. The inter-action between the colonial state and Indian society was, however, far more complex than such arguments would allow (Breckenridge and van der Veer, 1993). It has already been revealed that security considerations in the Punjab encouraged the construction of tribal allegiances which competed with reli-gious identities. Orientalist constructions were so versatile and pervasive that they were 'internalised' and even deployed by Indians in the nationalist struggle against colonial rule (for example, the notion of Indian spirituality and an ageless nation). This appropriation of Orientalism by nationalism has resulted, David Ludden has argued, in its not being the 'moribund legacy of colonialism that Said makes it out to be' (Ludden, 1993, p. 272). Rather it is 'embedded' in the subcontinent's contemporary political culture.

There was undoubtedly a colonial desire for order in its knowledge as well as its control of Indian society. Natives were more knowable if their behaviour was predictable. There was almost inevitably a tendency in colonial representations of Indian society to iron out the bumps of uncon-trollable multiplicities and to present the homogenised indigenous subjects desired by the state. Caste provided one manageable category by which the British could understand and control Indian society. It provided a useful key to knowing India because it could simultaneously describe complex multi-plicity and act as a totalising epistemology. Religion, along with caste, helped order colonial knowledge which might otherwise have remained resistant to fixity.

The intellectual baggage of Victorian muscular Christian servants of Empire helps in part to explain the viewing of Indian society through reli-gious spectacles. During the early years of British administration in the Punjab in the 1850s, for example, no official moved his camp on a Sunday, no regiments marched and no work was undertaken on public works projects. This was the result of the 'quiet and unostentatious example and orders of God-fearing men in authority' (Talbot, 1988b, p. 70). The

importance the British attached to religion as the principal organising feature
of Indian society was, however, already well established by this juncture.

British understandings of Indian society were 'skewed' from the late eighteenth century onwards by the impact of the increasing knowledge of Hindu
'great tradition' scripturalist understandings of social organisation. It was to
Brahmin *pandits* (scholars) and Brahminic sacred texts that the British first
turned to acquire knowledge of the society they had come to rule. They took
at face value the notions of a hierarchised and clear-cut Hindu identity which
they received. They did not at first concern themselves with the differences
between what scripture said and how society was actually organised. The
Dublin-born physician John Zephaniah Holwell (1711–98), who published a
number of early and influential works on Hinduism, had to study these scriptures in Persian or Hindi translation. Charles Wilkins was the first Englishman
to master their original Sanskrit language. The East India Company published
at its own expense his translation of the Bhagavad Gita into English in 1785.
Warren Hastings intended its deistic sentiments to appeal to a British intellectual elite influenced by Enlightenment thought and thereby to encourage a
'more generous feeling' for Indian 'natural rights'. The longer-term impact,
however, of this appreciation of the Gita was in India, where it came to be
viewed as the 'Hindu text par excellence' (Rocher, 1993, p. 228).

'Brahmanised' knowledge was seized on when the British rulers sought to
establish from the 1770s indigenous Indian laws relating to marriage and
inheritance. The Brahminical norm for 'Hindu' law encouraged first the
lumping together of tribals, Sikhs, Jains and Parsees as 'Hindus'. Complex
social structures and religious practices thus became homogenised.

Nevertheless, the colonial state, in order to legitimise itself, was not
adverse to the portrayal of Indian society as being mired in conflict between
homogenous 'Hindu' and 'Muslim' communities. The self-serving element in
the Orientalist perception has been highlighted by Gyanendra Pandey's
(1989) examination of the communal riot narrative in the colonialist reading
of Indian history. His analysis of riots at Banares and elsewhere in the United
Provinces isolates five major features in this colonial construction of communalism. First, it reduces popular politics to a problem of law and order;
second, it identifies crowd participants in terms of community and caste;
third, it assumes that doctrinal differences between Hindus and Muslims are
a 'natural' cause of violence; and fourth, it universalises particular riots and
clashes into an all-India discourse of communal conflict. Finally, it distinguishes the 'irrationality' of crowd violence from the 'legitimate' use of force
by the state. The 'convulsions' of the native society are quelled by the
presence of the colonial authorities. They thus acquire legitimacy as bringers
not only of modern civilisation and 'progress' but of communal stability.

The re-writing of Indian history in terms of a communal discourse can be
seen clearly at work in a different context in the account given below of the
Sikh uprisings against the Mughals led by Banda Bahadur. Before his capture

and death in 1715, Banda had carved a petty kingdom out of the Mughal *sarkar* (revenue subdivision) of Sirhind. The colonial account of his activities compiled in the *Punjab Provincial Gazetteer* recorded his activities as follows (this quotation and its following analysis is drawn from Alam (1986, pp. 134–55)):

> The severities of the Musalmans only exalted the fanaticism of the Sikhs and inspired a spirit of vengeance, which soon broke out into fury. Under Guru Govind's principal disciple, Banda who had been bred a religious ascetic, and who combined a most sanguinary disposition with bold and daring counsels, they broke from their retreat, and overran the east of the Punjab, committing unheard of cruelties wherever they directed their steps. The mosques were destroyed and the Mullas killed; but the rage of the Sikhs was not restrained by any considerations of religion, or by any mercy for age or sex.
>
> Whole towns were massacred with wanton barbarity, and even the bodies of the dead were dug up and thrown to the birds and beasts of prey. The principal scene of these atrocities was Sirhind.

The Orientalist reading of Indian history is very clear here. Banda Bahadur's career reflects fanatical religious animosity between Muslims and Sikhs. The phrase 'mosques were destroyed and the Mullas killed' encodes this as yet another example of communal conflict whose continuation was mitigated by the British presence. The objectivity of this representation was 'proven' by the support it drew from contemporary Persian chroniclers. If a clinching argument was required, Banda Bahadur had provided it himself by calling his struggle a *dharam yudh* (holy war).

In reality, Banda's call for 'Hindus' to join the Sikhs and defend *dharma* met with little response. Indeed Hindu Khatris from Lahore, disturbed by the disruption to their trade caused by the uprising, financed the Muslim Sayeds' fight against the Sikhs. Hindu Rajput landowners who were victims of the Sikh raids also consistently supported the Mughals. It thus appears that economic interest as much as religious community tilted the balance for or against Banda Bahadur. Even the considerable support which he received from Sikh Jats could in fact be understood in non-communal terms. Like the accounts of the 1809 riots in Banares which Gyanendra Pandey has investigated, however, the episode fed into the colonial construction of India's communal past.

The British not only overemphasised the role of communal conflict but perpetuated religious stereotypes. They were not, of course, alone in this. The great German Orientalist Friedrich Max Muller based his defence of Hindu character in part on the demonisation of the Muslim 'other', declaring that it was a 'wonder' that 'so much native virtue and truthfulness should have survived' the 'terrors and horrors of Mohammadan rule' (Chowdhury, 1998, p. 52). Mushirul Hasan (1996, pp. 185–208) has clearly revealed how a colonial paradigm of a bigoted, depraved, iconoclastic, undifferentiated Muslim community came into existence. This reflected deep-seated European anxieties concerning Islam and the challenge that Muslims provided as former rulers of India. It was 'empirically' grounded in uncontextualised translations of medieval chronicles. Hindu reformers and intellectuals widely disseminated this colonially constructed 'knowledge'. It fed into the popular pysche through the tracts of revivalists and the newly emerging form of literature, the popular novel. The Hindi writer, Kisorilal Goswami (1866–1932), for example, drew directly on British accounts in the depiction of the depravity of the Mughal Emperor Shah Jahan's court at Agra in his novel *Tara* (1902). Such popular writers as Bharatendu Harischandra (1850–85) and Pratap Narain Misra (1856–94) reduced pre-colonial Muslim rule to a catalogue of cruelty, debauchery and religious defilement. A major component of an emerging Hindu nationalism was thus the demonising of the Muslim 'other'. Hasan sees a clear link between colonial representations of Muslims and the 1980s' discourse of Hindutva (Hindu nationalism). Undoubtedly the exclusion of the Islamic influence in a consciously derived vision of a Hindu Indian civilisation has its historical roots in the European Orientalists' portrayal of Muslim culture as an 'extraneous' element in India's development.

The colonial state also reinforced caste as well as religious stereotypes. Census reports, district gazetteers and army recruitment handbooks are replete with references to 'wily' Brahmins, 'warlike' Pathans, 'sturdy' Jat peasants and 'effete' Bengali Babus. The latter were personified and immortalised in the character of the Bengali Hurree Babu in Kipling's great novel, *Kim*. Such understandings were drawn from *varna* (caste division) categorisations and the 'empirical' knowledge of local society distilled through social Darwinist understandings. In India, as elsewhere in the Empire, the British felt the greatest affinity with 'virile' races in which they could recognise some of their own traits and characteristics. The contemptuous attitude towards the 'effeminate' Bengalis comes out clearly in the following extract published in 1899:

> The Bengali's leg is either skin and bones; the same size all the way down, with knocking knobs for knees, or else it is very fat and globular, also turning in at the knees, with round thighs like a woman's. The Bengali's leg is the leg of a slave.
>
> cited in Chowdhury (1998, p. 4)

Physical weakness was equated with submissiveness. British rule was thus part of the 'natural' order of things. The cult of physical fitness and of the ideal of the armed ascetic, for example, which remains such an important feature of Hindu nationalist philosophy, was rooted in the response to the colonial stereotype of the Bengali (Chowdhury, 1998). As early as 1869, six gymnastic schools had been established in Calcutta alone.

The British tendency to view Indian society in terms of essentialised religious and caste categories was accompanied by the identification of language with national community. This was rooted in the modern European experience. It was to have important repercussions in the celebrated Hindi–Urdu controversy which along with municipal politics was so crucial in community consolidation in the UP at the close of the nineteenth century. Hindi and Urdu shared a common vocabulary, although they were written in the Nagri and Persian script respectively. Few Muslims, however, could read or write the Nagri script, which to them had an alien religious significance because it was the script in which Sanskrit was written. The noted linguist Sir George Grierson in (*The Modern Vernacular Literature of Hindustan* (1889) went so far as to claim that the British had created Hindi. This denies the agency of such figures as Bharatendu Harischandra (1850–85) in popularising the language and overlooks the fact that the late Mughal era had seen a gradual distancing of the languages which were to be later called Urdu and Hindi. Nevertheless, British rule did encourage the development of Hindi through the work of codification in grammars and dictionaries. Missionary tracts published in Hindi for a Hindu audience also helped to identify it as a Hindu language. Such publications built on earlier Orientalist speculations of a lineal linkage between Sanskrit and Hindi which marginalised the commonalities of Hindi and the 'Muslim' language Urdu.

The outcome of this colonial perception was thus likely to be a dichotomisation between Urdu and Hindi and their emergence as the 'national' languages of Muslims and Hindus. This process of differentiation was aided by the impact of print culture and by the role of Indian publicists and interlocuters of the colonial authorities, who helped establish a literary corpus of Hindi and Urdu which omitted influences from the other religious community. (For an authoritative examination of this immensely complex process see Dalmia, 1996, Chapter 4.)

The language issue became politicised with the rise of Hindu self-assertion in the United Provinces. There was a growing campaign in favour of Hindi and Nagri to replace Urdu which had become the official language of the provincial government following the abandonment of Persian in 1837. Such a move would put Muslim professionals' jobs at risk, as they used the Persian script and considered it degrading to learn Nagri. Their Hindu counterparts, however, were familiar with both the Nagri and Persian scripts because of its employment in the Muslim administrations which predated the British. The significance of the script/language controversy comes out clearly in the comment of a Hindu activist who wrote in 1868 that 'with the extinction of Hindi, the death-knell of Hindu nationality will begin to ring'.

The case for Hindi was put forward vigorously by a number of newspapers, including the *Kavi Vachan Sudha* of Bharatendu Harischandra, which was published from Benares. 'The Muslims', it declared in August 1873, 'it is true might suffer by the change [from the Persian to the Nagri script] but they are only a small portion of the community, and the interests of the few must always yield to the many' (Robinson, 1975, p. 71). A similar attitude led to the support for Hindi by Sivad Prasad through the columns of his newspaper the *Benares Akhbar.* Like Harischandra his cultural range included Urdu –

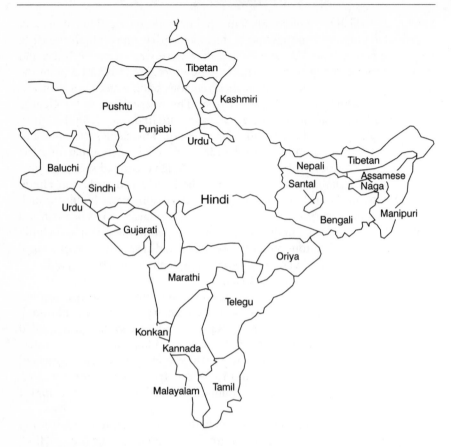

Map 1 Distribution of major languages. Note that although Urdu is Pakistan's official language it is the mother tongue in only a small area.

indeed he had written Urdu poetry in his youth. Other newspapers which supported the Hindi cause included Balkrishna Bhatta's *Hindi Pradip* of Allahabad, the *Bharat Bandhu* of Aligarh and the *Bharat Jiwan* of Benares.

The Nagri Resolution of 18 April 1900 declared that petitions could now be presented to the government in both the Persian and Nagri scripts. The sting was in the tail, however, of its last clause which laid down that 'no person shall be appointed, except in a purely English office, to any ministerial [clerical] appointment henceforward unless he can read and write the Nagri and Persian characters fluently'. Muslim protests were institutionalised through the formation of an Urdu Defence Association. Their spread into the districts and as far as Lahore, however, owed much to the coverage of the controversy by such newspapers as the *Indian Daily Telegraph* and the *Pioneer* of Lucknow. The Urdu–Hindi controversy gave a considerable fillip to Muslim separatism. It is important, however, not to view the agitation simply in terms of Hindu–Muslim conflict. Hindu Kashmiri Brahmin families and Kayasths also joined in, because they too would lose from the new importance attached to the Nagri script. The *Kayasth Reformer* published from Bareilly thus entered the lists on the side of the Muslim newspapers.

The colonial impact: socio-economic change

Muslim rulers had constructed canals and built such famous transport arteries as the fabled Grand Trunk Road, which helped to unify the subcontinent. The communications revolution which accompanied British rule, however, was qualitatively different in its impact. Not only did goods, people and ideas move more freely than ever before, but Indians were linked to the ceaseless business activity and cultural artefacts of an emerging world capitalist system. In this radically changed environment nationalist politics were able to take root and flourish.

The two decades after the 1857 revolt witnessed a communications revolution. During this period, for example, the number of miles of railway track increased from 34 miles in 1854 to 8,500 in 1880. This staggering advance had been driven forward by the twin demands of commerce and strategic interests. During the first year of its operation (1853–4) the short line which linked Bombay to Thana carried half a million passengers. One of the abiding images of modern India was created when after the opening of the Calcutta line, 12,000 third-class passengers each week grabbed whatever space was available inside and atop the inadequate carriages. The *Indian News* noted on 17 July 1855 that 'fondness for travelling by the rail has become almost a national passion among the inferior orders'. During the same period, the telegraph system had grown to 20,000 miles. A national postal service commenced in 1854 with the cheap standard rate of half an anna (an anna was one sixteenth of a rupee). Courier services for government officials and for villagers had traditionally been provided by Mahars. Within three months, there was a 50 per cent increase in the volume of mail in Calcutta. In the words of the historian Stanley Wolpert, 'The penny post served not only to unite the subcontinent as nothing else had done, but it became a most important new stimulus to learning, literacy, literature and sociocultural change of every imaginable kind' (Wolpert 1993, p. 231). While there is some hyperbole here, it is undeniable that ideas could be exchanged more rapidly and on a wider scale than ever before in the subcontinent's history.

Equally important was the growth of English as a 'link' language following the triumph of the Westernisers over the Orientalists in the East India Company Council debate over the language of instruction: a decision institutionalised in Macaulay's famous 1835 minute on education. Schooling in English for the elite who in Macaulay's phrase was to act as 'interpreters between us and the millions whom we govern' was crucially important in expanding horizons. It enabled communication across regional and religious barriers to a much greater extent than either the Mughal court language of Persian or the hybrid Hindustani had previously done. In 1837, English replaced Persian as the language of administration. Within 20 years, the universities of Calcutta, Bombay and Madras had been established to confer degrees in the arts, law, medicine and engineering through the medium of English. The importance of English as a lingua franca for an emerging all-India political community comes out clearly in the following extracts from the diary of Govindrav Babaji Joshi, a Marathi-speaking delegate to the third annual session of the Indian National Congress held in December 1887 in Madras. The first piece shows the way in which the delegates could communicate with each other in the sessions of the early Congress which were conducted solely in English. The second, in contrast, reveals the difficulties which faced the delegates outside the hallowed precincts of the Congress session.

> Today the conversation is with the delegate from the Bellari district, and tomorrow it is with the delegate from Trichanapalli. In a similar fashion, Bengali delegates interact with those from Bombay and the latter with those from Punjab. Every day one gets to talk with new delegates. The topics discussed are: the general condition of the country, the peculiarities of the regions and public affairs.
>
> [We] soon went in search of an inn for a meal ... The moment we set foot in the inn, we became utterly helpless. We tried our best to explain to the inn-keeper and his wife, in Marathi and in Hindustani, our need for a meal and at what cost. But all our efforts came to nought. We then made our intentions known ... by mimicking the act of eating. The reaction to our act was an expression *'evi, evi'* and then peals of laughter. The doctor at the rail-station had given us his peon to guide us to the rest-house. We fetched him to assist us. In Hindustani and a little English we explained to the peon our need to eat. He conveyed our wishes to the woman inn-keeper.
>
> Wagle (1991, pp. 123 and 118)

English also exposed the educated classes to Western notions of liberalism, democracy and self-determination. The 4,000-volume library of the early twentieth-century Calcutta Anushilan Bengali revolutionary group was stocked not only with anarchist materials and manuals on bomb-making material, but with histories of Mazzini, Garibaldi and the Italian Risorgimento. There was even a study of the First British Empire's main protagonist George Washington.

Western notions of community and nation were so powerful precisely because they were linked with the obvious European technological superiority. Early generations of the Western-educated almost lampooned themselves in their enthusiasm to imbibe 'modern' knowledge, manners and dress codes. Symptomatic of this atmosphere was the formation by students in Calcutta in 1838 of the Society for the Acquisition of General Knowledge. Within five years it boasted over 200 members, including such early nationalist figures as Ram Gopal Ghose and Debendranath Tagore. Significantly, the Western-educated Indian classes distanced themselves from the backward-looking revolt of 1857.

Attachment to liberalism inspired the nationalism of the early Congress moderates such as Gopal Krishna Gokhale (1866–1915) and Surendranath Banerjea (1848–1926). They argued for increased Indian political representation and share in the administration of the Raj in legalistic language, appealing to the British sense of justice and fair play. During the decades that followed, however, the British failure to live up to these values, along with the rising tide of educated underemployment following the '*babu* explosion', caused a shift in outlook.

Frustration at the illiberalism and racism which lay barely concealed behind the proclaimed high moral purpose of the Raj coincided with an increased awareness of India as a geographical unity and of a new sense of communal and caste identity. The Chiplunkar Brahmin family of Maharashtra reveals the generational conflict which emerged by the 1870s. Krishnashastri Hari Chiplunkar (1824–78) represented the old-style liberal Hinduism and nationalism. He was a social reformer who advocated widow remarriage. His son Vishnushashtri was a member of the new generation of Congress extremists who repudiated liberalism, praising 'traditional' Hindu values and claiming that the older graduates had become 'intoxicated' by the new learning and had 'heedlessly abandoned traditional values' in their 'uncritical' acceptance of the West.

The streams of nationalism and communalism ran close together with the rise in the 1890s of the cultural nationalism of the self-proclaimed Congress extremists. The Congress moderates and extremists were to come to blows at the 1907 Surat session (Tripathi, 1967). Even earlier, for many Congressmen notions of nationalism and religious identity were in fact inextricably linked. Joshi, for example, while calling for all in unison to manage the affairs of the nation, termed the Indian National Congress *arya lokamci rashtriya sabha* (national assembly of the Aryan people) and regarded his journey to Madras as a *punya kshetra* (holy pilgrimage).

The press mushroomed as a result of the communications revolution. The late nineteenth century saw the establishment of such influential papers as the Bengali-based *Bengalee* and *Amrita Bazar Patrika* and their Madras counterpart, the *Hindu*. Vernacular-language papers such as the Marathi *Kesari* and the Tamil *Swadeshamitram* laid the basis for a militant cultural nationalism. By the beginning of the twentieth century there were nearly 1,400 newspapers with an all-India subscription of two million. Effective readership was much greater, as newspapers were read aloud and passed from hand to hand.

The communications revolution not only knit India together as never before, but linked it far more closely into the wider world. The opening of the Suez Canal, which was accompanied by the transition from sail to steam, cut the voyage from Bombay to Bristol from three months to three weeks. This not only faciliatated the much vaunted arrival of the *memsahib* (European woman), but encouraged Indians to travel to the heartland of the Empire. Indeed attempts to organise politically on a national scale originated not in Calcutta, but London. Students living there in 1865 founded the London Indian Society which articulated Indian grievances and kept a watching brief on press coverage of subcontinental affairs. Within a year this body was superseded by the East Indian Association (Seal, 1968, Chapter VI). It sent political missionaries to the key Presidencies of Bengal and Bombay to establish local branches. The tradition of organising in London was continued by both the Congress and the Muslim League after their foundation. Indeed the League's securing of separate electorates in 1909 owed much to the assiduous lobbying by Syed Ameer Ali (1849–1928) who had retired to England the previous year to form a London branch of the Muslim League organisation.

While the overseas experiences of privileged Indians encouraged the emergence of moderate nationalism, those at the other end of the social scale who went either as indentured labourers to Malaya, Mauritius, Fiji, British Guiana and South Africa, or as 'free' labour to the Pacific coast of North America, sowed the seeds for its revolutionary variety. The experience of racial prejudice and discrimination bred a sense of militant nationalism. This bore fruit in the Ghadr movement of Indian settlers in British Columbia during the First World War.

Along with external migration, there was an increase in rural–urban migration. By 1901, the number of population centres with over 5,000 inhabitants had risen to 2,093. Brahmins were especially mobile, but towns also drew those right at the bottom of society, with the demand for unskilled porters and labourers, and of course a growing need, which did not exist in the rural village setting, for the removal of night soil from toilets. Urbanisation increased the constituency receptive to new identities, whether they were expressed in nationalist or communalist terminology. This was not just because town dwellers had, in Marx's phrase, escaped the 'idiocy of rural life', although they were far more likely to be literate, but because they found security in an alien environment by joining caste associations and Muslim *anjumans*. Caste and religious quarters were established in the new cities, often including migrants from the same region or even village. In later years, the Congress, in ways reminiscent of nineteenth-century American patronage politics, acted as an alternative Raj to the migrants, providing them with access to jobs, education and social services.

The educated classes' wider horizons were evidenced in the growth of voluntary social organisations. The emergence of caste associations (*sabha*) is of particular interest because they blended 'tradition' and 'modernity' in that they were both ascriptive and voluntary in character. They linked together the previously isolated *jatis* (occupational caste groupings). The Ahir *sabha* founded in 1912 was a typical example. It brought *jati* members together from across North India and published a monthly journal in addition to holding annual sessions. Another product of the changing social scene were the political associations formed by members of the professional elite in such cities as Bombay and Calcutta from the 1850s. Such bodies paved the way for the formation of the Indian National Congress. Indeed, the early Congress was to pursue many of the demands for administrative and political reform which these associations had pioneered.

It is of course tempting to exaggerate the processes of social change in late nineteenth-century India. The demographic growth and urbanisation of the post-independence years 1951–84, in which the population doubled, dwarfs the earlier historical period, when high deathrates held back this human explosion. Moreover, despite the urban migration, only one in ten of the population lived in cities at the beginning of the twentieth century. Many of the thousands of villages were still isolated from the distant cities and were untouched by railways and telegraph offices. Both metropolitan and industrial development was highly concentrated in what economists have termed enclave development. The main industrial centres were limited to Calcutta and its hinterland, Bombay City and Ahmedabad in Gujarat which became known as the Manchester of India. Moreover, it is easy to forget that two-fifths of the subcontinent, containing a third of its population, was not directly administered by the British. With such notable exceptions as Mysore, the 600 or so Princely States lagged socially, economically and politically behind the surrounding British provinces. In parts of central India and Rajasthan, slavery, female infanticide and forced labour ground down the ordinary people until the eve of independence.

Educational changes were similarly uneven in their impact, with greater financial support for education higher than primary level. As late as 1917, only one in three boys and one in 15 girls of school age were receiving primary education throughout British India. Hindu upper-caste males dominated access to schooling. In Bengal Presidency, the high-status *bhadralok* castes (see Broomfield, 1968) comprising less than one in 20 of the population monopolised the new educational opportunities. In Madras Presidency, Tamil Brahmins exerted a similar ascendancy which was to form part of the impetus for the anti-Brahmin movement which accompanied the rise of political consciousness in the south. Similarly, the educational backwardness of the Muslims relative to the higher castes of Hindus (6 per cent of Muslim men as opposed to 10 per cent of Hindu men were literate by 1900) was to be a major factor in shaping the emergence of a separatist Muslim political platform. The educated elite was, moreover, not only skewed in favour of the high-caste 'writer castes' but in favour of the Presidencies of Bombay, Bengal and Madras which had the longest interaction with Western culture. Up country, or in the hinterland of Bihar, the educated elite was spread even more thinly.

Regional cultural variations persisted in the colonial era. These were reflected in the South Indian emphasis on the temple as a religious centre and epitomised by the massive temple in Madurai to the fish-eyed goddess Meenakshi, or the especial veneration of the black earth mother, the goddess Kali, in Bengal. The western states of Maharashtra and Gujarat possessed a heritage of saintly figures fulfilled in the modern era by Mahatma Gandhi. Such variations were potent long after the Congress claimed to speak for the whole of India. The figure of the seventeenth-century Maratha warrior Shivaji who was to inspire a radical cultural nationalism in Maharashtra, as Joshi found when he displayed a photograph of the great hero (*param pratapi*), was unrecognised amongst the Kannada-speaking people of Madras.

Conclusion

A sense both of 'Indianness' and of religious community pre-dated British rule. The former arose from notions of sacred geography and the interactions brought by trade and pilgrimage. The latter was vested not just in the moral prescriptions of the Dharmashastra, Sharia and Rahitnama scriptures, but in historical developments such as Mughal and Sikh rule and in the eighteenth-century rise of the merchant classes of Marwaris and Gujaratis (Bayly, 1985). Nevertheless, such senses of identity solidified under the impact of the colonial state. The British were not the first rulers to bring administrative unity to large areas of the subcontinent. However, the technological advances they introduced enabled distant regions to be more closely knit together than ever before. English not only served as a unifying lingua franca for the Indian elite, but crucially introduced it to the notion of modern nationalism and the desire for self-determination. These sentiments intensified during the 1890s, although independence was not contemplated until after the First World War watershed. Nevertheless, the early Bengali Congress leader, Surendranath Banerjea, significantly referred to India as a 'nation in the making' in the title of his autobiography.

At the same time, the colonial state encouraged a heightened religious self-identity. 'The codification and elevation of brahminical practices' over local custom and practice made Indian society more 'knowable' and hence more controllable from a British perspective. For their Brahmin interlocuters it provided an opportunity to consolidate their position in the social and ritual hierarchy (Hansen, 1999, p. 66). The decennial censuses introduced a unique spur to the consolidation of community boundaries which might previously have been fuzzy, with heterogeneity arising from both the host of 'little tradition' beliefs and ritual practices and the great North Indian *sufi* and *sant* mystical traditions which transgressed the boundaries of formal religion.

The British not only viewed Indian society differently from their predecessors, but they encouraged Indians to organise themselves in religious communities as a result of their introduction of representative politics. Elites were inducted into arenas of political competition in which numbers not only counted in the scramble for profit and patronage, but in which official patronage encouraged organisation on a religious platform.

In succeeding chapters we shall examine in more detail the self-conscious efforts made by educated Indians to establish and institutionalise 'imagined' collectivities of community and nation. They reflected the constructive engagement with the new definitions of community and arenas for political participation provided by the colonial state. This process was far more complex than 'diffusionist' understandings of nationalism would allow.

|2|

Indian ideas and new senses of community

Say brother: 'the soil of India is my highest heaven,
the good of India is my good' and pray day and night:
'Oh the Lord of Gauri, O Thou Mother of the Universe,
Vouchsafe manliness unto me! O Thou Mother of Strength,
Take away my weakness, Take my manliness and *Make me
a Man!*'

Swami Vivekananda

Ideas were as important as interests in the forging of national, ethnic and communal identities. Yet many accounts underestimate their role and the breathtaking creativity of Indian intellectual responses to colonial rule. Indian nationalism, which had initially owed much to Western notions of liberalism and self-determination, dug deeper roots in Indian society. Such self-styled Congress 'extremists' of the 1890s as B. G. Tilak (1864–1920) utilised predominantly Hindu cultural and religious symbols. This process appeared threatening to the minorities and caused their educated elites to redouble their efforts to shore up community boundaries. History lay at the heart of both national and community reassertion. Hindu reformers, for example, utilised Western Orientalist writings of the myth of a golden Vedic age to justify their denunciation of 'corrupted' popular religion. History also played an important role in the later emergence of a militant cultural nationalism with the role models it provided of resistance to 'foreign' rule.

This chapter turns first to what has been termed the Hindu renaissance and looks at the key ideological components in the forging of a 'neo-Hindu' consciousness which was crucial for the later development of both Indian cultural nationalism and Hindu communalism. It then examines the Muslim and Sikh intellectual elites' responses to the challenges of colonial rule and the forging of the new Hindu identity.

History, nationalism and Hindu renaissance

An important stage in the development of nationalist consciousness, no less in India than in Europe, was the desire by subject peoples to replace foreign rulers' representations of the past by their own accounts. Control over the past was seen as crucial to the struggle for power in the present, hence the famous Bengali author Bankimchandra Chattopadhyay's clarion call in 1880, 'We have no history! We must have a history.'

In classical Hindu philosophy, the nearest equivalent to the term history – *itihasa* – possessed none of the connotations of the modern Western positivist search for 'facts'. Rather it encompassed the concept of 'thus it was' which could include mythology, genealogies, epics, eulogies and ancient lore and songs (*gathas*). It was only as a result of creative engagement with Western thought that such Indian intellectuals as the Bengali writer Rabindranath Tagore (1861–1941) could present the Mahabharata epic as a historical document of the Aryan era (Chakravarty, 1993, p. 163).

By the late nineteenth century, India's educated elite of some 30,000 graduates (around one to every 10,000 of the population) had become obsessed with historical writing. Pamphlets, tracts, novels and textbooks poured off the printing presses. Although these works mimicked the colonialist periodisation of Indian history and its speculations concerning the Aryan past, their production was a nationalist act. For Indians were now speaking for themselves about their past and carving out an autonomous space in the decolonisation of the mind.

The British claim that primordial attachments to religion had prevented the emergence of a sense of Indian unity and identity goaded nationalists. V. D. Savarkar (1883–1966), in *The Indian War of Independence, 1857* published in 1909, countered this charge by depicting the 1857 uprising as a united struggle for Indian independence. Nehru, in his famous work *The Discovery of India* (1946), provided a compelling if romanticised view of the past which stressed shared cultural history and the mixing 'of layer upon layer of thought ... yet no succeeding layer had completely hidden or erased what had been written previously' (pp. 38–9). Nationalist writings, however, not only challenged British histories but utilised their themes. A prime example was the Orientalist myth of a Vedic golden age. In the colonialist discourse this led to the assumption that India's decline could only be reversed under British tutelage. For nationalists, the golden era pointed to the possibility of future recovery and greatness.

The Vedic golden age and its uses

The myth of a golden age and its linkage with the status reversal of national renewal was a dominant trope in European nineteenth-century historical writing. 'The memories of a golden age mirror and point towards', in the words of Anthony Smith (1997, p. 51), 'a glorious *destiny* stemming from the true nature revealed in and by that golden past.' Zionists, for example, looked to the Mosaic era and the Davidic and Maccabean kingdoms for inspiration; Irish nationalists to the epics of the High Kings of Tara. The concept of a Vedic golden age should be understood in this universalised tradition. It encouraged nationalism by allowing the Indian people to 'realize themselves' and to restore their collective dignity lost by the degradation of foreign rule.

The Vedic myth also contributed to community renaissance. It enabled 'Hinduism' to enter the world of faiths as a primal and universal religion. Increasingly writers portrayed Hinduism as not only equal to Christianity, but superior to it because of its antiquity. Such sentiments are echoed in the extract below penned by the Arya Samajist leader, Lala Munshi Ram.

> The Veda was revealed in the beginning of creation for all races. It contains germs of all science physical, mental and psychical. But it cannot be denied that the glorious period of the supreme achievements of the Vedic Church was the bright period of Indian history. When India was the centre of Vedic propaganda and missionaries were sent from it to different parts of the world, it was also the seat of a worldwide empire and Indian kings exercised direct sovereignty over Afghanistan, Balochistan, Tibet etc. and Indian colonists colonised Egypt, Rome, Greece, Peru and Mexico.
>
> Jaffrelot (1994, p. 13)

Indian reformers contrasted the current degradation with this golden age. Decadence explained India's loss of political independence and was identified with popular religious practice. A return to the 'pristine' Hinduism of the Vedic era was a prerequisite for the recovery of national glory.

The myth of the glorious Vedic era rested on European writings. H. T. Colebrooke in his 1805 essay on the Vedas contrasted contemporary Hindu decadence with the monotheism of the ancient texts, a theme which was to become dominant in the writings of the Brahmo Samaj and Arya Samaj. The idea of a Vedic golden age was further popularised in the writings of the German-born Orientalist scholar Max Müller (1823–1900). Müller never set foot in the subcontinent. His armchair philological studies reinforced the idea of a linguistic kinship between Sanskrit, Greek, Latin and the Germanic languages earlier propounded by his fellow German Franz Bopp (1791–1867). Müller expanded the identification of Sanskrit as an Indo-European language into the theory of a common racial affinity between Europeans and Indians and the concept of an Aryan race, although he was later to reject the racial understanding of Aryanism. The Aryan race theory nevertheless still remains an important explanation for the caste divisions within Hinduism. Müller's appropriation of the Vedic past also included the idea that an 'instinctive monotheism' is present in the early hymns of the Rigveda and that modern forms of Hinduism were the result of subsequent 'decadent opulence'.

Thereafter, these ideas became fixed in the writings of such reformers as the Bombay judge M. G. Ranande (1842–1901) and Swami Dayananda. The former, picking up on the ideas that the English and the Aryans were 'parted cousins', regarded it as 'Providence' which had brought them to India to help in its 're-Aryanization'. This would free Hindus from the degraded customs relating to women which had arrived with the 'patriarchal Muslim tradition'. Dayananda based his social reformist movement on a return to the Vedas. He appears to have read these in a Bengali translation of Müller's German version of the Sanskrit original. While he disagreed with European theory concerning their recent origin (c.1500 BC) he appears to have been influenced by Henry Steel Olcott's Theosophical movement's claims that the Aryans originated in Tibet and migrated to America.

Dayananda came from a Gujarati orthodox Hindu family. The story is well known how his faith in 'idol worship' was broken when as a 14-year-old boy he witnessed a mouse nibbling the offerings to an image of Shiva whilst keeping a nighttime prayer vigil. Dayananda subsequently espoused a 'protestant' Hinduism with a fierce monotheism and 'fundamentalist' attachment to the Vedas. He declared that without 'faith in the Vedas … you cannot be certain what is truth and what is untruth' and preached that Hinduism was the eternal primal religion whose four Vedas were revealed for all races. Moreover, he maintained that they contained within them the germs of all modern Western scientific knowledge both physical and psychological. He depicted the Vedic era as a golden age when the Aryans dominated the world. Dayananda combated 'traditionalist' Hindus over such issues as caste and Brahminical domination. He also acrimoniously disputed with Muslim scholars and Christian missionaries.

Dayananda not only legitimised reform through the Vedic myth, he also turned to the past as the inspiration for a national identity which owed nothing to Western liberalism or British administrative structures. In his seminal work *Light of Truth,* Dayananda declared that 'this country is called Aryavarta because it has been the abode of the Aryas from the very dawn of creation. It is bounded on the North by the Himalayas, on the south by the Vindhyachala mountains, on the west by the Attok [Indus] and on the east by the Brahmaputra' (Dayananda 1975, p. 729).

By linking Indianness with ancient Hindu civilisation, the Vedic myth marginalised Muslims in an emerging cultural nationalism. The collapsing of Indian into Hindu identity, which is a marked feature of the current Hindutva philosophy, was presaged by the Bengali writer and organiser of the Hindu Mela, Manomohan Basu as early as 1873:

> The Hindus are the ancient inhabitants of this land and they have lived here for thousands and thousands of years; they are also the majority, even if they are defeated as a nation this is their country; not the rash usurpers, but only the Hindus are the true, legitimate children of the bharat Mata. No matter who confiscates their wealth, their dignity, their freedom, their princely status, their landed property, the Hindus will still retain the right to use the adjective 'National'.
>
> cited in Chowdhury (1998, p. 15)

The Vedic myth also alienated the non-Brahmin population living outside North India. The fight back was mounted by the western India low-caste social reformer Mahatma Jotirao Phule (1827–90). He not only claimed that the *shudras* and Untouchables of Maharashtra were forgotten descendants of the Kshatriyas, but that India's true golden age was the pre-Aryan Kshatriya era under the 'benign rule' of the mythological King Bali. This 'discovery' formed a key element in Phule's forging of a collective identity for the Maharashtrian cultivating classes in their struggle against the Brahmins' domination. Phule, in a pamphlet published in 1869 entitled *Priestcraft Exposed,* attacked the Brahmins' exploitation of the ignorant Marathi cultivators. Phule and his fellow workers in the Satyashodhak Samaj (Truth Seeking Society) which was founded four years later were not only reacting against the Brahmins' traditional social and religious influence, but its reinforcement by their domination of the local colonial adminstration.

A Tamil political identity was also constructed by inverting the Aryan myth and depicting the northern invaders as destroying a harmonious pre-existing society. Western scholarship on Tamil in South India laid the groundwork for a Dravidian historical myth, just as in North India work on Sanskrit had helped form the Aryan myth. The Reverend Robert Caldwell (1819–91) published in 1856 a work entitled *A Comparative Grammar of the Dravidian or South-Indian Family of Languages.* This argued for the antiquity of Tamil, and contended that it and such other Dravidian languages as Telegu were not derived from Sanskrit. Caldwell also maintained that Aryan Brahmin colonists had not only brought Sanskrit to South India, but had introduced idol worship and had termed the indigenous Tamilian chieftains, soldiers and cultivators as Sudras. The demand that the Sudra term should be dropped for the Tamil castes was to become a major element of the later non-Brahmin movement. A further component in a distinctive Tamil cultural identity was provided by another Society for the Propagation of the Gospel missionary, G. U. Pope (1820–1907), who maintained that the indigenous Saiva Siddhanta religious system was a fully fledged religious philosophy which pre-dated Aryan influences.

Such Tamil writers as Professor P. Sundaram Pillai (1855–97) built on these Orientalist speculations of a Dravidian golden age. Pillai originated the controversy that the Sanskrit version of the Ramayana, with its demonisation of Ravanna, had been written to make the 'Dravidians look small in the light of posterity'. In his and other Dravidian versions of the Ramayana, in a reversal of roles Ravana becomes a heroic figure and Rama is cowardly. By the turn of the twentieth century, such Tamil scholars as V. Kanakasbhai Pillai, and S. Somasundara Bharati, building on Caldwell's and Pope's ideas, had dated the existence of a Dravidian civilisation which owed nothing to Aryanism to the sixth century BC. They had also identified Tamil as a sophisticated language and had strongly argued that Saiva Siddhanta was the original Tamil religion. The Aryan invasions had destroyed this golden age by introducing the religious corruption of idolatry and the social evils of the caste system. This version of the Tamil past was popularised by an emerging press, and institutionalised in a number of Tamil associations or *sangams* culminating in the self-respect movement. It was eventually politicised by the Justice Party, a forerunner of the post-independence Dravida Munnetra Kazhagam (DMK).

History, Shivaji and the construction of community

Further evidence of the problems surrounding the imagining of a national Indian past are provided by the Shivaji myth. Recollections of this seventeenth-century Maratha warrior spurred militant resistance to British rule and divided both Hindus and Muslims, Brahmins and non-Brahmins.

Shivaji Bhonsle (1627–80) came from a Kshatriya family which had precariously exploited its distance from the Mughal authority and its borderland situation between the territories of the sultans of Ahmadnagar and Bijapur. Shivaji was brought up by his devout Hindu mother, Jiji Bhai, after his father's defeat by a joint Mughal–Bijapur army and his banishment. Shivaji was to emulate his career of guerrilla resistance, drawing on local knowledge of the mountainous Deccan terrain.

In a series of campaigns, Shivaji controlled a large area of the Deccan by capturing its hill-top fortresses. In 1659 the Sultan of Bijapur's military commander, General Afzal Khan, surrounded Shivaji's Pratapgarh (fortress of valour). Shivaji tricked and then murdered Afzal Khan under the pretence of surrendering. Soon after, he plundered Surat, even attacking the East India Company factory warehouse. Such exploits attracted the attention of the Mughal court. Alamgir's army, led by the Rajput Jai Singh, besieged Shivaji's forces at Purandhar in 1665 and he had to sue for peace and present himself at Delhi. His attitude at the court resulted in house arrest, but he escaped, hiding in a laundry basket. He raised new forces on his return to the Deccan and, flush with funds from a second assault on Surat, had himself crowned as a traditional Hindu ruler in a coronation at Rajgarh (the fortress of rule). Alamgir's campaigns in Afghanistan delayed the challenge to the assertion of Maratha power during Shivaji's lifetime. The Mughal rulers' eventual lengthy and bloody conquest of the Marathas' Deccan heartland imposed a severe strain on the imperial treasury.

Shivaji's daring exploits lingered in the memory of western Indian folk culture and he was frequently regarded as a reincarnation of the god Shiva. Nineteenth-century social reformers, nationalists and communalists alike, deployed myths about him to mobilise popular support. The lower-caste activist Mahatma Jotirao Phule pioneered this process. In a Marathi ballad published in 1869, he used the figure of Shivaji to project a new collective identity for lower-caste Marathas (O'Hanlon, 1985). The ballad portrays

Shivaji as their leader. Significantly, it is their force of arms, not the skill of the Brahmin ministers, that is depicted as holding the key to Shivaji's career. Phule's Shivaji was thus intended to inspire the anti-Brahmin movement.

Brahmin writers responded by depicting Shivaji as a unifying figure who was not the exclusive preserve of any caste. This approach is exemplified by the work of Rajaramashshtri Bhagvat and Mahadev Govind Ranade. The latter was a leading social reformer and Congress moderate. His disciple Gopal Krishna Gokhale was to become an even more famous figure. Ranade's Shivaji, as described in the work *Rise of the Maratha Power,* was a man cast in his own image: self-disciplined, humane and who in his later years eschewed violence. Shivaji's ability to bring both social and national cohesion, according to Ranade, was derived from the inspiration of the region's *bhakti* poet–saints. The message for his contemporary readers was clear: Shivaji provided a role model for a similar unifying nationalism which cut across caste and class divisions. It was, however, Balwantrao Gangadhar Tilak, a leading figure in what became known as the extremist wing of the Congress, who provided the most powerful reworking of the Shivaji story.

Tilak developed a reputation for rebellion and oratory from his days at Deccan College. He later derided the 'petitioning' approach of the Congress, epitomised by his great rival Gokhale. In order to reach a wider audience with his militant nationalist ideas, Tilak reinvented tradition in the development of an annual festival to honour Shivaji, whose cremation ground had lain forgotten and in disrepair until Ranade began to revive interest in the early history of the Marathas. In May 1895 Tilak convened a public fund-raising meeting in Poona to restore Shivaji's cremation ground. By the end of the year, thanks to his journalistic efforts, there were nearly 60,000 subscribers to the Shivaji fund.

The Shivaji tradition was increasingly reinterpreted in the columns of Tilak's *Kesari* ('The Lion') newspaper to justify violent resistance to the Raj. The 'terrorist' Chapekar brothers who assassinated the hated military administrator at the time of the 1897 plague, W. C. Rand, sang revolutionary verses at the Shivaji festival and claimed Shivaji's inspiration for their 'desperate enterprises'. In September 1897, the Bombay high court convicted Tilak of sedition for publishing a poem entitled 'Shivaji's utterances' in *Kesari*. This was a lament on the current condition of Maharashtra by a Shivaji called back from his sleep. The poem translated from Marathi read as follows:

> O, Shiv, Shiv! I see now with my eyes the ruin of the
> country!
> O, to build which I spent money like rain,
> And where to acquire which fresh hot blood was spilt.
> From which I issued forth attacking through the valleys
> roaring like a lion.

These forts of mine have toppled down.
What ruin is this!
The foreigners teasingly and forcibly drag away Lakshmi
[goddess of wealth] by the hand.
With her plenty has run away and health has
followed.

cited in Wolpert (1962, p. 99)

While Tilak deployed Shivaji as the symbol for militant nationalism, other writers highlighted the anti-Muslim potential in the story provided by the killing of Afzal Khan. The orthodox Brahmin Ekanath Annaji Joshi depicted Shivaji as the saviour of the Hindus from Muslim depredations. The humiliations Hindus faced in Shivaji's time were contrasted with the motif of a Vedic golden age. In the iconography of an emerging Hindu nationalism, Shivaji portrayed the need for strong leadership and for a Hindu state which preserved Hindu customs and laws and protected the cow.

The Hindu 'fundamentalist' Rashtriya Swayam Sevak Sangh (RSS – Association of National Volunteers), from its foundation in the mid-1920s, included the coronation of Shivaji (Shivajirajyarohonastava) in its ritual calendar. Obeisance was demanded to the saffron flag of Shivaji, known as the Bhagwa Dwaj. In contemporary India, the militantly Hindu Shiv Sena organisation of Bal Thackeray has perpetuated the Shivaji tradition with its strong Maharashtrian nationalism and anti-Muslim strain. Its neighbourhood offices are decorated to resemble Shivaji's hilltop fortresses. In one of his famous political cartoons in *Marmik,* Thackeray depicted Shivaji admonishing a Hindu politician for pampering Muslims for votes (Gupta, 1982, p. 139). On one notable occasion, the Shiv Sena *pramukh* (chief) Thackeray declared that 'whenever I am undecided, I think of how Shivaji would have looked at the problem, what would be his opinion and how would he act. Only then am I able to come out with a clear decision' (Gupta, 1982, p. 121).

The Muslim past in the construction of Hindu identity

Modern attempts to construct a unified Hindu national identity have contained a strong recurring anti-Muslim element. Hinduness has been constantly constructed in opposition to the attributes of the Muslim 'other'. Muslims, for example, are said to be licentious, Hindus are said to be sexually controlled. This is summed up in the phrases, *ham do, hamere do* ('We two, our two') to describe Hindus and *ham paanch, hamere pacchis* ('we five, a man and his four wives, we twenty-five') to describe Muslims. Muslims are barbaric, Hindus are civilised; Muslims are unclean (both ritually through meat eating and in physical terms), Hindus are clean. Another variant is that Muslims are violent, whereas Hindus fight only in self-defence.

Communal histories have legitimised the demonisation of the Muslim 'other'. How can we account for this? The 'authentication' of local communal narratives by Orientalist accounts, which were in turn recycled by late nineteenth-century Hindu writers, has been referred to in the previous chapter. The process was further encouraged by the use of resistance to Mughal rule as a metaphor for an anti-British stance. Its original purpose became overshadowed by the choice of Hindu heroic figures who reduced the past to conflict with Muslim 'tyrants'. Notions of India's 'glorious history' adopted a marked anti-Muslim bias even in such regions as Bengal, where in the absence of 'real' conflict heroes had to be 'appropriated' from elsewhere. Unsurprisingly, Bengali writers turned to the Orientalist work by James Tod (*Annals and Antiquities of Rajasthan*) to adopt Rajput heroes as part of their own past. (Chowdhury, 1998, p. 41). Finally, Muslim 'tyranny' could be conveniently blamed for the absence of the kind of cultural artefacts which Europeans sought as evidence for a 'glorious' civilisation in antiquity. 'It is not certain why our ancient countrymen, who were so learned and had achieved so much did not write down any descriptions of the country', Priyanath Mukhopadhyay noted in his *Children's History of Bengal* published in 1891. 'Some people say that they probably wrote such descriptions, but just in case reading histories of the glorious past should inspire people to rebel, the Muslims destroyed these books together with other good books when they conquered this country' (cited in Chowdhury, 1998, p. 52).

The historical device of the Muslim invasions destroying India's prosperity and harmony had in fact emerged as early as 1856 in the writings of the pioneer of Gujarati literature, Narmadashankar (1833–86). The prevalence of the stereotypical association of Muslim rule with plunder, rape and iconoclasm can be gauged by the fact that it appears in a variety of Indian languages. For example the talented Benares Hindi writer Bharatendu Harischandra (1850–85), in a poem published in 1877, wrote of the Muslim hordes continually harassing and ravaging the Hindus. Nabinchandra Sen's epic Bengali poem, *Palasir Juddha,* published just two years earlier, contains similar references. This reading of the 'dark age' of Muslim rule has enabled such Bengali authors as B. C. Chatterjee (*Betrayal of Britain and Bengal,* 1932) and J. Sarkar (*History of the Bengal Muslim Period 1200–1757,*1973) to portray Clive's defeat of Siraj-ud-Daula at the 1757 battle of Plassey as a liberation from tyranny, even though it ushered in British rule. 'The purity of domestic life was threatened by the debauchery fashionable at court', Sarkar wrote. 'Religion had become the handmaiden of vice and folly. On such a hopelessly decadent society, the rational and progressive spirit of Europe struck with resistless [*sic*] force. In the space of less than one generation, in the twenty years from Plassey to Warren Hastings ... the land began to recover from the blight of medieval theocratic rule' (cited in Chatterji, 1994, p. 184).

The idea of liberation from a Muslim 'static' 'theocratic rule' derives from Western modernism. Images of aggressive and lustful Muslims, however, can be traced much earlier to medieval European portrayals of Moors. Such stereotypes have fashioned contemporary Hindu communal consciousness. The BJP, in its rise to prominence in the 1980s, portrayed Muslim rape of Hindu women as a symbol not only of Muslimness, but of the Muslims' wider victimisation of the Hindu community.

Sultan Mahmud of Ghazni's destruction of the Somnath Temple at Prabhasa Patan (modern Gujarat) in January 1025 has become a historical shorthand for Muslim aggression. The site was connected both with Shiva and Krishna, who was believed to have left his human incarnation (*dehotsarga*) there. A thousand Brahmins daily attended the huge *lingam* (phallic aniconic form of Shiva), which was daily washed with water brought from the Ganges 750 miles away. Mahmud was of Turkish descent. He had established a military empire in the Punjab which was to survive for more than 150 years before it fell under Ghuri control in 1186. The account of the 'idol-breaking' at Somnath has become such a powerful historical motif because it links two key elements in stereotypes of Muslims: Muslims as aggressors and Muslims as foreigners. These representations are crucial components in contemporary Hindutva ideology, where Muslims are derided as *Babar ki aulad* (the progeny of Babar). Babar was the foreign half-Turkish and half-Mongol invader who after his victory in the first battle of Panipat (1526) founded the Mughal Empire. Such views disregard the foreign origins of the Aryans.

The sense that the Somnath desecration represented a national humiliation was reflected in the Congress mainstream as well as among the communalist Hindu groupings. At the Hindu Diwali festival shortly after independence, the powerful Indian Home Minister and Deputy Prime Minister Sardar Vallabhbhai Patel (1875–1950) announced that Somnath would be rebuilt. The installation of the images on the reconstruction of the temple was performed by the Indian President, Dr Rajendra Prasad (1884–1963), on 11 May 1951. While the Congress establishment professed secularism and disavowed the view that Muslims were 'foreigners', it nevertheless associated itself with the idea that Somnath's restoration was a 'point of honour' for Hindus and was an important symbol for a 'nation' which had liberated itself from British and Muslim 'foreign' oppression.

This symbolic restoration of Hindu national pride failed to assuage a growing tide of Hindu self-assertion in the 1980s. Many of the educated Hindus who took part in the July 1986 Ahmedabad riots, for example, which were so intense that they forced some 5,000 people to shelter in relief camps, claimed that they were avenging Mahmud of Ghazni's plundering of the Somnath Temple. Mahmud of Ghazni and Babar have been transformed into symbols of hatred by contemporary Hindu extremists.

Scripture and community formation

Scripture also formed a key element in the nineteenth-century reformers'
emphasis on Hinduism as an ideology. Hindus needed an infallible book, just
like the Muslims and Christians. Community boundaries were demarcated
by beliefs as never before. Dayananda sought a return to the Vedas. Ram
Mohan Roy (1772–1833), the outstanding Bengali scholar and social
reformer who was to die far away from his native Calcutta in Bristol, had
earlier emphasised the Upanishads. By referring to a single scriptural
authority, reformers believed that they could counteract Hindu disunity. In a
further strategic emulation of Christianity they sought justification in
scripture for social activism. This was provided for successive generations by
the Gita. Such activism eventually extended from socio-religious reform to
militant nationalism.

Such varied figures as Gokhale, Tilak, Gandhi and Aurobindo all drew
inspiration from the Bhagavad Gita. This 'Song of the Lord', which was
composed between about 400 and 200 BC, forms part of the great
Mahabharata epic. The conversation between the Pandavas warrior Arjuna
and his charioteer Krishna on the battlefield of Kurukshetra provides the
basis for teaching the importance of selfless devotion to duty which contrasts
with other Hindu teaching on quietism, devotionalism and renunciation.
Arjuna is revolted at the prospect of future bloodshed on the battlefield in a
fratricidal conflict. Krishna replies, however, that Arjuna should not back
away, but do his duty as a warrior. The key passages spoken by Krishna
include the tenets: 'In works be thine office ... in their fruits must it never be.
Be not moved by the fruits of works; but let not attachment to worklessness
dwell in thee' (cited in Sen, 1981, p. 24). The Vishwa Hindu Parishad (VHP),
a creation of the RSS, has attempted to accord the Gita a similar status for
Hindus as that held by the Quran and Bible for Muslims and Christians
respectively. Article 3 of its 1979 code of conduct for Hindu daily life
declared that: 'Bhagavad Gita is the sacred book of the Hindus irrespective
of various *sampradayas* [sects] which contains the essence of Hindu
Philosophy and way of life. Every Hindu must keep a copy of the Gita in his
house (cited in Jaffrelot, 1996, p. 348).

The Bhagavad Gita was popularised during the colonial era, through
greater accessibility and the interest displayed in it by such Orientalist
scholars as Max Müller. Gandhi first read the scripture in Sir Edwin Arnold's
translation, *The Song Celestial,* whilst studying in England (1888–91). Tilak,
on the other hand, was introduced to it through the classic Marathi translation and commentary of Dnyaneshvar. Bengali youths encountered it
through the philosophical treatise of the popular novelist Bankim Chandra
Chatterjee (1838–94) (*Srimad-Bhagavad-Gita,* 1888). The Gita's selfless
work ethic and activism inspired Gandhi's programme of social work,
including the uplift of the Untouchables whom he styled *harijans* (children of

God). Earlier, Gokhale exemplified its ideals in his Servants of India Society, which was founded in 1905 to assist through education and other means in the elevation of the 'depressed classes'.

Terrorists also claimed the Gita's moral authority. Jatin Mukherjee, the leading revolutionary figure in early twentieth-century Bengal, trained his followers in athletics including club (*lathi*) wielding and the Gita. This was read in English translation along with European anarchist literature. A raid on the revolutionary organisation Dacca Anushilan Samiti in November 1908 uncovered 13 copies of the Gita in the library, which according to the issue register were in great demand. Oaths of allegiance to revolutionary *dadas* (elder brothers) were made on the Gita. Indeed the archetypal image of a Bengali revolutionary of this era is a high-caste young man, bomb in one hand, Gita in the other.

At the 1897 Shivaji festival, shortly before the Chapekar brothers' murderous assault on Rand, Tilak had insisted that motive rather than action determined guilt. He expanded this concept of ethical relativism into a treatise during his second imprisonment for sedition following his trial in July 1908. The work was entitled *Gita Rahasya* ('The Secret Meaning of the Gita'). Its subtitle *Karma Yoga Shastra* ('The Science of the Religion of Action') conveyed the essence of Tilak's thought that action had primacy in the achievement of *moksha* (salvation) over meditation. Tilak also argued that 'bad' actions were not necessarily 'ethically sinful' if their perpetrators believed they were behaving beneficently.

Vivekananda, spiritual India and neo-Hindu identity

Narendranath Datta (1863–1902) who, on the death of his guru Ramakrishna (see below Chapter 3) in 1886 changed his name to Vivekananda, emphasised Indian unity in spiritual terms. More than any other writer, he based a sense of Indianness on the notion of its spiritual greatness. 'I see that each nation, like each individual has one theme in its life which is its centre', Vivekananda wrote.

> in one national political power is its vitality as in England, artistic life in another and so on. In India, religious life forms the constant centre, the keynote of the whole music of national life and if any nation attempts to throw off its national vitality, the direction which has become its own, through the transmission of centuries – the nation dies if it succeeds in the attempt.

This vision drew on earlier Orientalist speculations concerning the unique civilisational contribution brought by Hinduism's emphasis on holism, harmony and tolerance. Vivekananda boldly stated India's spiritual superiority over a materialist West at the time of the 1893 Parliament of the World's Religions in Chicago. His call for India to get 'Up and Conquer the

World with [her] spirituality' is echoed by contemporary Hindu nationalist claims that the 'twenty-first century will be the Hindu century'. In order to fulfil this destiny to save the West from itself, India must first be fully awakened. Contemporary ideologues see this in terms of political transformation. Vivekananda only implied this, but the colonial middle class recognised the logical outcome of his Hindu nationalist vision.

Hindu cultural nationalism, Bharat Mata and the cult of Kali

The icon of Bharat Mata (Mother India) played an immensely important role in the emerging Indian nationalist discourse. It combined elements of the Durga and Kali goddess cults with their emphasis on *shakti* (power) and of creation in destruction, along with the association of the Mother as nurturer of her sons and the worship of *gau mata*, the mother cow. Indeed the cow protection movement helped popularise the 'metaphoric feminisation' of the nation.

In such images as Kiran Chandra Bandyopadhyay's play *Bharat Mata,* first produced in 1873, Bharat Mata's emaciated and unkempt appearance was used as a symbol of India's dispossession under colonial rule. Patriotic songs of the period reiterate this theme and carry the appeal to her sons to restore Mata to her resplendent past (Chowdhury, 1998, p. 99).

The construction of nation as 'Mother' not only excited an oedipal emotional attachment, but provided a rationale for a masculinised Hindu culture. Only 'real men' could protect Bharat Mata. Moreover, the construction of 'real men' countered colonial charges of Hindu effeminacy, although another response was the Gandhian inversion of these charges by making strength out of 'feminine' characteristics of passivity and non-violence. The following passage from the Hindu nationalist figure Madhav Sadashiv Golwalkar (1906–73) powerfully illustrates the linkage between Bharat Mata and the call for the creation of 'real men'.

> Let us shake off the present-day emasculating notions and become real living men ... living and breathing the grand ideas of service, self-reliance and dedication in the cause of our dear and sacred mother-land ... Today more than anything else, mother needs such men – young, intelligent, dedicated and more than all virile and masculine. And such are the men who make history – men with a capital 'M'.
>
> cited in Hansen (1999, p. 83)

The dense mass of images surrounding Bharat Mata are not exhausted by her portrayal as victim/widow awaiting her sons' rescue. The image of India's current desolation is used by the leading Bengali writer Bankim Chandra Chatterjee's 1882 novel *Ananda Math* to conjure up the picture not of Bharat

Mata as victim, but in her terrifying aspect of the blood-thirsty Kali who was believed to stalk the cremation ground. The ability to call upon Bharat Mata's real power, despite her present powerlessness, was also testified to by identifying her with the figure of the widow Dhumabati in the tantric text 'Dasamahavidya'. In this, the frail and grey-haired Dhumabati retains sufficient supernatural power to destroy the demon Dhumasura with the fire that emanates from her eyes (Chowdhury, 1998, p. 97).

The image of the motherland as Bharat Mata carried especial resonance in Bengal with its devotion to the mother goddess cults. Aurobindo (1872–1950) used attachment to Kali as inspiration for nationalist militancy. Indeed both the Congress extremists and terrorists drew sustenance from his writings. Aurobindo was himself to dabble in terrorist organisations before withdrawing to spiritual exile in Pondicherry in 1910. As early as 1893–4, in a series of articles entitled 'New Lamps for Old', Aurobindo scathingly attacked the Congress for its 'timidity' and 'pathetic subservience' to the British. In his book *Bhawani Mandir* ('Temple of Goddess Bhawani' – one of the manifestations of Kali) Aurobindo called for the cultivation of *shakti* to bring in a new epoch for 'fallen' India. His ideas are summed up in the following extracts which Aurobindo penned in 1893–4.

> To play with baubles is our ambition, not to deal with grave questions in a spirit of serious enquiry ... while we are fussing with trifles (legislative councils, simultaneous examinations) the waters of the great deep are being stirred ... For what is a nation? What is our mother country? It is not a piece of earth, nor a figure of speech, nor a function of the mind. It is a mighty *shakti* composed of the *shaktis* of the millions of units that make up the nation, just as Bhawani Mahisha Mardini sprang into being from the *shakti* of all the millions of gods ... The *shakti* we call India, Bhawani Bharati is the living unity of the *shaktis* of 300 million people, but she is ... imprisoned in the magic circle of Tamas, the self-indulgent inertia and ignorance of her sons.

In a similar vein, Aurobindo declared:

> I know my country as Mother. I offer her my devotions, my worship. If a Monster sits upon her breast and prepares to suck her blood, what does a child do? Does he quietly sit down to his meal ... or rush to her rescue?
>
> Nandy (1983, p. 92)

Aurobindo interpreted the Gita in an activist way and like Tilak understood it as providing sanction for violence in the struggle to free India from foreign rule. Aurobindo's brother Barin gave this a practical dimension by producing a pamphlet called 'The Modern Art of War'. This maintained that war was inevitable when there was no other redress for oppression. *Shakti* should be worshipped in order to acquire the *karma* necessary to undertake warfare, which would result in personal salvation. The Bengali terrorist Ghose brothers were not only devoted to Kali but profoundly influenced by the writings of Bankim whose family was devoted to Durga's worship.

The Kali cult was also popularised by the Irish woman Margaret Noble (1867–1911) (Sister Nivedita). As a student she had studied Buddhism and moved away from her clergyman father Samuel Noble's Christian beliefs. She first met Swami Vivekananda at the London house of Lady Isabel Margesson in November 1895. She attended his public lectures on the Vedanta and answered the call to help his work in India in 1898. On her arrival in Calcutta at the beginning of the following year, she triumphantly recorded in her diary, 'Victory! I am in India' (Jayawardena, 1995, p. 187). In London she had moved in socialist and anarchist circles and had espoused feminism, but her romanticised view of 'traditional' India resulted not only in her devotion to Kali, but in her support of such social practices as child marriage, enforced widowhood and even on occasion *sati*, to the ire of both missionaries and Hindu reformers alike. When she arrived in India she was initiated into the Ramakrishna order and took the name Sister Nivedita (the devoted). She was dedicated to Shiva at the famous ice *lingam* at Amarnath in Kashmir, but increasingly devoted herself to Kali. Her selfless social work during an outbreak of plague in Calcutta in 1899, together with Swami Vivekananda's references to her as his daughter, ensured her acceptance within the mission. Sister Nivedita's advocacy of traditional devotionalism to Kali in lectures and in a book published in London in 1900 was a reaction to her childhood indoctrination into a patriarchal Christianity. Her emotive advocacy of Kali exerted a powerful impact on the Bengali Western-educated male mind. Significantly, female Brahmo Samaj social workers attacked Nivedita's writings for their 'blindness'.

Following Vivekananda's death in July 1902, Nivedita broke with the Ramakrishna Mission and adopted a more overtly political role. She maintained that India could only be truly spiritually free when India was politically free. While Ramakrishna and Vivekananda had stressed the realisation of 'God-consciouness', Nivedita emphasised the more concrete aim of the realisation of national consciousness. She supported the boycott of British goods during the agitation over the 1905 partition of Bengal and moved not only in the circles of the Congress extremists, but also in some of the terrorist organisations, to whom she donated her books on Irish revolutionaries. Indeed there is even some evidence that she may have been implicated in bomb-making activities. She was certainly being trailed by the police at this juncture. This background helps explain her decision to return to England for a time in 1907. When she died in Darjeeling 11 years later, she was hailed by Bengali supporters as the mother of the nation.

Even after the heyday of the *swadeshi* campaign, *shakti* philosophy continued to inspire revolutionaries prepared to sacrifice 'white goats' to Kali in the freedom struggle. Translations of revolutionary leaflets reveal the extent to which *shakti* beliefs had taken hold, with incitements to go and 'drink the hot blood of the Feringhees'. The terrorist outrages in Bengal from 1908 onwards can only be fully understood in terms of this intellectual background.

Shakti philosophy still influenced radical nationalist organisations in Bengal 20 years later, when the Oxford-educated teacher Latika Ghosh, who organised uniformed women volunteers at Subhas Chandra Bose's behest, asked women to think back 'to the battles between the *devis* [goddesses] and *asuras* [demons]. They should remember that just as the *devis* were losing, the fearsome goddess Durga appeared as *shakti* and the *asuras* were defeated.' The female volunteers were now the *shaktis* of the nation. 'Every one of you must be like a spark which will burn down all selfishness, all petty dreams – purified by fire, only the bright, golden love of the Motherland will remain' (cited in Forbes, 1996, p. 136).

Rallying around the cow

While the Kali or Shivaji cults were at least initially regional in their appeal, the cow carried an all-India Hindu significance. It was a symbol of fertility and nurture in the Vedic era, but was not treated as 'sacred and inviolable'. This was only widely accepted in the medieval era, although as early as the Gupta period (fourth century) Brahmins treated the cow as sacred. In the epics its veneration is attested to in such episodes as the attribution in the Mahabharata of the gift of immortality in the milk of Vasishtha's cow, Nandini. In popular culture, the cow was regarded as an auspicious omen in dreams and it was believed that if a person died holding on to a cow's tail their passage 'across the river of death' would be assured. Not only the cow, but its products were regarded as sacred objects and played a key role in many Hindu rituals.

The Muslim slaughter of cattle for both dietary and ritual purposes became a major cultural marker. The extent of slaughter also acted as a barometer for community relations and relative power status. The great Mughal ruler Akbar (1542–1604) banned cow slaughter in his attempt to create a Hindu–Muslim synthesis. The aged Shah Bahadur during the 1857 revolt attempted to unify Hindus and Muslims in Delhi by threatening to blow from cannons any Muslims apprehended for cow slaughter. The rise of Sikh power in eighteenth-century Punjab resulted in a banning of cow slaughter in the kingdom of Lahore. Finally, in the 1880s, Hindus used their powers on the newly established municipal committees in such places as Allahabad (UP) to prohibit the practice on the grounds of 'public hygiene'. Appeals challenging the Muslim right to kill cows were also brought before a number of courts.

While the cow divided Hindus and Muslims, it rallied the former, bringing together reformers and traditionalists. While Dayananda formed the first Cow Protection Society in 1882, traditionalist Hindus played a leading part in the spread of the movement in the United Provinces and Bihar. Its emotive power comes out clearly in the following description of a meeting held at Azamgarh in the former province early in the 1890s.

> A picture of a cow, representing the residence of all the Hindu gods, was placed on
> a stool before the platform, and copies of it were circulated. The speaker urged his
> listeners to only milk 'the cow' after its calf had been satisfied and told them that
> the cow was a 'universal mother' since every man drank cow's milk. It was
> therefore matricide to kill a cow.
>
> Freitag (1980, p. 609)

The cow protection riots which swept the United Provinces in 1893
profoundly influenced communal relations. The support of leading
Congressmen for cow protection convinced many Muslims that the
Congress was a Hindu organisation, despite its secular pretensions. This
appeared to be confirmed when a cow protection meeting was held in the
Congress pavilion immediately after the annual Congress session at Nagpur.
Although the organisational network of Cow Protection Societies did not
long survive the riots, the cow has continued to prove a potent political
symbol.

Indira Gandhi's Congress Party used the symbol of a cow and her calf as
an election symbol. Earlier, in the Constituent Assembly debates of 1948–9,
her father had attempted to demonstrate his secularist credentials by
preventing an all-India ban on cow slaughter. The compromise which left
legislation to the states' discretion formed a rallying point for Hindu nationalists. In 1962, for example, the Jana Sangh, the forerunner of the BJP,
circulated election pamphlets which depicted Nehru killing a cow with a
sword. In September 1966, a Committee for the Great All-Party Protection
of the Cow was founded. The following November a massive demonstration
in Delhi ended in disorder when, in a foretaste of later events at Ayodhya,
sadhus (Hindu holy men) got out of control and attempted to vandalise
public buildings. The police cordon on this occasion held and seven demonstrators died in the firing.

Sacred geography

The Ganges is another Hindu religious symbol which cuts across regional,
caste and sectarian divisions. Indeed images of the Ganges and the intermin-
gling of its holy water with that from local rivers and tanks were at the heart
of the Vishwa Hindu Parishad's Ekatmata Yatra (pilgrimage of one-soulness)
which was designed to bring about Hindu consolidation in November 1983.
The Yatra enacted on a massive and public scale the traditional practice of
some *sadhus* who take water from the Ganges' source in the Himalayas to the
Shiva *lingam* at Rameshwaram in the extreme south. Both Yatra and these
traditional pilgrimages attest to the belief that the land of India is an eternal
motherland demarcated by sacred shrines, rivers and mountains. The

Nagpur Brahmin philosopher and leader of the Rashtriya Swayam Sevak Sangh, Madhav Sadashiv Golwalkar, wrote, for example:

> Nothing can be holier to us than this land. Every particle of dust, everything living or non-living, every ... stone, tree and rivulet of this land is holy to us ... All our important religious ceremonies start with *bhoomi-poojan* worship of earth. There is a custom that as soon as a Hindu wakes up in the morning, he begs forgiveness of the Mother earth because he cannot help touching Her with his feet throughout the day.
>
> Golwalkar (1996, p. 88)

In Bengal the powerful icon of Bharat Mata became woven into a maternalised sacralisation of the Indian landscape. As Sudipta Kaviraj points out in his study of the writings of Bankim, the great Bengali author:

> Space is invested with sacrality ... It was not something which was fit to be geologically surveyed, but to be offered, a political form of worship. From a neutral space, India becomes an evocative symbol, female, maternal, infinitely bounteous, invested with the complex and convex symbolism of the feminine in the Hindu tradition – a sign simultaneously of vulnerability and invincibility.
>
> Kaviraj (1995, p. 114)

From Indian nationalism to Hindu nationalism

The neo-Hindu identity fed into Indian nationalism. It enabled Indians to be modern without denying their cultural roots. This intellectual autonomy from the West was crucial in making possible an eventual political autonomy. At the level of practical politics, a culturally based Indian nationalism was not only more authentic for the educated elites than Western liberal nationalism, but it possessed greater potential for mass mobilisation. Finally, the organisational skills obtained in socio-religious reform movements were to play a vital role in nationalist activity. It is therefore not surprising that such figures as Roy, Dayananda and Vivekananda are hailed as fathers of Indian nationalism, although they never took up political cudgels against the British.

The nineteenth-century revival also carried within it, however, the seeds of Hindu communalism, or Hindu nationalism (Hindutva) as it is more often called. The hailing of a glorious Hindu civilisation was at the expense of the Muslims who were cast as the villains who introduced 'corrupting' influences. Hindu spiritual superiority was trumpeted over both Christianity and Islam, although ironically part of the 'invented' Hindu tradition was the emphasis on tolerance. As we have seen, the Muslim 'other' became an important element in the new Hindu self-image, to be both feared and hated.

Communal sentiments thus coexisted from the outset with a Hindu-tinted Indian nationalism. The broad church of both Indian nationalism and the Congress held together these conflicting understandings. Political polarisation in the early decades of the twentieth century, however, led to a Hindu nationalist breakaway. The institutionalisation of Hindu nationalism in such organisations as the Hindu Mahasabha and the Rashtriya Swayam Sevak Sangh will form the focus of later chapters. Here we will briefly sketch the systematisation of Hindu nationalist or Hindutva ideology.

This process owed much to the writings of such figures as Vinayak Damodar Savarkar (1883–1966) and Madhav Sadashiv Golwalkar. The latter, because of his beard and long hair, was known as 'Guruji' from the time he taught zoology at Benares Hindu University. Savarkar, a Maharashtrian Brahmin, built his sense of Hindu national community not on religious considerations, but rather on common cultural characteristics and historical experience. In his work *Hindutva: Who is a Hindu?*, published in Nagpur in 1923, 'Hinduness' is depicted as being rooted in the soil and is linked back to the Orientalist construction of the Vedic golden age. Savarkar goes so far as to identify a sense of 'nationality' in the Vedic era. He also erroneously maintained that Sanskrit provided the origin for all Indian languages. Muslims and Christians, on the other hand, are 'foreigners', as they 'do not look upon India as their holyland'. For this reason the future of the Indian state lies with the Hindu nation whose past was most clearly bound up with the love of the 'fatherland'.

Savarkar's ethnic Hindu nationalism was given a racial twist by Golwalkar in his 1939 publication, *We, or Our Nationhood Defined.* He claimed, for example, that Nazi Germany's 'purging' of the Semitic races was 'a good lesson for us in Hindusthan to learn and profit by'. He also spoke of the Hindu race spirit in terms which obviously borrow both from the Nazi model and from the earlier writings on the notion of *geist* by such German writers as Fichte and Herder. He thus declared on page 21 of *We, or Our Nationhood Defined*:

> The ancient Race spirit which prompted the Germanic tribes to over-run the whole of Europe, has re-risen in modern Germany. With the result that the Nation perforce follows aspirations, predetermined by the traditions left by its depredatory ancestors. Even so with us: our Race spirit has once again roused itself as is evidenced by the race of spiritual giants we have produced, and who today stalk the world in serene majesty.

Although Golwalkar was influenced by German nationalist thinkers, he remained essentially within the Hindu cultural nationalist tradition. Indeed he was for a number of years, before he took up fulltime work with the RSS, connected with the Ramakrishna Mission and was initiated by Swami Akhandananda, a Gurubhai (brother guru) of Swami Vivekananda. Golwalkar drew from this tradition a sense of Hindu spiritual superiority and of the holiness of Mother India. Cultural unity rather than the racial purity of German National Socialism thus remained the predominant feature of his thought. This is provided by history and the language of Sanskrit. He wrote of the Hindu nation as Bharat, the name of the legendary Aryan unifier of the subcontinent. He also called Sanskrit the embodiment of the Hindu race spirit. Unity was also provided by sacred geography. 'Ganga is as holy to us as Cauvery', he wrote: 'the great Shivalinga formed out of ice in the Himalayan cave at Amarnath claims the same devotion from all of us as the Linga at Rameshwaram.' Despite his reference to German purging of the 'Semitic' races, Golwalkar's ideas about race fall short of a complete acceptance of eugenics and racial purity. Instead race is defined in cultural terms on page 26 of *We, or Our Nationhood Defined*:

> Race is a hereditary society having common customs, common language, common memories of glory or disaster; in short it is a population with a common origin under one culture. Such a race is by far the most important ingredient of a Nation.

Non-Hindus were thus not automatically debarred from sharing in this nation, but they would have to renounce their own culture. Hindu nationalists from Golwalkar's time onwards have invited Muslims to join the mainstream on these terms. This conception of nationality is of course very different from the composite nationalism of the Congress, where 'unity in diversity' is recognised and territoriality rather than culture is given significance. In a later work entitled *Bunch of Thoughts*, Golwalkar ridiculed the Congress's theory of territorial nationalism, because Muslims could never be called 'children of the soil merely because, by an accident, they happened to reside in a common territory under the rule of a common enemy'. Mere 'common residence' or birth could not imply that all held the same 'loyalties', 'qualities' or pattern of life. He also rejected territorial nationalism because it obscured the 'positive' and 'inspiring' concept of Hindu nationhood and reduced patriotism and nationalism to a mere 'anti-Britishism'.

The call for Muslim integration in a future Hindu *rashta* (nation) was set out uncompromisingly in *We, or Our Nationhood Defined*. 'The foreign races in Hindusthan', Golwalkar declared,

> must either adopt the Hindu culture and language, must learn to respect and hold in reverence Hindu religion, must entertain no idea but those of glorification of the Hindu race and culture … or may stay in the country, wholly subordinated to the Hindu nation, claiming nothing, deserving no privileges, far less any preferential treatment – not even citizen's rights.
>
> cited in Jaffrelot (1996, p. 56)

The palpable need for a united effort from Muslims and Hindus during the freedom struggle, together with the eclectic mix in Indian nationalism of secularism, socialism, Gandhism and cultural nationalism, however, consigned Hindu nationalism to the margins. Its main political representative, Jana Sangh, polled poorly in general elections from 1952 to 1967. In 1952, for example, it captured under 3 per cent of the vote. In an attempt to broaden its popularity, Deendayal Upadhyaya (d. 1968), a leading figure in the RSS, injected a strong element of Gandhian philosophy into the Hindu nationalist discourse. The Jana Sangh's new ideology was called 'Integral Humanism' and emphasised the Gandhian commitment to *swadeshi* (home-made goods) and political morality. Further respectability to the Hindu nationalist cause was lent by the Jana Sangh's movement into the political mainstream of opposition to Mrs Gandhi's emergency.

The final breakthrough for Hindu nationalism came with the rise to prominence of the BJP, Jana Sangh's successor. International, regional and domestic political transformations beyond its control were crucial in the upswing in its fortunes. The BJP, however, maximised its opportunity by its creative use of new methods of communication and by symbolising its message in the dramatic confrontation between Hinduism and its Muslim 'other' at Ayodhya.

The minorities, the colonial impact and Indian nationalism

The Muslim and Sikh elites had to grapple with both a new Western world view and a revived Hinduism. The Sikhs' fears of reabsorption into the Hindu fold stimulated attempts at boundary redefinition. The Muslim elites struggled with the loss of political power following the Mughal decline. Temporal power traditionally underpinned Islamic values: how then could these be safeguarded in the changed circumstances of colonial rule?

The introduction of political representation sharpened this question by raising the possibility that Hindus would one day rule Muslims. The Congress's inclusive nationalist ideology lacked reassurance on two counts: firstly, because of the presence of Hindu communalists in its ranks; and, secondly, because of the influence of Hindu cultural symbols in the nation-alist political discourse. Muslim separatism was also spurred, however, by cultural and intellectual revival. This pre-dated colonial rule but was greatly reinforced by it. At its heart lay a renewed interest in the glories of past Islamic civilisation.

Muslim historical awareness and community consciousness

Islam possessed a strong sense of history which pre-dated the modern encounter with colonialism. This was based on the events surrounding the revelation of God's word at a particular point in time and the responses this evoked, including the need for the Prophet and his followers to engage in *hijrat* (holy flight) from Mecca to Medina. It is from this event that the Islamic calendar is dated. Indian Muslims shared this inheritance with the worldwide community of believers because, in the words of the great reformer Sir Syed Ahmad Khan (1817–98), they 'were the progenies of a spiritual father' in a brotherhood which transcended nationality. When they sought to make sense of their situation in colonial India, they naturally looked back both to the splendours of the era of Mughal rule and to the early days of their faith in the deserts of Arabia.

Writers contrasted current decadence with past splendour. Not surprisingly, given the importance of poetry in Indian Muslim society, these ideas were most evocatively articulated in the epic poem *Musaddas Madd-o-Jazr-i-Islam* ('The Flow and Ebb of Islam') which was penned by the Urdu writer Altaf Hussain Hali (1837–1914) in 1879. Hali came from a respectable but poor family from Panipat, but it was in Delhi that he developed his interest in poetry. His patron for a number of years was Nawab Mustafa Khan, who was a friend of the great poet Ghalib. Hali experimented with a new freer poetic style (natural poetry) before producing his great work. In it, Hali both laments the fate of a decaying Muslim ruling elite and celebrates former Muslim glories. The call is for his contemporaries to once more 'make their mark' by drawing inspiration from this past. Significantly, the poem links political power with the glories of Islamic civilisation. The following two famous passages capture the flavour of the work, although much is lost in translation.

> Let someone go and see the ruins of Cordova
> The arches and the doors of its magnificent mosques
> The mighty palaces of Arab chiefs
> And their decayed pomp and grandeur.
> The glory of their race shines from beneath the debris,
> Just as poor gold glitters in a heap of ashes.
>
> In the desert, where I came upon a barren wilderness;
> On which, even in rains, there was no trace of verdure,
> Which the farmer had long ceased to have the heart to till,
> I was reminded of the desolation of my own people.
>   cited in Ikram (1977, p. 65)

The poem was so popular that it went through a new edition in each of the first seven years of its publication. Hali's attachment to a wider Muslim vision than that of India was echoed by the great poet–philosopher Mohammad Iqbal (1877–1938), in a work entitled *Anthem of the Muslim Community*, which was written after his return from Germany. The poem begins, 'China and Arabia are ours, India is ours, We are Muslims; the whole world is our country.'

This universalistic sentiment seems at first paradoxical, given Iqbal's espousal of a homeland for Indian Muslims: a vision implemented by Jinnah with the birth of Pakistan. Iqbal's inspiration for separatism did not come from European nationalism, which he rejected because it would result in secularism. Instead it arose from an acute understanding that political power was essential to the higher ends of establishing God's law. Iqbal, although he is revered as Pakistan's national poet, never lost sight of the worldwide community of Muslims. Territorial nationalism was a stepping stone to the achievement of Islamic universalism (Shaikh, 1989, pp. 202ff).

History and the construction of Sikh religious boundaries

The Sikhs shared with the Muslims a history of rule in their Punjab homeland which was shattered by the British. Colonial perceptions of Sikhs as a sub-sect of Hinduism, together with growing Hindu reassertion, threatened reabsorption into the Hindu fold. In such circumstances the Sikh elites sought to consolidate community identity. This process will be examined in greater depth in later chapters; in this section we shall focus more narrowly on the reformers' uses of history in the movement from a syncretic folk culture to a highly codified neo-Sikh identity (see Oberoi, 1994, for details).

Inspiration was drawn not from the founder of the Sikh tradition Guru Nanak (1469–1539), who emphasised 'interior religiosity', but from the eighteenth-century period of Mughal persecution. This was evoked to emphasise that 'true' Sikhs were those who maintained the five external symbols of the faith even if this led to their martyrdom. This Khalsa tradition had been initiated by the Tenth Guru, Guru Gobind Singh (1666–1708) in 1699. A whole genre of martyrdom literature was produced with biographies of martyrs appearing in tract, poetic, novel and historical form.

Such 'histories' were noted for their graphic description of Mughal (frequently conflated to Muslim) torture, execution and murderous assaults. In this context, themes of Sikh courage, heroism and martial prowess were deployed. Community survival was linked to the willingness to embrace martyrdom. This point emerges forcefully in the account below of the eighteenth-century martyr Bhai Taru Singh.

> To part with the *keshas* was to part with his emblem, which reminded the Khalsa of their high origin and of the lofty ideals which their noble progenitors lived up to. Now Bhai Taru Singh was a true Khalsa, thoroughly imbued with the spirit of the age. He could not submit to the insult. The Subah's [governor's] minions pinioned him and caught hold of his head and chin; but the barber found it difficult to bring his hand near the Bhai. With one shake of his head, he would push back his assailants and make them whirl on the ground like so many tops. A shoemaker was then sent for to try his skill with his tools and scrape off the Bhai's head; but he, too proved a failure. At last the services of a carpenter were requisitioned for the fell deed. With one stroke of his adze, he cut off Bhai Taru Singh's head which was triumphantly exhibited throughout the town.

cited in Oberoi (1994, pp. 331–2)

Bhagat Lakshman Singh who narrated the account was a leading figure in the reformist Singh Sabha movement in colonial Punjab. This was in the forefront of educational activities and of the removal of 'unhealthy' 'Hinduised' practices among Sikhs. It sought to identify a 'true' Sikh identity with the Khalsa tradition's emphasis on the physical symbols of Sikhism, including the wearing of uncut hair. The historical appropriation of martyrs such as Bhai Taru Singh perfectly served its purposes. Readers would draw the moral lesson that community survival depended on the maintenance of distinctiveness. They would also be inspired by the heroism and dedication displayed by such figures as Bhai Taru Singh, countless other martyrs and most notably by the Ninth Guru, Guru Tegh Bahadur (1621–75).

Gender, identity and nation

Recent feminist scholarship has uncovered the tensions between feminism and anti-colonial nationalism and the way in which debates over womanhood influenced the construction of the new images and symbols of the 'imagined community' of nation states (Kandiyoti, 1998). The centrality of female conduct, dress and appropriate activity to notions of cultural authenticity, on the one hand, and the need for 'reform' of women's condition, on the other, in the construction of modern 'nationhood' was especially marked in the subcontinent. This was rooted in part in women's exaggerated role as the bearers of cultural values through their identification with a community's *izzat* (honour). The notion of *izzat* lying in the control of female sexuality is summed up in Pakistan where rape is termed *bay-izzat karna* (causing one to lose one's honour).

The polemic surrounding womanhood also rested on the traditional division between what was termed *bahir* (the world) and *ghar* (the home). While Indian males accommodated themselves to the colonial state's norms in the world, in the home they still exerted their mastery to preserve 'true culture'. Thus, as Partha Chatterjee has maintained, 'In the world, imitation of and adaptation to Western norms was a necessity; at home they were tantamount to annihilation of one's very own identity' (Chatterjee, 1989, p. 239). The way women dressed and behaved and the type of education they received was therefore deemed crucial for the maintenance of an authentic 'tradition'. There were fierce debates about the maintenance of *purdah* or the seclusion of women. Even as eminent a Muslim reformer as Sir Syed Ahmad Khan upheld *purdah* and a traditional education for women in the seclusion of the home (Saiyid, 1998, pp. 65–7). Hali was more sympathetic, however, declaring in his work *Chup ki Dad* composed in 1905:

Even should a man of honour,
    Love you your whole life through,
Still good or bad, men all agree,
    That this one thing is true:
As long as you are living,
    of knowledge you'll be deprived.
You'll quit this world as uninstructed,
    As when you arrived.
In this way you'll stay passive,
    And hidden out of sight.
    [...]
That knowledge, which for men,
    Holds the elixir of life,
    Is considered, in your case,
    As deadly as a knife.

cited in Saiyid (1998, p. 71)

Purdah remained for many years a key issue in the debate on women's role in society. For Muslim women it increasingly turned around the extent to which it was a religious obligation according to the Islamic law *(shariat)*. The spread of education among elite women loosened its hold. Begum Rokeya Sakhawat Hossain (1880–1932), who pioneered education for Muslim girls in Calcutta, attacked the wearing of the *burqah* in her satirical short story, *Sultana's Dream* (1905), in which women ruled and men secluded them-selves in the house (Forbes, 1996, p. 56) The girls who attended her school nevertheless observed seclusion in their journeys from home. Inside the Sakhawat Memorial Girls' School, they abandoned the *burqah*, but covered their heads, signifying 'concern with both modesty and modernity'.

When women from all communities moved into the public sphere, unlike their menfolk who adopted Western dress, they safeguarded their modesty by maintaining traditional dress codes. The draping of a scarf *(dupatta)* to cover the head has become the acceptable style for Muslim women in the public eye from Fatima Jinnah in the 1940s to Benazir Bhutto half a century later. In addition Pakistani women have evolved a dress style which is an important national boundary marker, with the Indian sari being replaced by the 'authentic' and ubiquitous loose-fitting top and trousers known as the *shalwar qamiz*.

The final factor in the symbolic importance of women in the politics of national and communal identity arose from the attacks of Westerners on their 'degradation'. The oppression of women was used not only as a shorthand for oriental corruption but as a justification for colonial tutelage. James Mill, in his important work *The History of British India* (1826), main-tained that the level of civilisation was indicated by the 'condition of the weaker sex'. The low status of Indian women symbolised the Hindu deca-dence which made British rule inevitable.

The idea that Indians' sex lives made them unsuitable for self-government ironically received its crudest expression in the writings of the American authoress Katherine Mayo (1867–1940). Within ten years of its publication in July 1927, her work *Mother India* had gone through 42 reprints. Its notoriety stemmed from its explicit and prurient detail on the physical effects of the early consummation of marriage and childbirth. *Mother India* was not only more graphic than earlier attacks on social evils, but lacked balance in its portrayal of Hindu society, and scarcely hid its pro-imperialist sentiments. Typical of its essentialisation was the comment that all Hindu woes, 'material and spiritual poverty, sickness, ignorance, political minority, melancholy, ineffectiveness ... [possessed a] rock-bottom physical base ... [the Hindu's] manner of getting into the world and his sex-life thence forward' (Mayo, 1927, p. 22). Gandhi led the chorus of protests, terming the book the 'Drain Inspector's Report'.

'Traditionalists' rejected the notion that religiously derived notions of the ideal role of the sexes had anything to learn from European mores. Reformers responded to Western criticisms, but dressed these adaptations up as a return to the pristine original 'traditions' of their community. The emergence of the 'modern' Hindu/Muslim, Indian/Pakistani woman thus resulted not from secularisation, but from a blending of 'tradition' and 'modernity'. The initial impetus for female reform came from a response to the perceived attack by Christian missionaries regarding both their critiques of the condition of Indian women and their proselytising activities. In order to prevent girls being educated in mission schools, such organisations as the Arya Samaj and the Anjuman-i-Himayat-i-Islam (Organisation for the Defence of Islam) overcame 'traditionalist' hostility to establish women's schools and colleges.

Interest in female education drew strength from Hindu and, to a lesser extent, Muslim reformers' juxtaposition of contemporary 'degeneracy' with the myth of a 'golden age'. The Aryas trumpeted equality between the sexes in the Vedic period. Female education was thus an important step towards reviving this past. It would also enable women to play a role in the new community consciousness being constructed by men. Healthier and educated girls would be more able to fulfil their role of cultural and biological transmission. Ironically one of the clearest statements in favour of a conservative approach to female schooling was penned by the theosophist Annie Besant (1847–1933). Earlier in her life, as a single parent separated from her clergyman husband, she had striven to be allowed to read for a science degree at London University. A quarter of a century later she wrote:

the national movement for the education of girls must be one which meets the national needs, and India needs nobly trained wives and mothers, wise and tender rulers of the household, educated teachers of the young, helpful counsellors of their husbands, skilled nurses of the sick rather than girl graduates educated for the learned professions.

cited in Jayawardena (1995, p. 130)

The struggle to make female education socially acceptable limited its content. Begum Rokeya's school in Calcutta, for example, emphasised such practical subjects as handicrafts and home economics. In an essay entitled *Sugrihini* ('The Ideal Housewife') Begum Rokeya justified female education in terms of it enabling women to fulfil their 'traditional roles knowledgeably and professionally and hence contribute to the progress of the nation' (Forbes, 1996, p. 56). Religious teaching was accorded an important place in the curriculum of many girls' schools both to equip them for their role of bringing up future generations and to counter any charge that educated women might become lax in morals (Saiyid, 1998, p. 55). Thus the syllabus of the girls' schools opened in Lahore in the 1880s by the Anjuman-i-Himayat-i-Islam emphasised the teaching of the Quran. The pioneering Kanya Mahavidyalaya girls' high school established in Jullundur in the Punjab a decade later by the Arya Samaj stressed study of the Vedas, the writings of Dayananda and the daily performance of *havan*. Domestic skills were also taught, while by studying the history of 'great' Hindu men and women, they would be given the 'inspiration to build a modern nation' (Pal, 1995, p. 56). This sanitised curriculum acted as a model for other institutions and was only reformed as late as 1935. It was only on the eve of partition that the Kanya Mahavidyalaya became affiliated to the Punjab University and girls could sit its examinations.

By that time large numbers of women had become involved in the freedom struggles. However, they had either done so as appendages of men, or in terms of a reassertion of traditional values. Gandhi, who did most to feminise the Indian nationalist movement by, firstly, mobilising women into the public domain of nationalist politics and, secondly, by rejecting not only muscular Hindu responses to the Raj but 'masculine' rationality and modernisation in favour of 'female' intuition and spirituality, saw women as serving the nation as dutiful daughters and self-sacrificing mothers.

The colonial era thus bequeathed a legacy both of unresolved tensions between feminism and nationalism and of obsessive concern with female behaviour and appearance.

Conclusion

This chapter has stressed, more than many accounts, the key role that Indian ideas played in the construction of community identities that transcended localised social units. This is not to deny the importance of British methods of governing and categorisation in the establishment of new senses of community, or of the changing socio-economic and political circumstances brought by the colonial state. Nor is it to ignore the impact on educated Indians of such Western beliefs as self-determination, liberalism and democracy. But focusing on these alone both denies Indian agency in the sharpening of identity and plays down the intellectual interchange which was a crucial factor in the processes we have examined.

Nationalism was not simply an ideology borrowed from the West by Indian elites disaffected from the colonial power structure. It synthesised Western and largely Hindu cultural values. Conventional accounts that look at nationalism less as an ideology and more as a contest for political power ignore the creativity involved in what Partha Chatterjee has termed the forging of 'a modern national culture that is nevertheless not western'.

The notion of a Muslim territorial nationalism similarly cannot be understood in diffusionist terms. As we have seen, Iqbal, its greatest philosophical exponent, rejected as 'unthinkable' the replacement of the concept of Islamic universalism by a European concept of nationalism. National organisations for Muslims were 'temporary phases' in the movement to the establishment of Islamic universalism. His proposals for a separate Muslim homeland were predicated not on Western ideas of nationalism, but rather grounded in the traditional Islamic view that political power was essential to enforce the ethical ideals of the *shari'a*.

Muslim and Hindu ideas of community, however, had to be popularised and institutionalised. Their impact also depended on the historical contingencies brought by socio-economic and political change. In the next chapter we shall turn to the modern and traditional communication networks which articulated new senses of Indian identity.

| 3 |

Spreading the word: communicating new senses of identity

> Both my cousins, Rai Bahadur Bhagat Narain Das, MA,
> and Bhagat Ishwar Das, MA, were in those days [the 1870s]
> receiving instruction at the Government College at Lahore.
> Their library books filled any number of *almirahs*; in the
> course of time we had a big library consisting of any number
> of valuable books on any number of subjects.
>
> Singh (1965, pp. 19–20)

Print culture, according to Benedict Anderson, was crucial in nationalist invention. Colonial India certainly witnessed a revolution in the availability of the written word. Previously manuscripts were rare, expensive and not easily portable. Printed books were plentiful, cheap and could be read at any place and time. In Punjab, for example, the number of printing presses increased by over 70 per cent between 1864 and 1883 and there was a five-fold cumulative increase in the number of books published between 1875 and 1880.

Nationalists and communalists alike used newspapers and books to spread their ideas. But there were equally important methods, which find no place in Anderson's theory. The visual aids of drama, public spectacles and religious displays were necessary to reach out to a largely non-literate society. Both modern and traditional forms of communication played crucial roles in the transformation of customary culture into community consciousness.

The growth of the Indian press

Increased literacy, innovations in printing technology including steam presses and in road and rail communications together enabled the growth of a popular Indian press during the second half of the nineteenth century. It was also greatly assisted by the 1866 Post Office Act which not only set a low postal rate for books, newspapers and pamphlets, but ended the differential rates for imported and locally printed material which had disadvantaged the latter. Equally important, but seldom acknowledged, was the role of missionary printers in producing type which matched Indian scripts. In Punjab the Ludhiana Mission Press owned the only Gurmukhi typefaces for many years. Prior to this, the American Presbyterian missionaries had played an important part in the standardisation of languages by producing dictionaries and grammars. John Newton, for example, published a Punjabi grammar in 1851. Three years later he co-produced the first English–Punjabi dictionary. By the 1870s the printers of the Church Missionary Society had even adapted Braille type for Hindi and Urdu.

Finally, cheap rates increased Indian newspapers' circulation. These were made possible by advertising income and the relatively low capital startup rates. The influential Calcutta-based paper *Amrita Bazar Patrika*, which under the control of Motilal Ghosh ranged itself against Banerjea's *Bengalee*, commenced production in 1868 with printing equipment which had been purchased for just Rs 32. The Urdu paper *Paisa Akhbar*, which began publication in the Punjab in 1887, cost only a paisa (a sixty-fourth of a rupee). By 1901 its readership had risen to 13,000.

Circulation figures for papers and periodicals during the colonial era initially appear unimpressive. The leading Anglo-Indian newspaper, the *Statesman*, for example, had a circulation of just 4,000 according to a Bengal Special Branch Report of March 1908. The figure for the *Bengalee* at the same period was about 11,000. The radical *Comrade*, the first all-India Muslim paper in English, which moved from Calcutta to Delhi in 1912, possessed just 3,000 readers. Even the popular Lahore-based paper *Zamindar* only sold around 15,000 copies a day at this time. Newspaper audiences were, however, always considerably wider than their sales. Papers were not only passed from hand to hand, but read aloud in public gatherings.

The impact of the press

The press greatly influenced social and political developments in colonial India. Newspapers not only reported but propagandised fearlessly. From 1819, when Ram Mohun Roy founded the journal *Sambad Kaumudi* and used its columns to attack the social 'evil' of *sati*, the press was at the forefront of social reform. It was also deeply involved in politics. Many Indian politicians were proprietors or editors of newspapers. A third of the representatives at the 1885 founding session of the All-India National Congress were in fact journalists. Early nationalist editors included Dadabhai Naoroji (*Voice of India*) and Surendranath Banerjea who became the proprietor–editor of the *Bengalee* in January 1879.

The press's importance in the nationalist movement emerges clearly during the significant landmarks of the *swadeshi* movement and the Khilafat campaign. The *swadeshi* movement of 1905–8 popularised as never before the Congress extremists' ideals of the boycott of British goods and encouragement of self-reliance. Inspiration for militant nationalism borrowed heavily from Hindu attachment to Kali and *shakti*. The Khilafat campaign in 1921 marked the highwater point of Hindu–Muslim cooperation in the nationalist struggle. Muslims and Hindus joined hands in the non-cooperation movement. The press not only reported on these movements, but articulated the ideas which inspired them.

The press and the swadeshi *movement*

On 7 August 1905, the *swadeshi* movement was formally proclaimed during a packed meeting at Calcutta Town Hall. The resolution which launched it was moved by Surendranath Sen, the editor of the *Indian Mirror*. Protest meetings had been held from December 1903 onwards, when it became known that the British were to divide Bengal. This action was taken on sound administrative grounds given that the province contained about a quarter of the population of British India. Bengalis had not, however, been consulted. Moreover, inflation was making the educated classes discontented as it bit into their small fixed incomes following four successive poor rice harvests. Many of the upper-caste Hindus saw the creation of a Muslim eastern province as imperial divide-and-rule tactics. The partition proposals were roundly condemned in such newspapers as the *Bengalee*, *Hitavadi* and *Sanjibani*. Indeed it was the latter's editor, Krishnakumar Mitra, who was popularly credited with originating the idea of a boycott of British goods.

Calcutta observed a strike (*hartal*) on 16 October 1905, the day on which the partition took effect. Surendranath Banerjea addressed the largest gathering yet seen in the imperial capital. The crowd was estimated at 75,000. This was the precursor of a tumultuous round of protests. Women, in a foretaste of the later Gandhian campaigns, came out of their homes for the first time to join in the burning of foreign cloth and the picketing of stores selling foreign goods. Students were at the forefront of the campaign. Many of them were free for fulltime political activity as a result of abandoning their studies in government institutions for the new National Schools and College. Corps of volunteers (*samitis*) took the *swadeshi* message into the rural hinterland. By 1907 there were perhaps as many as 10,000 volunteers. The *swadeshi samiti* in Barisal town brought out its own extremist newspaper entitled *Barisal Hitaishi,* edited by Durgamohan Sen. This was the first district publication to be prosecuted for sedition. Other *mofussil* (interior) publications active during the *swadeshi* movement included the *Rangpur Vartabaha*, the *Howrah Hitaishi*, the *Khulnabasi* of Khulna and the *Pallichitra* of Bagerhat.

The singing of 'Bande Mataram' ('Hail Mother') became the rallying cry of the movement. This patriotic song was a source of great inspiration for educated Bengali youths brought up on the popular historical novels of Bankim Chandra Chatterjee. But its aggressive Hindu imagery alienated Muslims. Lower-caste Hindus could also hilariously misunderstand its meaning, as becomes clear in Prabhat Mukherjee's short story 'Khalsas' ('His Release') published in the *Prabasi* magazine in 1907–8. The children of an elite family during the *swadeshi* campaign are crushing imported biscuits under their feet as they are singing 'Bande Mataram'. This prompts an unlettered servant to ask, 'What are they saying? Banduk Maram [fire the gun]? A passer-by replies, 'It must be a term of abuse. Nowadays the boys say it whenever they see a sahib' (Ray, 1984, p. 163).

The Congress extremists endeavoured to convert the Bengal struggle into a national campaign for self-rule. Tilak, for example, attended a Shivaji festival held in Calcutta in 1906 and threw his weight behind the boycott movement. He launched the Swadeshi Vastu Prarcharini Sabha (Society to Promote the Use of Swadeshi Goods) in Bombay. Through the columns of the *Kesari*, he advised would-be businessmen how they could set up factories producing such Indian-made products as glass, matches and cigarettes. Tilak's campaign in Bombay secured the support of Gujarati- as well as Marathi-speaking businessmen through the backing of Iccharam Surajaram Desai, the editor of the influential weekly, *Gujarati*.

Tilak was arrested for sedition in 1908 following a series of articles in *Kesari* on the violence of the 'bomb'. These occurred against the background of such events as the Muzaffarpur bomb outrage (April) in which two English ladies were killed when their carriage was mistaken for that of the Chief Presidency Magistrate. The outrage led to the execution of Khudiram Bose and Prafulla Chaki's self-immolation. While Tilak deplored such 'nihilism', he believed it was inevitable when the people's 'urge for greater freedom' was repressed. Like other Congress extremists he did not distance himself from the rising tide of violence. Bengali publications like the weekly *Jugantar* expressed this in terms of the traditional adherance to Kali. In March 1908 it declared, for example, 'Without bloodshed the worship of the goddess will not be accomplished ... With a firm resolve you can bring English rule to an end in a single day ... Begin yielding up a life after taking a life' (Sarkar, 1973, p. 262).

Violent denunciations of British rule were also expressed in the weekly English-language *Bande Mataram*, edited by Aurobindo, and in *Sandhya*, the Bengali evening daily of Bramhabandhav Upadhyaya. Even some extremists described the *Sandhya* as a 'filthy rag' full of 'untruths, half truths and personal calumnies'. The two papers sought to outdo each other, before they were suppressed under fresh press laws which saw the prosecution of a number of extremist editors. Upadhyaya also briefly ran an illustrated weekly entitled *Swaraj*. This was militant in both its nationalism and espousal of

Hindu culture. The *Swaraj*'s articles and pictures of Bankim Chandra and Vivekananda ensured popularity with the Hindu lower classes.

British official hostility to the Bengali press was baldly stated by R. H. Craddock, the Home Member of the Viceroy's Council. 'There is not a single native paper which does not consistently blame the Government', he noted in 1913, 'either by carping criticisms, ill-natured imputations of bad motives, or in the worst cases, virulent calumny' (cited in Ray, 1984, p. 175). Such condemnation paid tribute to the press's effectiveness. This was also evidenced by the jump in circulation figures in 1904–5 for those papers that were active in the anti-partition campaign. In this period, for example, *Amrita Bazar Patrika*'s circulation increased from 2,000 to 7,500, the *Bengalee*'s from 3,000 to 11,000, *Hitavadi*'s from 16,000 to 30,000 over the period 1905–9 and, most spectacularly of all, the *Sandhya*'s increased from 500 to 7,000.

Pamphlets also popularised the *swadeshi* movement's ideals. Sumit Sarkar has traced 60 of these published during the period 1904–10. Some were compilations of articles published in *Bande Mataram* or *Jugantar*. Others justified the boycott of British goods by popularising the criticisms of such economists as William Digby and Rameshchandra Dutt of the 'drain of wealth' from India. One such pamphlet by Sakharam Ganesh Deuskar, entitled *Desher katha* ('Story of the Country'), went through four editions in the period 1904–7 totalling 10,000 copies. Two pamphlets which are especially interesting are those by Nikhilnath Roy and Ramendrasundar Trivedi. Roy's pamphlet, *Sonar Bangla* ('Golden Bengal'), published in July 1906, popularised the myth of a golden age in Bengal before the British intervention. This brought economic exploitation and degradation in its wake. The weapons of boycott and *swadeshi* are depicted as opening up the prospect of a return to the past glory. Travedi's colloquial pamphlet, *Banglakshmir brata-katha* ('A Vow for Bengali Women'), symbolised the *swadeshi* movement as a struggle to enable Lakshmi (the goddess of good fortune) to continue to reign over Bengal. She is portrayed as becoming restless because of the British cutting Bengal in two. If Bengali women take a *brata* (sacred vow) to abstain from foreign goods, Lakshmi can be made to stay (Sarkar, 1973, p. 273).

The press and the Khilafat movement

The Khilafat movement brought Indian Muslims on to the streets in large numbers for the first time. It sought to safeguard the temporal power of the Sultan of Turkey (the Khalifa of the worldwide Muslim community), who was on the losing side in the First World War, so that he could protect Islam's holy places. The Khilafat campaign coexisted, albeit briefly and uneasily, with the nationalist struggle. The basis for cooperation was a common anti-

British stance. It brought together the odd couple of the diminutive Gandhi and the strapping Shaukat Ali (1873–1938). There were, however, problems from the outset over the Muslims' adherence to non-violence and the rather superficial linkage between the two movements. Although the Congress and Khilafatists worked simultaneously on non-cooperation, the movements had their parallel volunteers, funds and organisations. It is safe to say that the joint struggle would not even have got off the ground without Gandhi's mediatory role between the Congress and Muslim leaderships.

The press made Indian Muslims aware of the Sultan of Turkey's fate. Pan-Islamic sentiments had been stirred in the period leading up to the First World War by a quartet of publications. These were Muhammad Ali's (1878–1931) English weekly *Comrade* and Urdu publication *Hamdard*, Zafar Ali Khan's *Zamindar* and Maulana Abul Kalam Azad's *al-Hilal*. Muhammad Ali, his brother Shaukat and Zafar Ali Khan all represented a younger generation of Aligarh graduates. While all four men were influenced by the Aligarh movement's Islamic modernism, by the time they began their journalistic enterprises they were disillusioned with its political outworking in the 'sycophancy' of the Muslim League to the colonial authorities. This intensified when it remained silent regarding the British government's neutrality in the 1911–12 Balkan wars. To many Muslims these seemed like a Christian plot to destroy the Ottomans, the last great Muslim power.

The quartet of papers, along with such less well-known Urdu weeklies as Hasrat Mohani's *Urdu-e-Mu'alla* and Syed Mir Jan's Lucknow-based *Muslim Gazette*, paved the way for the later Khilafat campaign by popularising the Ottoman cause during the Balkan wars. Appeals were made for Turkish relief and photographs were published of Turkish casualties. *Zamindar* and *al-Hilal* were also noted for their political poetry. The latter included verses penned by Shibli, which evoked the Ottoman Empire's former grandeur.

Muhammad Ali institutionalised the pro-Turkish sentiment in May 1912 when he founded the Anjuman-i-Khuddam-i-Kaaba (Society for the Defence of Muslim Holy Places). This emphasised that the preservation of the Sultan of Turkey's power was essential to his role as custodian and defender of Mecca and Medina, the holy places of Islam in the Jazirat-al-Arab. The president of the *anjuman*'s Delhi branch was the influential *imam* (prayer leader) of the Jama Masjid. Women were for the first time involved in public gatherings in support of the society. The Ali brothers' formidable mother Bi-Ammam addressed an all-women meeting at which gold and jewellery were pledged to help protect the Kaaba from the 'onslaught of Christian Europe'. By 1914, the *anjuman* boasted a membership of over 17,000.

The British interned the pro-Turkish Ali brothers during the First World War. The Press Act closed down all the radical 'young party' Muslim newspapers including *Comrade*, *al-Hilal* and *Hamdard*. When new papers emerged to fill the gap, such as Ghulam Hussain's English weekly *New Era* in April 1917, these too fell foul of the law.

Nevertheless, papers popularised the Khilafat campaign. The *Comrade* was revived in 1924. The weekly *Hindi* was founded by Khwaja Abdul Majid (1885–1962), the principal of the Jamia Millia Islamia college set up for Muslims independent of government control. Even existing conservative Muslim newspapers such as *Al Bashir*, which had been published in Etawah since 1899, briefly entered the anti-government lists. The British again limited the press's freedom. Among those arrested were Zafar Ali Khan, Tajuddin, who edited the *Khilafat* of Delhi, and Zafar ul Mulk. The latter, who had proposed the non-cooperation resolution during Khilafat Day on 1 August 1920, edited the Lucknow literary journal *An Nazir*. He was sentenced to two years' hard labour the following October for seditious writings.

Newspapers appealed for funds and Khilafatist volunteers. They carried detailed reports of meetings and *swadeshi* activities. They also popularised the Khilafat *fatwa* (ruling on a point of Islamic law) of Abdul Bari (1878–1926), the scholar from Firangi Mahal, which rallied religious support. Press reports of the large Khilafat processions described how 'poetic laments' moved those present 'to tears'.

Hasrat Mohani (1877–1951), nicknamed 'our mad mullah' by the Ali brothers, played a leading role before his internment in 1922. He called for complete independence for India at the December 1921 all-India Khilafat conference. Earlier he had presided over the Khilafat workers' conference in Delhi in April 1920. His journalistic activities dated back to 1903 when he had founded the weekly *Urdu-e-Mu'alla*. An accomplished lyricist, he turned his pen against British rule, as did Zafar Ali Khan who daily published Khilafat poetry in the *Zamindar*. Much of this was an apparently innocent lament for lost love deploying the traditional poetic devices of a neglected garden and vanished conviviality. Its readers would, however, have understood them as referring to the lost grandeur of Islam and have been inspired to work for its restoration. Typical were the verses below:

> The limits of sight were once too narrow
> To gauge that garden now seen in disarray.
>
> In your party is neither bowl nor cup.
> In your garden now sings neither dove nor jay.
>
> Consider then why your ship became
> of raging waves the thing of play.
>
> But even now if you bow before God,
> and on the Prophet's threshold lay.
>
> Dust will turn to gold in your hands,
> And you will fashion topaz from clay.

cited in Minault (1982, p. 156)

Caste and community-based publications

Newspapers devoted considerable attention to community as well as national issues. Religious controversies sold papers. Indeed much Muslim disquiet concerning the Congress's secular credentials arose from the fact that 'nationalist' pro-Congress papers such as *Tribune* or *Amrita Bazar Patrika* simultaneously supported Hindu communal issues. There was also a burgeoning of caste and community publications. The *Kayasth Reformer* was one of a number of caste-based papers dedicated to the spread of education and the uplift of their community.

One of the most successful and influential of this type of publication was the *Jat Gazette,* which was founded by the Hindu Jat reformer and political leader Chhotu Ram (1881–1945) shortly before the First World War. The newspaper popularised the emerging sense of community amongst the Jats of the south-eastern Punjab in part by reporting on the activities of the All-India Jat Mahasabha which had been formed in Muzaffarnagar in 1905. Its main contribution, however, was to assist in the articulation of *kaumi* (community) narratives. These included romanticised narratives of such historical figures as Maharaja Surajmal of Bharatpur, the 'invention' of a history of community unity and loyalty to the British during the 1857 revolt and the assertion of a Kshatriya status. The constant calls in the *Jat Gazette* for community consolidation and recognition of their martial prowess is summed up in the following poem, which was published late in December 1917.

> Those who possess a self-sacrificing spirit, they deserve to call themselves
> Jats. Warriors in war and those who are victorious in deeds, they
> deserve to be called the Jungilot [Army lord].
> They are the real spine of Hindustan, in helplessness they retain
> their splendour.
> They provide sustenance to others, it is they who make their home
> barren.
> In summer they toil and cultivate, they deplete their homes by providing
> grain.
> In winter, they retain their courage.
> Many among them are Raisahibs and Rai bahadurs, many in the army
> are captains.
> Many among them have access to the Government, and many among
> them enjoy the bliss of comfort.
> But in this *kaum* there are *lakhs* who lack provisions and wealth.
> As long as this *kaum* does not gain recognition,
> As long as it does not acquire the sense of self-respect,
> As long as everyone does not acquire education,
> The nation of the Jats will not be influential.
>
> cited in Datta (1997, p. 109)

Jats' claims of martial valour were rooted in their traditional stigma-tisation by the higher castes. This in part explains the community's receptivity to the Arya Samajist message with its strong anti-Brahmin over-tones. Indeed one chapter of Dayanand's *Satyarth Prakash* narrates the story of a Jat who ridiculed the authority of a Brahmin priest.

Social reform and revivalist organisations were as active as caste associa-tions in popularising their activities through the press. In Bengal, the Brahmo Samaj popularised reform in the monthly *Tatwa Bodhini Patrika*. The Punjabi equivalent was *Hari Hakikat*. In north-west India, community activists followed in the footsteps of the pioneering Christian presses of Allahabad and Ludhiana that were established in the 1830s. The latter produced the well-known paper *Nur-i-Ifshan*. The Arya Samaj was particularly prominent in the publication field. By the close of the nineteenth century, it published 30 papers in the Punjab alone. One of the leading English publications was the weekly *Regenerator of the Aryavarta,* which was produced in Lahore to serve as a 'popular forum where all questions that might interest the Arya Samaj could be discussed'. The *Arya Gazette*, another weekly, was the best-known publication. Its editor Pandit Lekh Ram (1858–97), a former police official who had joined the Peshawar Arya Samaj in 1880, became notorious for his vituperative attacks on the Muslim community. He wrote 32 books and pamphlets in all, the most infamous being his pamphlet, *Risala-i-Jihad ya'ri Din-i-Muhammadi ki Bunyard* ('A Treatise on Waging Holy War, or the Foundation of the Muhammadan Religion') which caused a considerable outcry when it was published in 1892. Five years later, Lekh Ram was murdered by a Muslim during a visit to Lahore, bringing communal tension to boiling point.

The Urdu weekly *Sat Dharam Pracharak* ('Herald of the True Religion') was another leading Arya publication. This was established in 1889 by Lala Munshi Ram (later known as Swami Shraddhananda). Through the columns of the weekly, Munshi Ram popularised the modification of the purification ritual – *shuddhi* – into a conversion ritual. A fellow member of the militant faction, Pandit Guru Datta, founded another Arya publication which circu-lated from 1888. This was the *Vedic Magazine*.

The emerging Tamil press, which can be dated from the weekly *Swadeshimitran* founded in 1880, played an important part in popularising a sense of regional nationalism. One of the earliest papers was the poet Subramania Bharati's journal *India* in which he published such compositions as *Sentamil natu* ('Country of Tamil') and *Tamil tay* ('Mother Tamil'). The Dravidianist ideology of the non-Brahmin movement was publicised in such Tamil newspapers as the *Dravidian* and *Justice,* which were both founded in 1917, and in the Telegu-language *Andhu Prakisha*. Non-Brahmin grievances were also voiced in the English weekly, the *Non-Brahmin*. The *Desabhaktan* weekly journal strengthened a sense of Tamil community consciousness amongst its readers as far afield as Ceylon, Burma and the Straits Settlements.

The self-respect movement of the former Congressman Ramaswami Naicker, which from the mid-1920s onwards inculcated a sense of pride in non-Brahmins based on the glories of their Dravidian past, spawned a vigorous press. This included the English-language *Revolt,* which was founded in November 1928, the Tamil daily, *Vidutalai* ('Freedom'), which was founded three years later and the monthly *Pakutarivu* ('Common Sense'), which began publication in 1935. The most influential paper, however, was the Tamil weekly *Kudi Arasu* ('People's Government'), which Naicker founded in May 1924. Its power stemmed from its simple and direct style of writing, which was similar to the popular idiom of Naicker's speeches. Naicker popularised, for example, the derogatory term *parppan* for the Brahmin with its connotations of cunning.

The leading Muslim *anjumans* in the Punjab ran their own newspapers: *Risala Anjuman-i-Himayat-i-Islam* and *Risala Anjuman-i-Islamia* respectively. They publicised their activities and refuted the criticisms of rival publications. The emerging sectarian groups also produced papers: for example, the *Ish'at-i-Sunnah* of the puritanically orthodox Ahl-i-Hadith. This paper directed much of its fire on the heterodox Ahmadiyah sect of the followers of Mirza Ghulam Ahmad. The Ahmadis defended their position in the late nineteenth century through such publications as the *al-Hakam,* which was produced in their Qadian headquarters.

The principal mouthpiece of the modernist Aligarh movement was the *Aligarh Institute Gazette.* This began life in 1866 as the newspaper of the Aligarh Scientific Society, which Syed Ahmad Khan had founded two years earlier. It soon emerged as the foremost weekly in the United Provinces, publishing articles in both Urdu and English on educational and social questions. Sir Syed contributed many pieces and was a regular correspondent during his sojourn in England in 1869–70. The newspaper created the greatest stir when he used it to voice his misgivings about the Congress and the impact of representative institutions on the Muslim community. The intra-community controversies arising from Syed Ahmad Khan's emphasis on reason, as opposed to authority, in religious interpretation were played out through another of his publications, *Tahzib-ul-Akhlaq* ('Muslim Social Reformer'), and such orthodox newspapers as *Nur ul Afaq* (Cawnpore), and *Terhawin* (Agra). Death threats accompanied the bitter condemnation of his 'progressive' views.

From November 1880 onwards, the activities and ideology of the Lahore Singh Sabha, a Sikh reformist body, were publicised by the Punjabi weekly, *Gurmukhi Akhbar.* Its editor Gurmukh Singh also launched the monthly journal *Vidyarak,* which combined historical accounts of the Gurus and the Khalsa with textual exegesis of the Granth and instructions on reform of Sikh rituals. The Singh Sabha's publishing really got under way with the opening of the Khalsa Press in Lahore in 1883. Its titles included the Urdu weekly the *Khalsa Gazette* and the highly influential Punjabi weekly *Khalsa Akhbar,* edited by Ditt Singh (1853–1901), which commenced publication in 1886. The growth of print culture assisted the reformers' aim of encouraging Sikhs to renounce popular religious practices and to ensure that the Granth took precedence over sacred texts belonging to 'others'. An editorial in the *Khalsa Akhbar* in April 1887 rhetorically asked its readers, 'Will the Beloved of the Khalsa Qaum, the firm followers of the tenth Guru, Gobind Singh, ever accept anyone else as Guru except the ten Gurus and the Adi Granth?' (cited in Oberoi, 1994, p. 320). The paper, along with the *Khalsa Gazette,* devoted a page each week to extracts from the Granth.

The *Khalsa Akhbar* also reported on reformist activities. Under the heading of 'A Joyful News' it published the following account on 6 November 1886.

> We have recently received news that on the occasion of the popular Gugga Naumi fair at village Kaudi in the Patiala state, Sabha activists spoke out against Gugga Pir and the holding of the fair … Through their incisive speeches they convinced thousands of peasants that Gugga was a mythical figure, purely a creature of imagination *without any history* [emphasis added]. He need not be followed. Instead they should all worship one Akal Purakh [the immortal God] whose glory is inscribed in each and every word of the Adi Granth. The *Khalsa Akhbar* prays for the success of all those brave Sikhs who are earnestly trying to eradicate the evil customs prevailing in the community.
>
> cited in Oberoi (1994, p. 310)

The dismissal of folk religion because of its lack of adherence to text or historical 'fact' baldly locates such endeavours within the Western modernist discourse. The campaign against Sikhs worshipping such folk saints as Gugga Pir and Sakhi Sarvar was also greatly boosted by the publication of Ditt Singh's tract, *Sultan Puara,* in 1896. During the next two years it went through three editions. Tracts provided a cheaper and more accessible means of communicating community values than newspapers. Like the press, they were adopted partly in response to the activities of missionary organisations. As early as 1848, the Bombay Tract Society was handing out Christian texts at railway bookstalls at nominal prices. Even earlier and more effective was the Native Bible and Tract Society established in Tinnevelly in the Madras district in 1822. In less than a decade it had published 45,000 tracts. The Ludhiana Mission handed out 25,000 tracts during a single visit to the Hindu gathering at the Hardwar Mela. By the end of the nineteenth century, over 300,000 Christian newspapers and tracts were being distributed annually in the Punjab alone.

Hindu and Muslim reformers responded in kind. The Muhammadan Tract Society of Lahore, for example, was established in 1882. Five years later, the Hindu Tract Society was established in Madras. Its editions of tracts ran to 10,000. The Brahmo Samaj was bringing out tracts in Hindi, Punjabi and Urdu in the Punjab from 1876 and the following year established its own printing press. Sikh reformers also joined the tract explosion. In 1894, the author and journalist Bhai Vir Singh (1872–1957) set up the Khalsa Tract Society. This produced pamphlets in simple language on Sikh scriptures, prayers and the lives of the Gurus, along with exhortations to eradicate superstitious beliefs and practices. By the turn of the century it was estimated that half a million copies had been distributed. This outpouring consolidated the Sikh community along both religious and cultural lines, as it provided a major boost for the promotion of Punjabi in the Gurmukhi script.

The endeavours to reach a mass Sikh audience were intensified with the establishment of the Khalsa Handbill Society in Lahore in 1908. This circulated free of charge printed handbills on religious and social issues. The aim was to reach the rural population which still persisted in 'un-Sikh' practices. Within two years of its creation, the society had published over 400,000 handbills, all but 20,000 of which were in Gurumukhi. The energies exerted by the Singh Sabhas and their publishing ventures undoubtedly strengthened community consolidation and paved the way for its politicisation in the 1920s.

Left-wing publications

The communist movement traditionally emphasised the importance of the articulation of its ideology of class warfare and scientific socialism. A vigorous left-wing press emerged in India in the wake of the 1917 Bolshevik Revolution. Its ideas spread far further than the ranks of the Communist Party of India (CPI) which was founded in 1925 and the provincial Workers' and Peasants' Parties which acted as communist ginger groups within the Congress. Indeed the strength, but also one of the weaknesses, of the left as a powerful individual entity was the extent to which its ideas fed into the nationalist mainstream through such figures as Jawaharlal Nehru and the radical Bengali politician Subhas Chandra Bose (1897–1945). Factionalism, lack of funds and the unpopularity arising from the opposition to the nationalist 1942 Quit India movement in keeping with the Comintern's new 'People's War' line all contrived to sideline the CPI as British rule drew to its close.

The initial appeal of communist ideas to the educated classes, especially students, meant that many leading publications were in English. The *Vanguard of Indian Independence* was published in Europe in the early 1920s by the leading left-wing figure M. N. Roy. Despite the efforts of customs officials, it circulated widely in the subcontinent. English-language CPI mouthpieces produced in India included the *National-Front* and *New Age*, *The Socialist Weekly* which was published from Bombay, and the *Labour-Kisan Gazette* which came out from Madras. They were read along with English translations of classic Marxist texts such as the *Communist Manifesto* and *Das Kapital*.

The need to disseminate communist ideas more widely, however, led to the development of a vernacular left-wing press. Typical of the early publications was *Inquilab,* which was begun by Ghulam Hussain in Lahore in August 1922 as an Urdu bi-weekly. This failed to survive its editor's arrest in the 1923 Kanpur Conspiracy case. A more lasting impact was made by the stable of papers published by the Workers' and Peasants' Party in the Punjab. These were in Punjabi and included the monthly *Kirti,* which was founded by Santokh Singh in February 1926. The *Kirti* appealed to the radicalised Sikh Jat population which inhabited the 'Big Red' villages of the central Punjab. Its sentiments towards the non-violent struggle of Gandhi were summed up in the derisive description, *Laghoti Bhan Mahatma* (the jockstrap Mahatma) (G. Singh, 1994, p. 49). The *Kirti*'s popularity owed much to its use of poetry. Above all, it linked contemporary socialist struggle against capitalism with traditional Sikh egalitarian sentiment.

Regular weekly newspapers also appeared in Bengali (*Ganavani, Jagaran, Gana Sakti*), Hindi (*Kranti Kari*), Marathi (*Kranti*), Telegu (*Navasakti*) and Tamil (*Janasakti*). Such publications were frequently repressed. In 1942, however, the CPI was legalised because of its pro-war stance in the Allied fight against fascism. A number of new publications appeared including the weekly *People's War,* which claimed a circulation of 33,000 by the beginning of 1943 (Overstreet and Windmiller, 1959, p. 449). Among the new regional publications at this time were such newspapers as *Janayuddha* in Bengali, *Deshabhimani* in Malayalam, *Muktiyuddha* in Oriya and *Jang-e-Azadi* in Punjabi, designed to strengthen local grassroots' support. Nevertheless, they also reflected the extent to which the communist movement had become fragmented and oriented towards local power. Its regionalisation was to become even more marked in post-independence India.

No analysis of left-wing publications would be complete without reference to the Progressive Writers' movement. This was launched in London in 1934, before being established at Lucknow in April 1936 under the leadership of the communist son of an Indian high court judge, Sajjad Zaheer. The move was undoubtedly encouraged by the establishment of the Union of Soviet Writers. Indicative of the ties between Congress left-wingers and the communists was the fact that Jawaharlal Nehru was invited to speak at the first All-India Progressive Writers' Conference. The progressive writers all came from the privileged upper and middle classes, but they brought a humanistic/socialist vision to their short stories, poetry and novels. Included amongst the supporters of the Progressive Writers' movement were such great names of South Asian literature as Krishan Chander, Saadat Hasan Manto, Faiz Ahmad Faiz, Ahmad Nadim Qasimi and Rajinder Singh Bedi. Some of their greatest creations were to emerge in the wake of the human tragedies of the 1947 partition (Talbot, 1996a, Chapter 4). It was not only progressive writers, however, who turned to fiction for didactic purposes.

Novels and the construction of community

Novels were also used in colonial India for purposes of community consolidation. Like nationalism, the modern novel was an import from Europe. In the subcontinent, as in its homeland, it was to be used for didactic purposes in the process of community invention. This purpose can be discerned most clearly in the works of Bhai Vir Singh and Bankim Chandra Chatterjee. We shall turn first, however, to a brief analysis of lesser-known authors.

Abdul Halim Sharar (1860–1926) pioneered the development of the Urdu novel. He is best known for his historical romances. In these he supported the ideas of the Aligarh movement. His best known work is *Flora Florinda,* which was originally published in serial form in 1893. Significantly the book is set in the Spain of the ninth century when Muslim power was at its height. Through the characters of Flora, the daughter of a Muslim father and a Christian mother, her brother Ziyad and the nun Florida who is to spirit her away to the Cathedral of Cordoba, Sharar explores the themes of Muslim nobility and Islamic superiority to Christendom. The latter's depravity is symbolised by the Patriarch's rape of Flora when she has taken refuge in a convent. Here in fictional form is the glorious past of Islam which inspired contemporary community consolidation.

Hindu writers of historical romances also looked to past heroisms to inspire the present. In their case, however, the 'other' was not the alien Christian, but the Muslim rulers of the past six centuries. These were invariably portrayed as 'tyrannical' and 'debauched'. Such representations as those of Kisorilal Goswami's (1866–1932) novel *Tara* (1902) fed into communal stereotypes which have become persistent. The Muslim characters in Bharatendu Harischandra's play *Nildevi* are similarly debauched, while the Hindus are courageous and honourable. Another Hindi writer, Radha Charan Goswami (1859–1923), in a translation of a Bengali play entitled (in Hindi) *Bharat Mein Yavan Raj,* has the character Vamadev thank an Englishman for rescuing the 'Hindustanis from the jaws of death' by overthrowing the Muslim rulers who had been 'killing cows', butchering children, defiling temples, raping women and robbing the people. A similar theme of Hindu resistance to Muslim tyranny can be found in the Bengali novels *Mahararashta Jibanprabhat* (1878) and *Rajput Jibansandhya* (1879) by the 'economic nationalist' Romesh Chandra Dutt (1848–1909) .

The most famous and influential historical novel is another Bengali work, *Ananda Math,* written by Bankim Chandra Chatterjee and published in 1882. Although the novel is set against the historical backdrop of Bengal's 1770 famine and the clashes between armed wandering ascetics and the forces of the Muslim Nawab, Chatterjee's didactic purpose leads him to omit mention of the role of the Muslim armed *faqirs* of this period. He also transforms the Hindu ascetics from Shaivites to worshippers of Vishnu and introduces devotion to Kali. The plot of armed uprising to foreign rule was used for inspiration by both militant Indian nationalists and Hindu nationalists. While the British led the troops of the Nawab, Chatterjee expresses the view we have seen in Goswami's play that the substitution of the Company rule for the Nawab's was providential, even although the ascetics' struggle ended in the apparent defeat of one foreigner ruler being substituted for another. The real enemy is thus the Muslims not the British. This point is reinforced by the graphic descriptions of assaults on Muslim villages. In a chilling but prophetic insight, a unified Hindu community is portrayed as emerging, through violence, as a people at war. The agenda of Ayodhya is articulated a century earlier, when the mob declares, 'Unless we throw these dirty bastards [Muslims] out, Hindus will be ruined ... When shall we raze mosques down to the ground and erect Radhamadhav's temples in their place?' (cited in Sarkar, 1996, p. 175).

The novel's fame rests in part on the fact that it contains the nationalist/communalist hymn 'Bande Mataram'. This was the rallying cry of the *swadeshi* movement, but has since been appropriated by Hindu nationalists. Bankim had in fact originally composed it in 1875, although he correctly saw that it would have greater impact contained within the novel. It was to be subsequently popularised by Aurobindo. The hymn identifies India with the icon of the Mother and portrays her as nurturer, demon slayer (Durga) and the embodiment of destructive force (Kali). The demon is unspecified and could be understood as either the British or the Muslims. What is important is the assurance of future triumph and the suggestion that the son empowered by the mother's *shakti* is militant and armed for conflict. This is a development of the theme contained in Bankim's earlier novel (*Kapalkundala*). Bankim's portrayal of militant Hindu ascetics appealed immensely to those upper-caste Bengali youths who by the end of the century were dedicated to the cult of physical fitness in response to the colonialist discourse of *babu* effeminancy. Equally inspiring were the tales of national uprising against foreign rule. Many who entered the revolutionary societies had been fed a diet of Bankim's romances and under Aurobindo's inspiration sought to re-enact them. Significantly, Bankim's works, especially *Ananda Math,* were prominent amongst the books uncovered by the raid on the Dacca Anushilan Samiti referred to earlier.

Bhai Vir Singh used the medium of the novel to popularise the major reformist themes of the Singh Sabha movement. The dangers to the community of an unreconstructed folk religion were summed up memorably by Bhai Vir Singh in his first Punjabi novel *Sundari* (1898). 'Leaving your God and your true Gurus, you worship stones, trees, idols, tombs and saints. Forgetting Sikh religion, you rot in another religion. Turning your back on the true Gurus you teach someone else's religion to your offspring too. Your children will grow to be half baked like you – Sikh on the head, Brahmin around the neck and Muslim below the waist' (cited in Oberoi 1994, p. 311).

Sundari was followed in rapid succession by the novels *Bijay Singh* (1899) and *Satwant Kaur* (1900), which are set at the time of the eighteenth-century Mughal persecution of Sikhs. The gruesome accounts of torture and martyrdom were included not to encourage anti-Muslim sentiments in his readers, but to move them to emulate the heroism of their forebears by standing fast to the physical symbols of their tradition. Sikh identity in these texts and in Bhai Vir Singh's final novel *Baba Nuadh Singh* (serialised 1917–21), which is set in the colonial era, is collapsed to mean Khalsa membership. The initiatory baptism rite is a leading motif in the works. The novelist uses the conversion from Hinduism of the second novel's hero Ram Lal, who becomes Bijay Singh, as an opportunity not only to describe the rite in detail, but to comment on its effects on moral character. In the third novel, it is a Muslim, Agha Khan, who converts, but again the transformation brought about by baptism is emphasised. These novels emerge from the context in which Arya Samajists were attempting to reconvert 'low caste' Sikhs to Hinduism and in which Sikh reformers were attempting to secure 'slow-adopting' Sikhs into the community fold through baptism and the wearing of the physical symbols of the Khalsa.

Traditional methods of communication

Print culture's limitations for propagandists in a predominantly non-literate society are self-evident. It is not surprising that traditional methods of communication were utilised to transmit new senses of identity. Bardic recitations, music and folk drama were important 'secular' oral media, while their religious counterparts were devotional poetry and the Ram Lila and Ras Lila religious dramas devoted respectively to Ram and Krishna. The role of the Ram Lila in bringing into existence a pan-Indian Hindu identity in its modern form has been much discussed.

Less attention has been devoted to such regional theatre forms as the *jatra* and the *nautanki* in encouraging nationalist sentiment. The Bengali *jatra* was an important medium of communication during the *swadeshi* movement. Its regional equivalent in the Urdu and Hindi-speaking world of North India was the *nautanki*. Its actors and musicians were drawn from an urban milieu, but the theatre troupes largely played to rural audiences, captivating them with their music and dance and professional costuming, which far outshone local folk entertainments. The importance of such peripatetic theatre troupes in the cultural exchange between urban literate society and the unlettered villagers, and in weaving a sense of regional identity, has yet to be fully appreciated by historians.

The surviving scripts and librettos provide some clues to the way in which *nautanki* theatre may have influenced cultural understandings through its transmission of urban ideologies to the countryside. There are, for example, a large number of scores of musical dramas (*sangits*) dating from the late nineteenth century, which emphasised Rajput martial virtues and resistance to Muslim rule. Such stories would not only have encouraged a developing sense of regional identification, but have underscored Hindu assertiveness and resistance to 'unlawful' authority. Such themes may have helped popularise the nationalism of the Congress extremists with its emphasis on Hindu values and defiance of British authority. Kathryn Hansen, the authority on *nautanki* theatre, has also unearthed later explicit political plays that retell the events of the Amritsar massacre. The Kanpur *sangit* writer Manohar Lal Shukla recounts the Jallianwalla Bagh massacre from a child's viewpoint in *Rashtriya sangit julmi dayar* (1922). The play concludes with a ghost of those killed taking revenge on General Dyer and forcing him to release his prisoners (Hansen, 1992, pp. 108, 134–5). The emotive impact of this play on its audience can be partially gauged from the surviving title page of the script with its allegorical portrayal of a kneeling woman (named Afflicted Punjab) praying to Lord Vishnu while a whip-wielding policeman (named Martial Law) pulls at her robe (Hansen, p. 109).

The costume, scenery, music and dance of the *nautanki* and other regional drama forms were especially suited for conveying messages to non-literate audiences. Poetry, songs and religious performance were equally able to reach out to those unable to respond to the modern medium of the printed word. For this reason traditional methods of communication were utilised alongside the press by nationalist, community and left-wing activists. Songs, poems and dramas were deployed, for example, by communists in the Punjab to 'demystify the socialist message' (G. Singh, 1994, p. 67). Left-wing members of the Kerala Congress used drama in the 1930s and adapted folk songs 'to the purposes of political mobilisation' (Hardgrave, 1979, p. 194). Demands for the reduction of land revenue or of rents to the Jenmi proprietors were popularised in such songs as the one below which was originally written in Malayalam by T. S. Subrahaniam.

Peasants! Workers!
The exploited! The Poor!
Come, rally behind the red flag
Let us resolve and prepare
In order to eradicate poverty
And to fight oppression
To burn and smash this
Capitalist fortress which creates famine
To change this social structure
Which perpetuates selfish interests
To smash imperialist domination
To tear apart the *Jenmi* system
To abolish exploitation
And to establish Socialism

cited in Gopalankutty (1983, p. 203)

In some controversies, such as that over widow remarriage in mid nine-teenth-century Bengal, orthodox opponents of reform sought to undercut the more modern methods of their opponents. Thus, while the reformer Vidyasagar petitioned the Legislative Council and popularised his views through the Brahmoist monthly *Tatwa Bodhini Patrika*, Hindu traditionalists ridiculed in song the demand for widow remarriage. Many of the verses were composed by the leading poets Dasarathi Roy and Isvar Chandra Gupta.

With respect to the cow protection movement of the 1890s, however, modern and traditional means of communication worked hand in hand. Its supporters in the United Provinces made effective use of print culture in producing pamphlets, books and handbills as well as using the columns of such newspapers as *Khichri Samechar* and the Kanpur monthly *Brahman*. Mobilisation was also encouraged by the use of relay letters (*patias*), which like chain letters carried an injunction to pass on their contents. Gyanendra Pandey has revealed that the basic form of these *patias* was the inclusion of religious invocations, information and appeal for action in terms of the sacred *dharmic* duty of cow protection. Recipients of letters who failed to respond were threatened with the 'de-merit flowing from the slaughter of five cows', or the consequences of a sin equivalent to that of incest (Pandey, 1997, p. 313). The message of cow protection was simultaneously spread by local holy men. One such figure, Sriman Swami, held nearly 50 meetings across the United Provinces in 1888. In addition to such wanderings, cow protection preachers addressed the large crowds which gathered at bathing festivals, most notably the Magh Mela at Allahabad and the Kumbh Mela at Hardwar. Emotive pictures were displayed symbolising the cow as both the abode of Hindu deities and the 'universal mother'. The horror of butchery combined images of inhuman monsters and clear allusions to Muslims as slayers of 'Mother Cow'.

From the time of Guru Hargobind (1595–1644) onwards, the *dhadi* tradition has been an important medium for communicating an awareness of Sikh political history and culture to rural Punjabi audiences (Pettigrew, 1992). *Dhadi* (eulogist) groups comprise three or four musicians and traditionally use two small drums and the *sarangi*. They perform in established centres at such places as Amritsar, Tarn Taran and Nawanshehar, as well as at village fairs and markets. Their songs are inspirational and designed to record the names of those martyred in the community's struggle against injustice. Various tunes and melodies are used in the performance, one of the most popular types of song being the *var*, which is sung in praise of a particular heroic figure. The political impact of the *dhadi* performance is enhanced by the spoken detailed explanation of the background to each song. It thus represents an especially effective tradition for recording history in song. The *dhadi* tradition, which significantly arose at the time of the Mughal persecution, was an influential means of communication in the troubled aftermath to the 1984 Indian Army operation in the Golden Temple at Amritsar.

The self-respect movement used songs and poetry to popularise its message in the Madras Presidency during the 1920s. Numerous songs about its leaders such as Ramaswami Naicker were distributed. Pamphlets used short stories to explain its message. One which appeared in 1929 under the title *Visittira tevarkal korttu* ('Wonderful Court of the Deities') used the device of a trial of the gods of the Pantheon to condemn the basis of Puranic Hinduism. Shiva, Vishnu and others were cross-examined and convicted of violent and sexual crimes (Irschick, 1969, p. 340).

Tilak was one of the earliest nationalist politicians to recognise the importance of song and festivals. He unashamedly sought to 'convert large religious festivals into political rallies'. Through these festivals results could 'be achieved', he declared, 'which it would be impossible for Congress to achieve'. We have already had cause to refer to his popularising of the Shivaji festival. From 1893 onwards, he also reshaped the Maharashtrian festival to honour the elephant-headed deity Ganapati, known as the 'overcomer of obstacles'. Public Ganapati celebrations can be dated to at least the thirteenth century in the region. Tilak systematised what had been spontaneous group immersions of clay images of the deity and increased the spectacle of the group celebrations by erecting decorated pavilions and ceremonial archways. At the same time as consolidating a sense of Hindu community in public display, something which Sandria Freitag has explored with respect to Ram Lila celebrations in North India, Tilak's 'invention' of *mela* (singing parties) to accompany the processions was designed as a vehicle for the dissemination of militant nationalism. Versifiers urged their hearers to wear Indian-made garments, to abstain from liquor and to oppose the policies of the government and the Congress moderates. By 1910 the British authorities had become sufficiently alarmed virtually to suppress the festival.

The flavour of the inaugural 1894 Ganapati festival in Poona emerges in the following description lifted from the pages of *Kesari*.

> [The procession] included a hundred ... ganapatis, conveyed in
> palanquins, carts, and horse-carriages, preceded by seventy-five
> bands of musicians, some seventy *melas*, twenty groups of
> *lejimvalas* [acrobats who dance to the music of the *lejim*] and
> a concourse of 25,000 people. They were in turn showered with
> sweets, parched rice and *gulal* [red powder used in religious
> celebrations] by an estimated crowd of 50,000 which watched from
> the streets and balconies. The procession took three hours to proceed
> from Reay market to Lakdi Bridge.
>
> Cashman (1975, p. 80)

In future years, the Ganapati celebrations were to become even more lavish and spread from Poona to Bombay and other towns and cities of the region. Nevertheless, the extent of the politicisation brought by the festival and its accompanying *mela* movement should not be exaggerated. Reports of the non-Brahmin *melas* of both Bombay and Poona declared, for example, that they were free from 'the political spirit and leaven' of the Brahmin parties. Their songsters instead concentrated on 'religious' themes. Moreover, like the Shivaji festival, political recruitment of a predominantly Maharashtrian celebration limited its wider appeal. Significantly, the festival in Bombay evoked little enthusiasm from the Gujarati-speaking Hindu population. In addition to failing to transcend linguistic barriers, the Ganapati festival, together with the development of the Shivaji celebrations, heightened tensions between Hindus and Muslims in the urban centres of the Deccan.

Three decades later the Muslim League also deployed pageantry and public display to deepen a sense of national identity. In this instance it involved the reinvention of Mughal processions rather than of a religious festival, although such occasions as Eid (the festival marking the end of Ramadan) were used for Muslim League propaganda as were the *urs* celebrations at *sufi* shrines. One such procession occurred in October 1938, when Jinnah arrived in Karachi to preside over the Sind Muslim League Conference. He was conveyed through the streets in a procession which stretched for three miles. On another occasion five years later, an estimated 50,000 persons processed with Jinnah through Quetta city with the entire route decorated with welcome arches and gateways named after Muslim heroes. On both occasions the British reported that Jinnah was conveyed in a manner 'befitting a king' or like a 'royal potentate'.

Such welcomes bear unmistakable similarities to coronation crowds using public places to honour the head of state. Much of the ceremonial deliberately re-enacted Mughal spectacle. Jinnah, it is true, did not ride on an elephant like a Mughal potentate, nor was he accompanied by slaves, servants and treasure chests, but all the roads were cleared, shops and houses were decorated and small tents and canopies erected to provide refreshments for spectators as had been the practice when the emperor had left his palace for Friday prayers at festival time. Furthermore, like the Mughals, Jinnah paraded his own uniformed bodyguard, musicians, horses and camels. Mughal processions were designed to generate a sense of pride and loyalty by displaying the emperor's wealth and power. The Muslim League processions which accompanied Jinnah had a similar psychological impact, heightening his symbolic role as the embodiment of Muslim unity and political aspirations. Moreover, his processions symbolised claims to control over the locality through which they passed. This was assisted by their slow pace. For as Sandria Freitag has commented in the context of the Muharram procession, 'onlookers had much time to observe and participate, to be incorporated in the process' (Freitag, 1989, p. 134). Routes invariably laid claim to the main bazaars and thoroughfares as well as taking in centres of Muslim community such as mosques and schools. A procession in Patna in October 1937, for example, pointedly stopped at places on the route which symbolised either Jinnah's leadership or the community's claim to unity. During one such halt the *imam* of the Jama Masjid, Bankipore, presented

Jinnah (1876–1949) with a sword and hailed him as the leader of the *millat* (nation).

By the closing period of British rule, political processions had become almost daily occurrences. All parties organised them and they sometimes merged imperceptibly with the crowds that marked important moments in the religious calendar. The morning *prabhat pheris* (nationalist processions) taken out by *mohalla* (ward-level) Congress committees in North Indian towns adopted such religiously symbolic behaviour as song, prayer and bathing in the Ganges.

Traditional methods of communication and the swadeshi *movement*

We conclude this brief examination of the use of traditional means of communication for transmitting new senses of identity by returning to the *swadeshi* and Khilafat case studies. How did 'traditional' means complement the use of print culture in these two important episodes in the nationalist movement?

The great Bengali writer Rabrindranath Tagore (1861–1941), in a famous Swadeshi Samaj speech of July 1904, debated how the *bhadralok* elite could put across their political message to the uneducated masses. He suggested the popularisation of *swadeshi* goods at traditional *melas* (fairs) and the use of *jatras* (folk dramas) and *kathakata* (recitals) to spread patriotic feelings, along with modern techniques such as *suhrid* (magic-lantern shows). Tagore, along with other Bengali writers, also brought out collections of *swadeshi* songs. A number were composed in regional dialects to ensure their popularity with village audiences. 'A new method of approaching the people is reported from the Tippera district', read a police report of 22 January 1907, 'where a band of young men is going about singing patriotic songs which are said to be far more effective than speeches … one song in particular, describing dawn as ushered in by Japan and hoping that India will one day assert her independence and see noon, is much appreciated by the people' (Sarkar, 1973, p. 291).

Another popular *swadeshi* song was directed to women and called on them to sacrifice their wealth on behalf of the wretched and dispossessed figure of the motherland.

> Leave your glass bangles, Oh women of Bengal,
> Never wear them again!
> Wake O Mothers and Sisters!
> Awake from this trance!
> …

Harki Mother Bengal calls out to you:
'Awake O my Daughters!
If you take the pledge my wealth need never leave the land!
For I am poor and unfortunate
And do not get even two meals in a day,
Alas! what have I deteriorated into –
And none of you have spared a thought!'
                                        cited in Chowdhury (1998, pp. 158–9)

The *swadeshi* activists also used the village entertainments of *kathakata* and *jatra* to spread their message. 'Patriotic ideas' were woven into the traditional stories from the Hindu epics in the *kathakatas*. These new forms of recitals were known as *swadeshi kathakatas*. For example, Girin Mukherji, a priest of the Calcutta Kalighat temple, wrote in 1907 a *Swadeshi Ramayana*. In Bankura, *bhadu* folk songs were similarly utilised for propaganda purposes.

Theatrical parties toured many Bengal districts with *jatra* plays which combined entertainment with *swadeshi* political messages. One of the most famous *jatras*, *Matri Puja*, was penned in 1906 by Mukunda Das, a 'minstrel' devoted to Shiva. The play depicts India as being exploited by foreigners, but Matangi, the goddess of war, is preparing herself for conflict. Das was eventually to be imprisoned in 1909. Further evidence of the anxieties the *jatras* caused the authorities emerges from a note recorded by the district magistrate of Bakargunj in the wake of the May 1907 regulation of meetings ordinance. The *jatra* had become 'an effective substitute for a *swadeshi* meeting as it reaches all classes and spreads seditious doctrines amongst them. At the same time it is very difficult to deal with' (Sarkar, 1973, p. 302). *Jatras* were not just adapted in this way by touring *swadeshi* activists. At Shikarpur in Chittagong district, villagers themselves initiated the use of plays to put across messages of an 'unequivocally anti-British nature'.

Ordinary people were drawn into the *swadeshi* movement through Kali *pujas* (religious devotions) and through the administration of *swadeshi* vows at temples. There are reports of a wide range of social groups including cobblers and washermen, labourers, sweetmeat vendors, barbers and cloth merchants taking such vows. A crowd of 50,000 took the *swadeshi* pledge at the Kalighat Temple in Calcutta on 28 September 1905. These were predominantly male gatherings, but women were involved in the *swadeshi* movement as they were called upon not to light household fires on the day annually observed as Partition Day.

There were attempts to involve Muslims in the movement through intercommunal functions like 'National Dinners' and during the Muslim Eid festival. Girischandra Ghosh's 'patriotic plays', published in 1905 and 1906 respectively, *Sirajuddoulah* and *Mir Kasim*, had their Muslim heroes. In December 1906 the revolutionary paper *Jugantar* hailed the revolt of 1857 as the first Hindu–Muslim war of independence. Just a few months earlier it had suggested a festival to honour Mir Kasim. It also cannot be denied that there were such leading Muslim *swadeshi* orators as Liakat Husain, described by the *Sandhya* as 'a lion amongst men', Din Mahomed, Abul Husain and Abdul Gafur. Despite such exceptions, the overwhelming Hindu character of the *swadeshi* movement alienated Muslims.

The pro-nationalist Muslim paper the *Soltan* expressed the feelings of non-communal Muslims in its comments on abortive attempts by *swadeshi* activists to spread the Shivaji festival to Bengal in June 1906. 'It has yet to be shown that Shivaji had any vast patriotic schemes in his contemplation', it editorialised. 'We know that the object of our Hindu brethren in celebrating the Shivaji festival is neither to wound Musalman feelings nor to vilify the reign of Aurangzeb ... But ... in order to give high praise to Shivaji, one cannot but censure Musalman rule' (Sarkar, 1973, p. 306). Bengali Muslims were not only alienated by the Hinduised imagery of the campaign, but by the social boycotts many experienced when they still used and sold non-*swadeshi* goods. The social boycott was not a new weapon in Hindu hands, but it was applied vigorously during the *swadeshi* campaign. Local markets (*hats*) were closed and services were withdrawn from those who ignored the calls of the campaign. Social boycott was, of course, practised against Hindu merchants and government employees as well as Muslims. The tensions it raised amongst the latter, however, played a part in instigating the communal riots which broke out in 1906–7 at such places as Iswargunj, Comilla, Mymensingh, Dewangunj and Phulpur.

Traditional methods of mobilisation and the Khilafat movement

The mass Muslim involvement in the Khilafat and non-cooperation movements depended on the temporary alliance that was forged between the modernist 'young party' of Aligarh and the *'ulama*. The latter had previously stood outside of politics, but because of their widespread influence as religious scholars, teachers and prayer leaders possessed an immense potential influence. The *alim* (plural *'ulama*) are literally those who possess (*ilm*) knowledge of Islam. This expertise lies in such areas as jurisprudence (*fiqh*) or Quranic exegesis (*tafsir*). This knowledge gave the *'ulama* power as educators in primary schools (*maktabs*), in the secondary Islamic school (*madrasa*), and in higher centres of learning such as the *dar-ul-ulum* which had been established at Deoband in 1857. Their expertise was also called on to issue rulings (*fatwa*) on points of law: for example, whether it was lawful for Muslims to learn English. Such rulings were regarded as infallible.

Members of the *'ulama* were also reciters of the Quran and led the prayers (*imams*) of the faithful. They also addressed the congregations in the mosques each Friday. These sermons focused on matters which concerned the community as well as on issues of Islamic belief and practice. Politics frequently featured within the sermons, as no distinction was acknowledged between the political and religious realms. The *'ulama* deployed the power of the sermon and the *fatwa* to popularise the Khilafat cause. The *fatwa* campaign began in November 1920 when a meeting of *'ulama* in Delhi, through the promptings of the scholar from Firangi Mahal, Abdul Bari, issued a *fatwa* which endorsed civil disobedience by declaring that non-coop-eration with the enemies of Islam was religiously lawful. It also permitted political alliances with Hindus. The *fatwa* was published under the title of *The Unanimous Fatwa of the Indian 'Ulama*. The government of India hurriedly banned it.

The following June, the *fatwa* was reiterated by a group of leading *'ulama* who emphasised even more starkly that service in the police or army was unlawful as it involved the 'sin' of firing on fellow Muslims. When the All-India Khilafat Conference, meeting in Karachi on 8–10 July 1921, endorsed the claim that Muslim law forbade Muslims to enlist in the army, this was too much for the British, who from the 1880s onwards had shifted the main centre of their military recruitment to the Muslim West Punjab. Conspiracy charges were alleged against a group of prominent Khilafatists, including the Ali brothers, who became known as the Karachi Seven. This action was to prove highly counterproductive. The British could not make the charges stick in a highly publicised court case. In the weeks leading up to it, the Khilafatists ran a successful campaign claiming that the authorities had no right to confiscate the non-cooperation *fatwa* because in doing so they were interfering with the Muslim rights to religious freedom. The *fatwa* was reproduced in leaflet form and read aloud in hundreds of meetings. The impact was particularly great in such cities as Lucknow, Agra and Delhi.

The British were sensitive to the non-cooperation *fatwa*, not just because of the recruitment issue. The power of a *fatwa* in influencing Muslim opinion had been graphically displayed earlier in the *hijrat* movement in the summer of 1920. *Hijrat* means religious flight and is linked in the Muslim mind with the original flight of the Prophet Muhammad and his followers from Mecca to Medina in the year 622. Muslims facing hostility to their faith in *dar al harb* (an abode of war) have traditionally been enjoined either to engage in *jihad* (holy war – this could be of a spiritual as well as a physical nature) or in *hijrat*. A spontaneous migration to the nearest abode of Islam (*dar al islam*) in Afghanistan began in July, following the issue of a *fatwa* in favour of migration by Maulana Abdul Bari and Abul Kalam Azad. By the time the number of *muhajirin* (refugees) had reached 30,000, the Afghan authorities could no longer cope and began turning them back. The *hijrat* ended in disillusionment and countless human tragedies.

Mosques and Islamic educational establishments were at the centre of the Khilafat campaign's mass mobilisation. The Muslim *julahas* (weavers) of the small town of Mau in the United Provinces, for example, raised funds and enlisted as Khilafat volunteers following the exhortations of the *imam* of the local mosque. Such volunteers, clad either in khaki or green Arab-style dress, kept order at political rallies, joined in protests and processions and enforced *hartals* (strikes). *'Ulama* joined in speaking tours during which the local mosques provided the venue for their rhetoric in favour of the Khilafat cause. They also tapped the networks of influence created by Islamic educational institutions. Political agents speaking in town and village halls could not have communicated so effectively. They would neither have possessed such a ready-made audience, nor have been given the latitude by the authorities which they had to accord to 'religious' gatherings. Mass contact methods were also aided by the entry of a number of *pirs* into the Khilafat struggle. With the exception of Sind, however, the *sufi* shrines and their vast networks of disciples lacked the importance they assumed in the 1940s when they played a crucial role in rallying support for the Pakistan movement.

Tensions in the Hindu–Muslim alliance existed from the beginning of the Khilafat campaign. Traditionalist Barelvi *'ulama* objected to Gandhi and other Hindu Congress leaders addressing Khilafat meetings in mosques. Even Muslims active in the Khilafat struggle differed from Gandhi's under-standing of non-violence. Gandhi's use of Hindu terminology to popularise non-cooperation like, for example, typifying British rule as *Ravanraj* (the rule of Ravan, a figure embodying evil), created echoes of the disquiet Muslims had felt during the *swadeshi* movement. The outbreak of econom-ically motivated violence in Malabar in August 1921 (known as the Moplah Rebellion), which had communal overtones as Muslim tenants turned on their Hindu landlords, also widened the rift. The two final fatal blows to the Khilafat campaign were Gandhi's suspension of civil disobedience on 5 February 1922 in the wake of the Chauri Chaura violence and the decision of the Turkish National Assembly on 21 November 1922 to separate the spir-itual and temporal power of the Caliph. The following July, in the Treaty of Lausanne, the Turkish leader Mustafa Kemal relinquished the historical tie with the Jazirat al-Arab. The cause of the Khilafat campaign was finished. The *'ulama* were relegated to the background as Muslim politics returned to more mundane 'rice and roti' issues.

Conclusion

This chapter throws a number of interesting lights on Benedict Anderson's work on the emergence of nationalism and print culture. Increased commu-nication undoubtedly made possible the imagination of community which transcended the narrow bounds of locality. But print culture did not result in the replacement of a sacred world view by a secular one. On the contrary, it paved the way for more 'fundamentalist' religious understandings by allowing a greater emphasis on dogma and doctrine. Rather than ushering in a homogenised civic secular culture, modern communications strengthened communities based on a sharply defined belief system at the expense of amorphous folk religion and culture.

Benedict Anderson's link between print capitalism and the ability of people to 'think about themselves' and to 'relate themselves' to others in 'profoundly new ways' thus requires extension from national to other new senses of community. The Indian case also points to the continued power of 'traditional' methods of communication based on the charismatic authority of *sadhus, pirs* and other holy men, and on the ability to address vast multitudes at the times of fairs, religious festivals and pilgrimage. Visual display, as in all semi-literate settings, was extremely important. This could take the form of street theatre, religious procession or the Ram Lila, *jatra* or *nautanki* theatres. Emotive pictures produced by the cow protection movement of cows standing meekly before a Muslim butcher or a demon, sword in hand, conveyed far more than the printed word. Traditional and modern means of communication thus complemented each other in spreading the awareness of new collective identities. In order fully to take root they needed to be institutionalised. This process forms the focus of the next chapter.

|4|

Anjumans, *associations and* sabhas: *the institutionalisation of new senses of community*

> Due to the establishment of the Singh sabhas in cities, all those who violated the teachings of Sikhism are now under great pressure. Consequently many of these people have now started to shift to villages where they find it easy to cheat and mislead innocent Sikhs ... It is very sad that these people do not know what their religion is and all that the Sikh Gurus did for them.
>
> *Khalsa Akhbar*, 11 September 1886, cited in Oberoi, (1994, pp. 296–7)

One of the sets of antinomies between 'traditional' and 'modern' societies, according to modernisation theory, is the replacement of ascriptive social organisation by voluntaristic associations. Indian historical reality reveals once again, however, evidence of a blending of 'tradition' and 'modernity'. The plethora of associations and societies which grew up in nineteenth-century India displayed 'traditional' aspects with their frequent reliance on charismatic founding figures. With their audited accounts, annual meetings, committees and published reports, they were, however, also very much 'modern' institutions, the by-product of the interaction between Indian society and the colonial state. At the most practical and obvious level this involved the registration of societies, which entitled them to legal protection to property. Modern organisational forms were adopted even by groups which sought to retain 'traditional' values. The Dharma Sabhas, for example, possessed their own presidents, membership rules and secretaries (Kopf, 1969, pp. 266ff). They were composed not just of learned Brahmins, but such leading lay figures as Bharatendu Harischandra in Benares.

This chapter reveals that while some associations institutionalised a re-defined religious identity, others strengthened caste consciousness by operating on a much broader basis than the 'traditional' village-level *jati* organisation. The burgeoning associations and societies could be analysed in terms of their caste, religious or national orientation. Another device would be to classify them as 'traditionalist', 'modernist' or 'revivalist'. We might cite as examples of the first category the Hindu Sanatan Dharma movement, or the Muslim Barelvi movement; of the second the Brahmo Samaj and the Aligarh movement; of the third the Arya Samaj and Deoband movements. This chapter, however, adopts a regional analysis. It both enables the reader to appreciate the all-India dimensions of this historical development and acts as a corrective to the North Indian bias which is often present in writings on Indian socio-religious movements. Each section commences with a brief study of the region concerned in order to contextualise the associations and institutions.

The Bengal Presidency

Ram Mohan Roy and the Brahmo Samaj

Bengal from the battle of Plassey (1757) onwards formed the heartland of the East India Company's power. By the beginning of the twentieth century Calcutta, with a population of over a million, was second in importance only to London of the British imperial cities. Calcutta's administrative and economic importance to the British as a port and jute-milling centre ensured a vigorous interaction between the colonial rulers and the indigenous elites, most especially the high-caste Hindu *bhadralok* drawn from the Brahmin, Baidya and Kayastha castes. They possessed both the tradition of literacy in vernacular languages and the wealth as rentier landowners eagerly to embrace the new Western learning. The lower castes and Muslims trailed in their wake, with important long-term political repercussions.

The early spread of institutions of higher education, such as Hindu College founded in 1817, encouraged a thirst for Western knowledge. Significantly the first vernacular newspaper in India (*Samachar darpan* – 'Mirror of the News') was published in Bengal on 23 May 1818. When Hooghly College was established 17 years later, within three days, 1,200 names were entered on the registers for the department of English. Educated Bengalis moved into the services and the professions in large numbers. A significant proportion migrated to other provinces in their capacity as administrators. From as early as the 1830s Bengali intellectuals were at the forefront of the 'modernist' Hindu Brahmo Samaj organisation and of 'secular' associations and debating clubs which fed into the liberal stream of Indian nationalism. Typical was the Association for the Acquisition of General Knowledge established by a meeting of 'Hindu Gentlemen' at Sanskrit College on 18 March 1838. It held monthly seminars in English and

Bengali, during which religious issues were barred. The association published three volumes of selections of the papers read at its meetings between 1840 and 1843.

Such student associations were forerunners of the British Indian Association (after 1876 named the Indian Association) which crossed 'the threshold of modern politics'. Such members as Surendranath Banerjea eventually became prominent Congressmen. Indeed, the Bengal branch of the Congress was the Indian Association writ large. The association pioneered the development of trans-regional linkages. It was more active than its counterparts in Bombay and Madras (the Bombay Association and the Independent Madras Association) because of the quicker tempo of political life in Calcutta, the imperial capital. Other regions of India, which lagged behind the three Presidencies' educational development and administrative importance, developed modern political associations more slowly and were marginalised in the life of the early Congress.

Ram Mohan Roy pioneered the Bengali Hindu elites' contribution to the development of journalism, social reform and institution building. Roy, who was born into a Brahmin family in Bengal in 1774, possessed a fierce attachment to Western ideals of liberty and freedom; a commitment to social reform in order gradually to prepare India for freedom; and a belief that the British would respond to reasoned Indian appeals for political and administrative reform. In 1830, on his way to represent the Mughal emperor at the Court of St James, he insisted on boarding a French ship flying the tricolour of liberty to pay homage to the ideals of the French Revolution. Unfortunately he slipped and injured his leg, thereafter walking with a limp.

Roy's most celebrated commitment to social reform was his campaign against *sati*. He not only published tracts against the practice of the immolation of Hindu widows on their husbands' funeral pyres, but used to go to the burning *ghats* (cremation grounds) in Calcutta and seek to prevent the practice. Roy maintained that this 'barbarity' was not a religious duty, because it contained no sanction in the Vedic scriptures. This strengthened the hand of those reformers in the East India Company who had eschewed intervention because they did not want to offend Hindu sensibilities. Largely as a result of Roy's campaign, the Governor-General Lord William Bentinck (Governor-General 1828–35) passed a regulation on 4 December 1829 which criminalised the practice. The *sati* figure remained, however, for many Bengali writers an 'adored nationalist symbol' (Sarkar, 1992), because she epitomised sacrifice and Hindu moral and spiritual energy. Bankim Chandra Chatterjee on one occasion described the self-immolating widow as the 'last hope of a doomed nation'. Rabindranath Tagore's writings during the *swadeshi* movement invoked the act of *sati* as one of glory and inspiration.

Roy also campaigned against the 'horrible' practice of polygamy and the sale of girls as temple prostitutes and advocated widow remarriage. These endeavours echoed the criticisms of Christian missionaries amongst whom

Roy spent much time following his retirement from East India Company service in 1814. To their disappointment, while he engaged in 'strategic syncretism', he never renounced his Hindu faith. Nevertheless, the monotheistic Hinduism that he propounded, with its social activism, was undoubtedly influenced by the Christian presence and Western rationalism. Like a later generation of reformers and revivalists, Roy argued that idol worship and the degradation of Hindu widows were the signs of a corrupted tradition whose original 'purity' could only be restored by returning to the precepts of the Hindu scriptures. Reform was intended to strengthen religious tradition not abolish it.

It was not just in campaigns of social reform that Roy pioneered the practice of petitioning the British authorities. He was also active in seeking to persuade them on such issues as the restrictions on the freedom of the press and the ruling that Indians could not sit as jurors in cases involving Christians. He also communicated with the Board of Control in advance of parliament's renewal of the East India Company charter in 1833, advocating such measures as trial by jury, codification of civil and criminal laws and Indianisation of the army. These activities were inspired by a sense of British fairness and liberalism. Roy emphasised the duties and responsibilities of both the Indian subjects and their British rulers. Such cooperation would ensure what he termed *lokshreya* – the goal of government for the good of the people (Grover, 1992, p.160).

Roy first attempted to institutionalise his ideas in the Atmiya Sabha in 1815, which met privately at his residence. It was not until August 1828, however, that a lasting organisation was created with the formation of the Brahmo Sabha (later to be renamed the Brahmo Samaj). No formal statement of aims and beliefs was produced before Roy's departure for England in November 1830, although it is clear that his attachment to rationalism, hostility to idolatry and belief in a universal theism marked out the society. It was renamed the Brahmo Samaj (House of God) and rescued from virtual extinction in 1843. Debendranath Tagore (1817–1905), the father of the great Bengali writer Rabindranath, brought about its revitalisation by both reforming its structure and providing it with a creed (Brahma Covenant) and scriptures (Brahma Dharma).

The Brahmo Samaj provided educated young Bengalis with experience of organisational work and the use of the press, which many later deployed in the Congress. It also paved the way for future political developments by establishing branches on a trans-provincial basis. This encouraged its members to think and act in all-India terms, although this aspect should not be exaggerated. Most of the society's branches were run by high-caste Bengalis who had been posted outside their home province in government service, rather than by 'locals'. Like other socio-religious movements, the Brahmo Samaj was active in social reform and missionary activities. While Brahmoist literature avoided religious controversies, the Samaj's hostility to caste, advocation of widow remarriage and female equality led to growing hostility from orthodox Hindus. In some orthodox Brahmin communities in East Bengal threats of suicide or of disinheritance were made to dissuade family members from joining its ranks. Brahmos were treated by the wider Hindu community as a sub-caste, to the chagrin of the reformers who sought to influence Hinduism at large.

One of the most articulate criticisms of the Brahmos came anonymously from the pen of the Hindi poet Bharatendu Harischandra in the form of a letter to the *Kavivachansudha* in 1877. 'What would you know of the essence of the Vedas, Puranas and image-worship', the author addressed the Brahmos:

> you only needed to learn a little English to don the turban of all the sciences of the world and to become so enlightened that you could proceed to censure the ways of your father, grandfather and great-grandfather (who were thousands of times cleverer and more learned than you). You who attach the tail of wisdom to your behind, have you paid heed that men of other faith, that is, the Christians and Muslims, continue to believe in the pronouncements of their prophets?

> cited in Dalmia (1996, pp. 388–9)

By the 1860s, tensions were increasing in the Samaj itself between the more conservative followers of Debendranath Tagore and the younger supporters of Keshab Chandra Sen (1838–84). Sen introduced Unitarian influences into the worship at the Brahmo prayer halls; he also sponsored inter-caste marriage and objected to Tagore allowing the wearing of the sacred thread. The split was formalised in November 1866, with Sen's followers joining the Brahmo Samaj of India and Tagore's grouping themselves in the Adi (original) Brahmo Samaj. The future, however, lay with the dynamic Sen and within six years there were 101 *samajes* spread throughout northern India. The Adi Brahmo Samaj struggled on as a sect comprising Tagore and his close associates and family. It was therefore hardly surprising that his death in 1905 dealt it a grievous blow.

This was not the only split in the Brahmo Samaj. A rift increasingly developed in the mid-1870s between the social activists within the Samaj and Sen's 'ascetic' faction of followers. The former were scandalised when Sen undermined the hard-won reforms laid down in the 1872 Brahmo Marriage Act by the marriage of his daughter to an orthodox Maharajah. On 15 May 1878, Sen's critics founded a rival Sadharan Brahmo Samaj. Sen's final years were marked by increasing religious experimentation. This included both an attachment to *bhakti* devotionalism and universalism. The latter was institutionalised in the foundation of the Nava Vidhan (New Dispensation) organisation, whose eclecticism was evidenced by the introduction of a type of Christian eucharist in worship, but with rice and water being substituted for the elements of bread and wine.

Within the Brahmo Samaj, the rationalistic religion and social activism of the Sadharan branch held the key to the future after Sen's death in 1884. In

Bengali society at large, the organisation was marginalised by a new generation of the Bengali *bhadralok* for whom it appeared too Western and too defensive in its dealings with occidental thought. The Ramakrishna Mission provided the organisational basis for the revived devotionalism which fed into the cultural nationalism of the Congress extremists.

The Ramakrishna Mission

The Ramakrishna Mission was part social service organisation, part missionary organisation and part revival of ancient Hindu monasticism. It started out as the informal group of disciples who had gathered around the charismatic teacher and mystic Ramakrishna (1836–86; his birth name was Gadadhar Chatterji) who lived at the temple of the goddess Kali at Dakshineshwar. The unlettered mystic appealed to a growing number of highly educated young Bengalis who were searching for their cultural roots and meaning in their lives. They were attracted by the 'otherness' of Ramakrishna's appearance and personality. He would fall into deep trances (*samadhi*) during which he became incapable of physical sensation. He also acted out roles, dressing as a Muslim and as a Hindu woman when taking the role of Radha (Krishna's wife). Ramakrishna's acting out of a number of female roles was not eccentricity, but in accordance with certain strains of Hinduism which allowed for male transvestic display and androgyny (Roy, 1998, p. 98). While he regarded women as sexually dangerous and barriers to spirituality, he eagerly attracted young males as his disciples, feeding them from his own hands and sitting on their laps. His teaching that all religions were equal had great appeal for educated Bengalis who had gone through the missionary schools. The emphasis which Ramakrishna placed on the Kali cult was also liberating for *bhadralok* youths who had been taught by the Brahmo Samaj to give up such superstitious idolatry. Finally, Ramakrishna appealed to the educated Bengali elite precisely because he rejected colonialism's rationality.

Narendranath Datta was one such youth who was attracted to Ramakrishna's group of disciples, after earlier being a member of the Sadharan Brahmo Samaj. For many years he remained highly sceptical of Ramakrishna's power, although the *swami* earmarked him from the outset as his favourite disciple. It was only after the death of his father that Narendranath formally accepted Ramakrishna as his guru. He exchanged the Brahmo Samaj's rationalism for the eclectic mix of Ramakrishna's thoughts. Three elements of 'traditional' Hinduism increasingly ran through them: the importance of *bhakti*; the following of traditional rituals surrounding the worship of a deity – in Ramakrishna's case Kali; and the importance of the realisation of 'God-consciousness' in each individual in keeping with the Monist philosophy of Advaita Vedanta. When Datta succeeded Ramakrishna as the leader of his group of disciples, he systematised these themes into a structured doctrine. In May 1897, he formally established the Ramakrishna Mission. This comprised Hindu monks and Western converts who had been captivated by his lectures in England and the United States and by his contribution to the World Parliament of Religions which was held in Chicago in September 1893.

By this juncture, Datta had taken the name Swami Vivekananda. His exotic appearance and emphasis on the Vedanta conception was attractive to Westerners who were seeking spiritual awareness outside what they saw as the confines of Christian orthodoxy. Indeed, Vivekananda did much to create the trope in the Western discourse of a juxtaposition between 'spiritual India' and the 'materialist West'. We have already noted that Vivekananda's most famous Western convert, Sister Nivedita, played a leading role in the emergence of a militant cultural nationalism. According to Parama Roy, his 'solicitation' of her and other female disciples was at least in part the result of his being 'the erotic object for female worship, specifically for western (white) female worship' (Roy, 1998, p. 114). Vivekananda's attraction to Western female followers was by no means unique, nor was he the first to evoke the sympathy of English women. Some 60 years earlier, Ram Mohan Roy had been lionised by the educationalist Mary Carpenter (1807–77) and her circle of Unitarian female friends.

Vivekananda used funds raised in the West to establish two monasteries, the second at Mayavati on the Himalayas. The tradition of social service activity was created during Calcutta's plague epidemic of 1899. Such activism contrasted with Ramakrishna's quietist spiritual practice. Nevertheless, by the turn of the century, the Ramakrishna Mission was well established and formed the main centre of restored Hinduism for those members of the educated elite who were dissatisfied with such liberal reform movements as the Brahmo Samaj.

Bengali Muslim associations

Bengali Muslims lagged almost a generation behind their Hindu counterparts in the formation of 'modern' community associations. Nearly 30 years after the creation of the Association for the Acquisition of General Knowledge, the Muhammadan Literary Society was founded in Calcutta in 1863. Its elitist character was revealed in its membership, in the leading role which Nawab Abdul Latif (1828–93) had played in its foundation, and the fact that a number of lectures including one by Syed Ahmad Khan were delivered in Persian. The Central National Muhammadan Association which was founded by the author and religious rationalist Syed Ameer Ali (1849–1928) in 1877 similarly struggled to evoke popular support. It aimed to present Muslim opinion to the government which it did successfully in a memorial to the Viceroy Lord Ripon (1827–1909) in 1882. Within half a dozen years, it had established 53 branches throughout the subcontinent, although it lacked the importance as a vehicle for Muslim community interests of the Aligarh movement. Syed Ameer Ali was on uneasy terms with Syed Ahmad Khan, but their rivalry did not prevent his presiding over the 1899 Calcutta session of the All-India Muslim Educational Conference. The Central National Muhammadan Association, like the Aligarh movement, discouraged Muslim participation in the Indian National Congress.

The United Provinces

The loss of political power to the British, together with the spread of representative institutions, opened up the awful prospect for the UP Muslim elites that they might one day be ruled by Hindus. They responded by giving birth to a rich variety of cultural and religious ideas. These were institutionalised in the Aligarh, Deoband and Barelvi movements.

The Aligarh movement

Sir Syed Ahmad Khan provided the intellectual inspiration for the Aligarh movement. He was born into the *ashraf* elite attached to the Delhi court and received a conventional schooling. After the trauma of the 1857 revolt, he worked to improve Anglo-Muslim understanding through such publications as the *Loyal Muhammadans of India* and to enable Muslims to meet the new intellectual and social challenges of colonial rule. He used the principle of *ijtihad* (independent judgement) in Islamic jurisprudence to reinterpret the Quranic revelation in the light of modern science. Such a view evoked considerable opposition from the orthodox *'ulama* and almost undermined his educational movement. After a visit to England in 1869–70, he emphasised the need for Muslims to receive a Western education alongside religious learning to equip them to take their place in government service. These ideas were institutionalised in the educational foundation located at Aligarh some 80 miles from Delhi which received its first students in 1875. Successive generations of Aligarh scholars assumed leadership roles in the Indian Muslim community.

Sir Sayed is even more honoured in Pakistan for giving birth to the two-nation theory than for his educational activities. It was only, however, when the Bombay Muslim lawyer Badruddin Tyabji (1844–1906) was chosen to preside over the third annual Congress session that Sir Sayed openly criticised the Congress. During the following two years, Sir Sayed publicly spelled out the incompatibility of interests between the North Indian Muslim elite and the Bengali *babu*s (clerks) who dominated the new nationalist organisation. He pointed to the dangers of democracy in India, which would consign the Muslim minority to permanent domination by the Hindus. This essentialisation of religious community was to become the creed of the Muslim League's freedom struggle in the 1940s.

The Deoband movement

While the Aligarh movement provided a means for Muslims to take their place within the new intellectual and cultural milieu, the Deoband movement of Muhammad Qasim Nanautvi (1833–77) and Rashid Ahmad Gangohi (1829–1905) sought to sustain their religion and culture apart from the colonial state. Like the Aligarh movement, its founders had grown up in the *ashraf* society of pre-1857 Delhi and saw education as the means to enable Muslims to survive the shock of the loss of political power. The *dar-ul-ulum* at Deoband was founded in 1867. Deoband was a country town in the Saharanpur district of the United Provinces some hundred miles north-east of Delhi. By the turn of the century there were 40 schools attached to the movement. It was there, however, that the similarities with the Aligarh movement ended.

The Deobandis emphasised the study of the Islamic revelation as opposed to modern science. English was not studied in the Deoband curriculum. They limited their involvement with the colonial state and refused to accept government grants-in-aid for their schools. While Aligarh turned out Muslim graduates able to compete with Hindus for employment in the professions, Deoband equipped its students to take their place among the *'ulama*. Deobandi *'ulama* were in fact to oppose the territorial nationalism of the Pakistan movement. Other groups of *'ulama*, including the even more puritanical Ahl-i-Hadith, shared this latter political stance. Indeed, one of the paradoxes of the freedom struggle is the fact that although the Pakistan demand was raised in the name of religion, it evoked little support from the majority of the *'ulama*. This reality was to be denied by official histories produced in Pakistan during the 1980s.

The Barelvi movement

The Barelvi movement was institutionalised much more weakly than either the Aligarh or Deoband movements. A mere handful of Barelvi *madaris* (Islamic secondary schools: sing. *madrasa*) were founded, the most important being in Bareilly and Lahore. The Barelvi movement reflected the ideas of its founder Ahmad Riza Khan of Bareilly (1856–1921). These focused on the need to defend customary Islam, especially the practices associated with the *sufi* shrines. The conflicts between Deobandi reformers and

Barelvi traditionalists were every bit as bitter as between the Aryas and Sanatanists within the Hindu tradition. Riza Khan called the Deobandis *kafirs* (unbelievers). However, he also entered into bitter controversy with Christian missionaries and such Hindu groups as the Arya Samaj.

Religious controversy, along with soci-economic competition in the towns and cities of British India's most urbanised province, spilled over into communal conflict. This ensured a ready hearing amongst Hindus for the Arya Samaj and RSS although, as we shall see later, their main centres of strength were in Punjab and the Central Provinces respectively. Cow Protection Societies (Gaurakshini Sabhas) were, however, to play an important role in the construction of Hindu community identity in the region in the last years of the nineteenth century.

Cow Protection Societies

Cow Protection Societies had originated in the 1880s as inoffensive associations dedicated to the care of sick cattle and to improving animal husbandry. Within a decade they were at the forefront of an attempt to create a Hindu identity which cut across caste and sectarian differences. They also spearheaded the attempt to take advantage of the colonial devolution of power into Indian hands by asserting Hindu supremacy over the former Muslim rulers of the region. The Cow Protection Societies' attempts to prevent the Muslim slaughter of cattle provoked a wave of riots which swept across north-west India in 1893. We have noted in earlier chapters the significance of the cow as a unifying Hindu symbol and the complementary roles of traditional and modern methods of communication in spreading the cow protection message.

The cow protection movement spread from such cities as Allahabad, Benares and Cawnpore into the countryside in the early 1890s. Its growth was accompanied by a sophisticated organisational framework which linked urban headquarters with village householders. Despite subscriptions from wealthy landholders and such Maharajas as Benares and Darbhanga, the need to pay itinerant preachers, buy cows destined for slaughter and maintain cow refuges (*gaoshalas*) placed heavy financial costs on the Gaurakshini Sabhas. In order to defray their expenses, collection networks were established in which contributions of rice known as *chukti* were realised from householders and later converted into cash. The collection of *chukti* explains the elaborate institutionalisation of the cow protection movement.

The Gaurakshini Sabhas both popularised the ideas of the need to protect and care for cattle and took action against cow killers. Muslim butchers, because of their trade, and weavers, because of their economic dependence on Hindu moneylenders, were threatened with social boycott if they continued to sacrifice cattle. Coercion was also exerted against Hindus who sold cows to Muslims. This could take the form of fines in trials conducted by the Sabhas, the cutting off of water to irrigated fields, the destruction of a family's earthen pots, or various forms of outcasting. The social boycott of Muslims created resentment which fed into communalism.

Another lasting legacy of the Cow Protection Societies was the orthodox Bharat Dharma Mahamandala. This grew out of the Gau Varnashrama Hitaishini Ganga Dharma Sabha (The Religious Association for the Benefit of the Cow, Social Order, and the Holy Ganges) which had been founded by Pandit Din Dayalu Sharma at the pilgrimage centre of Hardwar in 1886. The Pandit's subsequent travels in North India organising Sanskrit schools and *gaoshalas* convinced him of the need for an umbrella organisation for orthodox Hindus. The first gathering of the Mahamandala took place in Hardwar on the holy day of Ganga Dashmi in May 1887. This set the pattern for future gatherings with proceedings being conducted in Hindi only and modern-style discussion, debate and passing of resolutions being accompanied by elaborate religious ceremonies.

The Bharat Dharma Mahamandala upheld Hindu tradition both by lobbying the British government on such issues as the Age of Consent Bill and by rebutting the attacks of the Aryas. It perforce had to adopt many of the reformers' techniques. It thus established Sanatana Dharma (the Eternal Religion) schools, publicised its activities in journals such as the *Mahamandala Magazine* and the *Suryodya*, and also sent out paid missionaries. By 1900, it had over 800 Dharma Sabhas and had established a Hindu College in Delhi. The Mahamandala's organisational strength was further increased following the issuing of a new constitution in 1903 and the moving of its headquarters from Delhi to Benares.

Punjab

Punjab's unique historical and social features influenced the development of modern associations within the province. Not only were there three religious communities within the region, but both the Muslims and Sikhs possessed memories of rule before the advent of the British. The balance of economic and political power between Muslims, Hindus and Sikhs created the conditions for competitive mobilisation in the urban context and for cross-community accommodation under British encouragement in the countryside. The vigorous Christian proselytising presence which saw the Christian population grow forty-fold in the period 1881–1911 also encouraged the urban processes of religious reform and redefinition. What has been called the 'Punjab evangelical entente' was evidenced by official support for the founding of the Church Mission Association in Lahore in 1852 under the presidency of the leading administrator Sir Henry Lawrence. A decade later, officials freely mingled with missionaries at a Punjab

Missionary Conference in Lahore. Its president Donald Mcleod was shortly to be appointed Lieutenant-Governor. Given this environment, it was not surprising that the Arya Samaj, although not originally a Punjabi movement, acquired its greatest influence in the region. Its attempts to 'reconvert' Sikhs to Hinduism was a major factor in the emergence of the Singh Sabha movement, as were its claims that Sikhism was a reformist movement *within* Hinduism, encapsulated in such pamphlets as *Sikh Hindu hain* ('Sikhs are Hindus').

Muslim community organisation was largely 'defensive' and designed to counter both Christian missionaries and Aryas. Intra-community conflict also played a part in institutional growth, however, not only in the divisions between Muslim traditionalists and reformers, but in response to the emergence of the heterodox Ahmadiyah movement in the Punjab. The emphasis on the growth of religious communitarian institutions should not, however, obscure other developments. Ideas of a Jat community were institutionalised in the Jat Mahasabha which was one of the most successful caste associations in India. The Indian Association, the forerunner of the Congress, established a branch in Lahore which was headed by Dayal Singh Majithia (1849–98), the Sikh aristocrat who founded the famous *Tribune* newspaper which was originally a mouthpiece for the Brahmo Samaj. In Punjab, as elsewhere in the subcontinent, new senses of caste, religious and national identity were being coterminously constructed. These were both conflictive and accommodative of each other, a point that can be illustrated by the fact that Dayal Singh Majithia, in addition to supporting the Indian Association, patronised Sikh and Muslim community activities, as well as promoting the cause of the Brahmo Samaj. It is little remembered in Pakistan today, for example, that Majithia donated handsome funds to Aligarh College. It was not until their later politicisation that new senses of community became mutually exclusive.

Punjabi Muslim associations

Pakistani nationalist historiography has neglected the role of Punjabi Muslim community organisations because of its overemphasis on the Aligarh movement in the forging of a modern Muslim collective consciousness. In reality, during the period 1860–90, Punjab accounted for just over half of the 83 *anjumans* established by Indian Muslims. While Sir Syed Ahmad Khan made visits to the Punjab in 1873 and 1884 and had his close collaborators in the region, Punjabi Muslim organisations possessed their own agendas and independent institutional life. A pioneering role was played by the Anjuman-i-Matalib-i-Mufidah-i-Punjab (Society for the Propagation of Useful Knowledge) later known as the Anjuman-i-Punjab which was founded in Lahore early in 1865. Within a short space of time its membership had risen to 300. Like its earlier counterpart in Bengal, it sought to promote 'modern' knowledge amongst the Western-educated elite. In competition with Calcutta University, it successfully agitated for a Punjab University College to be established so that examinations could be controlled from within the province rather than from distant Bengal. As with a number of educational initiatives, it received support from the British. The Hungarian-born Orientalist scholar Dr Gottlieb Wilhelm Leitner, who took up the post of principal of Government College Lahore in 1864, was also a leading figure in the Anjuman-i-Punjab, which formed a role model for similar institutions in other Punjabi cities.

The Anjuman-i-Islamiyah founded in October 1869 was another pioneering Muslim association. Its original aim was to repair and maintain Lahore's famous Badshahi Mosque which had been used as a gunpowder magazine during the Sikh rule. Here we see an early linkage between sacred space and community identity which in the last century has become a dominant feature of the South Asian community landscape. The *anjuman* also looked after the relics of the Prophet Muhammad which had been kept in Lahore Fort. Its driving force was Muhammad Barkat Ali Khan (1821–1905), a Pathan from Shahjahanpur who in his retirement from government service devoted himself to community service. This earned him the title from the British of the 'Patriarch of the Lahore Muhammadans'. Under his aegis the *anjuman* extended its activities to include the provision of scholarships for Muslim students. It nevertheless remained an upper-class organisation as epitomised by the role of Sardar Muhammad Hayat, the father of Sikander, the future Unionist Prime Minister of Punjab and a leading landholder from Wah in the Attock district.

The Anjuman-i-Himayat-i-Islam, which was founded in Lahore in September 1884, was a more middle-class organisation. Its funds, like those of the Cow Protection Societies, were raised in part from individual householders who deposited handfuls of flour in earthen pots for collection and sale. The *anjuman* played a leading role in educational development, commencing with the Madrasa-tul-Muslimin in 1886 and culminating in the foundation of the 'Aligarh of the Punjab', Islamia College, Lahore. Like many reformist bodies, the *anjuman* published its own magazine (*Risala Anjuman-i-Himayat-i-Islam*), tracts and textbooks. These engaged in controversies with Christian publications. Also, to prevent conversion amongst orphans, it ran an orphanage in Lahore, as did the Arya Samaj.

The Ahmadiyah movement was the most divisive of the Punjabi Muslim organisations. Its followers (Ahmadis) are no longer regarded as Muslims in contemporary Pakistan. The movement was at first in the forefront of Muslim defence against the attacks of the Arya Samaj. But it increasingly became the target for Muslim critics because of the claims of its founder, Mirza Ghulam Ahmad (1835–1908). He not only identified himself with the promised Mahdi who would conquer the world for Islam, but blasphemously claimed prophetic revelations from God. These included visions concerning the birth of his son and the death of Dayananda.

The Ahmadis established their headquarters at Qadian, which was Mirza's birthplace, and henceforth they were known by some as Qadianis. Their founder engaged in public debates with both Hindu leaders and Muslim *'ulama*. His doctrine was also propagated in *al-Hakim* and in community educational establishments. *'Ulama* from a number of schools issued *fatwa* (religious edicts, opinions) against him. Not content with their enmity, he also disputed with Christian leaders, denying Christ's divinity and his death on the Cross, claiming instead that he had survived and travelled to Kashmir where he lived until the ripe old age of 120.

The Arya Samaj

The tract war between the Ahmadis and the Aryas was especially bitter. In 1887, for example, Pandit Lekh Ram published *Takzib-i-Barahin-i-Ahmadiyah* ('Accusing as False the Proofs of Ahmadiyah'). By this juncture, the Arya Samaj had established its main focus in the Punjab. The Lahore Arya Samaj had held its first meeting exactly a decade earlier. By the time that Dayananda left the Punjab in 1878 there were 11 branches in the province. Thereafter, local branches were established in most Punjabi cities, with the result that there were nearly 23,000 members by the turn of the century. A Dayananda Anglo-Vedic school (later a college affiliated to the Punjab University) had been established in Lahore in June 1886 in memory of the movement's founder. It taught 'modern' subjects, thus equipping its graduates for the government services, but at the same time remained independent of British control and influence. The college was immensely popular with the Hindu middle class, as it banished fears that Western education might also lead to conversion. Arya high schools grew up in many cities as also did *gurukuls* (seminaries) to train Arya *updeshaks* (missionaries) from an early age. They were despatched to preach Ved Prachar (Propagation of the Vedas) throughout the province. The Arya Samaj also pioneered female education, establishing a girl's school with the first female hostel at Jullundur in 1891. The new Arya woman who was its product, however, had not been educated on grounds of equality of opportunity, but because she symbolised community identity and pride, just as her degraded sisters represented for Aryas the 'degeneracy' of contemporary Hinduism.

The Arya Samaj's contribution to communalism within the Punjab has been extensively studied. Scholars have pointed out the acrimonious debates generated by its publications. Attention has also been drawn to the fact that the Arya Samaj thrived better in the more tense atmosphere of the Punjab than in Dayananda's native Gujarat and that its adaptation of the technique of ritual purification – *shuddhi* – into a weapon of conversion caused conflict with Muslims and Sikhs, as well as the Sanatanist guardians of Hindu orthodoxy.

The Arya Samaj's popularity in Punjab was not just the result of its communal appeal. Its major support came from the Khatri, Agarwal and Arora trading communities. These were upwardly mobile castes which had prospered under colonial rule. They had already displayed a willingness to utilise government and missionary schools in the drive for education, as attested by the fact that their literacy rates were many times higher than other castes (seven times higher than the average according to the 1891 census). They were especially attracted to Dayananda's teaching that caste should be determined by merit rather than birth. This chimed with their own experiences and offered the prospect of a ritual status commensurate with their material wealth. The Arya Samaj's creed of 'self-help' also appealed to them. It was involved in a number of commercial activities in the Punjab, including the initiating of the first bank with Indian capital and the retailing of *deshi* (local Indian-made) garments which were the precursors of the later *swadeshi* enterprises.

In 1893, the Arya Samaj split into its college and vegetarian factions. The division centred around such issues as vegetarianism, the role of Sanskrit in the syllabus of D. A. V. College and the importance of Ved Prachar. The moderates led by Lal Chand and Hans Raj controlled the management committee of D. A. V. College and were hence known as the college faction. The Mahatma or vegetarian faction of the militants was led by Guru Dutt (1864–90) and Munshi Ram (later known as Swami Shraddhananda, 1856–1928). Guru Dutt believed that any compromise on vegetarianism was a betrayal of Dayananda's inheritance, whereas the moderates maintained that a non-meat diet repeated the errors of the Jains who had deprived India of its manhood by their attachment to *ahimsa*. It should be noted here that many Indians, including the teenage Gandhi, tempted by a Muslim friend Sheikh Mehtab, equated meat eating with physical strength. This attitude was summed up in the ditty: 'Behold the mighty Englishman! He rules the Indian small; because being a meat eater, he is five cubits tall!' (cited by Rudolph, 1971, p. 248). The search for physical prowess through gymnastic exercises in order to respond to colonialist constructions of Hindu, especially Bengali, effeminacy was to be a lasting feature of cultural nationalism, although Gandhi turned upside-down notions of strength and weakness.

The militant faction of the Arya Samaj emphasised Ved Prachar and *shuddhi* and significantly the notorious Lekh Ram was drawn from its ranks. The college faction, on the other hand, was not only less confrontational towards the Muslim community but was prepared for local cooperation. The most striking instance was in the Jullundur heartland of Munshi Ram's power. The militant Aryas, it will be recalled, had established the K. M. V. girls' high school in Jullundur. The college faction replied under the leadership of Pandit Mehr Chand by attempting to establish its own educational institution there. Such was the resistance of the militants that the college party could only proceed with the help of the Khoja Muslim elite of Jullundur. They provided the land for both the Sain Das Anglo-Sanskrit

School and D. A. V. College, which were established in the city and in addition made monetary donations. Well-off Muslims continued to send their sons to the latter institution even after the opening of a local Islamia College. This situation does not fit in easily with conventional under-standings of communal relations.

The Singh Sabha movement and Sikh identity

Sikhs were particularly sensitive to missionary activities in the Punjab following the conversion of Maharaja Duleep Singh, son of Ranjit Singh, in 1853. When four Sikh students at a mission school declared their intention to convert to Christianity in 1873 a catalyst was provided for the creation of the first Singh Sabha at Amritsar. This organisation concerned itself with the codification of Sikh tradition, exemplified by its publication in 1883 of a biography of the Gurus under the title *Sri Gurpurab Prakas*. The Sabha was a conservative body dominated by its rich patrons who included Raja Bikram Singh, the ruler of the Sikh Princely State of Faridkot, and Baba Khem Singh Bedi who came from an immensely influential spiritual family. In November 1879 a Singh Sabha was founded in Lahore as a result of the efforts of Gurmukh Singh and Bhai Harsa Singh who were lecturers at Oriental College and had together established Punjabi as an academic subject. The following April, the Amritsar and Lahore Sabhas were declared branches of a new Sri Guru Singh Sabha General. The Lahore body was to prove the more active of the two original Singh Sabhas in its organisational meetings, publishing work and commitment to education and reform. It owed much to the leadership of Bhai Jawahir Singh Kapur (1859–1910) and Ditt Singh (1853–1901), both of whom had briefly flirted with the Arya Samaj before its divisive attempts to re-convert Sikhs.

Initially, the Singh Sabha movement spread to other towns of the Punjab as a result of the migration of members from Lahore and Amritsar, or their decision to set up branches in their home towns. Baba Khem Singh Bedi, for example, established a Rawalpindi branch in this way. Constitutions and membership rules were modelled on the Lahore body. In all 115 Singh Sabhas were established during the closing two decades of the nineteenth century. All but a handful were in Punjab, but the branches did extend as far afield as Malaya and Hong Kong. These were linked together under the umbrella of the Khalsa Diwan from 1883. Like the Arya Samaj, however, this organisation split. The conservative faction was based around the Amritsar Singh Sabha; however, most branches were loyal to the Lahore branch. One result of the split was the delay in establishing a Sikh college until 1897 (known as Khalsa College). Five years earlier the Sikh reformers had followed the Arya Samaj's example in establishing a school for girls in Ferozepore (Sikh Kanya Mahavidyala).

Despite the importance of personal and regional rivalries, divisions between the Lahore and Amritsar Singh Sabhas increasingly revolved around attitudes to the Tat Khalsa (pure Sikh) ideology. This involved a narrowing of Sikh identity to that of the Khalsa tradition. Physical appearance became an important diacritical marker. Tat Khalsa Sikhs wore the five 'k's'[1] and disapproved of Sikhs who wore *dhotis* or sported earrings. Women were encouraged to wear turbans. Just as Hindu reformers justified their actions in terms of a recovery of the Vedic golden era, Tat Khalsa Sikhs called for a return to the pristine Sikhism of the eighteenth century. The Lahore Sabha was at the forefront of the Tat Khalsa campaign. Its members were active in the Khalsa Tract Society and the *Khalsa Akhbar* newspaper. More traditionalist views were, however, held by members of the Amritsar Sabha, most notably by its founder-president Thakur Singh Sandhanwalia. As tensions increased between the Tat Khalsa and traditionalist Sikhs, Gurmukh Singh, one of the former group's leading activists, was excommunicated by the Golden Temple authorities at the instigation of Baba Khem Singh Bedi. The clash over Sikh identity was given further urgency in 1898 when, following a dispute over the will of the Sikh philanthropist Dyal Singh Majithia, the Punjab high court ruled that he was a Hindu and had thus legally bequeathed his wealth to charity under the Hindu law of inheritance. Khan Singh Nabha's riposte was to publish the famous tract *Ham Hindu Nahin* ('We Are Not Hindus').

The Central Provinces

Nagpur exerted a dominant influence in the Central Provinces. It was not only an important educational and administrative centre, but a railway node for the Bombay–Calcutta and Delhi to Madras lines. By the closing decades of the nineteenth century it had developed important textile, railway repair, brewing and pottery industries. It was shortly to become the birthplace of the Rashtriya Swayam Sevak Sangh which institutionalised the Hindu nationalist ideas of Keshav Baliram Hedgewar and Madhav Golwalkar. Given the important part played in their ideology by the stigmatisation of a threatening Muslim 'other', Nagpur appears at first an unusual location for the RSS's headquarters. Muslims comprised just 4 per cent of the Central Province's total population. Until the 1923 communal riots that precipitated the RSS's creation, relations had been on the whole harmonious. Even the riots had been caused by the hoary issue of Hindu processions playing music before mosques, rather than any new source of friction. The Muslim elite of Nagpur were well educated and noted for their low political profile and loyalty to the Raj as was demonstrated during the Khilafat campaign.

---

[1]   The five symbols worn by 'baptised' orthodox Khalsa Sikhs. They are *kangha* (hair comb), *kes* (unshorn hair), *kirpan* (steel dagger), *kach* (shorts) and *kara* (steel bracelet).

The emergence of the RSS examplifies the fact that internal competition rather than friction *between* communities was often a cause of communalism in colonial India. The traditional Marathi-speaking Brahmin elite of the Central Provinces faced a growing challenge to their political and socio-economic predominance from the spread of literacy amongst the lower castes. By the 1920s, Rajputs, Kurmis and Malis were all improving their literacy status relative to the Brahmins. Both Hedgewar and Golwalkar came from precarious economic backgrounds. Deshasthas Brahmins from Hedgewar's caste had taken to Western education more slowly than many other high-caste Hindus because of their close connection with the ruling elite of the Bhonsla Kingdom of Nagpur which was overthrown with the British annexation in 1854. Further insecurity arose from the traditional division between Marathi and Hindi speakers within the region.

The Muslims offered an easy target for those Hindus who sought to establish a unity based on Brahminism and hostility to the 'other'. It was not, however, only a crude instrumentalism which lay behind this approach. Early Hindu nationalists seem to have genuinely feared the Muslims in the wake both of the Nagpur riots and the 1921 Moplah Rebellion on the Malabar coast which was directed against Hindu landowners. Balkrishna Shivram Moonje (1872–1948), the Hindu Mahasabha leader who exerted an early influence on Hedgewar, admitted that 'we feel insecure', despite the fact that Muslims formed only one in seven of Nagpur's inhabitants.

The RSS

The RSS was conceived by its founders as a microcosm of the Hindu nation in the making. Shortly before his death in 1940, Hedgewar termed the RSS 'the Hindu *rashtra* in miniature'. Its cadres were to provide an inspiring example of unity and discipline. The contradiction between egalitarianism and Brahminical values was resolved through the traditional Hindu insti-tution of the sect and the concept of asceticism and renunciation. Hindu religious sects had always provided an alternative to localised caste hierar-chies, while with renunciation one left behind the caste-based world of the householder for the wanderings of a holy man. The RSS can best be under-stood as a nationalist sect designed to be the vanguard of a future egalitarian Hindu India.

Some writers have seen European fascist forms in its military-style features including uniforms and emphasis on drill. These were common to many other Indian organisations of the period, including the Congress volunteers, the Khaksars and the Muslim National Guards. Moreover, they had also formed an important aspect of the Bengali Revolutionary Societies with which Hedgewar was acquainted following his academic studies in Calcutta. The Bengali revolutionaries had in turn drawn inspiration for their martial exercises from the traditional *akharas* (wrestling centres), many of which had a temple attached. The extent to which the RSS drew on this tradition can be seen in the fact that its recruits not only took part in such 'Indian forms' of exercise as *lathi* drilling, but pledged themselves to the organisation before an effigy of Hanuman (the monkey god which in the Ramayana embodies physical strength), which was the presiding deity in the *akharas* of the Nagpur region.

The basic unit of organisation of the RSS remains the *shaka*. Its members (*swayamsevaks*) meet daily for physical and intellectual training. Hedgewar developed the *shaka* organisation, each with 200 members in the early growth of the RSS within the confines of Nagpur. By 1932, 66 branches had been established with their ideological emphasis on Hindu culture and history, in which, as might be expected, Shivaji's story played a leading role. Hedgewar toured Berar and the Hindi-speaking areas of the Central Provinces before casting his net further afield in Bombay province and the Deccan states. The first branches were established in North India at the holy city of Benares in 1931 and at Jullundur in the Punjab two years later. The relationship between Hedgewar and the RSS members increasingly resembled that between a guru and his disciples. His mausoleum Smriti Mandir (the temple of the memory of tradition) has become a leading pilgrimage centre for RSS activists. Golwalkar who was designated by Hedgewar as his successor as *sarsanghchalak* (supreme leader) was similarly regarded as a guru. This comes out clearly in the following poem which was recited in his honour on his sixty-first birthday.

> Oh, Guru, you are the defender of the over-all welfare of the Hindus,
> You know what is best for them,
> Throughout the year you exert yourself all over the country, without respite,
> You give us the light of your knowledge and captivate our hearts.
>
> cited in Jaffrelot (1996, p. 42)

In addition to the *swayamsevaks*, a corps of preachers (*pracharaks*) was formed. These were called to the ascetic life of the *sadhus*. Many still remain celibate today in order to devote themselves totally to the cause of developing the *shaka* network. Hedgewar gave so much attention to this because he regarded it as the framework of the future Hindu nation. Ideology without this institutional base would be useless, as he made clear in his last speech.

> Remember we have to organise the entire Hindu society from Kanyakumari to the Himalayas. In fact our main area of operation is the vast Hindu world outside the Sangh ... Our object should be to show to the people the true path of national salvation. That true path is none other than ORGANISATION [*sangathan*].
>
> cited in Jaffrelot (1996, p. 65)

Significantly the main RSS newspaper was called the *Organiser*. The RSS task was to penetrate society, 'improve' it and finally 'merge' with it when its values and those of the organisation had become identical. There are affinities here with European totalitarianism, as there is also in the RSS characteristic belief that the 'ideal' 'new man' was to subsume his personality to the Hindu nationalist cause. The *shaka* network spread as a result of the tireless propaganda tours of the *pracharaks* and the infiltration of colleges and universities. Many young recruits were drawn from an Arya Samajist background and the RSS also benefited from the support of the Hindu Mahasabha. At the outbreak of the Second World War, there were 60,000 *swayamsevaks* grouped in 500 *shakas*. The mounting communal conflict as a result of the Pakistan movement further increased the RSS's appeal, both for its protective role in riots and its relief activities for their victims. The organisation was thus able to expand from its Nagpur headquarters into the Punjab, the North-West Frontier Province and Bombay. Anti-Muslim sentiment and distrust of the Congress's ability and desire to uphold purely Hindu interests reinforced the earlier appeal of ethnic nationalism.

In assessing the RSS's strength, it is important to note the contradictions between its egalitarian and national ideology and its social composition. This marked it out as a Hindi belt and Maharashtrian organisation which drew support mainly from the high castes. Its Sanskritised culture lacked appeal in the Dravidian south and amongst the lower castes in North India. Furthermore, it is necessary to emphasise its self-conception as a vanguard movement with strict demands on its entrants in terms of ideological and physical discipline and lifestyle. The RSS was neither a mass-based and open social movement, nor did it ever aspire to be a political party, although it initially had close ties with the Mahasabha and latterly with Jana Sangh and its BJP successor. As we shall see later, the RSS, through its discipline, has wielded growing influence in post-independence India, despite its being branded as 'anti-national' and being banned after Gandhi's assassination.

Madras

We shall conclude this regional survey by examining developments in the Madras Presidency, the most extensive of all the British territories in India. Although Madras itself was acquired as early as 1639 by the East India Company, the relatively slow establishment of British dominance in the region and its remoteness from the seat of power in Calcutta and later Delhi delayed the emergence of new Indian ideas and institutions in reponse to British rule. The Presidency and South India more generally were notable for the extreme hierarchical organisation of Hindu society, dominated by the small Brahmin elite and by the existence of non-Aryan languages. Tamil and Telegu were the most important Dravidian languages, with the former dating from antiquity. The three other Dravidian tongues were Kannada, Malayalam and Tulu.

The emerging anti-Brahmin and Dravidian movements in the region need to be understood in terms of two sets of factors: first, the growing resistance to their classification as *sudras* by increasingly prosperous Tamil Vellala cultivators and their counterpart Telegu Reddis, and Vellamas and Malalayam Nairs; second, the increasing competition for literacy and careers in the government services between these cultivator groups and the Brahmin elite. Male literacy amongst the Vellalas rose from around 7 to 25 per cent in the period 1901–21. The Tamil Brahmins remained at the top of the literacy and professional tree at the time of the 1921 census with 71.5 per cent male literacy, followed by the Telegu Brahmins with 59.7 per cent, but they were under growing pressure. Parallels can of course be seen here with the situation in the Maharashtrian region. As elsewhere in the subcontinent, new senses of community consciousness were institutionalised in caste associations and religious reform movements. Before turning to these, we shall first look at the growth of the Theosophical Society in the region where it made its international headquarters.

The Theosophical movement

The roots of the Theosophical movement lay in the West, although India became its spiritual homeland. The closing decades of the nineteenth century saw free thinkers dissenting both from orthodox Christian world views and the increasingly dominant secular science-based alternative. Dabbling in the occult and spiritualism became fashionable and it was from this background that the Theosophical organisation was founded in New York in September 1875 by a Russian émigré Helena Petrovna Blavatsky (1831–91) and an American ex-army officer Colonel Henry Olcott. Its objectives were to oppose scientific materialism and 'dogmatic theology' and to acquire knowledge of 'occult manifestations'. Two years later, Blavatsky published *Isis Unveiled* which she claimed contained knowledge revealed to her by Tibetan spiritual 'masters' or 'mahatmas' of the Great White Brotherhood. Shortly after the work's publication, which drew on Hindu concepts of reincarnation and the law of *karma*, Olcott and Blavatsky left for India, proclaiming it the 'fountainhead' of all 'true religion'.

Olcott at first developed close links with Dayananda and the Arya Samaj, prompted by admiration for the latter's work on the Vedas. Indeed, the New York branch of the movement went so far as to rename itself the Theosophical Society of the Arya Samaj of India. By 1882, however, a split had occurred as the Theosophists did not want to replace the Christian orthodoxy they had left behind with Dayananda's dogmatic 'protestant' version of Hinduism. Bitter hostilities commenced with Dayananda's publication of a pamphlet entitled, *Humbuggery of the Theosophists*. Shortly afterwards, the Theosophical Society moved its headquarters from Bombay to an estate at Adyar just south of Madras.

Henceforth, the Madras Presidency became the main centre of its support. Amongst the Theosophists' eclectic beliefs was an emphasis on the Vedic golden age and the depiction of the Aryans as the progenitors of Western civilisation. In keeping with this view was Olcott's desire to encourage Sanskrit learning through educational institutions. In 1893 Annie Besant, the former Victorian free thinker and feminist, arrived in India following her conversion to Theosophy. To the chagrin of her Fabian friends, the former doyen of the National Secular Society had become attracted to the 'Hooey from the Orient' following her review of Blavatsky's major work, *Secret Doctrine*. The extent of both Blavatsky's influence and the break with her past was seen when she agreed to destroy all existing copies of her pamphlet on birth control (*Law of Population*) which had evoked immense controversy.

Annie Besant breathed new life into the Theosophical movement and became its president on Olcott's death in 1907. Before then she had been based in Benares where she had founded the Central Hindu College which taught Sanskrit along with mathematics and modern science. She was thus greatly exposed to the currents of North India Hindu religious reform and stressed the glories of the Vedic past. Like her Irish counterpart Margaret Noble in the Ramakrishna Mission, she moved increasingly from humanitarian to more political concerns. These were expressed through the columns of her twin publications, *The Commonwealt* and (from 1914 onwards) *New India*, and in the publication of a lecture series in 1913 under the title *Wake Up India*. Annie Besant's intellectual and political odyssey in India led her into the ranks of the Congress and eventually to become its president in 1917. Disillusionment soon set in, however, over the question of civil disobedience and the criticism of her claim to be guided by supernatural mahatmas. Besant withdrew from Congress to concentrate on the affairs of the Theosophical Society. She increasingly preoccupied herself with the claim that a young Hindu boy Jeddu Krishnamurti, spotted on the beach at Madras by C. W. Leadbeater, a bishop turned Theosophist, was the 'New Messiah and World Teacher' (Jayawardena, 1995, p. 133).

Although Annie Besant's influence at the all-India level of politics was short-lived, it sparked off a reaction in Madras, which with the formation of the Justice Party politicised the Dravidian movement. While the call to arms through appeal to the Vedic past played well in Benares, it did not meet with approval in the Tamil south. Significantly, the Brahmins (more particularly, the Smartha Brahmins) were the only groups in the Madras Presidency who sympathised with the Theosophical cause. The majority of the population was alienated by the harping on a past which it equated with the imposition of an oppressive caste system and alien culture. Annie Besant, as may be seen in the following extract, too enthusiastically expressed traditional Brahminical attitudes:

> The children of the depressed classes need first of all, to be taught cleanliness, outside decency of behaviour, and the earliest rudiments of education, religion and morality. Their bodies, at present, are ill-odorous and foul, with liquor and strong-smelling foods out of which for generations they have been built up: it will need some generations of purer food and living to make their bodies fit to sit in the close neighbourhood of a school-room with children who have received bodies from an ancestry trained in habits of exquisite personal cleanliness, and fed on pure food-stuffs. We have to raise the depressed classes to a similar level of physical purity, not to drag down the clean to the level of the dirty, and until this is done close association is undesirable.
>
> cited in Mendelsohn and Vicziany (1998, pp. 95–6)

Tamil associations

The growing interest in Tamil culture was evidenced by the formation of Tamil associations (*sangams*). The most famous was the Madura Tamil *sangam* which from 1903 onwards published its own journal entitled *Sen Tamil*. The various *sangams* encouraged the study of such Tamil literary classics as the *Silappatikarum*. They also emphasised the differences between Tamil culture and the Aryanism of the north. While the Theosophists praised Aryanism, the Tamil associations condemned it. Typical of the attitude was a 1921 lecture at the Madura association on the Aryan influence, entitled 'Deluge of the Dark Age'. Aryanism had not only undermined the Tamil language of the land, but had attempted to displace the original Tamil religion of Saiva Siddhanta. The speaker concluded that true freedom could only come about when the Tamil country was freed from 'Brahmin domination'.

The new Tamil collective consciousness was institutionalised not only in the *sangams*, but in the Desabhakta Samaj (Patriotic Association) which popularised the songs of the Tamil poet C. Subramania Bharati (1882–1921). The Saiva Siddhanta Sabha was another important institution. Its meetings popularised the reinterpretation of the Ramayana which reversed the hero status of the figures Ravana and Rama. The Saiva Siddhanta Sabha had been founded in 1886, not only to emphasise the superiority of the Saiva scriptures – the Agamas over the Vedas – but to increase interest in the Dravidian languages and culture. It was Tamil, however, rather than Telegu that was at the forefront of the Dravidian and anti-Brahmin movements.

The Brahmins responded by forming their own organisation, the Varnashrama Sabha in 1915. In the face of the attempts by the cultivating castes to shed the *sudra* status, it reaffirmed the four *ashramas* and the requirement of Hindus to adhere to their caste duties. These views were publicised in the journals *Varnashrama Dharma* and *Hindu Message*. Leaders of the non-Brahmin movement dismissed them as 'obscurantist'. The non-Brahmin movement was soon to espouse a new radicalism with the foundation of the Suyamariyatai iyakkam – the self-respect movement.

Conclusion

Anjumans, associations and *sabhas* were neither wholly 'modern' nor wholly 'traditional' organisations. Thus they do not fit into neat conceptual frameworks. This chapter has revealed, however, that they played an important role in the forging of new group identities within the arena of the colonial state. They assisted in the redrawing of boundaries by actualising the 'imagined communities' constituted by ideologues. This is seen most clearly in the case of the RSS because of its self-definition as the Hindu *rashtra* in miniature. But the same processes were at work in the Singh Sabhas, the Arya Samaj and the Muslim *anjumans* and the Aligarh movement. Sir Syed Ahmad Khan, for example, was aware that, in order to retrieve their fallen glory, the Muslims not only had to acquire new knowledge and skills, but also had to consolidate themselves as a *qaum* (community, nation) through participation in institutional activities.

Institutions for all communities provided a sense of identity based on participation rather than birth, and through their extensive organisational structure linked together diverse regional groupings. Their extensive educational institutions and publishing activities mobilised public opinion in favour of a more homogenised religious and cultural practice. The reformers' educational and publishing activities were so successful that traditionalists were forced to build similar institutions in the attempt to defend orthodoxy. Voluntary associations, with their schools and charitable work, had become so much a part and parcel of everyday life by the end of British rule that it was forgotten that these were still new forms of organisation.

The emerging forms of group consciouness were greatly varied within as well as between religious communities. The rationalist Brahmo contrasted with the traditionalist Sanatanist. An even greater contrast prevailed between the 'kshatriyaized Swayamsevak and the effeminate bhakti-inspired Gandhian.' The historic restructuring of senses of community culminated in their politicisation. This process can appear deceptively simple with, for example, an enhanced sense of Sikh community feeding into the Akali Dal and of Hindu and Muslim identity into the Hindu Mahasabha and Muslim League, respectively. But, as we shall see in later chapters, only sections of these communities followed this pattern. Moreover, the Congress embodied strands of both a secular, territorial nationalism and a cultural Hindu-tinged nationalism. The politicisation of community identity and its complex manifestation can only begin to be understood in terms of the interplay between the colonial state and historical contingency.

|5|

The politicisation of community identities

> Weak and divided we are and divided into
> various sects. But the remedy lies in bringing
> the sections on a common platform where they
> could realize that they are merely branches of the
> same stock and community, and not to lead them
> further astray and to teach them as if no such
> community exists or has a political status.

Lala Lal Chand, 'Self-Abnegation in Politics', *Punjabee*, 1909

The background to the Congress's foundation and the split within it between the moderates and extremists holds centre stage in most standard accounts of the emergence of Indian nationalism. The Muslim League appears in the wings, but otherwise Congress is depicted as operating almost in a vacuum. Such portrayals dramatise the clash between imperialism and nationalism. Anil Seal (1968) pointed out in his classic work, however, that neither the Congress nor the Raj were monolithic entities. An analysis which ignores the emergence of other regional and communal parties inevitably glosses over the compromises which the bearers of Indian and Pakistani nationalism had to make with ascriptive loyalties. It also leaves the reader to puzzle over their resurgence since independence.

This chapter therefore combines analysis of the Congress and the Muslim League with that of such neglected parties as the Punjab Unionist Party, the Justice Party of Madras, the Akali Dal and the Hindu Mahasabha. These parties were marginalised during the endgame of Empire, but the interests and identities they represented have continued to influence post-independence politics.

The emergence of the Indian National Congress

The Congress's roots lay both in the Brahmo Samaj and the Arya Samaj and in the secular associations which predated the 1857 revolt in the Presidencies of Madras, Bombay and Bengal. The latter associations represented the interests of the Western-educated elites and the landed and business communities. Rich *zamindars* dominated, for example, the British Indian Association which was founded in Calcutta in 1851. Its Bombay counterpart, the Bombay Association, which came into existence a year later, represented the interests of the emerging Western-educated elites and the *shetia* (commercial magnates) business communities. Indeed it was concern over local taxation and the running of the elected Bombay Municipality which brought the *shetias* into associational activities. Both associations petitioned parliament in 1853 at the time of the renewal of the East India Company's charter. They were not, however, national bodies and were restricted to small elite audiences in their own regions.

It was only with the formation of the Indian Association in Calcutta in 1876 that the concern with all-India cooperation was expressed. The second of its ideals set forth by Surendranath Banerjea was to unify the Indian races and peoples upon the basis of common political interests and aspirations. Nevertheless, it was the elite concern over the Viceroy Lord Lytton reducing the age limit for civil service examinations from 21 to 19 years of age, thereby reducing Indian opportunities, that prompted the first attempts at national organisation. Banerjea toured northern India in the summer vacation of 1877 and addressed a number of meetings on the civil service issue.

The Ilbert Bill controversy

The catalyst for the formation of an all-India political organisation was provided by the 1883 Ilbert Bill controversy. Sir Courtney Ilbert, the Law Member of the liberal Viceroy Lord Ripon's government, drafted a bill to remove 'every judicial disqualification based merely on race distinction'. Put simply, this was designed to enable Indian judges and magistrates to preside in cases involving European residents outside of the Presidency towns. What was seen as no more than ending the anomaly between the Presidency towns and elsewhere resulted in a furore. The up-country tea and indigo planters who would now fall under the jurisdiction of native judges protested vehemently. They secured support from the non-official English residents in Calcutta who disliked the reforming Viceroy. Protest meetings were held in Calcutta and other Presidency towns and the Anglo-Indian press entered the fray. Ripon was personally insulted and there was even talk of rebellion. A chastened government backed down. The Ilbert Bill was withdrawn in favour of legislation which allowed Indian district magistrates and sessions judges only to try Europeans in cases where the latter had a right to demand trial by jury, in which half the jury would comprise Europeans.

The agitation exposed the racism barely concealed beneath the surface of the Raj. It also demonstrated to the Indian professional classes that united action could win concessions. At the same time, the government recognised the need for the representation of Indian interests which could act both as a safety valve and a counterweight to the European interests. Significantly, in December 1884 the incoming Viceroy Lord Dufferin was favourably disposed towards the efforts of the retired official Allan Octavian Hume (1829–1912) to encourage the foundation of a 'responsible' Indian organisation. The inaugural session of the Indian National Congress was held in December 1885. The gathering was dominated by the Western-educated elite. Significantly, there were just two Muslims amongst the 72 founder members. The atmosphere was one of loyalism. The three-day session ended with Hume leading 'three cheers for her Majesty the Queen Empress'.

The rise of Muslim separatism

The rise of Muslim separatism was rooted both in the North Indian Muslims' responses to the loss of political power and Hindu resurgence. Its standard bearer was the Aligarh movement of Sir Syed Ahmad Khan. Sir Syed linked the strengthening of the consciousness and corporate will of the Indian Muslims with the wider advancement of Islam. If Indian Muslims were degraded, Islam itself would be weakened. In order to build up the community, Sir Syed exhorted its members to educate and economically advance themselves. Material impoverishment threatened Islamic culture. This was furthermore endangered by the principles of democratic representation brought by the British.

From the formation of the Congress in 1885, Sir Syed resolutely warned Muslims of its dangers. His communitarian approach to political representation was expressed most clearly in a speech in December 1887:

> Now let us suppose that we have universal suffrage, as in America, and that all have votes. And let us suppose that all Muslim voters vote for a Muslim member and that all Hindu voters for a Hindu member and now count how many votes the Muslim member will have and how many the Hindu. We can prove by simple arithmetic that there will be four votes for the Hindu to every one vote for the Muslim. Now how can the Muslim guard his interests? It will be like a game of dice in which one man had four dice and the other only one.
>
> cited in Malik (1970, p. 145)

The Aligarh old boy network facilitated greater trans-regional Muslim cooperation than had been provided by the earlier *anjumans*, most of which were localised in membership and influence. Further steps towards political community were provided both by the short-lived Muhammadan Anglo-Oriental Defence Association which, significantly, was set up immediately following the rash of cow protection riots in 1893, and Syed Ameer Ali's Central National Mohammadan Association. The latter became moribund when its founder departed for England in 1904, but at its peak in 1888 it boasted 53 branches throughout India.

Syed Ahmad Khan's Muhammadan Educational Conference advanced still nearer to the threshold of politics. Its function as a forerunner of the Muslim League was clearly stated by Muhammad Shah Din (1868–1918) who presided over its 1894 session.

> On account of the Conference, the nation [*qaum*] is provided an opportunity to bring round its centrifugal forces at one point. Mainly because of it men of one district and province have been able to meet with their counterparts from other provinces and places. This way they exchange their thoughts and strengthen national unity. Moreover, besides discussing their educational needs and means to remedy difficulties in the way, these men also think of practical methods to run their affairs in accordance to requirements of time.
>
> cited in Ahmad (1988, pp. 60–1)

A clear example of the latter process at work was given by the Bombay provincial Muslim Educational Conference which met in 1904. At the end of its formal proceedings, discussion took place about the establishment of a Muslim political association. The need to safeguard Muslim interests had been brought home by the Hindu opposition to Nasrullah Khan, a member of the Surat Muslim ruling family, when he unsuccessfully attempted to win a seat in the Bombay Legislative Council. The Bombay Presidency Muslim Political Association was duly established. It was to be eclipsed two years later, however, by the formation of the All-India Muslim League.

The background to the formation of the All-India Muslim League

The precipitating factors were, first, the further prospect of British constitutional reform and its likely impact on the Muslim community and, second, the effects of the *swadeshi* movement in Bengal on Muslim opinion.

Constitutional reform was mooted by the Liberal Secretary of State John Morley (1838–1923) in 1906, in the light of the tussle between the moderates and extremists within the Congress. The new Viceroy Lord Minto (1845–1914), who had been sent out in 1905 on a peace mission following the hostility evoked by his predecessor Curzon (Viceroy 1899–1905), was also prepared to give a hearing to such Congress moderates as Gokhale. After discussions between Morley and Gokhale, an official announcement was made that the government would consider proposals for reform.

This was unwelcome news for Muslim leaders in the main centres of Hindu population. They had already seen the very limited powers devolved to municipal committees used by Hindu revivalists to their advantage. This process was especially marked in the towns of the western UP. Newly elected Hindu leaders introduced municipal regulations to control butchers' shops and slaughterhouses and to alter procession routes at festival times. In Agra, almost immediately after the passage of the 1883 Municipalities Act, Hindu leaders had claimed the right to hold festivals which clashed with the Shia Muslim period of mourning (Muharram). In Moradabad, the newfound powers were used to force Muslim butchers to dry their hides outside the city, while in Chandpur a ban on cow slaughter was introduced. For a North India Muslim elite which already felt itself under pressure because of the assertion of Hindi over Urdu, such actions were straws in the wind.

Muslim leaders were not just concerned with how Hindu representatives used their newfound powers; they also feared that the situation at the local level would be reproduced in the provincial and all-India arenas of politics. Muslims had been consistently underrepresented in municipal committees because they lacked the educational and property qualifications to vote. At Muzaffarnagar in the UP, for example, Muslims formed 42 per cent of the population, but there was just one Muslim amongst the 12 elected municipal committee members. Similarly, at Allahabad there was just a single Muslim representative, although Muslims formed a third of the population. Not a single Muslim was elected to the new UP Legislative Council from 1893 to 1906, although Muslims numbered seven million and formed 14 per cent of the inhabitants. In the light of these figures, it is hardly surprising that UP Muslims headed the movement towards political separatism.

Muslim disquiet intensified during the agitation against the partition of Bengal. This was accompanied, as we have seen, by the extensive use of Hindu religious symbolism. Kali was evoked by the *swadeshi* activists who also adoped 'Bande Mataram' as their rallying cry. Educated Bengali Muslims had not sought the division of their province, but they were quick to recognise the advantages this might bring. In order to ensure that Muslims remained aloof from the anti-partition movement, the Governor of the new East Bengal and Assam province Bampfylde Fuller (1854–1935) leaned heavily in their favour. When Minto accepted his resignation in August 1906, it seemed to many Bengali Muslims that the British had succumbed to Hindu agitation. Their attitude was summed up by Syed Nawab Ali Chaudhry (1863–1929) in a letter to Mohsin-ul-Mulk. 'Up till now the Mohammedans of Bengal have been careless', he declared.

> If only Mohammedans of Bengal instead of following the Government, had agitated like the Hindus and had enlisted the *sympathies of the Mohammedans of the whole of India* [emphasis added] and raised their voices up to the Parliament, they would never have seen these unfortunate consequences.
>
> cited in Ahmad (1988, p. 74)

The successful campaign to unseat Fuller also worried elite Muslims in other areas of India, primarily because it might encourage educated Muslim youths to join the Congress bandwagon. There was certainly evidence of growing impatience with the conservative and loyalist stance of the Aligarh elders. In August 1906, a correspondent to the *Times of India*, for example, urged:

> The interests of the silent millions of [Muslims] demand prompt and steady action ... let [the Muslim leaders] be active ... They should come at once on the political arena and fight out their battles abreast with the rest of the world; or the very existence of the Mohammadans in India will become a shadow and a name.

cited in Ahmad (1988, pp. 76–7)

It was against this background that on 4 August 1906 Mohsin-ul-Mulk (1837–1907) the Aligarh college secretary wrote to its English principal W. A. J. Archbold (1865–1929) for advice on whether Muslims should submit a memorial to the Viceroy Lord Minto and ask him to receive a deputation. This would provide an opportunity for a public affirmation of the Aligarh stance from the highest possible authority in India. When Minto intimated his agreement, the stage was set for the famous Simla deputation.

Indian nationalists in later years criticised the Simla deputation and memorial as a command performance (i.e. a put-up job by the British). Muslim writers hailed it as speaking for the whole Indian Muslim community. In reality it was neither. The Simla deputation and the subsequent formation of the Muslim League was not simply the result of Machiavellian divide-and-rule tactics by the British. The final transition to Muslim political community reflected growing self-consciousness and fears arising from the spread of Hindu revivalism. The memorial was drawn up following hints of British sympathy, but it was the work of Mohsin-ul-Mulk, Imad-ul-Mulk and Syed Husain Bilgrami (1844–1926). The latter had good personal cause to be wary of Hindu intentions as he had encountered bitter opposition when he was appointed by Lord Curzon to the University Commission in 1902. The memorial called for a 'due proportion' of Muslims to be represented in the services where they had suffered with the introduction of competitive examinations and for representation in the legislatures to reflect the 'numerical strength, social status, local influence and special requirements of either [i.e. Hindu or Muslim] community'.

If the members of the Simla deputation were not 'puppets to counterbalance the Congress', nor were they representatives of the whole Indian Muslim community. The deputation led by the Agha Khan was largely comprised of landowners and members of Princely States or their officials. Prince Bakhtiyar, for example, was a direct descendant of the legendary Mysore ruler Tipu Sultan (d. 1799). There were just seven representatives from the Punjab and the Frontier to 11 from the UP, although these provinces possessed twice as many Muslim inhabitants. The Bombay Presidency, which at this time also included Sind, had four representatives for its four million population. The five representatives from the two Bengal provinces came from the Urdu-speaking elite which had no cultural roots in the soil of the region. Naseer Hussain Khayal (1878–1934), for example, was a renowned Urdu poet who wrote under the pen-name of Khyal. Not surprisingly most of those who journeyed to Simla for their meeting with Minto on 1 October 1906 were connected either with the various Aligarh institutions or with Ameer Ali's National Muhammadan Association. The dominating influence of the Urdu-speaking elite from the UP amongst the deputationists established a pattern for the future development of the All-India Muslim League.

Minto offered tea and sympathy. His acknowledgement that there was such a thing as a Muslim community political interest which transcended differences of region and class was of inestimable value to the deputationists. It reflected the traditional British policy of understanding Indian society in terms of religious categories. Nevertheless, the decision to establish a separate Muslim political platform following on from the deputation was not as smooth as some writers have portrayed it. The Agha Khan's doubts were only dispelled by the need to head off a unilateral attempt by Nawab Salimullah (1884–1915) to found a 'Muslim All-India Confederacy'. The disadvantage of such a body would have been its domination by Bengali interests as far as the UP *ashraf* elite was concerned.

The All-India Muslim League was thus created at the Dhaka 1906 Muslim Education Conference. Salimullah was allowed to propose the foundational resolution, but thereafter he was sidelined, a symbol of the future marginalisation of Bengali influence in its counsels – a process that has been called by some writers a foreshadowing of Bangladesh. In its early years, the Provincial League branches were independent of the all-India organisation and possessed their own rules and regulations. The All-India Muslim League membership was limited to just 400, seventy of whom were from the UP quota.

The achievement of separate electorates

The League's principal aim was to voice Muslim views during the discussions which took place from October 1907 onwards concerning constitutional reform proposals. In a dispatch of 27 November 1908 to the Viceroy, the Secretary of State acknowledged the need for a system of representation for Muslims which protected them from exclusion. He suggested, however, that this could be achieved by means of an electoral college rather than the separate electorates demanded by the Muslim League. While the reform bill was being discussed at Westminster, the League coordinated protest meetings in different parts of India, relying on local Muslim *anjumans* to provide leadership where it did not possess a formal organisation. Around 30 meetings were held between April and May 1909 and a crowd of 12,000 was attracted to the meeting at Lucknow, for example, held on 27 April.

These efforts intensified the anxieties of Morley that a bill without separate electorates would not pass through the Conservative-dominated House of Lords. Earl Percy, for example, a former Conservative Under-Secretary of State for India had pointed out that the bill's proposals appeared to contradict the impression Minto had given to the Simla deputation. Separate electorates, together with reservation of seats in the Imperial Legislative Council, were duly included in the Indian Councils Act of 15 November 1909.

'Religious nationalism' had received official validation through the linking of religion with political representation, power and patronage. In reality the Muslim community was not monolithic. Separatism was of far more interest to those Muslims living in Hindu-dominated areas than in the main centres of Muslim population, in which support for the Muslim League was muted. Much was to depend on whether separate electorates were seen as the answer to the demand for Muslim safeguards in an increasingly demo-cratic India, or merely as the beginning of a much wider quest.

The rise of Hindu communal political parties

Just as the formation of the Muslim League was founded on the the fears of the Muslim minorities living in UP and Bombay, the Hindu Mahasabha was precipitated by the anxieties of Hindus living in the Punjab where they formed around 36 per cent of the total population. The word 'Hindus' should be used carefully, however, as it was only certain sections of the Punjabi Hindu community, just as it was the elite *ashraf* Muslims, who were behind the drive for communal representation. Despite the claim of the Hindu Sabha (Hindu Forum) to speak for Punjabi Hindus, the interests of the Jat cultivators of the Rohtak district and of the Khatris, Aroras and Bania moneylending and commercial castes were at variance. Indeed they were to follow two completely different political trajectories: the Hindu Jats formed an important component of the cross-community Unionist Party which dominated the region's politics until the eve of the British departure; the commercial castes oscillated between the Congress and the Hindu Sabha depending on the contingencies of the day.

What should now be familiar features to the reader of increased community consciousness and a 'race for positions' in government service following the spread of literacy formed the background to the emergence of a Hindu political platform in the Punjab. Just as the Muslim professional elites closely associated with the Aligarh movement spearheaded the formation of the Muslim League, so the Hindu Sabha was the work of the Hindu commercial castes who had been active in the Arya Samaj. At one level they saw the Hindu Sabha as a protector of their interests which were threatened by the rise of an urban educated Muslim class and by the British decision during James Lyall's governorship (1887–92) to break the Hindus' monopoly of government posts by a policy of positive discrimination. During the decade 1891–1901, the rate of growth of Muslim literacy at 28.4 per cent was twice that of the Hindus who had declined to a proportion among the literate of 61 per cent. At another level, they were responsive to the ideological appeal of Hindu nationalism. The Arya Samaj had inculcated a pride in the Vedic golden age. The Punjab had a special place in this mythology, leading as early as 1909 to the Arya Samajist missionary Bhai Parmanand arguing for a partition of the north-west subcontinent to ensure that this holy land was under Hindu control. The commercial castes had previously entered the Congress's ranks, but a series of events, both within the Punjab and at an all-India level from 1900 onwards, convinced them that it inadequately safeguarded Hindu interests. This sentiment was encapsulated in the ideological charter of the Hindu Sabha which was published by the Arya Samajist leader Lal Chand in a series of letters to the *Punjabee* newspaper under the title 'Self-Abnegation in Politics'.

Separate electorates wiped out the Punjabi Hindus' advantages in local bodies arising from their superior education and organisation. Such power had not always been wielded wisely, for example when the Hoshiarpur municipal committee had attempted to ban the sale of beef within the city. Forebodings about the impact of democratisation on the minority community – a mirror image of Muslim misgivings in UP – were intensified by the perceived bias of British officials in favour of the Muslims. Hindus had been appalled in 1904 when Lyall's recommendations for increasing the number of Muslim entrants to the bureaucracy had become public. Soon every government appointment from the lowliest village *patwari* (record keeper) to the most exalted high court judge was keenly scrutinised for its effect on the communal balance within the services.

While the Hindu intelligentsia believed that its traditional monopoly of education and the government services was under threat, the moneylenders were hit by the raft of agrarian reform measures which entered the statute book between 1900 and 1904. The cornerstone of the reforms, and indeed the stimulus for the cross-communal politics which dominated the Punjab region for the next four decades, was the 1900 Alienation of Land Act. This measure prohibited the transfer of land from 'agriculturalist' cultivators to 'non-agriculturalist' urban moneylenders. In order to understand the political significance of what became termed the 'Magna Carta' of the Punjab's rural population, a brief examination of its background is required.

British rule had seen a rapid commercialisation of agriculture in the Punjab. Improvements in irrigation and transportation had seen the region transformed into the bread-basket of the subcontinent by the beginning of the twentieth century. The rising land values which accompanied the commercialisation of agriculture had been accompanied by a private property land market. Peasant indebtedness partly resulting from social extravagances had seen land change hands rapidly in a number of districts. This process received great publicity as a result of a book entitled *Mussalmans and Moneylenders in the Punjab* published by S. S. Thorburn (1844–1924), the Deputy Commissioner in the Dera Ghazi Khan district. The emergence of an absentee moneylending landholding class threatened rural stability in a region which had become the major recruitment centre of the Indian Army from the 1880s onwards. The large Muslim landowners of the trans-Indus districts were not, however, the moneylenders' only victims. The Hindu Jat cultivators of the 'famine tracts' of the Hissar and Rohtak districts also suffered from exploitation. Their subservience was vividly illustrated in village meetings where the moneylender sat in a place of honour at the head of the *charpoy* (stringed bed) with his peasant clients at his feet.

After a sharp internal debate concerning the virtues of intervention against sticking to *laissez-faire* principles, the Punjab government implemented the 1900 Alienation of Land Act. It barred the transfer of land from agriculturalist to non-agriculturalist tribes. These were designated on a district-wide basis. The agriculturalist grouping included not only the Rajput 'martial caste' landowners and Jat, Arain and Gujar cultivators, but also the Muslim religious elites – the Syeds, Sheikhs and Qureshis. The measure not only halted expropriation by the non-agriculturalist moneylenders, but also provided the framework for the structuring of politics around the idiom of the 'tribe' rather than the religious community. It was, however, the regionalist Unionist Party rather than the nationalist Congress which benefited from politics being placed on this secularist basis.

The Congress, which ranked many Khatris and Banias amongst its supporters and financial backers in the Punjab, vacillated in its reponse to the Alienation of Land Act. It ended up with the worst of all possible worlds. It failed to convince the rural population that it upheld their interests at the same time as appearing to be a weak reed to the non-agriculturalists. The Hindu Sabha eagerly replaced it as the upholder of urban Hindu interests. It was no accident that one of the earliest Hindu Sabha communications to the government demanded that traditional landholding Brahmin and Khatri castes be classified as agriculturalist tribes.

In 1907, the college faction of the Arya Samaj founded the Hindu Sabha. This action followed hard on the heels of the Chenab Canal Colony disturbances. These had broken out when the Punjab government announced that, despite the poor harvests, the water charges for the colonists would be increased. The canal colonies had been created following the large-scale irrigation schemes of the final decades of the nineteenth century. Six million acres of land had been transformed from arid wasteland populated only by nomadic herders into the richest farming area in the whole of the subcontinent. The canal colony areas were neatly laid out into plots of land known as squares, with market places, towns and villages spaced at regular intervals along the roads and railways which criss-crossed them. The blame for the agitation in what were regarded as model settlements by the British was placed on the Arya Samajist leader Lajpat Rai (1856–1928), who had addressed a large meeting of the colonists in Lyallpur. Rai was subsequently convicted and transported. The Arya Samaj was put under surveillance as a potentially seditious organisation. This repression convinced a number of Aryas that they needed a political organisation to defend their interests. Congress, in the grip of the moderates, appeared unable to do so either in national or provincial politics.

The Hindu Mahasabha

Between 1907 and 1909, a number of local Hindu Sabha branches were formed in the Punjab and neighbouring areas of North India. These came together in the all-India federation of the Hindu Mahasabha in 1915. It was only in the wake of the Muslim peasant uprisings against Hindu landlords in the Moplah riots six years later, however, that the Hindu Mahasabha stirred itself into real life. In 1923, B. S. Moonje, the leader of the Central Provinces' Hindu Sabha, produced a report into the violence on the Malabar coast. In this he diagnosed the weakness of the Hindu community in comparison with the Muslims. His main findings were to provide ideological sustenance both for the Mahasabha and the RSS. It should be remembered that Hedgewar, the founder of the RSS, was in many respects Moonje's protégé in Nagpur.

Moonje placed himself in stark opposition to Gandhi's teaching by first attributing Muslims' 'virility' and 'readiness to kill and be killed' to their meat diet. He claimed that *ahimsa* was an 'un-Vedic' principle and attempted to popularise the Vedic institution of *yajnathag* so that Hindus would be accustomed to 'the sight of spilling blood and killing'. Whereas this animal sacrifice had traditionally been performed for a single household, however, Moonje sought to transform it into a sacrificial assembly (*yajnasamarambh*) held in a temple. The idea that the temple could form a unifying community centre similar to the role of the mosque with its large spaces for congregational assembly for the Muslim community was to be taken up by Swami Shraddhananda (formerly Lala Munshi Ram) in his influential work *Hindu Sangathan – Saviour of the Dying Race*, published in 1926.

> The first step I propose is to build one Hindu Rashtra Mandir [Temple of the Hindu Nation] in every city and important town, with a compound which could contain an audience of 25,000 and a hall in which *katha* [prose selections] from Bhagavad Gita, the Upanishads and the great epics Ramayana and Mahabharata could be daily recited. The Rashtra Mandir will be in charge of the local Hindu Sabha which will manage to have *akharas* for wrestling and *gatka* etc. in the same compound. While the sectarian Hindu temples are dominated by their own individual deities, the Catholic Hindu Mandir will be devoted to the worship of the three mother-spirits, the Gau-mata [the Cow-Mother] the Saraswati-mata

[goddess of knowledge] and the Bhumi-mata [motherland] ... Let a lifelike map of
Mother-Bharat [India] be constructed in a prominent place, giving all its characteristics in vivid colours so that every child of Matri-Bhumi [earth-mother] may
daily bow before the Mother and renew his pledge to restore her to the ancient
pinnacle of glory from which she has fallen.

cited in Jaffrelot (1996, p. 22)

This proposal is yet another another striking example of the invention of
tradition in the attempt to construct community. The Orientalist-inspired
themes of decline from a golden age, the cult of physical fitness and of a
nationalism inspired by India as holy motherland are all present. The temple
is transformed into a centre of congregational assembly and the tradition of
household worship is ignored because of its lack of political utility.

Lying behind the idea of temple as mosque, according to Moonje, was the
second cause of Hindu weakness: that of social disunity. The answer to the
problem created by the disunity of the caste system was given in the title of
Shraddhananda's book – *Sangathan* – which means 'self-strengthening'. Its
most controversial elements were the *shuddhi* movement of conversion and
the encouragement by Moonje of the Vedic 'custom' of Anuloma and
Pratiloma inter-caste marriages. These were referred to in the legal code of
Manu, but were disapproved of. In Moonje's eyes, however, they would
assist the organic development of a national Hindu unity. The most popular
form of the *sangathan* movement was the cultivation of physical fitness.
There was considerable progess in the Punjab in the construction of *akharas*
and Mahabir Dals (associations of the strong named after Mahabir/Hanuman
the monkey god who embodied strength). The growing number of
communal riots in the Punjab's towns in the 1920s both reflected the growth
of the *sangathan* movement and contributed to it. Gandhi's appeal to non-
violence evoked little interest in a region deeply infused with martial values
following centuries of invasions through its plains.

The *sangathan* movement was a major factor in the Hindu Sabha's capture
of the Hindu vote in the urban constituencies in the 1926 Punjab Legislative
Council elections. These were the first polls contested by the Punjab branch
of the Congress since the 1919 Government of India Act had enlarged the
provincial Legislative Council. It fared badly, as in addition to its loss of
urban Hindu support, the rural Jats voted overwhelmingly for the Unionist
Party which placed curbs on the moneylenders at the centre of its platform.
Despite a few token Muslim Congress figures, its appeal was infinitesimal to
the majority community in Punjab. With the rise of the Sikh Akali Dal it was
also marginalised amongst the Sikhs. The leading Congressman Motilal
Nehru (1861–1931) (Jawaharlal's father) conceded that 'We have not only
been defeated, we have been routed.' Not surprisingly, the Congress fared
little better in the 1934 Council elections when the Sabha again made a good
showing in the urban seats. The Congress recovered a little ground following
the introduction of provincial autonomy in 1937, but it was always aware of

the danger of being outflanked by the Hindu Sabha on communal issues. A strong current of Hindu nationalism thus pervaded the Punjab Congress Committee. The lesson Muslims drew from the state of affairs in the Punjab Congress was that a gulf existed between its lipservice to secularism and realities on the ground. The Hindu Sabhas had succeeded in their task as ginger groups for the main vehicle of Indian nationalism.

The political institutionalisation of Sikh community consciousness

The Singh Sabha movement and the voluminous tracts and pamphlets published by the reformers had prepared the ground for the political institutionalisation of Sikh community conciouness in the Punjab homeland. The first step in this process occurred when 29 out of 150 of the Singh Sabhas agreed to merge into the Chief Khalsa Diwan. This body had been formed in Amritsar on 30 October 1902 to represent the Sikhs' political demands to the government. By 1910 its membership had risen to 10,000, grouped within four important regional branches: the Manjha Diwan at Taran Taran, the Malwa Khalsa Diwan at Choohar Chak in the Ferozepore district, the Doaba Khalsa Diwan at Jullundur, and finally, the Khalsa Diwan centred in the neighbouring Princely State of Patiala.

The 1909 Morley–Minto reforms had been hugely disappointing, as Sikhs were not granted separate electorates along with the Muslims. Thereafter Sikh representation on the Provincial Council was limited to those members nominated by the British. Lobbying by the Chief Khalsa Diwan ensured that separate electorates were conceded by the 1919 Montagu–Chelmsford reforms, but the Sikhs received only 10 out of 58 Council seats, despite their demands for 30 per cent weightage to reflect their importance to the Indian Army. This setback encouraged the radicalism which manifested itself in the *gurdwara* reform movement. It was also rooted in the impact of the First World War on the Sikh community.

War, recruitment and the Ghadr movement

The Sikhs, along with the Muslim Rajputs of the north-west Punjab and the Hindu Dogras, were designated as a 'martial caste'. From the 1880s onwards, a Punjabisation of the Indian Army had taken place in which three-fifths of its recruits were drawn from the 'martial castes'. This process was justified in terms of the inherited fighting capabilities of these Punjabi communities, but nationalist opponents claimed that the policy was designed to ensure 'docile' recruits from a conservative and educationally backward region. During the First World War, the number of Sikh soldiers peaked at a record level of 150,000. Wartime recruitment was an unsettling experience both for the servicemen who fought in terrible conditions on the Western Front as well as in the Mesopotamia campaign and for the extended families they left behind. The war also brought in its wake high prices and shortages of goods for the Sikh farmers of the Punjab.

The second major radicalising impact of the war came in the shape of the abortive uprising in the central tracts of the Punjab by members of the Ghadr (Revolution) movement. It had been formed by Sikh emigrants to the Pacific states of North America under the leadership of Lala Har Dyal (1884–1939) in October 1913. The background to its emergence was the increasing racial discrimination highlighted in the 1907 and 1908 anti-Asian riots in British Columbia and California respectively. The Canadian government had tightened entry for Asian immigrants in 1910. Anger at this situation was deflected onto the government of India and the weekly *Ghadr* newspaper was soon calling for an armed revolt against the British.

Animosity increased still further following the celebrated Komagata Maru affair when a party of Punjabi Sikhs who had sailed in a Japanese vessel from Hong Kong were refused the right to disembark in Canada in May 1914. The authorities were acting within the law, but in a discriminatory manner. Immigration regulations which stipulated that migrants should travel directly from their home country to Canada had been drawn up in the knowledge that there was no direct passage from India. Following a series of meetings in California, around 2,000 Indians (mainly Sikhs) volunteered to go back to lead a revolt. The date set for a revolution which was expected to involve a rising by the army was 21 February 1915. The scheme was poorly organised and thought out and was soon uncovered by the Punjab police. The Ghadr ringleaders were rounded up and later tried in the Lahore Conspiracy case. Eighteen were hanged and 58 were transported for life. A conspiracy trial was also held in San Francisco which resulted in the winding up of the Ghadr Party. Although the revolution had failed, there was some support and sympathy in the central Sikh villages which had always been noted for their loyalty to the Raj. This was a testament both to the Sikh emigrants' genuine grievances and to the disquiet arising from the Punjabi Sikhs' sense of political marginalisation. The scene was set for the mass mobilisations of the *gurdwara* reform movement. Finally it should be remembered that the infamous Amritsar massacre of 13 April 1919 claimed many Sikh victims amongst the unarmed crowd fired upon by the troops commanded by Brigadier-General Reginald Dyer.

The gurdwara reform movement

The 'de-Hinduisation' of Sikh *gurdwaras* was a long-term aim of the Sikh reformers. In May 1905 the Tat Khalsa supported the manager of the Golden

Temple, Arur Singh, when he ordered the removal of idols from its precincts. Hindu opposition to the move was backed up by a 13,000-strong petition to the British administration.

The *gurwarda* reform movement centred around the wresting of the control of *gurdwaras* from Sikh priests (*mahants*). Some of the latter were deemed by reformers to have lived immoral lives, encouraged idolatry and superstition and used the income of the shrines arising from the land attached to them for personal rather than community purposes. These concerns might appear to be purely community matters without any political significance. The struggle for the control of the *gurdwaras*, however, brought the Sikhs into conflict with the British who felt they had to uphold the *mahants*. Such action was prompted, firstly, because they were useful rural collaborators, some of whom had even assisted in army recruitment during the First World War. Secondly, the British felt obliged to uphold the private property rights of those *mahants* who had registered titles to the *gurdwara* property. Moreover, the government itself had granted revenue-free land to the *gurdwaras*.

The highly politicised character of the *gurdwara* reform movement was revealed when the campaign was inaugurated by a new Sikh political party known as the Central Sikh League rather than by religious reformers. Legal methods were first used to evict the *mahants*. From the autumn of 1920, however, tired by the law's delays, the Sikhs turned to direct action. Two new political institutions were created to carry out the struggle of the Sikh Akalis (immortals). Their emergence completed the politicisation of the Sikh community. They still remain the most important centres of power within it.

The first institution was the Shiromani Gurdwara Prabandhak Committee (SGPC) (Society for Gurdwara Protection) whose 175 members were elected at a general Sikh meeting on 15 November 1920. Its task was to act as a managing committee for all Sikh *gurdwaras*. In order to facilitate this, the SGPC took responsibility for launching a movement to liberate the *gurdwaras* from their *mahants'* control. The following month, the second institution came into being to spearhead this struggle. It was known as the Akali Dal (army of the immortals) and its role was to coordinate the bands of volunteers (Akali Jathas) who were to engage in direct action. The *jathas* emulated the Gandhian techniques of non-cooperation and non-violence. The *mahants*, however, resorted to force in a struggle which became increasingly bitter following a violent clash at Guru Nanak's shrine at Nankana Sahib on 20 February 1921. In this incident many Akalis were killed by the hired armed guards of the *mahant* Narain Das. Their bodies were burnt on the spot in an attempt to cover up the massacre.

The episode thrust the Akalis into the mainstream of the nationalist movement, as in its wake the SGPC passed a resolution in support of Gandhi's non-cooperation movement. By the time that the *gurdwara* reform movement came to an uneasy conclusion in October 1925, 4,000 persons had died, 2,000 had been wounded and over 30,000 arrests had been made in what was at that time the largest mass movement in the colonial Punjab's history. It centred around three main agitations, the so-called 'Keys Affair', the Guruka Bagh (Garden of the Guru) agitation in the Amritsar district and the Jaito 'Morcha' in the neighbouring Princely State of Nabha.

The 'Keys Affair' revolved around the attempts of the SGPC to secure the return of the keys to the *toshakhana* (treasury) of the Golden Temple in Amritsar from the Deputy Commissioner. He had taken them into his safe keeping when Baba Kharak Singh, president of the SGPC, had sought them from the temple manager Sunder Singh Ramgarhia. Non-violent protests continued from October 1921 until the following January, when the keys were handed over and the imprisoned Akali workers were unconditionally released. Gandhi, who had been following the affair closely and recognised the *gurdwara* reform movement as part of the wider non-cooperation movement, telegraphed Baba Kharak Singh with the words, 'the first decisive battle for India's freedom is won' (Grewal, 1990, p. 160).

The Guruka Bagh agitation began early in 1922 and lasted for over 15 months. It was caused by the Akalis' challenge to the *mahant* of the *gurdwara* (built to commemorate the visit of Guru Arjun, 1563–1606) situated near Ajnala in the Amritsar district, by cutting wood from the land which adjoined it. By October 1922, nearly 2,500 volunteers had been arrested because of their unlawful assembly at the *gurdwara*. Police brutality against the daily non-violent protests was a source of acute embarrassment. When a *jatha* of ex-servicemen was involved in the protests, the British, who were eager to maintain the Sikhs' loyal connection with the army, intervened to engineer a compromise solution. An Indian official was encouraged to buy the land next to the *gurdwara* from the *mahant* Sunder Das. He then allowed the Akalis to gather the firewood in peace.

The Akali agitation in Nabha State was less successful, partly because it was more overtly political, but also because the state officials were less sensitive to criticism of their policing techniques. Its initial cause was the abdication on 9 July 1923 of the state's Maharajah Ripudaman Singh in favour of his son who was a minor. The Akalis claimed that the British had forced him to step down because of his sympathy with the *gurdwara* reform movement cause. The dispute widened into a struggle for the right to freedom of worship, following police disruption of an Akali-sponsored *akhand path* (lit. unbroken reading; a ceremony involving the entire reading aloud of the Adi Granth scriptures) at the village of Jaito. Sikhs flocked from the neighbouring districts of the Punjab to join the Akali protests. They also secured support from the Indian National Congress: indeed Nehru visited Jaito and was arrested. The Congress interest waned, however, following Gandhi's release from prison in February 1924.

The *gurdwara* reform movement ended with the passage of the 1925 Gurdwara and Shrines Act which gave the SGPC control over most of the

gurdwaras including the Golden Temple. This had important political consequences as it meant that it not only controlled the substantial financial
resources of the shrines, but also their vast powers of patronage. Henceforth
these became available to the Akali Dal which dominated the SGPC, which
became a kind of parliament for the Sikh community. From 1925 onwards
the Akali Dal secured a considerable advantage over other Sikh parties. In the
words of the American political scientist Paul Brass, it not only acted as a
'political expression of pre-existing Sikh aspirations', but was to play a
'critical role in creating a modern Sikh nation' (Brass, 1974, p. 433).

In a pattern reminiscent of the earlier Khilafat campaign, the highpoint of
Sikh involvement in the national struggle resulted as much from community
concerns as nationalist sympathies. It was to be followed by a drifting apart.
The Congress's acceptance of Ramsay MacDonald's Communal Award in
1932 marked a definite 'parting of the ways' between it and the Akali Dal.
Although the Sikhs had separate electorates, they hoped for reservation of a
third of the seats in any future Legislative Assembly. The Communal Award
gave them just 33 out of 175 seats (i.e. 18 per cent). In the wake of the
growing influence of the Pakistan movement, some Sikhs were to raise the
claim for their own Sikhistan/Khalistan homeland.

The politicisation of regional identities

The British devolution of powers to elected Indian politicians in the
provinces during the interwar period, while at the same time holding on to
control at the centre, encouraged the emergence of regional parties which
challenged the dominance of the mainstream nationalist organisations. The
dyarchy system introduced by the 1919 Government of India Act transferred
for the first time to elected Indian politicians control over such administrative functions as local self-government and education and made the
provinces an important political arena. At the same time the provincialisation
of politics disadvantaged nationalist politicians who lacked a strong local
electoral powerbase. Mohammad Ali Jinnah was the most famous victim of
this process. Frustrated by the lack of opportunities under the conditions
created by the 1919 constitutional reforms, he set sail from Bombay in
October 1930 to begin his self-imposed exile in London which was to last
nearly five years.

While regionally based parties may have been an outgrowth of the
colonial state's administrative structures, they also drew sustenance from the
transition from localised identities to wider linguistic and caste-based
community consciousness. Provincial historical contingencies were also
crucial. An important factor, for example, in the development of the two
most influential regional groupings, the Justice Party of Madras and the
Punjab Unionist Party, was the domination of local Congress branches by

high-caste Brahmins and Banias who were popularly perceived as being both socially and economically exploitative.

The Punjab Unionist Party

Throughout much of the closing two decades of British rule in India, the Unionist Party dominated politics in the Punjab. Its cross-communal support from the rural population enabled it to sideline both the Congress and the Muslim League. Indeed the latter was never able to form a pre-independence government in this Muslim majority region dubbed by Jinnah the 'corner-stone' of Pakistan. Despite its historical significance, little was written about the Unionist Party until the 1980s, however, because it fitted awkwardly into both a triumphalist Indian and Pakistani nationalist historiography.

The Unionist Party was founded in 1923 as a loose organisation of land-holders elected to the Legislative Council. Landlord parties existed in a number of provinces by this time including the neighbouring United Provinces. But the Unionist Party differed in that it appealed to peasant proprietors as well as large landholders and it drew support from the Hindu Jats of the south-east Punjab as well as the Muslim 'tribes' of the west. Indeed the Hindu Jat leader Chhotu Ram was the star Unionist public speaker. He addressed crowds of peasants for hours on end without the use of a micro-phone. His slow delivery captured the directness and simplicity of the Punjabi language. His violent and sometimes lewd diatribes against the moneylenders whom he dubbed 'black banias' and blood-suckers was quintessentially Punjabi. In his famous tract *Bachara Zamindar* ('Helpless Zamindar') he passionately declared: 'Leave religion to the four corners of the temple, the mosque and the Gurdwara. Release yourself from the bondage of the Maulvis, the Pandits and the Granthis. Do whatever you feel in observing your religious tenets but keep it strictly outside politics' (cited in Talbot, 1996b, p. 135).

The Unionist Party's cross-community appeal was amply demonstrated in the 1937 provincial elections, when it captured all but one of the rural Hindu seats in the Jat heartland of the Ambala division. It secured, in total, 99 of the 175 Legislative Assembly seats. The Muslim League recorded a single victory, while the Congress did little better, capturing just 18 constituencies. Chhotu Ram's boasts that the Unionists were the 'real' Congress appeared to ring true.

At one level the Unionist Party's foundation represented a continuation of the informal alliances the British had forged with the rural elites since 1857 when their support had been crucial in suppressing the civilian and military revolt. The decision in the 1880s to make the rural Punjab the major recruitment centre of the Indian Army added a further incentive for the British to link their authority with important local intermediaries. The judicious use of patronage and the skewing of representation in favour of landholders and retired servicemen ensured the emergence of a strong loyalist lobby. Equally significant was the establishment of an 'agriculturalist' cross-community political interest. This was rooted, as we have noted, in the 1900 Alienation of Land Act.

Following its passage, both the justification of British rule in the Punjab and the programme of the leading men of the tribes and clans who eventually banded together to form the Unionist Party was the protection and 'uplift' of the agriculturalist tribes. Significantly, only members of the agriculturalist tribes as defined by the 1900 legislation were allowed to stand as candidates for rural seats in the new Legislative Council created by the Montagu–Chelmsford reforms. British administrative decisions thus created a favourable environment for the predominance of rural interests which were committed to 'tribal' rather than religious identification in politics.

The Unionist Party was not merely, however, the landowners' opportunistic response to the colonial political setting. The rural population shared a common language, songs, poetry and folklore.The tragic love tales of Hir Rajha, Sassi Punnu and Sohni Mahival were popular with all communities. Sufism acted as a cross-community focus of religious devotion, although religious reformers increasingly warned of the dangers of such syncretic practices. A further indigenous underpinning for the Unionist enterprise was provided by the growing self-consciousness of the Jats. The Muslim League had repeatedly to denounce 'Jatism' and 'tribalism' in its attempts to emphasise religious affiliation over all other loyalties. Even as late as the 1946 Punjab provincial elections, however, Muslim, Hindu and Sikh Jats provided an important base of support for the Unionists.

The Muslim League breakthrough in these elections paved the way for Pakistan while sounding the death-knell for Unionism, although a rump Unionist–Akali–Congress coalition government took office after them. The Unionist political era was thereafter consigned to the dustbin of history for many years. However, it is once more the focus of attention. Its espousal of power-sharing, cross-community cooperation and decentralisation of power has much to teach politicians in the contemporary subcontinent, while for historians, it provides illuminating insights into the real stuff of politics in the late colonial period. Most importantly of all, the Punjab case warns against narratives which focus too narrowly on the triumph of Indian and Pakistani nationalism.

The rise of the non-Brahmin movement in the Madras Presidency

By the closing decades of the nineteenth century, a myth of a Dravidian golden age prompted in part by Orientalist speculations had emerged in the

Madras Presidency as a counter to Brahmin domination. The Tamil *sangams*, like other new Indian institutions, carried political undertones, although they were community organisations. The final push in the direction of politicisation was provided by the increasing national prominence of the Theosophical Society president Annie Besant who was seen by the non-Brahmin movement as a steadfast upholder of both the Vedic myth and the contemporary caste system.

Annie Besant signalled a more active concern in politics by joining the Congress in 1914. She immediately revealed her sympathies for Tilak who was seeking to re-enter the party following his release from prison. Stalwart moderates like Gokhale and Pheroze Shah Mehta were determined to block this as they did not want the old moderate–extremist division to re-emerge. They also publicly associated themselves with support for the imperial war effort. Annie Besant, through the columns of her newspapers, the *Commonweal* and *New India*, was increasingly critical of the latter stance. Finally, on 25 September 1915 she announced in *New India* that a Home Rule League was to be formed as an 'auxiliary' to the Congress. The opposition of the Congress moderates, however, slowed her efforts. The impatient Tilak responded by founding his own Home Rule League in Maharashtra, although this was subsequently to cooperate with Annie Besant's organisation. The Home Rule Leagues used religious songs, street corner preaching techniques and a flood of pamphlets translated into various Indian languages to publicise their message.

Annie Besant's activities were particularly intensive in Madras because it was the headquarters of the Theosophical Society, which provided much of the backbone for the Home Rule League movement. Her tub thumping was disquieting for the non-Brahmin elites who had no wish to see British rule replaced by a Brahmin-dominated state. Such anxieties were based not only on the traditional influence of the Brahmins, but, as we have seen, on their dominance of the colonial public services arising from their educational attainment.

On 20 November 1916 around 30 leading non-Brahmin figures met in the Victoria Public Hall in Madras to create a joint stock company to found English, Telegu and Tamil-language newspapers to ventilate non-Brahmin interests. The company rapidly transformed itself into a political party known as the Justice Party and its three papers, the *Andhu Prakasika*, the *Dravidian* and the *Justice*, entered the lists against the Home Rule League. The Tamil-language paper the *Dravidian*, which began publication in mid-1917, ran such banner headlines as, 'Home Rule and Brahmana's Rule'. The Justice Party also issued a pamphlet entitled 'Home Rule and Caste'. Its tone is summed up in the following sentences: 'It is a misrepresentation to say that Brahmins belong to the same Indian nation as the non-Brahmins while the English are aliens ... Indian Brahmins are more alien to us than Englishmen' (Irschick, 1969, pp. 51–2).

A parallel can be seen here with the Muslim League's two-nation theory and critique of the 'unrepresentative' character of the Indian National Congress. Both the Justice Party and the Muslim League were favourably disposed to the British who were regarded as holding the ring between conflicting community interests. Both parties were also from the outset elitist in outlook and support, although they claimed to speak for the illiterate non-Brahmin and Muslim masses.

The Justice Party

The Justice Party was the dominant party in the Madras Legislative Council following the 1919 constitutional reforms. It was now in a position to break the Brahmins' much resented monopoly on government service posts at both elite and district levels. Parallels can be seen here with the rise of the OBC (upwardly mobile peasant communities such as the Yadavs of Uttar Pradesh) in North India in the late 1980s and the attempt to undermine high-caste privilege through positive discrimination. In both historical instances, however, the lower-caste Hindus were to find it difficult to extend their concerns to include those right at the bottom of society – the Untouchables. Indeed as early as 1923 there was a bitter break between the Justice Party and the nascent Untouchable movement whose leaders accused it of shedding only 'crocodile tears' on behalf of the depressed classes.

As Andre Beteille has shown, Brahmins held 93 out of 128 permanent district *munsifs* (judges) posts in 1914 and had accounted for 15 out of 16 successful ICS candidates from the Madras Presidency during the years 1892–1904 (Beteille, 1997, p. 80). The Justice Party deployed its power in 1922 to achieve the promulgation of what became known as the Second Council Government Order. This ensured a greater distribution of administrative posts among non-Brahmins. Many Tamil Brahmins switched their attentions to trade and commerce; a large number left Madras for the less hostile environment of Bombay. Their identity was increasingly rooted in a sense of discrimination. Indeed some termed themselves the Jews of South India.

The Government Order marked the highwater mark of the Justice Party's influence. One reason for its subsequent decline was the growing tensions between its Tamil and Telegu members arising from the latter group's dominant position. Indeed, a rival Tamil Nadu non-Brahmin conference was held in August 1923 at Trichinopoly. Later demands for Dravidistan were linked to this strand of the Justice Party movement, as the Telegu speakers were always more ambivalent about Dravidianism. Sanskrit had exerted some influence on Telegu, unlike Tamil. Moreover, the non-Brahmin Telegu elites such as the Kapis and Kammas were less opposed to the Brahmins than the Tamil Vellalas. Finally, the Telegu speakers had their own historical myth to pursue – that of the Kingdom of the Andhras.

The Justice Party's decline was also precipitated by the death of such leading figures as Tyagaraja Chetti. Following its setback in the 1926 council elections, the Coimbatore Resolution was agreed which permitted Justice Party members to hold dual membership with the Congress. At one level this can be understood as part of a wider process during the interwar period that saw the demise of regional parties outside the Congress or Muslim League mainstream, with the notable exception of the Punjab Unionist Party. It reflected the overriding of local interests by national considerations in an intensifying freedom struggle. At another, it marked a radicalisation of Tamilian identity as the formal politics of the Legislature were exchanged for the social activism of Ramaswami Naicker's *Suyamariyatai iyakkam* (self-respect movement). Naicker, who had been born in 1879 into a respectable middle-class family, had spent six years of his life as a religious mendicant. This experience had created a strong personal distaste for what he regarded as the Brahmins' exploitation of the lower castes.

The self-respect movement

The trigger for the creation of the self-respect movement had been a speech made by Gandhi in Madras in March 1925 in which he had upheld the caste system and the duties of each separate caste. Naicker, who had been a member of the Congress, broke with Gandhi when he could not be persuaded to modify his views. In an editorial in his Tamil newspaper *Kudi Arasu* Naicker called for the destruction of the Congress and Brahminism. The self-respect movement set about the task by sponsoring religious cere-monies which did not employ Brahmin priests. The cause dear to Gandhi's own heart of allowing Untouchables freedom to worship in temples was also espoused. The self-respect movement not only attacked the Brahmins but the 'bogus' patriotism of the Congress. In May 1931 Naicker denounced what he termed 'the superstition of khadi'. Such sweeping criticisms required great courage at a time when the wearing of homespun cloth had become the symbol of Indian nationalism and Gandhi, its main advocate, held immense moral sway. As we shall see in the next chapter, the self-respect movement resuscitated the Justice Party in the late 1930s and raised the cry for a Tamil homeland in opposition to the Indian nationalism of the Congress. The demand for Tamil Nad for the Tamilians was the climax of the growing awareness of a collective Tamil/Dravidian identity.

Conclusion

Nationalism jostled with other sources of identity during the late colonial era. Between the 1880s and early 1920s, communal and regional identities were politicised, although they have often been neglected in mainstream histories which have taken their cue from the nationalist discourse. Communal parties blended the modernity of voluntaristic organisation with the tradition of ascriptive loyalties. Historical contingencies determined the timing of their emergence and the main focus of political mobilisation in a given locality. Fears of the impact of democratisation led a number of minority communities to create organisations designed to safeguard their own specific community interests. Interesting parallels can be drawn in this respect between the behaviour of the UP Muslims and the urban Hindus of the Punjab.

The provincialisation of politics by the British during the interwar era under the dyarchy system undoubtedly boosted regionally based parties. It is true that the Congress, as we shall see in the next chapter, mounted mass nationalist campaigns during this period, but they were episodic. Day-to-day politics were dominated by the patronage concerns of provincial politicians. It was only when the British departure became imminent that the spotlight shifted to all-India issues, to the immense advantage of the mainstream nationalist parties.

|6|

Nationalism, communal and ethnic identities and the partition of India

Indian nationalism is not exclusive nor aggressive, nor destructive ... I would like to see India free and strong so that she might offer herself as a worthy and pure sacrifice for the betterment of the world.

Gandhi (1957, p. 119)

The Hindus and Muslims belong to two different religious philosophies, social customs and literature. They neither inter-marry, nor inter-dine together ... they have different epics, their heroes are different, and ... very often the hero of one is a foe of the other ... To yoke together two such nations under a single state, one as a numerical minority and the other as a majority, must lead to growing discontent and the final destruction of any fabric that may be so built up or the government of such a state.

M. A. Jinnah, presidential address, Lahore Session of the All-India Muslim League, 22 March 1940

The three and a half decades from the outbreak of the First World War to the British departure from India witnessed an intensification of the nationalist struggle and the emergence of the Pakistan movement. The political landscape was increasingly dominated by the triangular relationship between the British, the Congress and the Muslim League. This did not, however, mean that other sources of political identity had been obliterated. There were calls for a Tamil state, Sikhistan/Khalistan and Pakhtunistan during the endgame of Empire. Almost immediately after independence the Nagas called for separation from India, heralding the beginnings of a secessionist movement in the hill districts of Assam which had become an armed struggle by the mid-1950s. Within Princely States such as Hyderabad there were some who

Map 2 The Indian subcontinent on the eve of independence.

harboured the desire for independence. Moreover, Indian and Pakistani nationalism had compromised with other sources of community in the drive for territory. The Congress in both Punjab and Bengal, for example, was hardly distinguishable from the Hindu nationalism of the Mahasabha. The Muslim League had used localist identities based on kinship (*biraderi*) and *sufi* allegiances to break through in the key Punjab region.

The outgoing Raj, for a variety of strategic and economic reasons, had set its face against the Balkanisation of the subcontinent. The princes were thus coralled into the Indian and Pakistani camps. The 1947 referendum in the North-West Frontier Province disallowed the option of a separate Paktun-Pakhtunistan state. Sikh and Tamil claims for separate states had similarly received short shrift. Indeed, the British were so attached to the concept of a United India that even with respect to the demands of the Muslim League, which clearly could not be denied, Jinnah was only offered a Pakistan of the 'moth-eaten' variety.

This chapter examines the interplay between national, communal and regional identities at the close of British rule. It explains both the circumstances in which nationalism 'triumphed' and the legacies of the freedom movement for the new Dominions of India and Pakistan.

The Congress, mass nationalist struggle and the British departure

The Congress's growing base of support

The closing decades of British rule raise the crucial question of how the Congress was transformed from an elitist to a mass organisation. Its answer lies both in the radicalising impact of the First World War and Gandhi's emergence on the Indian political scene. Gandhi transformed the freedom struggle by increasing its appeal to wider groups than ever before and by introducing the unique philosophy of non-violence.

Gandhi insisted that attachment to truth (for God was truth according to Gandhi) meant that *ahimsa* (non-violence) was the 'highest religion' (*paramo dharma*). This philosophy was to guide the individual's life and be the driving force of the freedom struggle. The goal of independence (*swaraj*) could not justify the means of violence. Gandhi explained this in terms of the image of a seed and a tree with the same 'inviolable connection' between means and end as between seed and tree. The wrong sowing would bring forth a bitter harvest. The link between non-violent struggle and the search for truth is revealed in the Gujarati term *satyagraha*, meaning truth-force or soul-force. This has sometimes been misleadingly translated into English as 'passive resistance' which robs it of its moral content. Gandhi declared in his seminal study *Hindu Swaraj* that *satyagraha* would not only 'purify' those engaged in its struggle, but also 'bless' those against whom it was used as they would not be forced to abandon their understanding of truth.

Satyagraha was culturally rooted in the Gujarati tradition of Hinduism that was influenced by the Jain emphasis on the sacredness of life and hence the need for non-violence. *Satyagraha* was remarkably successful as a tactic against a ruling power that prided itself on its moral authority to govern. Those on the left of Indian politics, however, saw the Gandhian *satyagraha* campaigns against the Raj in more cynical terms. They believed these obscured Indian exploitation of fellow Indians and ensured that independence would not be accompanied by a social revolution. Undoubtedly Gandhi's presence at the head of nationalist struggle was immensely reassuring to the upper-caste business and industrial class. Significantly, they increasingly bankrolled the Congress in its struggle with the British.

The Mahatma's non-violent philosophy thus ensured conservative support for the old extremist weapons of direct action and boycotting of the

Raj. Moreover, his style of leadership enabled the Congress to appeal well beyond its traditional supporters from the urban educated classes. Rich peasants, some of whom had first been alerted to Gandhi's leadership by his local *satyagraha* on behalf of the Gujarati Patidars in the Kaira district in 1918, played a key role in the nationalist movement in such provinces as UP, Gujarat, West Bengal and Bihar. Indeed D. A. Low has seen the alliance between the rich peasants, the educated classes and the commercial classes as being of crucial importance in this climacteric period (Low, 1991, pp. 101–19). The leadership still tended to be drawn from the educated Hindu upper castes. But as Gopal Krishna has perceptively remarked:

> The significant difference between the pre-1920 and the post-1920 Congress leadership lay in the fact that before 1920 it was social position which automatically conferred a leading position in the movement; after 1920 it was the renunciation of social position and the demonstration of willingness to accept that sacrifice was demanded of those who aspired to lead.
>
> Krishna (1971, p. 267)

The commercial castes

D. A. Low explains the commercial castes' support for the Congress partly in terms of the fact that Gandhi himself was from a merchant Modh Banya caste. Indeed the word Gandhi means 'grocer' in Gujarati. Equally important was his religious appeal as epitomised by his relationship with the Marwari businessman G. D. Birla (1894–1983). Support from the commercial classes ensured not only massive previously untapped finances for the Congress, as seen in the successful Tilak Swaraj Fund in 1921, but the use of their connections for nationalist purposes not only with the local peasant economies, but with fellow traders across the subcontinent. Moreover, post-independence India's commitment to economic planning and state control of the public sector was presaged by the 1944 Bombay Plan which had been drawn up in consultation between Congress leaders and such industrialists as Birla.

The dominant peasant castes

The dominant peasant castes' support was equally important. The Congress was increasingly seen as a vehicle for the interests of these upwardly mobile groups. It offered not only the prospect of patronage, but land reform and tenant reforms directed against the rich non-cultivating *zamindars*. Indeed the Congress's commitment to agrarian reform in the UP in the 1930s was a significant factor in its alienation of the Muslim landed elite which turned to the Muslim League to safeguard its interests. Moreover, the non-revolutionary and non-violent character of the nationalist struggle appealed to the rich peasantry, who at the same time as seeking to overthrow the landlords feared violence from the poor peasants and the landless. Although the Congress organised Kisan Sabhas, its provincial ministries dampened down their activities during 1937–9.

The rural poor including Untouchables participated in some of the Congress's *satyagrahas* like, for example, the 1930 Forest Satyagraha in Madhya Pradesh, but the Congress was never a party of these groups. Instead, it gained support from the wealthy Patidars in Gujarat, the Bhumihars in Bihar, the Jats, Rajputs, Ahirs and Kurmis in UP and the Reddis in the Andhra region. Gandhi's leadership here is in marked contrast with the earlier extremists who seldom looked beyond the Brahmin community for support. His local *satyagrahas* in Gujarat and Bihar during 1917–18 had involved peasant communities for the first time. This was not so much a strategy on Gandhi's behalf as a response to local initiatives. He championed the peasant tenants at Champaran in Bihar and the Patidar cultivators at Kaira in order to right what he saw as injustices, not to mobilise new peasant communities. The contacts he developed with such people as Rajendra Prasad (1884–1963) and Sardar Vallabhbhai Patel (1875–1950), however, earned him influential allies who could link dominant peasant communities with the wider world of national politics.

The rich peasants' support for the Congress enabled it to dig deeper roots into Indian society than ever before. The Indian nationalist movement was no exception to other nationalist struggles in that its ability to exert pressure on the authorities depended on its mobilising villagers as well as townspeople. The British always feared rural agitation because it was more difficult to control than urban unrest. Moreover, it threatened the land revenue system which remained the financial underpinning of the imperial edifice. The rich peasants had their own reasons for fearing widespread disorder in the countryside. They faced the twin dangers of having their land confiscated by the British and of a rising by the dispossessed who might not draw a fine distinction between their British and Indian exploiters. There was thus no war to the death in the countryside between the British and their nationalist opponents. The most violent rural disturbances were either communal in character, like the 1921 Moplah uprising, or the work of the communists, like the 1946–51 Telengana uprising. Nearly 25,000 peasants and party workers had been arrested in this insurrection by August 1949 (Dhanagare 1986, p. 200).

The Congress, to the contrary, sought to confine agrarian disturbances within the bounds of non-violence. Moreover, while it supported calls to withhold land revenue from the government, it did not want disaffected tenants to engage in no-rent campaigns against the landholders. The Congress leaders at first supported the Eka (Unity) movement in the northern UP districts of Hardoi, Bahraich and Sitapur late in 1921. They disowned this, however, when the lower castes turned to violence in protest at the landowners' extraction of illegal rents. The Eka movement is also interesting because it reveals the importance of Hindu symbolism even to class-based agitations. The Eka meetings were accompanied by a religious ritual in which those assembled vowed over a representation of the river Ganges dug in the ground not to do forced labour or to pay rent over and above the legally recorded level (Chandra, 1989, p. 200).

The rich peasants' greatest value to the Congress was not as *satyagrahin*, but as voters. Their support held the key to the Congress's sweeping victories in the 1937 polls. Two important consequences stemmed from this success. First, the victory accorded the party legitimacy in British eyes. The Muslim League achieved a similar standing following its victory in the 1946 elections. Second, the Congress was regarded by large sections of the population as an 'alternative raj'. This undermined the power of regional opponents, although conversely it encouraged the Muslim League to redouble its efforts.

The role of women in the freedom struggle

From the time of the local *satyagrahas* in 1917–18, Gandhi not only encouraged a widening of the freedom movement to include the rich peasantry, but also actively sought female support. During the three decades which followed, they were to be involved in the 'constructive programme', mass civil disobedience and in legislative politics. Gandhi especially appealed for female support because he believed that women possessed the moral strength required of the *satyagrahin*. On a number of occasions he said that India's moral salvation rested with them and that if 'non-violence is the law of our being' the 'future is with women'. Like earlier Hindu reformers, he linked the strength of society with the removal of social disabilities affecting women. He thus saw their involvement in the freedom movement as not only broadening it, but serving as an education. Women flocked to the Congress partly because of Gandhi's charismatic personality which caused many to worship him as a saint and Mahatma. Importantly, he also couched his appeals in terms of the traditional role model of Sita, the devoted wife, while at the same time likening British rule to that of the evil Ravana in the Ramayana. Finally, he politicised the routine female activity of spinning. This revolutionary 'reconfiguration' of women's traditional domestic activity comes out clearly in the following extract from Madhu Kishwar:

> Gandhi's relentless propaganda in favour of *charkha* [spinning] and wearing of *khadi* was designed to bring the spirit of nationalism and freedom into every home, even the remotest village. In this way, abstract political ideas such as struggle against colonial rule, assumed concrete form for ordinary people. This was a very remarkable way of reaching out to women and bridging the gap between their private lives and the economic-political life of the country. The decision of what to wear or not to wear is one of the decisions likely to be in the control of women, and Gandhi was able to imbue this seemingly mundane sphere of life with a new political and moral significance.
>
> Kishwar (1985, p. 1695)

During the first non-cooperation movement, women's role was largely confined to spinning clubs, although in Bombay and Ahmedabad they publicly burned foreign cloth. From the time of the 1928 Bardoli campaign, women were involved in much larger numbers in public demonstrations and engaged in law breaking. When Gandhi attempted to limit female participation in his famous 1930 salt march to Dandi, declaring that just as it would be cowardly for Hindus to keep cows in front of them in time of war, similarly it would be cowardly to have women with them on this march, he drew angry responses. On 10 April 1930, when he reached Abhrama, two-fifths of the audience were women. Over 500 women greeted him when he arrived at Dandi three days later. Daily processions were taken out at this time in Ahmedabad by women wearing the saffron saris of the Videsh Kapade Bahishkar Samiti. On 23 April the procession stretched for half a mile. Women volunteers daily went around the city of Bombay singing patriotic songs and selling salt which they had converted from sea water in defiance of the government's monopoly on its manufacture. They waded out at low tide at Chowpatty beach to fetch pitchers of salt water. A group of 45 women on Tilak Day in August squatted all night on the road in the Fort area of Bombay. Their protest in mixed company without their husbands created a moral sensation (Basu, 1984, p. 11). Not all of the women who joined in civil disobedience campaigns were from elite families. In Bardoli in 1928, for example, some came not from Westernised families but from the rural Patidar castes. Similarly, the majority of the women involved in the 1930–1 *satyagraha* in Gujarat could not read or write English and had only received elementary education in their native tongue (Basu, 1984, p. 12).

Contemporary Indian feminists point out that Gandhi's involvement of women in the freedom movement did not challenge patriarchy. 'They marched and picketed', as Geraldine Forbes has pointed out, 'in sex-segregated groups, usually wearing distinctive orange or white saris to emphasize their purity and sacrifice' (Forbes, 1996, p. 156). Female participation was linked both with traditional role models such as Sita, and with women's sense of devotion and duty which was extended from the family to the nation. Gandhi also perpetuated stereotypical representations of women concerning their greater religious devotion, moral quality and ability to suffer than men. The invitation to women to involve themselves as 'national' actors whether as mothers, educators or even as fighters, at the same time as reaffirming 'the boundaries of culturally acceptable feminine conduct' was by no means unique to India, and was present in numerous anti-colonial struggles (Kandiyoti, 1998, p. 13). Women may have joined the nationalist movement on men's terms and feminism was denied autonomy, but their own agency should not be denied. For some at least who were brought out of the seclusion of their homes this was a liberating experience. Such an attitude was epitomised by the women marching in processions in Bombay at the time of the salt *satyagraha* when they chanted 'Free India means free womanhood.'

The Congress in office 1937–9

The strategy of direct action or council entry was contingent on the political circumstances of the moment. It enabled the Congress to wear down the Raj's stock of moral and political capital as well as providing Indian politicians with the opportunity to acquire experience of government. This has been linked by a number of scholars to the Congress's much greater success than freedom movements elsewhere in the Empire in making the post-colonial switch to a party of government. The psychological impact of the formation of Congress governments comes out clearly in the passage below taken from Nehru's *Discovery of India*:

> At the headquarters of the Provincial Governments, in the very citadels of the old bureaucracy, many a symbolic scene was witnessed ... Now, suddenly, hordes of people from the city and the village, entered these sacred precincts, and roamed about almost at will ... It was difficult to stop them for they no longer felt as outsiders; they had a sense of ownership in all this ... The policemen and the orderlies with shining daggers were paralyzed; the old standards had fallen. European dress, symbol of position and authority, no longer counted. It was difficult to distinguish between members of the legislatures and the peasants and townsmen who came in such large numbers.
>
> cited in Chandra (1989, p. 324)

The Congress was also unique in the strength of its grassroots support and organisational strength. This development was underpinned by the financial backing it received from wealthy Marwari commercial groups and such emerging industrialists as the Birlas. Between 1921 and 1923, the Congress collected over Rs 13 million. This huge war chest funded Gandhi's 'constructive programme' of *khadi* (i.e. the production and wearing of homemade cloth) and the removal of untouchability as well as political campaigns. It enabled the growth of the new phenomenon of the fulltime paid Congressite political worker. By the eve of the Second World War, the Congress boasted a membership in excess of four and a half million. No other nationalist movement was to ever attain this level of support. Indeed a number of freedom movements (like, for example, Kwame Nkrumah's struggle in the Gold Coast in the early 1950s) adopted it as a role model for its organisational success as well as for its famous attachment to non-violence.

There were drawbacks as well as advantages for the Congress when its local organisations held office either in the Legislative Councils from the mid-1920s onwards, or in the new provincial legislatures following the granting of provincial autonomy by the 1935 Government of India Act. Factional tensions arose between those who had access to the new sources of patronage and party men who were excluded. Differences frequently emerged between the so-called ministerial and organisational wings of the party. The divisions were so bad in the Central Provinces that the Prime Minister Dr N. B. Khare (1882–1969) resigned. In November 1938 another problem arose when Congress ministers in Bombay had to repress trade union and peasant activity. Earlier in September the All-India Congress Committee had been driven to pass a resolution condemning those including Congressmen who, 'in the name of civil liberty', advocated arson, looting and class war by violent means. Indeed some writers have gone so far as to say that the high command's order for its provincial ministries to resign, in the wake of the Viceroy Lord Linlithgow's declaration that India was at war in 1939 without consulting Indian opinion, was a useful get-out from these growing problems.

The transfer of power

Nationalist struggle, although crucially important, did not alone cause the British departure. Other factors included: the diminishing economic value of India from the First World War onwards (Tomlinson, 1979); the decline in the administrative 'steel framework' of the Raj (Epstein, 1982; Potter, 1973), in part the result of the attrition of the nationalist movement; the changed postwar domestic priorities and the Labour government's need to extricate itself from India (Moore, 1983); the anxiety to avoid being caught in the middle of a communal civil war; the desire to transfer power to 'friendly' Indian politicians who would keep India within the Commonwealth as a Dominion and not undermine Britain's economic and strategic interests in the region (Krishan, 1983); and the desire on behalf of an increasingly dominant Congress right wing in the post-1942 period to ensure that independence did not involve social revolution even at the cost of accepting partition (Sarkar, 1985).

The official view of the British departure was of course that it was not a defeat, but in a real sense the fulfilment of the Raj's tutelage. Whether or not this was self-deception, the British retained a sense of achievement regarding their rule. This led them to share with the Congress high command the concern to prevent the breakup of India. In these circumstances, any British Viceroy would have regarded Jinnah as obstructive, and shared a closer community of interests with Nehru, even if he had not possessed Mountbatten's personal rapport with the Congress leader. Jinnah was marginalised in the final negotiations which led to the 3 June 1947 Partition Plan. It is also true that later authors have taken their cue from Mountbatten and his publicists in their unflattering depiction of Jinnah. Akbar Ahmed (1997) ignores the convergence of British and Indian nationalist interests when he entertainingly reduces the decision-making process to an affair of personalities in which Jinnah was excluded from the Nehru–Mountbatten–Edwina *ménage à trois*.

What is clear is the fact that Jinnah was forced to accept the minimum territorial extent for Pakistan. The result was that the country inherited the less developed areas of the subcontinent, a factor which was to influence its political development. Other minority leaders, such as the combative head of the Sikh Akali Dal, Master Tara Singh (1885–1967), received even shorter shrift from the Congress–British combination. The loss of the rich Sikh agricultural lands in West Punjab along with the holy shrine of Nankana Sahib was a major factor in the partition-related disturbances of August 1947. In the longer run, the sense of betrayal by the Congress fuelled Sikh separatist urges in post-independence India.

The legacy of the Indian nationalist movement

India's democratic 'exceptionalism' in the third world has been linked by a number of writers to the legacy of the freedom struggle. This bequeathed a highly institutionalised political party in the Congress whose support structure reached down into the villages. Moreover, the Congress, because of Gandhi's 'genius' in fund-raising had established its cadre of fulltime political workers. The Congress's 'struggle–truce–struggle' strategy, moreover, ensured that the nationalist movement was not just an oppositional force, but had produced leaders schooled in the arts of government.

The seeds for democratic success had also been sown by the Congress's ability to bring new social groups and classes into politics. By the close of the freedom struggle, mobilisation extended well beyond the Brahmin elites to include upwardly mobile rich peasants, the commercial castes, and for the first time ever groups of women. Another marked feature of the nationalist movement had been its idealism, whether expressed in terms of Gandhian philosophy or in the socialism of Nehru and the Congress left wing. Hundreds if not thousands of Congress activists had demonstrated their commitment to a free India by submitting to the blows of the police and to extended periods of imprisonment. This sacrifice gave India a high public service ethos as it embarked on independence, as well as ensuring the prestige of the Congress above all other parties.

There were also, of course, warning signs for the future. The nationalist discourse, despite its professed secularism, was suffused with Hindu religious symbolism. It also contained hegemonic tendencies which made it difficult for the 'difference' of minorities to be accepted on anything other than the majority's terms. The partition-related upheavals were to increase hostility to the Muslim 'other' well beyond the narrow bounds of Hindu communal organisations. Indeed, for Gandhi at least, partition represented a defeat for all that he believed in, causing him to dub freedom a 'bitter loaf'.

The Muslim League and the achievement of Pakistan

Muslims from all over India gathered on 22 March 1940 in the huge tent set up in Minto Park, Lahore, within sight of the imposing Badshahi Mosque. Jinnah's two-hour presidential address given in English surveyed the developments which had occurred since the preceding year's Patna session. These included the celebrations which had been held throughout India on 22 December 1939. This day had been termed Deliverance Day by Jinnah in thanksgiving for deliverance from the 'tyranny, oppression and injustice' of the Congress provincial ministries following their resignation. The ceremonies in the local mosques or public spaces had included the hoisting of Muslim League flags. Most importantly, Jinnah's Lahore address spelled out the two-nation theory justification for the demand for a separate Muslim state. It portrayed the Muslims and Hindus as irreconcilably opposed monolithic religious communities.

Pakistan was not mentioned by name, although the resolution was subsequently dubbed the Pakistan Resolution. Its third paragraph called for the grouping of contiguous Muslim majority areas in north-west and north-east India into 'Independent States in which the constituent units would be autonomous and sovereign'. This vagueness may well have been deliberate to give Jinnah room for manoeuvre. It encouraged ideas of a confederation which were not fully put to rest by the 1946 removal of the plural 'states' from the Pakistan scheme.

Pakistan should not be regarded as inevitable from the time of the Lahore Resolution onwards. The Muslim League first had to demonstrate its support in the major centres of Muslim population where it had traditionally lacked influence. It had won just one seat in Punjab and was empty handed in both Sind and the Frontier in the 1937 provincial elections. It was only in Bengal that the Muslim League put up a respectable performance, capturing 37 out of 119 seats reserved for Muslims. Less than a decade later it had turned the tables on its opponents. In Punjab it captured 75 of the Muslim seats, in Bengal 115, in Sind 30. Throughout India in the 1946 provincial elections it secured 75 per cent of the total Muslim vote in comparison with 4.4 per cent in 1937. Jinnah had been given the mandate for Pakistan.

How had this remarkable transformation come about? An immediate response is that the two-nation theory rallied support for the Pakistan demand as it linked the powerful themes of 'Islam in danger' and religious community. Scholarly opinion is, however, divided on this question and many of the explanations shed more heat than light.

Explanations for the Muslim League breakthrough

Indian nationalist writers have denied that a mass upsurge in support for the Pakistan demand lay behind the Muslim League's advance. They rather link the achievement of Pakistan with the long-term British divide-and-rule policy epitomised by the granting of separate electorates and the bolstering of the Muslim League during the war years. While the Cambridge school of Indian historiography diasavows a conscious divide-and-rule strategy, Pakistan is seen as the outcome of the colonial state's patronage policies and dealing in terms of religious categories (Robinson, 1975). Pakistani nationalist historiography, in contrast, focuses on the role of Islam and of Jinnah in the creation of the Muslim homeland. Jinnah's leadership is considered as vital in bringing moral authority and unity to a community which was 'naturally' set apart from the Hindu community. Recent works have sought to explore how Jinnah came to symbolise both the unity and aspirations of the Indian Muslim community (Ahmed, 1997).

Important differences, however, surround the interpretation of Jinnah's intentions in demanding Pakistan. Ayesha Jalal's revisionist understanding (Jalal, 1985) questions whether Jinnah ever regarded this as more than a bargaining counter for a greater Muslim say in a united India. This view has been criticised for reducing the causes of Pakistan's creation to deliberations in 'smoke filled rooms'. My own work (Talbot, 1996a) emphasises that Jinnah did not create Pakistan single-handedly and that there was immense popular enthusiasm and participation in the closing stages of the Muslim League struggle. This opens up again the role of Islam in the creation of Pakistan. Writers such as Paul Brass (1974) maintain that this was instrumental, i.e. that Islamic ideology was chosen and manipulated by political elites in order to legitimise their bid for power which arose from other, predominantly economic and social, compulsions. Opposed to this modernisation thesis paradigm are primordialists such as Hafeez Malik (1963), I. H. Qureshi (1965) and Riazul Islam (1976), who maintain that Islam did not just legitimise political action, but impelled support for the Muslim League.

The spotlight has increasingly turned away from the Muslim League's development in its UP heartland, or at the all-India level, to rest on the precise reasons for its breakthrough in the future Pakistan areas. Both David Gilmartin (1988) and myself (Talbot, 1988b) have directed attention to the battleground of the Punjab which held the key to the credibility of the Pakistan demand. The demise of the Muslim League's powerful Unionist Party opponents can be understood in part in terms of the unpopularity which they engendered by loyally carrying out British wartime economic and recruitment policies. Other factors include the increasing factional weakness of the Unionist Party in the wake of the deaths of such powerful figures as Sikander Hayat (1882–1942) and Chhotu Ram (1882–1945). The Unionist Party, under its last leader Khizr Hayat Tiwana, also suffered because of communal polarisation elsewhere in North India and because of its unquestioning loyalty to the outgoing Raj (Talbot, 1996b). The Muslim League for its part linked Islamic appeals with solutions to the rural population's economic and social difficulties. Crucially, although it had earlier criticised the Unionist Party for using 'tribalism' and the peasants' superstitious reverence for *pirs* to win political support, the Muslim League did not hesitate to use these same methods when it was in a position to do so. Punjab League candidates were chosen from representatives of leading *biraderis* in a constituency, sometimes even if this involved passing over loyal activists. The fevered atmosphere at the time of the 1946 Punjab elections was summed up by a Unionist worker from the Jhelum district who reported, 'Wherever I went everyone kept saying, *bhai* [brother], if we do not vote for the League we would have become kafir ... We did not vote for individuals; if we did so, it was only to vote for the Quran' (Talbot, 1996a, pp. 95–6).

This type of electioneering was by no means confined to the Punjab. *Sufis* played an important role in Sind in popularising the Pakistan cause (Ansari, 1992). The Muslim League sought to advance in the Frontier by utilising loyalty to *pirs* and to *gundis* (factions based on tribal descent). The Pir of Manki formed an organisation known as the Anjuman-us-Asfia to coordinate the activities of the province's *pirs* on behalf of the Muslim League. It relied on localist Islamic identities and kinship and landholding ties to mobilise support for Pakistan, in part because of the urgency of what it regarded as a life and death struggle. It also lacked the institutional base to channel the popular but unfocused enthusiasm for its separatist demand. The Muslim League was poorly organised in most of the future Pakistan areas. The one exception was Bengal where a mass membership had been built up in a number of districts as a result of the efforts of Abul Hashim who had become the secretary of the Bengal Muslim League in November 1943. He aimed to establish the League as a broad democratic institution, based on 'clarity of purpose' capable of 'fighting for liberation from all forms of oppression' (Harun-or-Rashid, 1987, p. 164). In addition to extensively touring the *mofussil* (interior), he employed fulltime workers who received training and accommodation at party houses. Amongst those based at the Calcutta centre was Sheikh Mujibur Rahman (1920–75), later chief of the Awami League and architect of Bangladesh. These activities brought a rapid increase in membership in the districts of Tippera, Barisal and Dacca during 1944. Enthusiasts hailed this rising tide of support as 'revolutionary' and rejoiced in the fact that the League had become a 'really mass movement'. The League old guard of the Nawab of Dacca's family (Khwaja faction) looked askance at these activities which threatened its traditional domination. Hashim and his supporters were dubbed communists in such papers as *Azad*, which were controlled by the Khwaja group.

Elsewhere in the subcontinent the Muslim League organisational situation was bleak. The Sind Muslim League had a total of just 48,500 members. Its institutional weakness was mirrored in the shallow support for the Pakistan ideal. This resulted not only from the backwardness of the overwhelmingly rural population, but from the emergence of a Sindhi political consciousness amongst sections of the Muslim elite. This coexisted uneasily with support for Pakistan. It was rooted both in the politicisation which had accompanied the campaign to separate Sind from the Bombay Presidency and in the increasing anti-Punjabi sentiment amongst Sindhis following the influx of cultivators from the neighbouring province in the wake of irrigation development in the late 1920s.

In the Punjab, the 'cornerstone' of Pakistan, League membership stood at just 150,000. Factional infighting in the Frontier League prompted an enquiry by the All-India Committee of Action in June 1944 which admitted that 'there was no organisation worth the name' in the province. The tendency of local officials to bolster their influence by enrolling bogus members may mean that even these modest totals overestimate the Muslim League's true membership. Moreover, its provincial branches were further handicapped by lack of funds, paid workers and sound techniques of office management.

The Muslim League's electoral breakthrough in 1946 occurred in spite of this weak organisational base. It also masked it. The British accepted Jinnah's claim that the outcome was a referendum on Pakistan. Despite the difficult months of negotiations which lay ahead, the claim of independent Muslim nationhood was no longer questioned. The 3 June Partition Plan and the Boundary Commission's subsequent findings, particularly regarding the award of the strategic Muslim majority Gurdaspur district of the Punjab to India, was of course a very bitter pill for the Muslim League to swallow. But the freedom struggle had achieved a goal which would have seemed impossible a decade earlier.

The legacy of the Pakistan movement

The movement for Pakistan, like that for Indian independence, had been played out to a background of competing political identities and a revolution of rising expectations for social and economic reform. The Muslim League's exclusion from office and weak institutionalisation equipped it less well than the Congress for the twin tasks of development and nation building. In the future Punjab heartland of Pakistan, none of the provincial leaders possessed appreciable ministerial experience. Despite the Muslim League's emergence as the single largest party after the 1946 polls, a Unionist–Akali and Congress government survived in office in the province until shortly before the emergence of Pakistan. When the Unionist Prime Minister Khizr Tiwana resigned in the wake of a Muslim League direct action campaign, the province remained under Governor's rule for the remaining five months of the British Raj. This meant that, in the fight against Unionism, of its famous 'three musketeers' the Nawab of Mamdot, Mian Mumtaz Daultana and Shaukat Hayat, only the last had experienced office in the pre-independence era. Nor had his brief term as Minister of Public Works in the Khizr cabinet been a productive learning experience. Indeed he had been dismissed in controversial circumstances on a corruption charge.

Even in Bengal, where a favourable inheritance from mass nationalist struggle might have been expected, the freedom struggle bequeathed an ambiguous legacy. This was rooted in the political and cultural tensions between the Bengali- and Urdu-speaking elites. Abul Hashim's activists had fought for the ideal of a sovereign East Pakistan state. Indeed Hashim prophetically warned that a united Pakistan would result in the imposition both of Urdu and an alien bureaucracy and reduce East Bengal to a stagnant backwater. The vision of a sovereign Bengal was based both on the reference in the 1940 Lahore Resolution to Muslim states and on the distinctiveness of a Bengali cultural identity (Harun-or-Rashid, 1987, pp. 177ff). The United Bengal scheme raised by the Muslim League Prime Minister Husain Shaheed Suhrawardy (1893–1963) in April 1947, which was supported by the Congressmen Surat Bose and Kiran Shankar Roy, should thus be viewed not as a belated response to the threat of the province's partition, but as emerging from these long-held ideals.

Crucial to future developments in East Bengal was the incipient conflict between the Urdu- and Bengali-speaking elites and the marginalisation of Bengali interests in the councils of the All-India Muslim League. The Urdu-speaking business classes of Calcutta, along with the Khawajas of Dacca, remained loyal to Jinnah's conception of an East Pakistan zone within a single Pakistan state. They also subscribed to the belief expressed as early as July 1933 by the All-Bengal Urdu Association that 'Bengali is a Hinduised and Sanskritised language' and that 'in the interests of the Muslims themselves it is necessary that they should try to have one language which cannot be but Urdu' (Harun-or-Rashid, 1987, p. 45). This was, of course, firmly in step with the AIML's official two-nation theory ideology. Diametrically opposed to this were the views of Bengali-speaking Muslim League members active in the East Pakistan Renaissance Society. This had been formed in 1942 in order to articulate intellectually and culturally the 'ideal of Pakistan in general and Eastern Pakistan in particular'. In his May 1944 presidential address, the Muslim League journalist-cum-politician Abul Mansur Ahmed maintained that Bengali Muslims were not only different from Hindus, but from Muslims of other provinces. 'Religion and culture are not the same thing', he maintained. 'Religion transgresses the geographical boundary but *'tamaddum'* [culture] cannot go beyond the geographical boundary ... Here only lies the differences between *Purba* [Eastern] Pakistan and Pakistan. For this reason the people of *Purba* Pakistan are a different nation from the people of other provinces of India and from the "religious brothers" of Pakistan' (Harun-or-Rashid, 1987, p. 181).

It was, however, the Urdu-speaking elite that had a direct line to Jinnah. He never nominated Abul Hashim or Suhrawardy to the All-India Muslim League Working Committee despite their tremendous organisational achievements. He preferred to deal with such trusted lieutenants as Hasan and Ahmed Ispahani who knew little of Bengal outside of Calcutta, or with the Dacca Nawab family which was bitterly opposed to the progressive group within the Muslim League. Both the language issue and the marginalisation of Bengali political influence were subsequently to dominate East–West Pakistan relations and contribute to the Bangladesh breakaway of 1971. An indication of the disregard for the Bengali Muslims' interests which waited in a future Pakistan state was provided by the AIML's decision in October 1946 to fill the province's quota on the interim government with a scheduled caste representative, Jogendra Nath Mondal. Bengal with its 33 million population in fact possessed just ten more members on the All-India Muslim League Council than UP with its seven million Muslims.

The continued dominance of politicians from Bombay and UP, the new February 1938 constitution notwithstanding, on such powerful Muslim League bodies as the Council and the Working Committee gave the Muslim League organisation a top-heavy look. It also meant that many of Pakistan's future leaders would lack a popular powerbase. The future Prime Minister Liaquat Ali Khan (1895–1951), a leading UP landowner, for example, was eventually nominated a place in the Constituent Assembly from an East Bengal constituency. As Yunas Samad has perceptively pointed out, 'the establishment of a strong centre was a lifeline' for many *mohajir* politicians who lacked electoral support in the country (Samad, 1995, p. 127).

The centralisation of power within the All-India Muslim League was compounded by its exclusivist claims. In order to justify its claim to be the sole representative of the Indian Muslims, the AIML had adopted a strident approach. Its Congress Nationalist, Unionist or Red Shirt rivals were denounced as both traitors to Islam and the Indian Muslim community. This attitude was perpetuated in the post-independence period. In October 1950 Liaquat Ali Khan, for example, declared that 'the formation of new political parties in opposition to the Muslim League is against the interest of Pakistan'. Earlier, at its December 1947 Karachi Council Meeting, the Bengali Muslim League leader Suhrawardy had unsuccessfully attempted to open the Muslim League's membership to all communities. This would have enabled the large Hindu minority in East Pakistan to have entered mainstream politics. Ideology, however, took precedence over the task of nation building. Such a move 'would finish the League', Sardar Abdur Rab Nishtar (1899–1958), a former leader of the Frontier Congress, explained. 'I say if the League exists, Islam exists, Musalmans exist' (Zaheer, 1995, p. 18).

Such an ideological standpoint could not, however, wish away the incipient clash between regional interests and a Pakistani identity. Within Bengal, the Muslim League's popular base of support rested on regional outlooks which were difficult to harmonise with Jinnah's all-India understanding of the Pakistan demand. Similar ambiguities were present in Sind, Punjab and the Frontier. In these circumstances it was hardly surprising that provincialism, as it was termed, became a barrier to nation building almost immediately after independence.

A further problem centred around the role of Islam. The freedom struggle had been deliberately vague about the nature of a future Pakistan state. Nevertheless, many of the leading *'ulama* had opposed what they called the 'secularist' Muslim League leadership. Followers of the Deoband movement (Metcalf, 1982) who had sought to sustain their religion and culture apart from the colonial state could not reconcile territorial nationalism with concern for the solidarity of the worldwide Muslim community, the *umma*. Led by Maulana Madani, they mustered under the banner of Jamiat-ul-Ulema-i-Hind, while the smaller number of Deobandis who backed the Muslim League joined the Jamiat-ul-Ulema-i-Islam which it formed in November 1945.

The most influential exponent of what would today be termed an Islamist discourse was Syed Abul A'la Maudoodi (1903–79) who founded the Jamaat-i-Islami in August 1941. He unequivocally opposed the campaign for Pakistan as it was based on such secular notions as nationalism. 'As a Muslim', he declared in 1942,

> I have no interest in the prospect that Muslims may form governments in those areas of India where they are the majority. The most important question for me is whether the system of government in this Pakistan of yours will be based on the sovereignty of God or on the sovereignty of the people. In the former case, it will surely be 'Pakistan' [land of the pure], but in the latter case it will be just as ungodly as that part of the country where, according to your plan, non-Muslims will rule ... In the sight of God, Muslim nationalism is just as cursed as Indian nationalism.
>
> Syed (1982, p. 35)

Once Pakistan was created, however, Maudoodi migrated from India and sought to bring its laws into conformity with Islam. But this goal was in conflict with Jinnah's famous speech to the Pakistan Constituent Assembly of 11 August 1947 in which he held out the prospect of its future development as a plural secular society. Ambiguity concerning future national aims rested in part on the fact that the Pakistan movement was simultaneously a 'movement of Islam' and of Muslims. Later generations of Pakistani leaders have, however, ignored the complexities and ambiguities of the freedom struggle. For example, the acting Prime Minister Ghulam Mustafa Jatoi declared early in October 1990 that 'it was imperative to constantly keep an eye on the objective behind the creation of Pakistan which was *nothing but seeking the glory of Islam*' (emphasis added) (*Dawn*, Karachi, 5 October 1990).

Given the exigencies which faced the all-India leadership in the early 1940s, it could hardly be blamed for attempting to be all things to all men. But by presenting Pakistan as a panacea for all social and personal ills, the seeds were sown for the disenchantment which has been so palpable in the post-colonial era.

Unfulfilled nationalist demands

History has always been written by the victors. This is especially the case with respect to the end of the British Raj. The achievement of Indian independence after years of struggle and the dramatic transformation in the Muslim League's fortunes which enabled the creation of Pakistan have inevitably dominated historical accounts. The towering figures of Gandhi, Nehru and Jinnah and the sheer human drama of the closing stages of their struggles against the might of the British Raj have captured the imagination of historians. The ideological requirements of nation building in the subcontinent have further reinforced this tendency to look no further than to the Pakistan and Indian nationalist movements. There were, however, other claimants to the inheritance of the colonial state. Although they 'lost' in 1947, we can learn as much from their unfulfilled aspirations as from the triumph of Pakistani and Indian nationalism. We shall turn first to the demand for a separate Sikh state.

Sikhistan/Khalistan demands

The demand for a Sikh state was first raised by an All-Parties Sikh Conference in Amritsar in mid-1944. This idea was stated most forcefully, however, by the Akali Dal on 22 March 1946 during submissions to the three-member Cabinet Mission of Pethick-Lawrence, Secretary of State for India; Stafford Cripps, President of the Board of Trade; and A. V. Alexander, First Lord of the Admiralty. The mission had been dispatched to India by the Attlee cabinet in an attempt to break the constitutional deadlock which had developed since the collapse of the Simla Conference the previous July. The Muslim League's electoral breakthrough in the Punjab provincial elections earlier in 1946 raised the real possibility of the creation of Pakistan. In one sense, therefore, the demand for Sikhistan/Khalistan was a response to this situation. British officials who were dismayed by the implications of this demand for the Punjab, 'sword arm' and 'bread basket' of India, emphasised the 'reactive' nature of the call for a Sikh state. Alongside the opportunism of the Akali Dal's stance, however, there were deeper historical causes.

Without the Singh Sabha movement's enhancement of the sense of community and of the history of martyrdom at Mughal hands, it is unlikely that the Sikh community would have reacted so violently against the prospect of Pakistan. Without the forging of the Akali Dal in the *gurdwara* reform movement, it would have been impossible for one party, whether justifiably or not, to claim to speak on behalf of the whole community. Moreover, the increased sense of a history of Sikh rule in the Punjab before its annexation by the East India Company encouraged the feeling that Sikh sovereignty should be restored in any transfer of power. Finally, the Akali

Dal's mistrust of the Congress, from the 1932 Communal Award onwards, encouraged the feeling that the community should look to its own salvation. This culminated in the tragedy of the 'ethnic cleansing' of the Muslim minority population in East Punjab during the anarchy of August 1947.

The Akali Dal leader, Master Tara Singh, made the uncompromising response to the Lahore Resolution that he would 'fight Pakistan tooth and nail'. The first stage of this struggle involved hostility to the Unionist government of the Punjab, but in June 1942 this policy was reversed as it was realised that the Unionists presented a formidable barrier to the Muslim League's advance in the province. At the same time, the Akali Dal opposed the Congress's non-cooperation with the British war effort in order to secure the maximum political leverage arising from the Sikhs' traditional association with the Indian Army. Sikh wartime recruitment was encouraged by the Khalsa Defence of India League.

The Akali Dal's first constitutional response to the Pakistan demand was to float the idea of Azad Punjab in March 1942. This scheme called for a readjustment of the boundaries of the Punjab. The whole of the Rawalpindi division and most of the Multan division, with the exception of the Lyallpur district where Sikhs possessed considerable irrigated land, would be detached. Thus shorn of many Muslim majority districts, Sikhs with 20 per cent of the population in Azad Punjab would hold the balance between the Muslims and Hindus with 40 per cent each. Not surprisingly, the scheme incurred the hostility of both the Congress and the Muslim League. Sikh Congressmen dubbed it 'anti-national and reactionary'. The most significant opposition was provided by the British authorities. Sir Bertrand Glancy (1882–1953), the Punjab Governor, regarded the scheme's practical objections to be 'even greater than those' that lay in the path of Pakistan. The Viceroy Linlithgow concurred, regarding the Sikhs as only 'a small nuisance' and counselling that the British should be careful not to lend any substance to such a 'preposterous claim'.

Sikh unease increased in 1944 following the Gandhi–Jinnah talks. Even after their failure in September, many Akalis believed that the Congress might come to an agreement concerning Pakistan over their heads. Equally worrying was the growing Muslim League pressure on the Unionist government of Khizr Tiwana. It was mainly because the Akali Dal seemed the best able to protect community interests that Sikh voters in the 1946 Punjab elections handed out a drubbing to the Congress and Communist candidates. After abortive negotiations with the Muslim League, the Akali Dal sought to prop up a coalition government comprising the Muslim rump of the Unionists and the Congress which had squeezed out the Hindu Unionists in the Rohtak and Hissar districts. Merely keeping the Muslim League out of office in the Punjab was insufficient to safeguard Sikh interests. The Akali Dal accordingly raised the Sikhistan demand. The proposed Sikh state was to be a federation comprising the most populous Sikh districts of the eastern and central Punjab, and the neighbouring Sikh Princely States of Patiala, Nabha, Jind, Faridkot, Kalsia and Kapurthala.

The scheme singularly unimpressed the Cabinet Mission team because it further complicated the task of securing an all-India, Congress and Muslim League agreement. Moreover, there was no one of Jinnah's calibre to bring his skilled advocacy to the Sikh representations. The Sikhs were further handicapped as they lacked a majority in any area of the province which could form the territorial basis for a separate state. To make matters worse, the Akali Dal was divided partly on factional grounds and partly along regional lines within Punjab. Given the British reluctance to concede to the demands of the Muslim League, which could claim to represent a far larger minority population in the subcontinent, it is small wonder that the Sikhs received such short shrift. They were unhappy with the Cabinet Mission proposal for lumping them without consent into a grouping of provinces that despite retaining an Indian union 'made it possible for the Muslims to secure all the conditions of Pakistan'.

The failure of the Cabinet Mission proposals opened up the even grimmer prospect, from the Akali viewpoint, of Pakistan's creation. The communal situation in the Punjab deteriorated following the Muslim League's launching of a direct action movement against the Khizr coalition ministry in January 1947. The powder keg exploded in widespread communal disturbances following Khizr's resignation on 2 March. Muslim attacks on the Sikh minority population in the Rawalpindi division sowed the seeds for the future partition of the province and the communal holocaust which accompanied the British departure. Sikh politicians demanded the partition of the Punjab, a move which suicidally divided their community in two. Some clung to the forlorn hope, following the acceptance of the 3 June Partition Plan, that 'other factors' including the extent of Sikh landholdings in parts of the Multan division, along with the presence of shrines and *gurdwaras*, would ensure that significant proportions of the Muslim majority districts of Lahore, Lyallpur and Gujranwala would be included in India.

The Punjab's civil administration collapsed during the closing weeks of British rule. All communities stockpiled weapons and made preparations for a communal war of succession. The British received CID reports of a Sikh plan designed to drive out the Muslims from East Punjab and to consolidate the Sikhs into a majority there. Whether the widespread killings in the area were a result of the cycle of revenge or deliberately planned, they reversed the demographic equation which had sidelined Sikh demands for a separate state.

The Pakhtunistan issue

If the Akali Dal demanded a separate state in part to avoid 'Muslim tyranny' in a future Pakistan, the Khudai Khidmatgars (Servants of God) raised the cry for Pakhtunistan partially to counter Punjabi domination in any new Muslim homeland. In November 1931 Abdul Ghaffar Khan, the Khudai Khidmatgar leader, outraged non-Pushtun audiences in Hazara by denigrating Punjabi language and culture and declaring that 'When we have self-government we will have everything in Pushtu' (Rittenburg, 1977, p. 176). The catalyst for the Sikhistan demand, as we have seen, was the Muslim League break-through in the 1946 Punjab elections. For the Pakhtunistan demand it was Congress acceptance of the 3 June 1947 Partition Plan and of the holding of a referendum to decide the Frontier's constitutional future without consulting its Khudai Khidmatgar allies. Pakhtunistan, like Sikhistan, however, was not merely a 'knee-jerk' reaction at the end of British rule, but rather was rooted in the earlier emergence of a politicised community consciousness.

The philosophy of Pakhtun nationalism was first articulated by Abdul Ghaffar Khan in the monthly Pushto journal the *Pakhtun*, which he launched in May 1928. The journal, which was repeatedly banned by the British, rose in circulation from an initial 500 to around 3,000 copies. It carried articles on Pushto language and literature and on loyalty to the Pakhtun homeland (*watan*). Like other sources of political identity that we have examined in colonial India, politicisation followed an earlier process of socio-religious reform which placed a premium on the establishment of educational institutions. The key institutions in the earlier phase of development were the Azad schools and the Anjuman-i-islah-i-Afaghna (Society for the Reformation of Afghans) which Ghaffar Khan had founded at the beginning of the 1920s. The twin goals of reformed social practice and pristine religious faith common to socio-reform movements throughout the subcontinent were at the forefront of the *anjuman*'s activities. The 70 or so Azad schools that were established in the Frontier emphasised not only Islam, along with such vocational skills as weaving and carpentry, but also promoted an interest in Pushto language and culture.

In 1929, Abdul Ghaffar Khan institutionalised the ideals of Pakhtun nationalism in a new grassroots party called the Afghan Jirga. This was rapidly overshadowed by the Khudai Khidmatgars, which was established in November of that year on quasi-military lines. Its members wore uniforms dyed with red brick dust, since their ordinary white clothing showed the dirt too easily. Henceforth they were popularly known as the Red Shirts. The cultural roots of Pakhtun ethno-nationalism lay in the language of Pushto, the code of conduct known as *pakhtunwali* with its emphasis on agnatic rivalry, the preservation of women's honour and the obligation to both protect and provide hospitality to guests and to take revenge for insults to kinsmen. Another important feature of Pakhtun collective consciousness was the tracing of descent through the male line to a common ancestor known as Qais. Alongside these 'tribal' senses of identity was pride in Islam and a belief that Pakhtuns were descended from amongst the first converts to the faith.

Parallels can be drawn between the Akalis and the Pakhtun activists in that both groups were drawn under the umbrella of the Indian nationalist movement because their local grievances coincided with the wider freedom struggle. British repression in what was a key strategic part of their empire exerted an abiding impact on the Pakhtun activists' outlook. For this reason there was not a later parting of the ways as happened with the Akalis. This is not to argue that the interests of the later Khudai Khidmatgar movement and the Congress were identical. Both movements nevertheless needed each other. The Khudai Khidmatgars received support from Congress in their anti-British struggle and over issues of infringements of civil liberties. For the Congress, the Khudai Khidmatgars represented important Muslim allies, particularly as the Pakistan movement intensified. Abdul Ghaffar Khan, because of his simple lifestyle, deeply religious but non-communal outlook and commitment to the cause of Indian independence by the means of non-violent struggle, became dubbed the 'Frontier Gandhi'.

Abdul Ghaffar Khan toured the Frontier to enrol Khudai Khidmatgars. He called on the people to reform their social and religious condition, and articulated the poorer classes' grievances against the pro-British large landholding Khans, many of whom were later to play leading roles in the Frontier Muslim League. The alliance between Abdul Ghaffar Khan's organisations and the Congress was cemented by the 1930 civil disobedience campaign. The April riots in Peshawar created the martyrs and myths of the Khudai Khidmatgar movement which were to sustain it until the eve of independence.

The post-1946 Muslim League breakthrough in the Frontier has been analysed at length by Jansson (1981) and Rittenberg (1988). Four key factors emerge from their examination: first, the polarisation of opinion following reports of Pakhtun victims in communal riots elsewhere in India; second, the tension within the Frontier itself in the wake of the Muslims League's direct action movement; third, the bad impression created by Nehru's visit to the tribal areas in October 1946 in his capacity as head of the External Affairs Department in the interim government; and, fourth, the influential Pir of Manki's increasing prominence in the Pakistan campaign.

It was against this background and an increasing realisation that the Congress high command was throwing the Khudai Khidmatgars 'to the wolves' that the Pakhtunistan demand was raised. Mountbatten, citing Nehru's opposition, flatly rejected Abdul Ghaffar Khan's demand that a third option for a sovereign Pakhtunistan be included in a referendum on the constitutional future of the Frontier. Despite the Khudai Khidmatgars' long association with the Congress, Ghaffar Khan could only secure a handful of support when the issue of the referendum was discussed by the Working Committee and the All-India Congress Committee. Gandhi sympathised with the Pakhtuns' viewpoint, but he was an increasingly marginal figure in the Congress's counsels, which were dominated by Nehru and Patel. The Mahatma discreetly withdrew from Delhi to work amongst riot victims in

Bihar. The Khudai Khidmatgars responded to their abandonment by peacefully boycotting the referendum which they dubbed a 'farce' and a 'one-sided
affair'. Ninety-nine per cent of the votes cast in the July 1947 referendum
were for accession to Pakistan. The turnout, however, was just 51 per cent.
The Muslim League victory ensured that, for the moment at least, the
Pakhtunistan issue was shelved, although the Khudai Khidmatgar/Congress
ministry remained in office at the time of independence.

Tamil nationalist demands

At the beginning of the 1930s, the Congress had absorbed many non-
Brahmins who had previously supported the Justice Party. Symptomatic of
the changed atmosphere was the rise to prominence in the Tamil Nad
Congress Committee of a Tamil-speaking Vellala, Muthuranga Mudaliar.
Tamil political consciousness, however, lay beneath the surface of many of
the new Congressmen, while outside its ranks the enfeebled Justice Party and
self-respect movement became more outspoken in their support for
Dravidian culture. Naicker and a number of his supporters were arrested
following violent protests against the Congress provincial government's
policy in 1937 of making Hindi a compulsory subject in school. The
campaign, which was marked by the death of two demonstrators, forced the
government to back down and make Hindi an optional subject only
(Hardgrave, 1979, p. 27). Naicker built on this achievement to reinvigorate
the Justice Party by becoming its president the following December.

In 1939 he organised a Dravidia Nadu Conference which advocated a
separate Dravidian state. Calls for an independent Dravidistan were stepped
up following the launching of the Pakistan demand. Naicker maintained that
there were three nations in India: the Muslims, the Dravidians and the
Aryans. They should each have a separate state, to be called Pakistan,
Dravida Nad and Aryavarta (Irschick, 1969, p. 347). In August 1944 the
Justice Party changed its name to the Dravida Kazhagam (Dravidian
Federation) to emphasise that its aim was the creation of a non-Brahmin,
Dravidian country. Its black flag with a red circle in the centre symbolised
both the mourning of the Dravidian people and the hope for a future
Dravidistan. Presaging the later Tamil nationalist movement's use of the
cinema to popularise its ideas, the Dravida Kazhagam sought to attract
support by staging plays presented by travelling troupes, especially the alternative Dravidian reading of the Ramayana in which Ravana is the hero. The
circumstances of 1947 nevertheless foreclosed the establishment of
Dravidistan as a realistic option. Naicker felt betrayed by the British and
boycotted the Independence Day celebrations. The Dravidistan demand,
however, should not be overlooked, as it was the climax of the process of
interest in Tamil culture initiated by the Reverend Robert Caldwell. It also, in

another important respect, presaged the challenge to the Indian state posed by the Dravida Kazhagam's successor, the Dravida Munnetra Kazhagam (the Dravidian Progressive Federation), which was founded in September 1949 by the film writer C. N. Annadurai (1908–69) (Hardgrave, 1979, pp. 33ff).

The impact of partition on identity

The magnitude of the social upheavals of 1947 was so great that elites involved in the construction of national and collective identity have seized on partition as a benchmark to confirm their reading of South Asian society and history. The communal holocaust which accompanied the partition of the subcontinent in 1947 created the greatest refugee crisis of the twentieth century. Some seven million people migrated to Pakistan. Around 5.5 million Hindus and Sikhs crossed over in the opposite direction from West Pakistan to India. The largest of the foot columns of refugees (*kafilas*) took around eight days to pass the same spot (Butalia, 1998, p. 77). Vast amounts of property were abandoned with many individuals never receiving adequate compensation. Hindu and Sikh refugees, for example, vacated 9.6 million acres of land in Pakistan, and abandoned 1,789 factories and around 400,000 houses. Muslims left behind 5.5 million acres of land in India. In total, it is reckoned that Hindus and Sikhs left property worth Rs 500 *crores* (a *crore* is 100 *lakhs* or ten million) in West Punjab. Muslims left property worth Rs 100 *crores* in East Punjab. The migration to and from East Bengal occurred episodically over a longer period, but also involved millions of refugees.

Many people never made it to their new homeland as a result of attacks on refugee trains and foot columns which were planned with military precision (Aiyar, 1995). The exact death toll will never be known, although the figure is likely to lie between 200,000 and one million fatalities. Families were separated, as upwards of 100,000 women were kidnapped in the upheavals on both sides of the border. They were especially victimised because they were culturally understood to uphold their community's 'honour' (Major, 1995). Those who were returned often had political slogans tattooed on their bodies and the dates and names of the men who had raped them (Agarwal, 1995, p. 29).

An Inter-Dominion Treaty of 6 December 1947 launched what became known as the Central Recovery Operation to rescue abducted women. Both its operations and the debates in the Indian Legislature on abduction have led the feminist historian of partition, Urvashi Butalia, to declare that national pride rather than concern with women as individuals dominated the issue of their recovery. Forceable 'recovery' continued until the mid-1950s. Women were returned to their home of origin, even if this involved separation from their children of new families. Such action was deemed necessary to restore the 'moral order' of the nation. As one speaker in the Indian Constituent

Assembly put it, 'As descendants of Ram, we have to bring back every Sita that is alive.' The RSS mouthpiece the *Organiser* reinforced this sentiment, declaring that the recovery of 'our pious mothers and sisters ... is a challenge to our manhood, no less than to our nationhood' (Butalia, 1998, p. 186). Significantly, while the *Organiser* linked the abduction of Hindu and Sikh women to stereotypes of 'lustful', 'barbaric' Muslim behaviour, it did not acknowledge that Hindu men had behaved similarly. It merely acknowledged that they had 'sheltered' Muslim women during the turmoil of partition.

Indian 'official' histories have traditionally relegated partition to a footnote in the freedom movement's triumph. The massacres are acknowledged primarily as 'proof' of the need for secularism. They are seen as directly resulting from the communal passions unleashed by the Pakistan movement. This nationalist understanding intersects with Hindu communalist depictions in its portrayal of the Muslims as instigators of violence. Stereotypes drawn from the partition, along with portrayals of Muslim iconoclastic destruction of Hindu sacred space from the medieval period onwards, have played a crucial role in the 'essentialisation' of the Indian Muslim identity in Hindutva philosophy. A key element in this stereotype is the Muslim 'other' as a sexually rapacious and a violent aggressor. Hindu violence in this discourse is always justified as self-defence. This is not only a self-serving attitude, but reflects a deep sense of injury.

Pakistani histories also subordinate partition to accounts of nationalist triumph. Partition sits uncomfortably with the reality that the creation of Pakistan involved not just the division of territory but, despite the two-nation theory, of Muslims. It is little acknowledged outside narrow academic circles that the Indian Muslim population in contemporary South Asia outnumbers that of Pakistan. Mushirul Hasan (1997) has chronicled the economic, political and emotional depression of an Indian Muslim community left leaderless and traumatised by the partition. Even in the so-called golden era of Nehruvian secularism, the Muslims' relations with the Hindu majority were marked by a sense of insecurity and desire to disprove any charges that they represented a fifth column. One working out of collective insecurities little remarked upon by historians was the adoption of Hindu names by leading Muslim actors in the Bombay cinema. Dilip Kumar went even further and avoided Muslim roles except in K. Asif's 1960 production, *Mughal-e-Azam*. This projected backwards, to the time of the great Mughal ruler Akbar, Nehruvian ideals of 'unity in diversity' and a composite Indian national identity.

Despite the ambiguities for Pakistan of the partition of Muslims, the state has used the event for nation-building purposes by emphasising the sacrifices it entailed.

Official histories in Pakistan have linked the partition-related violence with stereotypes of Hindu treachery and a desire to destroy Muslim culture. These are expressed most clearly in school textbooks sanctioned by the state which distort the events leading up to partition and the upheavals themselves. Such distortions find their counterparts in India where state governments led by the Hindu nationalist BJP have influenced textbook production.

The continuing influence of such ideologically constructed accounts of partition was brought home dramatically by the anti-Muslim riots in India in 1992–3. After the devastating Bombay riots which followed the demolition of the Babri Masjid at Ayodhya in December 1992, the news magazine *Communalism Combat* was founded in Bombay to open up dialogue between Indian and Pakistani citizens. On Independence Day 1996 a small letter-writing exchange called Peace Pals was launched between selected Karachi and Bombay schools. One of the major areas of prejudice and stereotyping encountered was the understandings of the partition experience.

A selective replaying of the bitter memories of partition has been used by the contemporary Hindutva movement to both fix the stereotype of the Muslim 'aggressor' and to attack the Congress's secularist inheritance. The archetypal secularist Nehru is blamed for the acceptance of partition and Pakistan's emergence. This version of the partition event was set as early as 14 August 1947 when the *Organiser*, the mouthpiece of the RSS, carried on its front page an illustration of Mother India in the form of a map of the country with a woman lying on it, one limb severed, with Nehru holding a bloody knife (Butalia, 1995, p. 96). Articles in the *Organiser* constantly equated the creation of Pakistan with the 'violation' of Bharat Mata. Rape, Muslim men and Pakistan were made synonymous through lurid accounts of assaults and the claim that lust for Hindu women and property had motivated the demand for a separate state. Hindu men, in contrast, were portrayed as only occasionally succumbing to the 'aberration' of violence because they were the inheritors of a 'tolerant' and 'glorious civilisation' (Butalia, 1995, p. 68).

The *mohajir* (refugee) community in Karachi and Hyderabad and the East Bengali *bhadralok* refugees now settled in Calcutta have experienced especial 'identity' problems in the wake of partition. Both communities contrast their perceived post-independence marginalisation with their sacrifices in the freedom struggle. Political dissent in the case of the former has taken the shape of support for the MQM and an autonomist if not secessionist stance. MQM publications talk of the death of two million *mohajirs* at the time of partition and portray this community alone as sacrificing themselves for the establishment of Pakistan. The *bhadralok*'s commitment to the Communist Party is motivated by a similar sense of displacement and loss of prominence.

It is difficult for those outside these communities to appreciate the sense of alienation and loss brought about by the uprooting from an ancestral homeland. It may be glimpsed in the autobiographical account of a Muslim refugee from Amritsar. In his imagination he returns to his home declaring, 'Even the footprints [ruins] of Muslim culture were not visible. The Mosques seemed to be reciting elegies. Hindu women were plastering with cow dung, the walls of rooms which once formed the rendezvous for Kashmiris' (cited in Talbot, 1996a, p. 183).

Strikingly similar sentiments are struck by Hindu refugees from East Bengal. As recently as 1993, a souvenir brochure of a *bhadralok* refugee gathering included this heartfelt lament:

> Sometimes, at night, I awake in tears. With this so-called Independence my own golden village became someone else's. The *desh* [homeland] was divided and we had to move away forever ... The tragedy of the partition uprooted everybody ... the household broke down and people's lives broke down. The deity's room [*thakur ghar*] in our old house ... who knows if it is still standing even. I imagine there are no evening bells letting everyone know that the devotional songs in the temples have begun, no one lights the lamp under the *tulsi* plant now ... it must be an eerie place now.
>
> cited in Ghosh (1998, p. 52)

God had become a refugee.

Conclusion

This chapter has revealed that it is facile to regard the emergence of independent India and Pakistan as a triumph of nationalism over ethnic and communal identities. Secular territorial nationalism not only jostled with competing identities at the point of British departure, but also made significant compromises with communalism and parochial loyalties. Pakistani nationalism was further questioned by the very creation of a territorial unit that itself inevitably transgressed the two-nation theory ideology by leaving millions of Muslims behind in the Indian state. The division of the subcontinent also represented, however, a defeat for the Indian secular nationalist vision by acknowledging the 'communal' demand of the Pakistan movement. Hindu nationalists regarded Nehru's acceptance of the 3 June Partition Plan as nothing less than a betrayal. Communalists in both India and Pakistan also drew strength from the massive social disruptions which accompanied the British departure.

A host of modern-day Somnaths fed into the 'commonsense' Hindu view of the rapacious and fanatical Muslim, while those Muslims who had crossed the killing fields of the East Punjab to Pakistan were determined to justify their sacrifice by transforming Jinnah's dream of a Muslim homeland into an Islamic state. The secular elites on both sides of the Wagah border thus found themselves having to face a renewed communalist challenge. Simultaneously they had to weld together diverse peoples into a sense of nationhood in the territories which they had inherited from the Raj. Their populations included not only host communities, but large numbers of refugees who carried the physical and emotional scars brought by the savage uprooting of partition.

In such circumstances, independence could not, despite the triumphalist rhetoric of freedom's dawn, mean the completion of the nationalist project but rather, as Dr Ambedkar the Untouchable leader openly acknowledged, its beginning for India and Pakistan. 'In believing that we are a nation, we are chasing a great delusion', he declared on the eve of his drafting of India's 1950 constitution. 'We can only attempt to become a nation in the making' (cited in Das, 1994, p. 8).

|7|

Nation building in India: ideas and institutions

Humanity with all that is good, bad or indifferent
about it, finds its reflection in democracy. You
may call it weakness, but really in the long run, it gives
it immense strength ... It is the only insurance of the
continuation of our national policies against reaction.

Jawaharlal Nehru, 1960

The present election is a *Dharma Yudh* [holy war]...
the BJP–Shiv Sena alliance is bound to sweep this election
because Shri Krishna is on our side and Lord Ram's
dhanushya baan [bow and arrow] and Goddess Laxmi's
kamal [lotus], such sacred and holy articles are our election
symbols.

BJP election pamphlet, Maharashtra, 1990

When India received its freedom at the midnight hour of August 14 1947, decolonisation was still a novel rather than routine event. Like later generations of African nationalists, the subcontinent's new rulers were faced with the problem of converting freedom movements into political parties and transforming themselves from opposition figures to responsible rulers. They also faced what was to become the familiar post-independence task of establishing a sense of unity amongst peoples divided by language, ethnicity and religion now that the common colonial enemy had been removed.

Just as the struggle against the Raj had taken on epic proportions, so the problems which faced the new leaders of India and Pakistan were immense. In addition to those attendant on all decolonisations, they were confronted with the administrative and human legacies of partition. For Pakistan, the worst affected of the two states, there was also the problem of building the state from scratch with extremely limited resources. As we shall see in the next chapter, longer-term nation-building requirements had to take second place to the need for survival. India, as the inheritor of the Raj's capital and administrative system, was better placed, but still had to rehabilitate refugees and oversee the integration of the former Princely States before it could turn to longer-term goals. We shall thus begin this chapter by examining responses to the immediate aftermath of partition before adopting a more thematic approach to some of thce ideas and institutions which dominated India's nation-building enterprise during its formative decades.

The aftermath of partition: refugees and rehabilitation

In the immediate post-independence period, all the energies of the Indian government were diverted to the refugee crisis. The machinery of the state was called on to evacuate refugees, recover abducted women and resettle and rehabilitate the millions of people flooding across the new international borders. Following the failure of the British-led Boundary Force, Indian and Pakistan Army units organised the safe evacuation of around six million people from each other's territory. Early in October the government of India even formally requested the US government to make available ten transport planes to evacuate 50,000 non-Muslims from the North-West Frontier Provinces. Nehru had made this request because the Indians could themselves only muster sixteen BOAC Dakotas, most of which were un-airworthy.

The government was similarly unprepared for the tasks of housing and rehabilitating refugees. Indeed Hindu Bengali refugees who ended up in Calcutta had to rehabilitate themselves in squatter colonies or face years of languishing in government relief camps in the absence of a planned response to the refugee problem. Rehabilitation, which was a provincial government responsibility, was carried out by understaffed administrations operating in an atmosphere of hysteria and bitter communal hostility. Responses to the unprecedented population movements were made still more difficult by Indo-Pakistan rivalry, which undermined the effectiveness of the joint inter-Dominion conferences on the refugee situation, and by the almost complete breakdown of the East Punjab government. Unhindered bands of armed Sikhs ethnically cleansed Muslims in the killing fields of the East Punjab.

By the beginning of September 1947 the Indian capital New Delhi itself was awash with blood and refugees in a situation which for a number of days threatened anarchy. In addition to the 150,000 refugees from Pakistan who poured into the city, attacks on the Muslim residents of the Old City forced them into makeshift camps like the one at the Old Fort where over 50,000 huddled without food, shelter or sanitation. The situation was little better at another camp at Humayan's Tomb. Order was only finally restored in the city as a result of the combination of Gandhi's temporary residence and the patrolling of the streets of Delhi by 5,000 Indian troops.

Nehru's insistence that the Muslims left behind by partition were not a 'fifth column' but equal citizens appears even more courageous in the light of his difficulties with the Deputy Prime Minister Patel. According to US reports, relations between the two men had become so embittered that the impression prevailed in many quarters that Patel was 'determined to get Nehru out of the Government'.

Within a fortnight this particular crisis had passed. According to Matthai, the Minister of Transport who was the Americans' New Delhi informant, Gandhi had once more come to Nehru's rescue, making it clear to Patel that if 'he took any steps against Nehru he [Gandhi] would be finished with him for life'. Such an admonishment could not be taken lightly by Patel who had been the Mahatma's associate since the 1920s.

Partition provided not only immense human challenges for the new Indian state, however, but the opportunity to stamp its authority. The state was able to prove its paternalistic credentials by establishing orphanages and grants and monthly cash allowances for refugee dependants who legally became 'permanent liabilities' of the state. The tentacles of refugee rehabilitation spread far into the economy with support for small businesses, custodianship of evacuee property and a sliding scale of land allotments for refugee agriculturalists in Punjab.

Nevertheless, the state could never do enough to meet the myriad of partition-related problems. The Hindu nationalist discourse seized on this. Failure to protect the symbolic body of Mother India was linked with the reality of the violation of countless Hindu and Sikh women. We have seen in the previous chapter how the call for the rehabilitation of abducted women was linked with national honour. Such Hindu nationalist writers as Chaman Lal called for a 'strong and virile state backed up by a powerful army' to respond to the aggressor Pakistan state which preyed on Hindu women and property (Butalia, 1998, pp. 183–4).

The aftermath of partition: the Princely States

British fear of the subcontinent's Balkanisation ensured that when Mountbatten turned his attention late in the day to the future of the Princely States, which were linked to the crown in the special relationship known as Paramountcy, such options as Dominion status or confederation were summarily dismissed. The Princes' lack of unity and tardy responses to the demand for democratisation did not help their cause. Many Princes as late as 1947 still utilised state funds for private purposes. Although such rulers as the Nawab of Bhopal who was the Chancellor of the Chamber of Princes harboured a deep mistrust of the Congress, and especially of Nehru's republican sentiments, Mountbatten's

Map 3 Territorial disputes and boundary changes since 1947.

Gwadar ceded by Oman 1958; Rann of Kutch fought over 1965; Junagadh acceded to Pakistan August 1947, occupied by India November 1947; Diu and Goa, Portuguese territories, annexed by India 1961; Mahe and Pondicherry ceded by France to India 1954; Chandernagore also ceded in 1954; Bhutan made Indian Protectorate 1949; Sikkim annexed by India 1975; Arunachal Pradesh fought over by India and China in 1962; Hyderabad occupied by India Army September 1949, acceded to India in November; Jammu and Kashmir contested by Pakistan; India claims legal right not only to Jammu and Kashmir but to the Northern Areas which are administered separately from Azad Kashmir.

cajolery ensured that the majority of the Princely States had opted to join the Indian or Pakistani Dominions by the time of the British departure. Such exceptions as Junagadh, Hyderabad and most notably Kashmir became major sources of Indo-Pakistan tension. Concern with their fate has tended to overshadow the importance for the fledgling Indian state of the integration of the 600-odd other Princely States.

Shortly before independence, with Mountbatten's consent, a States Department under Sardar Patel's control was established to 'oversee matters of common concern' with the states (Copland, 1997, p. 255). The Princes' accession to the Raj's successor states was ensured when the generous concession was made in their instruments of accession that they would only have to cede power in the three areas of defence, foreign affairs and communications. The ink on these documents had hardly dried, however, before Patel and his secretary V. P. Menon (1894–1966) at the States Department had begun to plan a 'final solution' for the states 'problem' (Copland, 1997, p. 261). By November 1949, only a handful of states remained as separate entities; the remainder had been amalgamated (like for example, PEPSU, the Patiala and East Punjab States Union) or merged into neighbouring provinces. The Princes had also transferred the remainder of the powers left to them in the original instruments of accession. The bitter pill of the ending of the old princely order had been sugared by tax-free pensions linked to the former state's revenue levels and by making some of the rulers of large states *rajpramukhs* (governors) of the new administrative entities.

Although Patel and Menon faced criticism for duplicitously repudiating earlier guarantees, the former hailed the integration of the Princely States as a peaceful political revolution. Their absorption compensated for the losses brought by partition in that over half a million square miles and 90 million people were added to the political map of the Indian Union. Administrative integration was not of course the end of the matter, for with the exception of such states as Baroda and Mysore, levels of both political and economic development in Princely India had lagged far behind those attained in the neighbouring British provinces. Lord Hastings, for example, remarked of the state of Cutch after a visit in 1932, 'If any European has been here before he hasn't left any traces' (cited in Copland, 1997, p. 9). Indeed, despite decades of development programmes, the former Princely heartland of the subcontinent, Rajasthan and Madhya Pradesh, still trails behind other parts of India in human and economic development terms. Rajasthan remains one of the most socially conservative regions in India as seen, for example, in incidents of *sati* and continuing female infanticide. Scions of the Princely class have also continued to exert a political influence albeit now through the ballot box. The most spectacular demonstration of this occurred in the 1962 Lok Sabha polls when the Maharani of Jaipur secured a world record electoral majority of 175,000 votes (Copland, 1997, p. 268).

India's foundational ideas and nation building

Nehru's influence as Indian Prime Minister (1947–64) grew steadily after his shaky start and was definitely assisted by the death of his deputy Patel in 1950. By the middle of the decade, he was able to put his personal impress firmly on the nation-building programme. The key ideas he articulated dominated the national discourse until the emergence in the 1980s of the challenges posed domestically by Hindutva and internationally by globalisation. Five ideas underpinned the Indian nation-building process, all of which had their roots in the earlier independence movement. Secularism and democracy occupied the leading positions in the nationalist pantheon, followed by statism, socialism and non-alignment. They were regarded as the hallmarks of a modernising and progressive Indian nation state eager to cast aside both its 'traditional' and colonial past. By adopting them, India would, in Nehru's telling phrase, be able to clothe herself in the 'garb of modernity'. Significantly, Gandhian thought with its anarchist vision of a decentralised polity and economy based on the village was reduced to the margins of the nationalist enterprise, although the Mahatma was mythologised as the founder of the nation.

Secularism

Secularism did not imply, as in the Western sense, a separation of religion and politics, but rather an equality of religions. 'I believe in India being a secular state with complete freedom for all religions and for cooperation between them', Nehru declared in a letter to the Nawab of Bhopal on 8 July 1948. 'I believe that India can only become great if she preserves that composite culture which she had developed through the ages' (Hasan, 1997, pp. 135–6). The continued attachment to a composite national identity was epitomised by the billboards in New Delhi sponsored by a leading English-language daily newspaper at the time of the fiftieth anniversary celebrations five decades later. Under the slogan 'Let's Keep the Light of Freedom Alive', they displayed flames set on red, white and green candleholders. These, like the tricolour of the national flag, respectively represented the Hindus, the other minorities and the Indian Muslim community.

Shortly after independence, the All-India Congress Committee publicly committed itself to a democratic and secular polity. Secular principles were embodied in the fundamental rights in Part III of the 1950 constitution. These included cultural and educational rights along with the right to freedom of religion. It was not, however, until the 42nd constitutional amendment in 1976 that India was explicitly called a 'Sovereign, Socialist, Secular Democratic Republic'. An early sign of the commitment to national integration on secular lines was found in the abolition of separate electorates and the reservation of seats for Muslims which many Congressmen had blamed for bringing disunity during the colonial era.

Nehru put his personal stamp on secularism as he did on much of what became 'modern' India. Secularism was seen as countering the internal threat to national unity provided by communalism, as well as differentiating 'progressive' India from 'reactionary' Islamic Pakistan. 'It will be with pride', a Constituent Assembly member declared in May 1949, 'that our nation will be remembered by the nations of the world that in our Constitution we have kept no room for communalism and that we are in the true sense of the word a secular State' (cited in Hasan, 1997, p. 141). Nehru himself had declared:

> India is a secular nation which guarantees equality of citizenship to people of all religions. We consider our Muslim population – we have some fifty million of them – as part of our nation, the Indian nation, and not some other Muslim nation ... if we consider this two nation theory which Pakistan is sponsoring what happens to our Muslim population? Do we have to consider them as a different nation just because they have a different religion? The very concept is fantastic. It might lead to further trouble, division and disruption of the nation.
>
> cited in Hasan (1997, p. 139)

A number of writers have linked India's unyielding stance on the Kashmir dispute to the fear not only of Balkanisation if the region became independent or went to Pakistan, but to the importance for India's secular self-image of having this sole Muslim majority state safely within the Union. It could be argued, however, that the Kashmir issue has been far more important to Pakistani than Indian nationalism, because it has provided a rallying point in an otherwise fractious political environment.

Formidable Hindu nationalist challenges to secularism existed from the outset. The fact of partition challenged the secularist understanding of Indian society. The traumas arising from the mass migrations and massacres of August 1947 both increased hostility to Muslims and created a refugee constituency for the Hindu nationalists. Hindu Mahasabhite spokesmen castigated the Congress's 'appeasement' which had resulted in the 'vivisection' of the 'motherland'. Even within Congress circles such leading figures as the UP chief minister Govind Ballabh Pant publicly questioned the Muslim community's loyalty to the Indian Union. We have already referred to the bitter private tensions between Nehru and Sardar Vallabhbhai Patel which threatened the still fragile ship of state. Symptomatic of the poisoned atmosphere was the assassination of Gandhi, the 'father' of the nation, on 30 January 1948, primarily because his public fast had secured the release of Rs 55 million by the Indian government as compensation to Pakistan for the assests lost at partition.

Gandhi in death, however, achieved as much for the goal of Hindu–Muslim unity as in life, for Nehru was able to utilise the public revulsion to clamp down on the activities of the RSS. Over 16,000 of its dedicated activists (*swayamsevaks*) were arrested in the space of five days. The Hindu Mahasabha was, however, unaffected and the ban on the RSS itself was lifted on 15 July 1948. By the mid-1950s, it controlled a set of affiliated organisations known collectively as the Sangh Parivar (the RSS family). These included the Jana Sangh political party which had been founded independently in 1951, the Akhil Bharatiya Vidyarthi Parishad student movement and the Bharatiya Mazdoor Sangh labour union.

Even during the heyday of Nehruvian secularism, a number of compromises were made with both Muslim and Hindu religious traditionalists which with hindsight endangered the nation-building enterprise. Partly to reassure the Muslim minority and partly in order to secure the important Muslim bloc vote in elections, the national government did not reduce the sway of the *shariat* in Muslim personal law. This resulted in Muslim women being deprived of the equal status provided by the constitution in matters relating to divorce, maintenance and inheritance. Simultaneously, leading Congress figures associated themselves with Hindu nationalist concerns such as the rebuilding of Somnath Temple. Sardar Patel went so far in January 1948 as to invite Hindu Mahasabhites to join the Congress. In a repetition of the freedom movement, local Congress governments in such states as Uttar Pradesh and Bihar gave the lie to Nehru's professed secularism by enforcing bans on cow slaughter and privileging Hindi over Urdu as the language of administration.

Democracy

India's post-independence ruling elite had been schooled to value the merits of democracy in the prisons of the Raj. In contrast to Pakistan's bureaucrats and generals, the Indian Congressmen saw participation rather than administrative fiat as the key to long-term economic and political development. Nehru consciously rejected Chinese-style solutions to India's growing agrarian problems in the 1950s because of his commitment to the democratic process. This principled stance was beset with frustrations and ironies.

Democracy, which was supposed to underpin not only secularism but the wider nation-building enterprise, was in fact a two-edged weapon. Local Congressmen in the bid to acquire or retain office were encouraged to placate communalist demands. Despite the incessant talk of national integration and secularism, votes were sought, especially at the state level, through appeals to caste, language and communal identities. 'What has the Congress done to pull up its party organisations in those states which have flagrantly violated the principles of integration of the people which it swears by?' questioned a political analyst in January 1961. 'Is there any guarantee ... that in selecting candidates for the next election, the Congress will not be guided in its choice by caste or communal considerations?' (Hasan, 1997, p. 145). Almost a decade earlier, Gandhi's long-time disciple Mira Behn had warned that patronage could replace principles. 'The Congress should recognise', she wrote to Nehru, 'that it was the ideals that conquered, and it is those ideals alone that can successfully overcome the dangers and difficulties which today surround us on all sides' (cited in Hasan, 1997, p. 153).

Patronage politics, nevertheless, encouraged processes of bargaining and accommodation. When they have been absent in subcontinental politics, minority groups have become alienated and even in extreme circumstances felt driven to take up arms in order to secure justice. The Congress system of one-party dominance, as political scientists have termed it, also enabled the interests of newly politicised communities to be articulated under its broad umbrella. The Indian political system was accordingly spared the crises of legitimacy which bedevilled its Pakistani neighbour and most newly independent states. The 'exceptionalism' of Indian democracy in the third world was not only increasingly remarked upon by political analysts, but along with secularism and non-alignment constituted India's claim to moral authority and leadership in the developing world. It formed another important differentiating marker in the Indian self-image from the Pakistani 'other'.

'Humanity with all that is good, bad or indifferent in it, finds its reflection in democracy', Nehru declared in 1960.

> You may call it weakness, but really in the long run it gives immense strength, permanent and durable strength. It is the only insurance of the continuity of our national politics against reaction. Therefore, it is not right to change the basis of our stand on democracy simply because we are going through a crisis of something or other.
>
>   Israel (1991, pp. 63–4)

Democracy, like secularism, was, however, little more than a paper promise for those at the base of society where inequalities arising from gender, class and caste persisted, despite the promises of the constitution and the periodic round of elections.

Statism

Nehru, like many leaders of newly independent countries, shared a statist outlook which emphasised the need for government-led processes of economic development and social reform in order to achieve the twin goals of modernisation and nation building. Experience of wartime planning, admiration for the Soviet economic model and a belief that only the 'dead hand' of colonial bureaucracy had held back advance fed into this outlook. Nehru also emphasised the need for economic planning so as to develop a strong industrial/military base that would safeguard independence. This policy became even more pressing after the 1962 conflict with China, leading Nehru to declare in a Lok Sabha debate in the following August: 'It is essential for our strength, for our military strength ... to have an industrial base ... I say you cannot even remain free in India without an industrial base' (cited in Israel, 1991, p. 37). This goal of planning to increase the productive powers of industry rather than to oversee redistributionary measures ensured the support of those sections of the Congress which did not share Nehru's professed socialist ideals. Sardar Patel, for example, earlier declared:

We must industrialise our country quickly and efficiently in certain directions. Otherwise we are doomed in the modern world because a modern army requires many things which only machines can produce apart from arms and ammunition, uniforms and stores, jeeps and motor cars, aeroplanes and petrol. If industry is not developed in the country, we have to depend on external sources.

Israel (1991, p. 161)

Statism involved not just economic planning but an attempt to achieve social progress. 'When we talk about a secular state', Nehru lectured his chief ministers in 1954, 'this simply does not mean some negative idea, but a positive approach on the basis of equality of opportunity for everyone, man or woman, of any religion or caste, in every part of India' (cited in Brown, 1999, p. 118). This was to be achieved through legislative enactment, exhortation through the state-controlled media, All-India Radio and Doordarshan television, and by a policy of positive discrimination for disadvantaged minorities such as the Untouchables, now known as the scheduled castes and tribes.

Discrimination arising from untouchability had been made illegal by the 1955 Untouchability Offences Act. This was strengthened in an amendment introduced during the 1975–7 emergency, which in addition to discrimination regarding temple entry, access to shops, restaurants and wells, made it an offence to 'insult' Untouchables. Implementation of the law, as in many other areas, however, was limited. During the Nehruvian era only around 300 cases were annually brought to court. Penalties on conviction could be as little as fines of 3–4 rupees. Legislation introduced in 1989 introduced stronger penalties, but it remains extremely doubtful that the law can by itself remove discrimination. Relaxations of ritual discrimination have owed far more to increased social mobility and urbanisation. In the words of a recent study, they have engineered a 'new civic culture ... of pragmatism which allows ample scope for compartmentalisation and social hypocrisy' (Mendelsohn and Vicziany, 1998, p. 126).

The continuation of a reservations policy for access to government employment and educational institutions from the colonial era appeared problematic given the Constituent Assembly's resistance to the principle of separate electorates for religious minorities. Ultimately reservation was perpetuated for the scheduled castes and tribes at the national level and permitted for the 'backward castes' at state level. The move in the late 1980s to implement the Mandal Commission's recommendation that 27 per cent of all government jobs and education places should be reserved for members of the OBC administrative category resulted in an almost hysterical outburst from the upper castes. There were incidents of self-immolation by Brahmin students. Criticism of compensatory discrimination has focused on the creation of a perpetuating Untouchable elite distanced from the bulk of the village-based *dalit* community and on the encouragement it has lent to caste-based politics in the states. By the 1990s, such new identities as the OBCs had come into existence in response to the Indian state's positive discrimination policy and the opportunities provided by representative politics. Ironically, the Indian state, despite its foundational resistance to ascriptive identities, has encouraged their perpetuation by making caste identity the basis for increasingly elaborate programmes of affirmative action.

The increased importance of the OBCs in North India must be understood in terms of the furore surrounding the Mandal Commission's positive action programme in the early 1990s and the 'instrumentalist' decision by educated lower-caste leaders to create an umbrella OBC political identity to advance their struggle for social and political power. The decision of the OBCs to desert the Congress for such parties as the Janata Dal also reflected the increasing gulf between its rhetoric in favour of reform and the reality of continuing hierarchical power relations. Some writers have seen the rise of the OBC caste-based politics in contemporary North India as part of a second wave of democratisation from below. This is also constituted by the scheduled caste-based Bahujan Samaj Party which in the early 1990s made electoral inroads in the Punjab and momentarily held office in UP. Others have regarded it as a barrier to political stability in which parochial concerns are 'subverting' national politics.

Lower-caste activists reject such suggestions and rightly point to the upper castes' use of ascriptive loyalties in the past for political mobilisation. Patronage on the basis of caste has been a driving force in modern Indian politics and is only now being dubbed a 'corrupting' influence when lower groups are joining the game. Even the BJP, whose organicist ideology with regard to Hindu society explicitly denies caste, in informal practice has accommodated itself to aspects of India's caste-based politics. The rise of the OBC identity in contemporary India, no less than the classic case of the emergence of a 'Muslim' political identity during the Raj, raises issues concerning the interplay of the role of the state, collective self-consciousness and the competition for power. By the 1980s there was growing intra-caste violence in such states as Gujarat over reservation policy, while the Congress's alleged 'pampering' of the Muslim minority had become an important ideological plank of Hindu nationalism. In reality, however, the Brahmins felt under pressure from the rise of the lower castes, rather than those at the bottom of society. The scheduled castes, after 40 years of reservations, accounted for just 10 per cent of the class 1 administrative posts.

Socialism

Nehru had repeatedly linked his support for the freedom struggle with socialism. 'I should like the Congress to become a socialist organisation', he told the 1936 Lucknow Congress session, 'and to join hands with other forces in the world who are working for a new civilisation' (cited in Lall,

1976, p. 185). According to Nehru's vision, socialism would consolidate the state by removing inequalities and ensuring redistributive justice. Moreover, the democratic and non-violent transition to a socialist society would provide for developing countries a rival role model to the Soviet and Chinese versions of socialism.

In 1955 at its Avadi Session, the Congress stole the clothes of the Praja Socialist Party by publicly committing itself to a socialist pattern of society. Nehruvian socialism, however, embraced the mixed economy. State ownership and national economic planning coexisted in a partnership with the private sector which was rooted in the experience of the freedom movement and the 1944 Bombay Plan. Land reform legislation during the 1953–5 period was limited because of the loopholes in the 'ceiling legislation'. Moreover, by removing the absentee *zamindar* class in such states as UP, it strengthened the rich peasant cultivator class which had become an increasingly important support base for Congress in colonial India. After independence it was crucial for delivering votes in both national and, even more, state elections. Its ability to block radical rural reform was increased by the constitutional division of powers between the Union and the states delivering to the latter most matters affecting the rural population. The success of the rising 'backward' caste cultivators at the expense of both Brahmin and Rajput ex-landlords and Untouchable landless labourers, as exemplified by the Yadavs and Kurmis, has been one of the most important political and social developments of post-colonial India. The other main gainers have been the urban middle classes. In the cities, the fruits of India's import-substitution-led industrial development have not trickled down to the base of society and here, as in the countryside, massive inequalities remain in terms of access to resources and political power.

Despite its socialist rhetoric, property relations have remained basically unchanged in both the towns and countryside. Privileged social groups who had supported the Congress during the freedom movement thus continued to feel comfortable with it, despite its redistributionary pretensions. In the longer run, however, the gap between rhetoric and reality sufficiently widened to inject cynicism into a once highly idealistic political culture. As Atul Kohli has noted, India's current crisis of governability is rooted in the politicisation of depressed groups as a result of electoral competition without a corresponding increase in 'the state's limited capacities for redistribution of wealth' (Kohli, 1997, p. 388).

Non-alignment

Non-alignment with either the Western or Communist blocs was the final ideological pillar of the post-independence state. Like secularism and socialism, it was rooted both in the freedom struggle and Nehru's personal beliefs. The Congress had taken an interest in international affairs throughout the latter stages of the freedom struggle. Indeed it had created its own Foreign Department headed by Nehru in 1928. He soon became the party's acknowledged expert on foreign affairs and articulated a policy which was critical of colonialism. The 1928 Calcutta Congress Session, for example, sent fraternal greetings to the peoples of Egypt, Palestine, Syria and Iraq in 'their struggle for emancipation from the grip of western imperialism'. By the end of the Second World War, the Congress's outlook was that India's freedom could influence the wider international system and that a free India could exert leadership in the Asian region. The holding of an Asian Relations Conference in New Delhi in March 1947, which was attended by over 200 delegates drawn from 28 countries, was a dress rehearsal for this self-perceived post-independence role. Its vehicle was commitment to the anti-colonialist struggle and attachment to the concept of non-alignment in a world increasingly dominated by the Cold War. 'We in Asia', Nehru declared, for example, at the UN General Assembly meeting in Paris on 4 November 1948, 'have committed ourselves inevitably to the freedom of every other colonial nation ... We do not conceive it possible that other countries should remain under the yoke of colonial rule' (cited in Israel, 1991, p. 81).

Nehru was quick to point out that non-alignment did not simply mean neutrality. It was portrayed not as a strategy in a dangerous Cold War riven world, but rather as a moral imperative rooted in India's traditional values of tolerance and non-violence. This idealist approach to India's international role had first been expressed by the great Bengali intellectual Rabindranath Tagore. 'That the measure of man's greatness is in his material resources is a gigantic illusion', he had declared. 'It lies in the power of the materially weak to save the world from this illusion, and India, in spite of her penury and humiliation, can afford to come to the rescue of humanity' (cited in Bandyopadhyaya, 1976, p. 176). By the time that the non-aligned movement formally came into being at the 1955 Bandung Conference in Indonesia, India had secured the moral high ground for itself in international relations.

Leadership of the non-aligned movement ensured that India wielded greater international influence than its economic or military muscle warranted. Non-alignment's sharp break with the colonial past underlined national sovereignty. As with secularism and democracy, it provided India with a sense of moral superiority over its Pakistan neighbour. By the end of Nehru's period in power, however, the lustre was wearing off non-alignment, just as it had faded from the secular, socialist and democratic underpinnings of the state.

Following the disastrous war with China in October 1962 after the Chinese invasion of the North-East Frontier Agency, India had been forced to accept arms from the West. Moral posturings on the international stage calling for peaceful resolutions of conflicts had been belied by the 17 December 1961 invasion of the Portuguese Indian enclave of Goa.

Moreover, a resolution of the dispute with Pakistan over the former Princely State of Kashmir remained as distant as ever. Pakistan may have introduced the Cold War into the subcontinent by its security pacts with the United States, but there were already signs that India might reply by moving into a closer relationship with the Soviet Union.

The Hindutva movement and the re-invention of India

By the middle of the 1980s, India's foundational ideas were under attack by the Hindutva movement which sought to remake the country in the image of a Hindu *rashtra* (state). The recovery of Ram's Ayodhya birthplace from its Muslim 'occupation' and the building of a temple there became the symbol of a restoration of Hindu national pride. Inchoate upper-caste anxieties arising from the 'Mandalisation' of politics and the breakdown of order and society under population pressures and globalisation were displaced onto a demonised Muslim 'other'. Muslims were not only blamed for Babur's past iconoclastic behaviour, but were dubbed both a threatening and 'pampered' minority. The repertoire of stereotypes which had been in circulation since the late nineteenth century now solidified into a communal 'commonsense' prejudice of the Muslim other. This was reinforced by the limited social interaction between Muslims and Hindus. Further 'evidence' was provided by the rumours which circulated following sporadic bouts of rioting.

The strident anti-Muslim tone of the Hindutva movement was epitomised in the speeches of the female activist Uma Bharati. They were widely distributed on audio-cassettes, a new technology which, as we shall see in Chapter 9, the BJP quickly mastered. The following, tape-recorded in 1991, captures the flavour of Bharati's tone.

> Declare without hesitation that this is a Hindu *rashtra*, a nation of Hindus. We have come to strengthen the immense Hindu *shakti* into a fist. Do not display any love for your enemies ... The Quran teaches them to lie in wait for idol worshippers, to skin them alive, to stuff them in animal skins and torture them until they ask for forgiveness. [We] could not teach them with words, now let us teach them with kicks ... Tie up your religiosity and kindness in a bundle and throw them in the Jamuna. Any non-Hindu who lives here does so at our mercy.
>
> cited in Hansen (1999, p. 180)

Bharati expressed Hindutva ideas more crudely than many other activists. Nevertheless, beliefs which had once been confined to the RSS sub-culture gained wide acceptance in 'respectable society'. The post-colonial state's policy of equal rights was increasingly condemned for its violation of the political and cultural rights of the Hindu majority. One mid-1990s survey of Brahmin opinion in UP found that even among 'long-time INC supporters or ideologues' the BJP anti-secular discourse had acquired 'legitimacy' (Brotel, 1998, p. 93).

From the early 1980s onwards, the BJP launched a full-blooded assault on what it dubbed the 'pseudo-secularism' of the Congress. Secularism was denounced not only as an alien implant, but as unjust in that it encouraged the overriding of Hindu rights in its rush to 'appease' the Muslims. Hindu nationalists also portrayed secularism as a source of national weakness. India would be strong, they argued, if it acknowledged the genius of its Hindu culture. It was, however, the aggressive masculine strand of Hindu belief that was held up for emulation, not the non-violent Gandhian strain. The will to power in domestic politics was matched on the international stage with the nuclear weapons testing of the Vajpayee government in May 1998.

Nehru accorded an important place for the peaceful development of nuclear power in his modernist outlook. Indeed he attached so much importance to atomic energy that he ensured that he was Minister for the Department of Atomic Energy. Nehru's ability to control nuclear policy, like foreign policy, was only to decline following the debacle of the 1962 Sino-Indian War. Up until this time, his influence and that of his close associate Krishna Menon (1897–1974), the Defence Minister from 1957 to 1962, had marginalised the bomb-making lobby amongst the scientific elite led by Dr Homi Bhabha and the bureaucrats, although significantly it was during this era that the technical expertise in plutonium reprocessing was acquired which would make an Indian bomb a possibility. Nevertheless, Nehru, both in public and in private, was an ardent supporter of the nuclear disarmament movement. Significantly it was only after his death that the recognition of a defence use came to the forefront in India's atomic energy activities. Nehru's short-lived successor Lal Bahadur Shastri (1904–66) broke with previous policy and authorised a 'peaceful' nuclear explosion, although this was to be delayed until 1974, a decade after Nehru died. It was only with the advent of a BJP government that India adopted an unambiguous stance on nuclear arms.

India and Pakistan's testing of nuclear devices at Pokhran and Chagai respectively in May 1998 shocked the international community. Their emergence as overt nuclear weapons states in the teeth of condemnation and economic sanctions ended two decades of what strategists had termed policies of nuclear ambiguity in the subcontinent. From the time of the 1974 'peaceful' Indian nuclear test onwards, Pakistan had acquired, frequently by clandestine means, the technology to enrich uranium in sufficient quantities for bomb-making capabilities. The threat and later imposition of US economic and military sanctions had not led to a capping of the Pakistani programme. Rather, a capability was acquired, but at the same time the state refrained from an overt weaponisation including test explosions and the assembly of warheads. This stance was only abandoned in the wake of the series of Indian detonations on 11 and 13 May 1998.

India's nuclear tests were motivated by the political need of the BJP to stamp its authority on its recalcitrant coalition partners in the two-month-old New Delhi government. They also reflected the influence behind the scenes of the hardline RSS, despite the mild-mannered public persona of the Prime Minister Atal Behari Vajpayee. Finally, they were in keeping with the party's traditional views. The BJP's 1991 election manifesto, for example, in its chapter on 'Towards World Fraternity' had talked of giving India 'nuclear teeth'. In the immediate post-test euphoria, India's joining of the nuclear weapons club was portrayed as a triumph for Hindutva. Its cult of manliness and virility rooted in nineteenth-century rejections of colonialist charges of Hindu effeminacy was reflected in the popular headlines which hailed the tests as 'Vajpayee's Viagra'. The BJP turned to another well-established theme in the Hindu nationalist discourse by dubbing the tests 'Operation Shakti'. The invocations to potency and primal power which had once inspired the bomb-throwing Bengali revolutionaries were now hymned to the potentially most destructive technology devised by modern man. In another echo of the extremist struggle against the Raj, the '*swadeshi* bomb' was celebrated in India.

Apart from the BJP government's sharp break with the earlier policy of nuclear ambiguity, there is thus cause to term the events of May 1998 as the Hindutva bomb. The Hindu nationalist discourse's urge to power and belligerence was encapsulated in Vajpayee's comments on the tests that they would 'show our strength and silence our enemies'. The Hindutva philosophy with its undercurrent of nineteenth-century-inspired social Darwinism had found a short cut to India achieving global status on the eve of the second millennium. From the days of the freedom struggle onwards one of the strands of nationalist thought had contained a primal urge to power and assertion of the superiority of the Hindu civilisation. This vision of Indian greatness has gained in strength with the rise of the BJP. Physical force has become substituted for moral authority, nuclear apartheid for the goal of economic self-reliance, although there were echoes of this when gangs of Hindu youths assaulted lorries carrying Pepsi and Coca Cola in response to US sanctions.

At the time of the military clashes in Kargil in June 1999, Hindutva activists spoke openly about the use of the bomb 'to finish off Pakistan'. A VHP gathering at Hardwar, for example, declared that '1999 was the year to wipe Pakistan off the globe'. The RSS mouthpiece *Panchjanya* exhorted Vajpayee to fulfil his destiny, for 'after all, why have we made the bomb?' (cited in Seshu, 1999).

India's foundational institutions and nation building

Traditional accounts of Indian politics in the early years of independence focused on the role of the constitution (Austin, 1966) and the formal institutions of government – legislature, executive and judiciary – in assisting the nation-building process. With the so-called behaviouralist revolution in political science in the 1960s, the emphasis shifted from structures to processes, with emphasis on the role of political actors, such as parties and interest groups, rather than government. In this section, we will first look at the formal organisation of government, before moving on to an examination of the informal institutions of the political system which played a significant role in the nation-building enterprise.

Formal institutions of government

The 1950 constitution retained the federal structure of government established under the 1935 Government of India Act. At the centre there was the all-powerful Lok Sabha, the House of the People and the Rajya Sabha or Council of States whose members were elected from the state legislatures roughly on an equal territorial representation. The government was formed from the majority in the Lok Sabha. The 27 Indian states, following the integration of the former Princely States, each had their own Legislative Council and government. Some states possessed a bicameral legislature. The Union List gave the centre control over matters of national importance including defence, foreign affairs and income tax. The State List gave the states responsibility for such items as agriculture, land revenue, welfare, public order and police. The centre and the states shared authority in what was known as the Concurrent List for such responsibilities as social and economic planning. This left responsibility for implementing many national policies with the states. An increasingly important issue has been the states' ability to implement changes in textbooks arising from their governments' responsibility for education.

In 1991 the BJP government of UP led by Kalyan Singh altered textbooks in the state-run schools to enable students to understand the 'Hindutva truth'. This policy was later adopted by other BJP administrations. In 1996 a new chapter entitled 'Religious policies of Babar' was introduced into the history textbooks of Delhi's state schools by the BJP administration which reproduced the party line on Ayodhya. Additional chapters were introduced to refute the suggestion that the Aryan invasion had led to the 'enslavement' of Dravidians and tribals. Finally, new material was included on the RSS's founder, Hedgewar. The national government was constitutionally unable to prevent such 're-writing' of history for propaganda purposes.

The division of powers between the central (Union) government and the states has been dubbed by some scholars as 'cooperative federalism' in which national integration is enhanced by the bargaining process between state and central leaders. Other writers have maintained, however, that the system is at best quasi-federal. They point to the fact that residual power (i.e. responsibility for administrative matters not mentioned elsewhere) lies with the Union and that emergency powers can be and frequently have been invoked by the President to supersede state power. A final piece of evidence for the centralisation of power in the Indian political system, it is claimed, is the national parliament's ability to create new states, to alter existing states' boundaries or even abolish them without the necessity of constitutional amendment. The most important changes to state boundaries came from their reorganisation along linguistic lines following the States Reorganisation Act of 1956. This is held up as an example of Nehruvian accommodationist politics which stands in stark contrast to the handling of linguistic demands in neighbouring Pakistan. In reality, Nehru acceded to this process with extreme reluctance. Nevertheless, the creation of the new southern linguistic states of Andhra Pradesh and Tamil Nadu helped 'domesticate' regional linguistic loyalties. In Robert Hardgrave's words, the DMK 'was transformed from a secessionist movement, nurtured on vague dreams of a glorious past and an impossible hope for the future, to a party of increasing political maturity and parliamentary discipline. As it was drawn into the political system, interests became more specific and were formulated as pragmatic political demands' (Hardgrave, 1980, p. 192).

The Planning Commission

The Planning Commission, with its headquarters at Yojana Bhavan in New Delhi, was established in 1950 as an extra-constitutional advisory body with Nehru as its *ex officio* chairman. During the remainder of his period in power, it acted as a kind of 'super-cabinet' which was unaccountable to parliament. The three five-year plans (1951–66) of the Nehruvian era were increasingly more ambitious in scope, although they shared the common characteristic of an emphasis on industry rather than agriculture as the key to India's development. This proved one of a series of weaknesses in the planning process. In Baldev Raj Nayar's perceptive phrase, however, 'Nehru's economic policies, whatever their concrete ... results, served important legitimation functions' for the Indian state. Intervention in the economy for developmentalist purposes drew a clear line between independent India and the Raj, which had always been marked by its desultory efforts in this respect. Development, in Nehru's thought, however, was not just about providing the Indian state with a *raison d'être*; involvement in its project would strengthen a sense of common citizenship.

Self-reliance, the encouragement of heavy industry and the belief in state control of key sections of the economy continued the freedom movement's quest for Indian independence in the modern world and continued to hold in tension the prospect of greater social equality along with the interests of a nationalist-minded industrial elite. The Planning Commission, which sought to institutionalise these goals, was itself the heir to the National Planning Committee which had first met in December 1939.

While Nehru had in the early 1930s admired the Soviet model, he was well aware by the time of independence of the human costs involved in its forced march to industrialisation. Hence he adhered to the social democratic rather than communist path to modernisation in the political sphere. In the realm of planning, he emphasised coordination of the economy rather than centralised command. The plans were indicative, i.e. did not have the force of law. Nevertheless, Nehru vigorously encouraged their implementation and government intervention extended to the fields of consumption, production, investment and trade, thereby giving birth to what was called the licence-permit raj.

By the 1990s, academics and politicians had grown increasingly critical of the consequences arising from a 'grace and favour' state in which the Congress and bureaucracy presided over extensive industrial regulation. Not only did it encourage political corruption (Singh, 1997), but it also undermined flexibility and initiative in both the public and private sectors of industry. Opportunities for export-led growth, shared by other Asian countries, were neglected. India's annual rate of economic growth of around 3 per cent was not only easily surpassed by the 'Asian tigers', but by neighbouring Pakistan. The planning exercise achieved the goal of self-reliance, but it was increasingly realised only at the cost of highly subsidised and inefficient state enterprises. Indeed, the poor production performance of the public sector was a factor in the slow annual rate of economic growth from the mid-1960s onwards, dubbed by some economists 'the Hindu rate of growth'.

Nehru's grandson Rajiv Gandhi (1944–1991), who came to power in the wake of his mother's assassination in October 1984, began dismantling the bureaucratic system of economic management in the 1985–6 budget. The liberalisation process accelerated in the wake of the 1990 foreign exchange crisis and the impact of globalisation (Rothermund, 1993). The longer-term negative economic consequences of Nehru's economic policy should not, however, be allowed to obscure the important part which planning played in the opening decades of independence, first in the 'ideological ensemble' of Indian nationalism and second in the physical process of nation building.

The sinews of the nation were knit more closely together by the allocation of 21 billion rupees for transport and communications by the third five-year plan (1961–6). There were also considerable achievements in the field of human development. The first four decades of Indian independence saw infant mortality halved (79 per thousand in 1993), life expectancy doubled (61 years in 1993) and adult literacy trebled (51 per cent in 1993). Despite a virtual doubling of India's population from the 1950s to the 1980s (442 million in 1960; 902 million in 1993), there was no repetition of the periodic famines of the colonial era. Higher up the social scale, by the eve of the fiftieth anniversary of independence, the 100–150-million-strong middle class had never had it so good. Nevertheless, alongside this advance there remained almost unimaginable human distress which could only begin to be understood in stark statistics. In the mid-1990s, 290 million adults were illiterate, 135 million people were denied access to primary healthcare, 44 per cent of the population lived in absolute poverty and India contained nearly one-third of the world's poor (Haq, 1997, p. 33).

There were not only persisting imbalances in class, community and gender terms, but also regionally. Over two-thirds of the female population remain illiterate in comparison with the Indian national adult average of 49 per cent illiteracy. Among males, the literacy rate varies from 72 per cent for Hindus to 55 per cent for Muslims and 53 per cent for scheduled castes (Haq, 1997, p. 32). Gender disparities are also very clearly marked with respect to malnutrition. In low-income families in rural Punjab, for example, seven times more girls (21 per cent) suffer from malnutrition than boys (3 per cent). While just over a quarter of Haryana's population, for example, live below the absolute poverty line with an income of less than one US dollar a day, in Orissa this figure rises to over 50 per cent. Punjab's per capita income is twice that of West Bengal's. Indian literacy rates vary from 41 per cent in Rajasthan to 90 per cent in Kerala. A state-level disaggregated analysis of the Human Development Index reveals that Kerala, which records the highest score, would rank internationally with China in status, while Madhya Pradesh would take its position in terms of score for life expectancy, access to education and income alongside Rwanda.

The Congress system and its post-Nehruvian decline

The Congress Party itself was as crucially important as the formal institutions of the state in providing a 'steel frame' for national integration. It was able to play this role for five main reasons: first, because of its historical prestige; second, its heterogeneous base of support; third, its broadly based ideological appeal; fourth, its access to patronage; and fifth, its accommodationist political stance which enabled it to become the voice of regional interests at the state level. The party's over-arching predominance in the political process was termed by analysts the 'Congress system' (Kothari, 1964).

Throughout the opening two decades of independence, the Congress 'system' ensured stability for the world's 'largest democracy'. It differed from the one-party state in that it was flexible and responsive to public opinion. Political competition, nevertheless, largely took the form of competition within the Congress Party rather than between it and opponents. The Congress's political dominance was such that in the three national elections of the Nehruvian era (1952, 1957 and 1962) it won three-quarters of the seats in the Lok Sabha. Flexibility and the politics of patronage came at a price. This was increased factionalism and an inability to redress social inequalities. Judith Brown has recently explained why Nehru's visions could not be realised during his lifetime (Brown, 1999, ch. 5). Many reforms relied for their implementation both on administrative services schooled in the conservative ways of the Raj and on state governments which represented the vested interests of the locally powerful. They dragged their feet, for example, over restrictions on the amount of land holdings. Moreover, those at the bottom of society lacked knowledge of their constitutional rights and the power and resources to fight for them through the courts.

Despite Indira Gandhi's (1918–84) populist sloganeering, the chances of meaningful socio-economic transformation further diminished with her weakening of the Congress structures as she grabbed more and more power to herself. The Congress thus sowed the seeds of its own post-1967 demise. Indira Gandhi hastened the process of decline by substituting centralisation of power for the malfunctioning Nehruvian system. Regional Congress organisation was allowed to atrophy and fiat from New Delhi replaced bargaining and accommodation. Damaging consequences resulted not only for the Congress but for the country.

Mrs Gandhi's 'deinstitutionalisation' of the Congress resulted in the 'nationalisation' of local crises. Justifiable grievances concerning the operation of the federal system were dismissed as 'anti-national' in character. In these circumstances, the coercive power of the state was increasingly called on to safeguard national integration. This included not only curbs on the press (the Press Objectionable Matter Act), detention without trial (the Defence of India Act and the Maintenance of Internal Security Act) but the imposition of President's Rule in the states. Mrs Gandhi increasingly utilised what had been intended as a power of last resort in time of national emergency to remove troublesome opposition governments. It should be remembered that this was not without precedent. In July 1959 Nehru had removed the democratically elected CPI-led Kerala state government headed by E. M. S. Namboodiripad (Hardgrave, 1979, p. 225). Following Tamil agitation, an anti-secession law was passed in 1963 as a constitutional amendment.

The centralisation of authority and coercion reached its peak during the 1975–77 emergency. Political opponents of Mrs Gandhi were arrested under the provisions of the Maintenance of Internal Security Act. A rigid press censorship was imposed and a presidential order suspended the light of legal redress. Under the Defence of India Rules, 26 'extremist' organisations including the RSS were banned. In all over 100,000 people were detained without trial during the emergency era.

Apologists for India's democratic achievement have pointed out the unique circumstances of the emergency, which included Mrs Gandhi's personal insecurities arising from the threat of her political disqualification because of conviction for 'corrupt electoral practices'. They have also maintained that the strength of democratic norms was confirmed both by Mrs Gandhi's attempts to justify her actions within the framework of the constitution and by her acceptance of the unforeseen outcome of the 1977 elections which voted her out of office. A more pessimistic assessment emphasises the speed with which the emergency was implemented and the continued existence of the Maintenance of Internal Security Act on the statute book. Further evidence for the coercive power of the Indian state is provided by the burgeoning paramilitary police services and the ruthless counter-insurgency which has been mounted in the troubled states of Punjab and Jammu and Kashmir in recent years.

India's diversity meant, however, that the process of constructing a national coalition to challenge the Congress was arduous. Significantly, it was at the state level that its political fortunes first declined. Regional parties such as Telegu Desam, and earlier the DMK and AIADMK made inroads into its power in the south, and the CMP in Bengal. It was, however, the BJP which aimed to fill the vacuum left by the Congress at the centre. Its rise to prominence in the 1980s accelerated the decline in public support for India's foundational beliefs. Its initial breakthrough occurred in the 1989 general elections, when it secured 89 seats in the Lok Sabha, although it polled less than 12 per cent of the votes. Two years later, in an election whose tone was changed by Rajiv Gandhi's assassination, it emerged as the second-largest party with 119 seats, having obtained nearly 20 per cent of the popular vote.

The BJP successfully articulated Hindu nationalist beliefs, in part because of the exhaustion of the Congress. It was also able to build on the years of patient organisational work laid by its 'Mother' organisation the RSS. As we shall see in the next chapter, it benefited both from the insecurities brought by globalisation and by the new opportunities this provided for transmitting its message. The palpable sense of the upper castes being under siege from the insubordination of the rising lower castes and from the threat both within and externally of Islamisation was also a powerful factor which enabled it to ride the Ayodhya wave to national prominence. The party represents a blending of neo-traditionalism and modernity. The latter is evidenced in its slick PR and use of the 'new media'. Indeed one theme of the BJP is the desire to make India strong in the modern world by acquiring through economic liberalisation the fruits of a high-technology economy to India. This is countered, however, by the attachment of RSS members to a reworked Gandhian *swadeshi* approach to economic development. Neo-traditionalism is also attested to by the use of religious slogans and symbols and by the continued drive to homogenise the Hindu faith tradition.

It was clear by the mid-1990s that the BJP faced a dilemma in the drive for national power. Its upper-caste, North India composition limited its appeal at the time when politics were becoming both increasingly regionalised and caste-based, as seen in the rise of the Samajwadi and Bahujan Samaj parties. Once in government, the BJP suffered the same claims of corruption as its Congress rival. The 'victory' of the demolition of the Babri Masjid on 6 December 1992 did not prevent the defeat of 'corrupt' and inefficient BJP governments in state polls in Uttar Pradesh, Himachal Pradesh and Madhya Pradesh in 1993. Although the largest single party following the 1996 general elections, the BJP national government, in the absence of coalition partners, survived for just two weeks. Pragmatists within the BJP argued for an expansion in its support base, but the RSS purists would brook no compromise with the traditional disavowal of caste divisions within the Hindu *jati*. The outcome was what some scholars have termed 'indirect Mandalisation' in that while the BJP still remained an upper-caste organisation, it constructed regional alliances with parties whose support base rested on the OBCs. The strategy culminated in the establishment of a BJP government following the February 1998 Lok Sabha elections.

The resulting Vajpayee national BJP-led government was, however, an unwieldy coalition which, to the dislike of RSS purists, backtracked on earlier promises regarding the repeal of Kashmir's special constitutional status and on establishing a uniform civil code. Like earlier BJP state governments in Gujarat and Madhya Pradesh, the exercise of power encouraged a breakdown in discipline. RSS ideologues unfavourably dubbed this as the 'Congressisation' of the BJP. In economic policy, for example, divisions opened up between the RSS-dominated Swadeshi Jagaran Manch with its emphasis on austerity and *swadeshi* and the Vajpayee government's attachment to domestic liberalisation with its attendant consumerism at home and a 'calibrated globalisation', i.e. encouraging foreign investment in pursuit of technological advance in selected sectors. Thomas Blom Hansen has wittily labelled such differences in outlook as 'Kar Sevaks [temple volunteers] Versus Car Sevaks' (Hansen 1998, p. 306).

The media and nation building: Doordarshan, the Ramayana and the image of the nation

The Congress not only inherited the coercive instruments of the colonial state, but its monopoly of radio and later television broadcasting. This has been deployed to assist nation building, both in the cultural field in the proliferation of Hindi and Hindu values and in the use of satellite technology in the mid-1970s in the attempt to disseminate rural development educational messages.

Private radio transmitters had been established in Bombay and Calcutta in 1927, but within three years the colonial authorities had taken them over and banned private broadcasting. The 1935 Government of India Act provided a legal cover for centralised control of broadcasting. After independence, officials from the Ministry of Information and Broadcasting maintained a close control over All-India Radio and later over the television network, Doordarshan. The first television broadcast was made in 1959. Its expansion was limited by the shortages of transmitters and sets. India's successful indigenous INSAT satellite programme, however, eventually provided the technological base for a Delhi-centred national network. By the late 1990s, signals could be received by over 80 per cent of the population, the vagaries of power supply notwithstanding. The number of sets had risen from three million at the beginning of the 1980s to 35 million by the early 1990s. The impetus for growth, as acknowledged by the 1966 Chanda Committee Report, was to link television with the goal of nation building rather than to provide mass entertainment. This sphere was left to the market-orientated cinema industry.

Programming was designed to promote national values. As recently as 1996, the Ministry of Information and Broadcasting stated that Doordarshan's 'main aim is national integration, inculcating a sense of unity and making people proud that they are Indians' (Ohm, 1999, p. 82). Doordarshan took its cue from the earlier example of All-India Radio in broadcasting its news reports in Sanskritised Hindi. This not only increased Urdu's marginalisation, but clearly subordinated regional languages which were relegated to their own special cultural slots. Pakistan Television (PTV) served a similar role in national integration in privileging Urdu which was spoken by a relatively smaller minority than Hindi in India. PTV, if anything, was even duller than Doordarshan. This was certainly the case during the Zia era, when hours were given over to devotional programming. Before the advent of trans-national satellite television, Pakistanis escaped by watching their videos or by tuning into the Doordarshan Amritsar transmitter. PTV signals can equally be received in parts of North India. They were in fact jammed by the Indian government, during the 1999 Kargil conflict.

From the time of the fortieth anniversary of independence celebrations onwards, Doordarshan broadcast a series of promotional clips around the theme of Mera Bharat Mahaan (My India is Great). They included scenes from military displays on Republic Day, shots of such independence movement figures as Mahatma Gandhi and Subhas Chandra Bose, and increasingly new national icons including cricket stars.

Doorsdarshan simultaneously shed a part of its stilted image with the advent of commercials, which were frequently more entertaining than the main programmes, and the networking of such soap operas as *Buniyaad* ('Foundation') and *Nukkad* ('Street Corner') produced by independent studios. These soap operas paved the way for the serialisation of such historical/religious epics as *Tipu Sultan*, the *Mahabharata*, the *Ramayana* and *Chanakya*. The first of these productions about the eighteenth-century Mysorian Muslim ruler was only broadcast after a court case. This defeated its attempt, if this was intended, to bring Muslims into the Indian main-stream, by forcing each episode to be introduced by a disclaimer to the effect that the contents were fiction rather than historical fact. *Chanakya* appeared intentionally to equate Indian history with Hindu history, for its central focus in the account of the ancient Mauryan Empire was not the Emperor Ashoka who converted to Buddhism, but his Hindu advisor Chanakya (Farmer, 1996, p. 207).

The most significant production in terms of its impact, however, was the adaptation of the religious epic, the Ramayana. This was broadcast to a spell-bound nation on Sunday mornings from 25 January 1987 to 31 July 1988. The independent Punjabi producer Ramanand Sagar had struggled to acquire bureaucratic support for the project. Some critics (Z. Hasan,1996, p. 92) have linked its broadcast with the wider 'Ayodhya strategy' of Rajiv Gandhi's government, designed to conciliate the rising influence of the BJP. This included the government-controlled Hindi Language Trust's publication of low-priced editions of Tulsidas's version of the Ramayana. As is well known, the Congress state government in a sense made the campaign to 'liberate' Ram's alleged birthplace at Ayodhya possible by in 1986 encouraging the unlocking of the mosque built by Babar which stood on the disputed site. However, at the time of the first televised episodes no one anticipated the eventual success of the production, whether in terms of the massive income generated by advertisements during its screening, or the profound impact it was to exert on the viewing public. The cessation of public activity during the course of the weekly transmission; the instances of mass devotion including the transformation of television sets into makeshift altars decorated with garlands and sandalwood paste; the pooling of village resources in order to rent television sets; and the fervour which greeted public appearances of the actors and producer have all been well documented (Lutgendorf, 1990).

There has been considerable controversy concerning the serial's 'inad-vertent' promotion of Ram iconography and increased awareness of Ayodhya, which were to be appropriated by the BJP in its mobilisation around the 'liberation' from Muslim control of the Ramjanmabhoomi (birth-place). Moreover, it has been argued that the production also fed indirectly into the current of Hindutva by promoting a North Indian homogenised standardised version of the Ramayana epic which marginalised tribal and regional variants, including the role reversal of the Tamilian account. It is true, however, that there are countercurrents to this hegemonic tendency in the production. Sager, for example, depicted Ravan more as a 'magnificent Dravidian monarch' than as the demon of traditional Ram Lila theatrical productions. Tamil sensibilities were also pandered to in the inclusion of speeches in which Ram praises their 'divine' language. The early episodes dealing with Ram and his brother Bharat's education stressed 'humanistic' values. Nevertheless, the popular reception of the televised broadcasts appears to bear out the argument that they assisted the BJP 'project of funda-mentalism' (Farmer, 1996, p. 102). Festive illuminations and the distribution of sweets greeted the visual depiction of the establishment of Ramraj following Ram's return to Ayodhya from his exile. While it is not possible to link the later Muslim–Hindu clashes at Ayodhya to the television imagery, there were instances of attacks by Sikh militants on public viewings of the production both in Punjab and neighbouring Haryana. In the most serious incident, 15 people were killed and 30 injured in an attack on an audience viewing Ramayana outside an electronics shop at Kurukshetra in June 1988.

Three years after its final transmission, the BJP was still intent on appropriating the appeal of the series for its own cause. Deepika Chikalia, the previously unknown actress who had played the role of Sita in the production, was given a BJP ticket in the parliamentary elections of that year. The ceremonial chariot processions (*rath yatras*) which accompanied the intensification of the campaign to liberate Ram's birthplace at Ayodhya significantly copied aspects of the costuming and iconography of the Doordarshan series. This reflected in part the BJP leader L. K. Advani's previous ministerial responsibilities with respect to the media which made him, in Victoria Farmer's phrase, 'probably the most media-savvy figure in Indian politics' (Farmer, 1996, p. 207). It also resulted from the Vishwa Hindu Parishad's (VHP or World Hindu Congress) approach to Hindu consolidation.

The VHP had been founded in 1964 as an offshoot of the RSS with the goal of creating an umbrella Hindu organisation that would counteract sectarian and caste-based divisions. We have noted in earlier chapters how fears of Hindu disunity had greatly exercised the minds of nineteenth-century reformers. Such varied figures as Dayananda, Vivekananda and Aurobindo had looked to ideological reformulation to solve the 'weakness' arising from pluralism. Such an approach, with its emphasis on the reworking of scripture, had its limitations in a semi-literate society. Moreover, as the Arya Samaj experience illustrated, it could also increase the very sectarianism it sought to eradicate. The VHP has instead brought a 'cumulative' rather than 'reformist' approach to consolidation. Its activities have been focused on the development of unifying symbols rather than intellectual argument. Although not a creation of the video and television age, it has benefited from the ability to use this new media. In 1984, in a Dharam Sansad (Assembly of Faith) in Delhi, the VHP adopted the goal of ' liberating' temple sites occupied by Muslims in North India as a means to achieve Hindu consolidation. The Ramjanmabhoomi at Ayodhya was singled out as the initial focus of its efforts. In such circumstances the serialisation of the Ramayana was a veritable godsend in raising popular consciousness and providing a repertoire of powerful visual images for appropriation.

Kargil: India's first televised war

Television was dominated during June and July 1999 by the Kargil conflict with Pakistan. Everything from light entertainment to advertising was linked to the events in the remote Tiger Hills. Television reporters like other journalists were kept well away from the battleground, although shots of them in combat gear near disused military bunkers gave the viewers the feeling of closer proximity to the events than in any previous Indo-Pakistan conflict. Television, like newspapers, also went to town on 'human interest' stories concerning the discomforts of the troops and the support for their bravery 'from the home-front'.

Newscasts of funerals of martyred Indian *jawans* sustained an intense pro-war feeling. The outpouring of national pride and fervour also included a strong 'Anti-Paki' sentiment. Television even less than the press did not question the costs, human and economic, of the conflict. Nor was there anything in the coverage other than ready acceptance of the army's daily briefing. The Belgrano-type debate which occurred in Britain during the Falklands War was conspicuously absent, even when there were obvious contradictions in army assessments of intelligence failures and Pakistan's preparedness for conflict, and in the continuing numbers of casualties after victory had been announced.

Bollywood, popular culture and Indian identity

The Bombay-based cinema, popularly known as Bollywood, has been driven by market forces, and despite the censorship imposed by the 1952 Cinematograph Act has never been totally controlled by the Indian state. Heavy-handed restriction has been avoided both by the precensorship of scripts and by the personal desires of writers and producers not to indulge in 'objectionable' subject matter. These pressures combined to place films on partition 'off limits' for many years. Indeed it was not until 1973 that a young Hindu film-maker from Kerala, M. S. Sathyu, traversed this uncharted territory with a Hindi production centring around the experiences of a Muslim family from Agra in the aftermath of partition. Although *Garm Hawa* ('Scorching Wind') was an adaptation of the respected female novelist Ismat Chugtai's work, Sathyu had to lobby hard before the censor board's ban on the production was lifted.

Cinema has been a far more popular medium than the state-controlled television. Its influence is revealed by the fact that, at the beginning of the 1990s, 12 million Indians viewed films every day. Moreover, many more were exposed to *filmi* culture by listening to music tapes, especially those of the prodigious 'play-back' songstress Lata Mangeshkar with her 30,000 or so recordings. The Bombay-based film industry is the most productive in the world in terms of its output. To the outsider this may frequently appear formulaic and escapist in content, but it is undeniably popular and one must reluctantly concur with Peter Manuel's (1993, p. xiii) judgement that the Allahabadi cinema megastar turned Congress politician Amitabh Bachchan is 'a far more significant and familiar name to most North Indians' than the freedom fighter Subhas Chandra Bose or the great Mughal Shah Jahan.

Film-makers have been happy to assist nation-building purposes. Early post-independence films stressed the themes of Hindu–Muslim unity (*Mughal-e-Azam, Taj Mahal*) and in their iconography and patriotic songs (as in, for example, Satyen Bose's 1954 production *Jagriti*) assisted in the invention of a national tradition. Mehboob Khan's 1957 production *Mother India* was not only the greatest box-office success of its day, running for 50 weeks in Bombay, but has been most commented upon as a nation-building picture. While it borrowed its title from the freedom movement's identification of India with the Mother, it projects through the character of Radha, played by the leading Muslim actress Nargis, the stereotype of the suffering woman who provides continuity and keeps her community together despite the depredations of the village moneylender, Sukhilala. This stereotype of suffering motherhood, as we have seen, was deployed by Gandhi to good effect during the freedom struggle. Radha, despite losing two of her sons and her husband in a flood, refuses to become Sukhilala's mistress in return for his support. She eventually rebuilds her life and is acknowledged as the 'mother of the whole village'. As she sings to the peasants, in the name of the Mother, a map of pre-partition India forms on the screen. The film is, however, more than the traditional celebration of ideal Indian womanhood and of Bharat Mata, as it also alludes to the Nehruvian goals of nation building through modernisation with its shots of tractors, machinery and dams. Scenes of cheerful communal agricultural endeavour, including one in which Radha is silhouetted on the skyline hoe on her shoulder, would not appear out of place in Soviet films, perhaps hardly surprising as the hammer and sickle formed the logo of the Mehboob productions (Chakravarty, 1993, p. 156).

Within the space of two decades, however, such films as *Godhali* (1977) and *Manthan* (1976) were far less self-confident in associating modernisation and nation building. Both films focus on the clashes arising from the onset of change in village India. Indeed the dusk of the title of the former production is symbolic of the transition between old and new. The character Nandan who returns to his village after some years abroad is portrayed as ultimately defeated and confused in his endeavours to introduce new farming techniques (Chakravarty, 1993, p. 258). The cinema of the past two decades has not only reflected the fading blush of Nehruvian enthusiasm for state-led modernisation, but, as Akbar Ahmed (1992) has pointed out, has mirrored changing social attitudes, with increasing recourse to sex (with the obligatory wet sari scene) and violence marked by such films as *Bobby, Satyam, Shivam*, and *Sundaram*. The decline of Muslim stars and producers, Akbar Ahmed maintains, mirrors the growing marginalisation of the Muslim community within Indian society (see Hasan 1997). Chidananda Das Gupta (1991) has concurred that the Hindi cinema marginalises minorities. He also argues that since the 'revenge films' of Amitabh Bachchan in the 1980s, it has glorified 'nihilistic violence' and helped promote the 'macabre marriage of consumerism and fundamentalism' which threatens the social fabric.

Nationalism is undoubtedly now portrayed in an aggressive way in oppo-sition to the Pakistani 'other' as seen most clearly in the controversial but successful film *Border*, which was released just two months before the fiftieth anniversary of independence celebrations. This picture, set at the time of the 1971 Bangladesh War, directed by J. P. Dutta and starring Sunny Deol, drew packed houses in India to its portrayal of a battle in which 120 lightly armed Indian soldiers successfully combated a Pakistani tank unit with over 1,500 troops. *Border* aroused similar enthusiasm and misgivings when it was released in Britain. Rumours that it contained a scene in which the Quran was burnt sparked a riot involving 300 youths in Leeds outside a video store selling pirated copies. Dr Siddique, then head of the self-styled Muslim Parliament, claimed that it was irresponsible to distribute the film in Britain.

Bombay (1995), directed by Mani Ratnam, has aroused similar contro-versy because of its subject matter of the Hindu–Muslim riots which wreaked havoc in the wake of the destruction of the Babri Masjid at Ayodhya. Alongside a graphic portrayal of violence there is, however, a return to the theme of composite national solidarity. A riot is prevented when one of the characters douses himself in kerosene and face to face dares the crowd to torch him. As the mob throw their torches to the ground, one is disposed of in a puddle in which is the inverted outline of a map of India. There follows a Hindi song which translates as follows:

> Everyone full of hope and full of dreams
> At last finds peace
> But out of that night
> Comes a new dawn
> Nothing else matters
> A ray of bright light
> Will shine down on us
> There will be no fear
> For it will pass
> Even if the garden is ravaged
> Spring will come again.[1]

The rise of Shiv Sena which will be explored in Chapter 9 has inevitably impacted upon the Bombay cinema. From March 1970 onwards, the Shiv Sena institutionalised its relations with the film industry through the Chitrapat Shaka (the Shiv Sena-run film production board). It aimed both to promote Marathi films and artists and to raise funds for its parent organ-isation. The Chitrapat Shakha also makes Oscar-type academy awards. Since Shiv Sena's emergence as the dominant political force in Bombay, the large number of Muslim actors have found it more difficult to secure roles. In August 1968, Bal Thackeray called upon the renowned actor Dilip Kumar to

---

[1] I am grateful to Rajinder Kumar Dudrah for bringing this clip to my attention.

publicly apologise for criticising Shiv Sena or face a boycott of his films. A Bombay cinema showing him in a starring role was vandalised at this time. Shiv Sena agitation against 'unsuitable' films was well established even by this early date (Gupta, 1982, pp. 87, 167, 169). The veteran director Avtar Kishan Hangal was forced on another occasion to publicly apologise to Shiv Sena for depicting Muslim characters in too favourable a light.

Film-makers such as G. Shiduke and N. Patekar have been closely associated with Shiv Sena. The latter's 1986 production *Ankush* epitomises Shiv Sena culture. Thackeray has taken a great interest in Bollywood and has increasingly adopted the persona of an ageing matinee idol, making up his face and dyeing his hair. Drawing on the popular concern that sections of the film industry had financial connections with Dubai-based Muslim criminal mafias, Thackeray has increasingly sought the suspension of 'anti-national' producers and actors and called for films which respect 'the Hindu way of life'.

Finally, it is important to note that it is not just the content of Bollywood films but their medium of expression that has impacted on nation building. Indeed the Bombay-based film could be seen as the most effective vehicle for the promotion of Hindi as the national language.

Colonial legacies and nation building

Nehru with his statism and attachment to non-alignment and the Hindutva movement with its cultural nationalism have both represented the conception that the creation of a modern India involved a sharp break with the colonial past. We have already alluded, however, to the important institutional continuities which smoothed the path of nation building. Until 1950 India was governed under the terms of the 1935 Government of India Act. The Indian Administrative Service inherited the traditions of the so-called 'steel-frame' of the Raj, the Indian Civil Service. The Indian Army was also bequeathed the professionalism of its colonial counterpart. The decision to widen recruitment from the martial castes did represent a break with the past, but it was as much the strong functioning of democratic institutions and values as this innovation that marked India's different post-colonial career compared with its Pakistani neighbour. The Congress itself, of course, bridged the British and independence eras and derived much of its moral authority in the 1950s and 1960s from its role in the freedom struggle.

We have spoken much of the significance of Hindi as a national language, but it is also important to note the role of English in the Indian nation-building process. It has not only continued to provide a common language at elite level, but has increasingly proved an asset in India's opening up to the processes of globalisation. There was fierce debate in the early post-independence era as to whether English should continue to receive official recognition. The political decision was made, however, to retain it as a link language, for administrative purposes, between the Hindi-speaking north and the Tamil-speaking south of the subcontinent.

If English at the local level has been indigenised since independence, the same can be said for cricket, another imperial inheritance that has played a crucial role in both India's and Pakistan's national self-perception. Cricket, like a number of other sports, acquired a global audience with the shrinking of the world in the twentieth century. While global economic activities and the transmission of information have undermined the sovereignty of the nation state, national identity has been given a new arena for focus in international sporting events. Success in these arenas enables, in the words of a Pakistani journalist, 'poor nations of the third world' to 'cover-up for their backwardness in all other modern fields'. The opportunity to take on and defeat their former colonial master and originator of the game has certainly boosted self-esteem both in the subcontinent and among their teams' supporters settled in England, notwithstanding the strictures of the Tebbit test for the diasporas' citizenship.

The keenest rivalry, however, has been evoked by matches between India and Pakistan, which have sometimes been billed as 'war minus the shooting'. During the course of such 'hostilities' India in particular has perpetuated its own stereotype of secularism counterposed to the Pakistani 'other'. Going into the 1996 Cricket World Cup, for example, much was made of the fact that the Indian squad was captained by a Muslim, the monosyllabic Azharuddin, included a Sikh opening batsmen (Navjot Singh Sidhu) and that its two young-gun pin-ups were the bulky Brahmin Sachin Tendulkar and the pony-tailed Dalit, Kambli. Pakistani cricket, on the other hand, was portrayed in both India and England as demonstrating the country's and Islam's worst traits of fanaticism, corruption – involving betting, cheating and the notorious ball-tampering claims – and factionalism. In reality, personality clashes were as great in the Indian as in the Pakistani game and beneath the facade of a 'secular' selection policy were claims of favouritism based on regional and caste lines. It certainly appeared coincidental that Muslims and Gujaratis who had once been important components of the Bombay Ranji Cup team had disappeared from view following the rise of the chauvinist Shiv Sena to political prominence in Maharashtra.

It is important to note that the rivalry between India and Pakistan was once regarded as being that of a game, rather than encapsulating national strength and identity. Indeed it was the Indian Cricket Board that proposed in July 1952 that Pakistan be admitted to coveted test match status. The early contests between the countries in the mid-1950s were marked by sportsmanship from the players and good humour from the spectators. When sporting contact was resumed in 1978 after an 18-year gap (occasioned by the 1965 and 1971 conflicts) partisanship was noticeably keener. This was intensified by the advent of wider television coverage and by the one-day game with its drama and the removal of the traditional option of a face-saving draw, which had been a marked feature of test matches between the countries.

The rise of communal forces also took its toll. Indian defeats by the Imran Khan-inspired Pakistan team of the 1980s were used by Hindutva ideologues both to castigate Hindus for their 'softness' and to reinforce the stereotype of the 'macho Muslim male'. The Shiv Sena leader Bal Thackeray, in a subcontinental version of the Tebbit test, claimed that he wanted Indian Muslims to prove their national loyalty with 'tears in their eyes' whenever India lost to Pakistan. On the eve of a 1990–1 tour, the Shiv Sena press ranted that the presence of the Pakistani team was an 'insult to the nation's integrity' and a security threat. The visit was eventually cancelled after Shiv Sena supporters poured oil on the test match square at the Wankhede stadium in Bombay. Three years later another Pakistani tour was called off at the last minute.

The advent of satellite television and the presence of large numbers of Pakistani and Indian migrant workers in the Gulf meant that the cricket rivalry between the two countries was increasingly fought out on the 'neutral' territory of Sharjah. The most celebrated contest occurred in April 1986 when the pugnacious Pakistani batsman Javed Miandad hit a winning six off the final ball of the Austral-Asia Cup. This was immortalised in Pakistan in Saleem Lodhi's pop song 'Sharjah ka chhekka kargaye hukka-pukka' ('Six in Sharjah devastated the world'). National pride in the Pakistani team reached its climax some six years later when Imran Khan's team lifted the World Cup in Melbourne. By the time of the 1996 trophy, the link between cricket and nation building had become explicit in a plethora of songs and videos. These ranged from the joint Pepsi and PTV-sponsored 'Hum jeetain Gae' ('We Will Win') with its images of the Pakistan squad practising in the elegant surroundings of the elite Aitchison College, Lahore, to the rock group Junoon's anthem 'Jasbaan-e-Junoon' ('The Joy of Madness'). The video juxtaposed the group performing the song with footage of the Pakistan squad and *galli* (back alley) cricketers. The verses included the repeated refrain, 'Pehchaan kabhina bhulo' ('Never forget your identity') and talked of 'apne ghar, apne sarzamin' ('our home, our native land'). The nationalist chord emerged most strongly, however, in the chorus: 'Pakistan kabhina bhulo, Pakistan hai tumhara, Pakistan hai hamara' ('Never forget Pakistan, Pakistan is yours, Pakistan is ours') (Marqusee, 1996, p. 70).

The 1999 World Cup played in England occurred against the background of the fighting in the Kargil region of Kashmir as Indian forces tried to displace Pakistani-backed 'infiltrators'. The *Times of India* reported that troops at the front were closely following the competition, including one who was reported as declaring, 'Tell Sachin [Sachin Tendulkar, the Indian master batsman] to take some rest as we blow the daylights out of Pakistan. They'd better know that this is not cricket, they just cannot win.' Journalists dubbed the meeting between India and Pakistan on the cricket field as a 'battle'. The *Indian Express* in its report of 8 June declared that the match 'seems the next best thing to war'. The Indian victory was greeted with such headlines in the *Asian Age* as 'Reborn India kill Pak'. Every bit as distasteful was a computer game available at the time entitled 'I love India' in which the user could destroy Lahore.

For corporate India, Kargil and India went hand in hand as events that could be 'milked for financial gain'. Advertisements featuring prominent players had appeared in newspapers for weeks leading up to the tournament. Similarly products were advertised with part of their proceeds going to war victims. There were Kargil television entertainment specials and Kargil designer shows, leading one prominent columnist, Nivedita Menon, to write in the *Times of India* about 'Plastic patriotism in times of war'.

Conclusion

At the dawn of the twenty-first century India remains a nation in the making. The pressures of globalisation and of Hindu nationalism have transformed some of the key institutions and ideas in the nation-building process. The Congress and the Planning Commission have lost their significance, although legacies from the era of their dominance such as a professional army, an apolitical bureaucracy and an independent election commission have eased India's development in comparison with neighbouring Pakistan.

The Hindutva enterprise of the reinvention of India as a Hindu *rashtra* may not succeed in the face of rising caste and regional allegiances. It has, nevertheless, both contributed to and benefited from the discrediting of India's foundational secular ideal. It is important, however, to avoid a simplistic association of Congress with secularism and the BJP with communalism. The Congress under Indira Gandhi's and Rajiv Gandhi's leadership utilised religious symbolism to undercut both lower-caste-based rivals and the emerging BJP. Indira Gandhi sought to consolidate Hindu support by playing up a 'Sikh menace'. Rajiv, in 1985, placated Muslim 'fundamentalists' in the Shah Bano case involving a Muslim woman's right to maintenance and simultaneously reopened the disputed religious site at Ayodhya. Four years later he commenced the general election campaign in neighbouring Faizabad and spoke of creating a Ram Rajya (rule of Ram) (Hansen, 1999, p. 150).

Proponents of Hindutva argue that politics are being indigenised, while its opponents lament the loss of Nehru's internationalist vision. Community and national identity has become increasingly forged on the basis of hostility to a Muslim/Pakistani 'other'. This was demonstrated most clearly at the time of the military clashes in the Kargil region of Kashmir in the summer of 1999.

The Indian Army's decision to dispatch home the bodies of ordinary soldiers, instead of just officers as it had done in the past, contributed to the whipping up of an almost hysterical war fever. Martyrdom was celebrated in funerals which were attended by political functionaries both of the BJP and the Congress. Such events encouraged emotional reporting with such photographs and captions as 'tears of pride' showing a widow saluting her husband's coffin. The demonisation of Pakistan reached its peak with unsubstantiated claims of Pakistani torture of six Indian soldiers. Earlier, a headline on 28 June had screamed 'Pakis, play dirty, booby trap body of army officer' (sic). National remembrances were held and collections were made for these victims of the conflict. Indian national pride, however, still did not extend to the erection of a single memorial for the hundreds of thousands of innocent civilian victims of the 1947 partition upheavals.

8

Nation building in Pakistan: ideas and institutions

You are free; you are free to go to your temples, you
are free to go to any other place of worship in this State of
Pakistan ... You may belong to any religion or caste or creed –
that has nothing to do with the business of the State ... We are
starting with this fundamental principle that we are all citizens
and equal citizens of one State ... Now, I think we should keep
that in front of us as our ideal and you will find that in course of
time Hindus will cease to be Hindus and Muslims will cease to
be Muslims, not in the religious sense, because that is the personal
faith of each individual, but in the political sense as citizens of the
State.

Mohammad Ali Jinnah, presidential address to the Constituent
Assembly of Pakistan at Karachi, 11 August 1947

Pakistan which was created in the name of Islam, will continue
to survive only if it sticks to Islam. That is why I consider the
introduction of [an] Islamic system as an essential prerequisite
for the country.

Zia-ul-Haq, 1977

The freedom struggle had left unresolved the question of whether Pakistan
should be run on secular or Islamic lines. Indeed, the debate about Islam's
role in Pakistan's public life still rages on over half a century since independence. Equally contested is the relationship between Pakistani nationalism and
ethnic and linguistic allegiances. The latter were partially submerged during
the freedom struggle. Their power in comparison with a state-centred
identity of recent construction was summed up by the famous phrase of the
Pushtun nationalist Wali Khan, son of Adbul Ghaffar Khan the 'Frontier
Gandhi', when he declared in the 1980s 'I have been a Pushtun for 4,000
years, a Muslim for 1,400 years and a Pakistani for 40 years'.

The Pakistan state has been manifestly unsuccessful in accommodating diversity. This was evidenced most dramatically in its increasingly bitter conflict with Bengali nationalists which culminated in the breakup of the country in 1971. The mere fact of diversity cannot solely explain Pakistan's post-independence travail, as India has in the main successfully accommodated an even more bewildering range of languages, ethnic groups and religions. One explanation which has been frequently proffered is that democracy has served the Indian nation-building process well and its absence in Pakistan has dealt a major blow to national unity. We saw in the last chapter that such a view ignores the two-edged nature of Indian democracy with respect to particularist identities. It is nevertheless undeniable that successive bouts of military rule in Pakistan have reinforced centrifugal ethnic, linguistic and regional forces. Difference has not only gone unacknowledged, but there has been a tendency to treat all dissent as a law-and-order rather than a political problem.

Depoliticisation, populism briefly under Zulfiqar Ali Bhutto, and Islamisation have all been deployed to bring about a sense of national unity. Depoliticisation – the reduction of participation in the political process – was designed to keep the lid on pluralist demands. Under Pakistan's first bout of martial law, which began in October 1958, guided democracy was accompanied by a strong commitment to socio-economic modernisation. Under the second, following Zia-ul-Haq's 1977 coup, however, depoliticisation and Islamisation went hand in hand. Indeed, in the early years of Zia's martial law it was maintained that democracy and Islam were incompatible.

Unlike in India, neither the constitution nor political parties have been the central institutions in the nation-building process. In their absence, the bureaucracy and the army have played a key role. Indeed, the generals have wielded great influence behind the scenes even during periods of civilian rule. Ironically, given its self-perception as a pillar of Pakistan, the unrepresentative ethnic composition of the army has none the less proved a stumbling block to national integration. Before examining the major ideas and institutions in Pakistan's nation-building enterprise, it is necessary to focus initially on the massive problems which threatened to strangle the country at birth. Pakistan's survival in the aftermath of partition provides important clues both to its resilience and to the long-term problems which have beset the state.

The aftermath of partition

It is easy to overlook the fact that Pakistan's survival hung in the balance in the immediate post-independence era. India had inherited both the colonial state's central apparatus in the former imperial capital New Delhi and the Bengal provincial secretariat in Calcutta. Pakistan, on the other hand, had to improvise its federal government in the provisional capital at Karachi. Basic office equipment and even accommodation space were in short supply as a result of the almost total cessation of building activity during the war years, even though Karachi's population had risen from about 375,000 in 1941 to 600,000 on the eve of partition. By July 1947 even prominent British government officials were being evicted from their homes to furnish accommodation for incoming Pakistani bureaucrats. A new provincial government also had to be created at Dhaka in East Pakistan.

The state was not only to be constructed from scratch, but with scanty industrial and financial resources. Partition left most industrial development in India, and separated Pakistani raw materials from their markets. The main cotton-producing areas of what became West Pakistan, for example, had supplied the raw materials to mills in Bombay and Ahmedabad. Just 14 of the subcontinent's 394 cotton mills were located in Pakistan at the time of partition. East Pakistan, which produced the bulk of the world's raw jute supply, did not in fact boast a single mill, as during the colonial era all the crop was dispatched to Calcutta where it was made into hessian and exported. As British officials acknowledged before the partition of Bengal, East Bengal without Calcutta would be reduced to a 'rural slum'. East Pakistan during the 1950s and 1960s was unable to overcome its relative backwardness at the time of partition, with increasingly dangerous political consequences.

Shorn of industry, the new Pakistan state entered into existence desperately short of cash. In the two months before independence, three billion rupees had been transferred out of the Punjab and Frontier alone by Hindu and Sikh capitalists, while the Chartered Bank of Sind informally reckoned a capital flight of a tenth of a billion rupees each week of June 1947. Bankruptcy was further threatened by Pakistan's meagre share of the assets inherited from the Raj. In principle it was entitled to 17.5 per cent of the assets of undivided India, but the growing mistrust between the two governments prevented a smooth division of the spoils. It was not until December 1947 that an agreement was reached on Pakistan's share of the cash balances. The bulk of this (Rs 550 million) was held back by the government of India as a result of the hostilities in Kashmir following the former Princely State's controversial accession to India. It was only paid on 15 January 1948 after Gandhi's intervention and fast which led to his assassination.

The refugee problem's magnitude is brought home by the stark fact that one in ten of the population, some seven million people, were enumerated as of refugee origin in Pakistan's 1951 census. In the three and a half months which followed independence, 4.6 million Muslims were evacuated from the East Punjab alone. This flood of refugees was totally unexpected and had never been an intended consequence of the Pakistan demand. Indeed, the so-called 'hostage' theory saw the advantage of the existence of large minority populations in both India and Pakistan. The only anticipatory migration which Jinnah had encouraged was the establishment of some 'nation-building' enterprises in the Pakistan areas.

The bulk of the migrants were 'acute' refugees, driven out by ethnic cleansing in East Punjab. Urdu-speaking refugees from UP and Delhi drawn from the Muslim professional and commercial elite regarded themselves, however, as true *mohajirs* who in keeping with the Prophet Muhammad's flight from Mecca to Medina in AD 622 had left India for a religious cause. They settled mainly in Karachi, the new state's administrative and commercial capital, and in other urban centres of Sind such as Hyderabad and Sukkur. While East Punjabi migrants soon dropped the *mohajir* label and slotted culturally and economically into the West Punjab scene, the UP *mohajirs* retained their separate entity and grew increasingly estranged from the Sindhi population amongst whom they had settled. Their growing disillusionment with the Pakistan state itself, which they saw as dominated by Punjabi interests and unmindful of their sacrifices for its creation, has exerted an increasingly profound political impact. In the words of their controversial leader Altaf Hussain (b. 1953), 'We have a right to Pakistan, and it is a right of blood, we gave blood for it' (Jalal, 1995a, p. 83).

While the aftermath of partition in India resulted in growing tensions at the heart of the national government, in Pakistan it pitted the centre against the provinces and especially the government of Sind. Its Prime Minister, the Larkana district landholder Mohammad Ayub Khuhro (1901–80), strongly opposed the demand that Sind should accept those refugees who could not be absorbed in West Punjab. By December 1947 Sind had only resettled 244,000 displaced persons, while West Punjab had resettled over four million. That month its government agreed to take another 500,000 refugees provided that they were relocated in the Sukkur, Shikarpur and Mirpurkhas districts, as Karachi was 'super-saturated'. Within a month, Khuhro had reneged on this promise, declaring that Sind would be unable to rehabilitate more than 150,000 refugees during the first half of 1948. This 'uncooperative' attitude was criticised by the West Punjab Governor. In a letter to Jinnah early in 1948 he cited census figures to demonstrate that Sind had a net loss of 600,000 Hindu and Sikh agriculturalists and therefore should have no difficulty in meeting its reponsibilities.

Khuhro was severely upbraided by Raja Ghazanfar Ali (1895–1963) the Pakistan Minister for Refugees and Rehabilitation at a sub-committee meeting of the Pakistan Muslim League Council held on 23 February 1948. His defence that the local populace was suffering from the burdens imposed by the refugee influx was dismissed by Ghazanfar Ali as raising 'the virus of provincialism'. 'This is not only against the teachings of Islam and in direct contravention to the principle on which we fought for the achievement of Pakistan', Ghazanfar Ali added, 'but is a deadly weapon which if allowed to operate unchecked will destroy the foundations of our newly-born state' (*The Statesman*, Calcutta, 25 February 1948).

Unlike in India, where less land was available for resettlement, there was no attempt at land reform, although the Oxford-educated left-leaning Mian Iftikhar-ud-Din (1907–62), the Minister of Refugees and Rehabilitation in the West Punjab cabinet, in fact pressed for the kind of policies of tenancy reform and redistribution of land which were to be pursued in the resettlement programme in East Punjab. Iftikhar-ud-Din called for a 50-acre ceiling on landholdings, the nationalisation of basic industries, the provision of a dole of Rs 5 a month and the exchange of refugee property through officially appointed trustees. When the Punjab Prime Minister the Nawab of Mamdot (1906–69), himself a refugee from East Punjab, refused to countenance these demands, Iftikhar-ud-Din sensationally quit his post. His departure brought the organisational and ministerial wings of the Punjab Muslim League virtually to blows. The feudal landholders' grip thus remained and in some respects tightened as they 'illegally' acquired evacuee property and took over the moneylending activities of the departing Hindus. This reinforcement of the rural elite possessed important consequences for Pakistan's future development.

An opportunity was crucially lost for constructing a popular base for the Muslim League. The tradition was also established of emphasising administrative action rather than political initiative in dealing with Pakistan's problems. In the absence of a political lead, the British Governor of the West Punjab Sir Francis Mudie left the responsibility for the settlement of refugees on the land with the overworked Deputy Commissioners and *tehsildars* who acted as Assistant Rehabilitation Commissioners for the areas under their jurisdiction. The Deputy Commissioners were also responsible for furnishing each refugee camp within their jurisdiction with medical, food and sanitary requirements.

The immediate post-partition era also provides an important key to the future course of Indo-Pakistan relations. The refugee crisis and disputes over the division of assets, and most importantly the defining moment of the Kashmir War, established an atmosphere of hatred and mistrust. This was not something Jinnah had anticipated when on the eve of partition he was negotiating to purchase a houseboat on the idyllic Dal lake at Srinagar, the Princely State's summer capital. Pakistan turned first to Britain and ultimately the United States to counterbalance its 'strategic deficit' with India. Internally, the need for a strong central authority was accepted despite the loose federal structure envisaged by the 1940 Lahore Resolution. This in itself took the country further away from the direction of democracy, given the likely effects of centralisation on an ethnically plural society.

Pakistan as an ideological state

Pakistan has been dubbed an ideological state because of the importance of its foundational two-nation theory myth to the process of nation building.

Throughout the post-independence era the ideology of a monolithic Muslim community has countered the 'other' of Indian nationalism and 'provincialism' within Pakistan. The hegemonic tendencies of the Muslim League ideology were intensified by the successful conclusion of the freedom struggle, for this ensured the deployment of the state's resources in support of the two-nation theory. Control of educational curricula and textbook production, resort to press censorship and legislative enactment could all protect the ideological boundaries of the state. This 'brazen' process reached its peak during the Zia-ul-Haq (1922–88) era (1977–88) with the increase in censorship and the Islamisation of the history curriculum with the compulsory introduction of Pakistan Studies from secondary to university level of education. The leading Pakistani scholar K. K. Aziz (1993) has pointed out the encouragement of xenophobia and the glorification of military struggle given to an impressionable younger generation by the one-sided view of history provided in the government-approved texts. Those like myself who have been involved in the Pakistan Studies examination process for pupils of private schools studying in English can endorse his criticism of the impact of such texts on the historical imagination and understanding.

In May 1982 Zia declared that the 'preservation of that Ideology [Pakistan ideology] and the Islamic character of the country was ... as important as the security of the country's geographical boundaries' (Hasan-Askari, 1988, p. 242). The official discourse swept to one side the ambiguities of the freedom struggle, as the goal of an Islamic state was deemed to be its main basis. Jinnah the secularist became Jinnah the upholder of Islam in such writings as Karam Hydri's *Millat ka pasban* (1981), while the *'ulama* whose influence had been marginal in the creation of Pakistan were elevated to a vanguard role. By making a hegemonic Islamic ideology the pillar of the state Zia sought to solve at a stroke the identity problems which had beset it since 1947.

Newspaper articles on the occasion of the anniversary of Jinnah's birth in December 1981 omitted the words from his speech to the Constituent Assembly which we have already quoted. When the veteran Muslim Leaguer Shaukat Hayat objected to such puerile attempts to show Jinnah favouring the establishment of an Islamic state (as did the former Chief Justice Muhammad Munir in his book *From Jinnah to Zia*), a resolution was moved in the advisory body called the Majlis-i-Shura that sought to ban any verbal or written comment that 'would in any way, directly or indirectly, detract from, or derogate [Jinnah's] high status, position and achievements'. Newspapers had been subject to full pre-censorship from October 1979 onwards whereby proofs had to be submitted for scrutiny and approval prior to publication. They were also sent so called 'advices' concerning how stories should be covered, or whether they should be included at all.

There were similar attempts to censor film production in the 1979 Motion Pictures Ordinance. In addition to immorality and the undermining of religion, a film would be deemed unsuitable for public exhibition if it either contained 'propaganda in favour of a foreign state bearing on a point of dispute between that state and Pakistan' or undermined Pakistan's 'integrity or solidarity as an independent state' (Gazdar, 1997, pp. 170–1). The Ordinance served only to suffocate creative talent within Pakistan, for the state could not control the 'new media' of the video-cassette and the flood of pirated copies of Hollywood and Bollywood films into the domestic market. The Zia regime, like that of Ayub earlier, also sought to use the film industry to popularise its ideology. The main endeavour was the attempt to rewrite history by presenting Jinnah as the proponent of an Islamic state. In 1982, the year in which Richard Attenborough's acclaimed portrayal of *Gandhi* was released, production began on a film on Jinnah's life, which was entitled *Stand Up From the Dust*. The Ministries of Information and Broadcasting and of Culture were involved in the project along with the Pakistan Television Corporation and scholars and journalists sympathetic to the regime. The script was required to meet the following three requirements:

Not to be in conflict with the policies of the Martial Law regime.

To portray Jinnah as a greater leader than Gandhi and show that the creation of Pakistan was the outcome of the Quaid's [Jinnah's] supreme command over the Muslim League and his followers.

To emphasize that the Quaid-i-Azam's main motivation for founding Pakistan was to form an Islamic State as had been established by the Martial Law regime.

Gazdar (1997, p. 187)

Zia's lukewarm response to the rushes ensured that the film was never publicly released, despite the considerable costs it had incurred. In contrast to Akbar Ahmed's 1998 production, it depicted Jinnah as a cold and aloof man. Ironically, this was precisely the one-dimensional stereotype that British detractors, from the Mountbatten era onwards, had perpetuated. While the Lahore Resolution speech was included in full, there was significantly no room for the Quaid's equally important speech to the Constituent Assembly. The opening sequences of armed horsemen by the Arabian Sea reproduces the two-nation theory linkage of Pakistan's genesis with the emergence of Muhammad Bin Qasim, the first Muslim invader of India. A similar didacticism is present in the narrator's concluding comments: 'His achievement was Pakistan, an independent homeland for the Muslims of India, a sovereign state where Islam could flourish freely not merely in its religious rituals, but in culture, law, economics, in fact in every aspect of life' (Gazdar, 1997, p. 191).

This sentiment faithfully reproduced Zia's attempt to impose a unitary vision of Pakistan based on religion. In his first televised speech he had declared that 'Pakistan which was created in the name of Islam, will continue to survive only if it sticks to Islam. That is why I consider the introduction of [an] Islamic system as an essential prerequisite for the country' (Richter, 1979, p. 555). Islam was, however, less effective in providing a national cohesive force than Zia anticipated.

Lollywood and the promotion of Pakistani culture

The Urdu cinema based in Lahore (popularly known as Lollywood) has played an important role in promoting Pakistani culture. Lahore has, however, always been overshadowed by Bombay as a centre of film production, partly because of the time it took to overcome the disruptions brought by partition, which included the burning down of the famous Shorey film studios, and because of successive martial law regimes' constraints on artistic expression. Lack of investment and training facilities has meant that its products could not competete with the slicker Indian output. Hindi films have proved immensely popular in Pakistan, whether at the cinema or more recently on video. This is witnessed by the number of plagiarised versions produced in Pakistan and interestingly by Zulfikar Ali Bhutto's adoption of an Indian film title for his famous PPP slogan, *Roti, Kapra, Makan* ('food, clothes, house'). The loss of middle-class Urdu-speaking audiences to Indian-produced Hindi videos which could be viewed at home led both to the rise of downmarket Rambo-type productions and of the regional-language Pushtu and Punjabi cinemas in the 1980s.

The leading Pushtu actor Badar Munir, the son of a *maulvi* (Muslim theologian) from rural Swat, alone starred in over 250 films. Urdu cinema has made a comeback in the 1990s through such releases as the actress-turned-director Shamim Ara's 1993 film *Hathi Mera Sathi*, which was shot on location in Sri Lanka and starred the former cricketer Mohsin Khan, and her even more successful *Munda Bigra Jaey*. Throughout much of the previous decade, however, it was eclipsed by Punjabi productions. These action-packed dramas, epitomised by *Maula Jat* which became the biggest box-office success in the history of the Pakistani cinema, shot Sultan Rahi (1938–96) to stardom. He was eventually to feature in over 500 productions. In a 'one man film industry', Sultan Rahi was simultaneously engaged in as many as 35 productions. The settings altered, but his role as the protector of the oppressed was always the same until his shocking murder on 8 January 1996. Punjabi cinema undoubtedly encouraged a revival in interest in the Punjabi language and culture which, partly in the interests of national integration, had been relegated to the language of the home in the region in favour of Urdu.

Before the rise of regional cinemas, Urdu films were the home-produced mainstay of Pakistani cinema-goers. Their producers used this medium to support a 'national' identity. This is seen most clearly in films dealing with the anti-colonial struggle (*Shaheed, Farangi*), with the Mughal era (*Anarkali*) or biopics such as, for example, the 1961 film *Ghalib. Gharibon ka Badshah*, a melodrama set in riot-torn Karachi, represents a more recent attempt to promote national cohesion. Urdu films, like their Indian Hindi counterparts, have turned increasingly to violent drama to attract a younger lower-class audience. This new direction was highlighted by the 1975 production by the rising director Mumtaz Ali Khan, *Dulhan Ek Raat Ki*. This film, with its violence and provocative dance sequences, slipped through the censor's net because of political influence (Gazdar, 1997, p. 138). Again, in a mirror image of events across the border, nationalism was promoted through hostility to the 'other', rather than by stressing positive cultural values in such films as Sajjad Gul's *International Guerillas* (1990), which portrays Salman Rushdie as an Indian agent.

Despite Zia's interest in the cinema as a propaganda tool, it was used most in this respect during the earlier martial law regime of Ayub Khan. The Department of Film and Publications within the Ministry of Information and Broadcasting produced a series of documentaries designed to popularise the regime's nation-building programme. The most famous project was *Nai Kiran* ('A New Ray of Light') which was made in the five major languages of Bengali, Punjabi, Sindhi, Pushto and Urdu. The 80-minute documentary depicted Ayub as the nation's saviour from corrupt politicians (Gazdar, 1997, p. 74). During the ten weeks of its production, prominent artists such as the songstress Noorjahan were coerced to take part if they did not volunteer their services. When *Nai Kiran* was released every cinema had to show it without charge for a week.

The Department of Films and Publications also inaugurated Pakistan News Pictorial, designed to 'acquaint our people effectively with the day-to-day events of our national life'. The newsreels were given a compulsory screening before the main feature in all cinemas. Documentaries and newsreels were used throughout the Ayub era for indoctrination purposes. In other respects, however, Pakistan's first martial law regime was more 'modern' and enlightened in cultural matters than its successor. The Zia era's philistinism was epitomised by the ban on the celebrated *kathak* dance performer Naheed Siddiqui performing in public. While the writer and director Zia Sarhardy had to spend the second period of martial law in exile in London, he wrote the screen play for perhaps his greatest work *Lakhon Mein Eik* (1967) under Ayub. Another sensitive cinematic portrayal of the 1947 partition upheavals which passed the censor during the Ayub era was Saifudin Saif's classic Punjabi film *Kartar Singh* (1959). The Censor Board also allowed the social realist production *Jago Huwa Savera* (1959) portraying the life of an East Pakistani fisherman, which had been scripted in part by the progressive poet Faiz Ahmad Faiz (1911–84).

Depoliticisation and modernisation: the Ayub Khan era, 1958–1969

Ayub Khan (1907–74), Pakistan's first military ruler, sought to establish a new constitutional order more suited to the 'genius of the people' than the 'failed' parliamentary democracy. Indeed he blamed the 'unruly' politicians for Pakistan's ills. Depoliticisation marked a return to the colonial administration's ideas of political tutelage through indirect elections and official nomination of representatives. This approach was formalised in the Basic Democracies scheme. Ayub further clipped the politicians' wings by the introduction of the Public Offices (Disqualification) Order and the Elective Bodies (Disqualification) Order in March and August 1959 respectively. These established the concept of 'accountability'. Politicians who had engaged in 'misconduct' could either be tried by a tribunal or voluntarily 'withdraw' from public life.

Ayub used his control of the media to malign the politicians and later without much success to trumpet the achievements of his regime. The press was the first weapon in his propaganda campaign, but the cinema, as we have just seen, also took on an increasingly important role. The Ayub regime not only used the Public Safety Ordinances already on the statute book to control news items, but in 1963 promulgated the Press and Publications Ordinance 'to make the press conform to recognised principles of journalism and patriotism' (Niazi, 1997, p. 182). News management was further enhanced the following year with the establishment of the supposedly independent National Press Trust. It acquired ownership of such former radical papers as the *Pakistan Times* and transformed them into government mouthpieces. 'Sycophancy and servility' replaced a true 'patriotism' born of honest reporting. The press as an institution and the wider nation-building process suffered in the long run. The damage has only recently begun to be repaired with the repeal of the Press and Publications Ordinance in 1988 and the dismantling of the National Press Trust in 1996. During the course of 1999, however, Nawaz Sharif's government was to become increasingly hostile to independent news groups such as Jang and journalists such as Najam Sethi, the celebrated editor of the *Friday Times*.

Modernisation

Ayub's modernisation programme centred around social reform, land reform and a commitment to economic development. The most important social reform was the 1961 Family Laws Ordinance. This established the principle of arbitration in divorce cases. It also granted gender equality for grandchildren in inheritance cases. Conservative Muslim opinion was highly critical of this 'un-Islamic' measure. The *'ulama* were vociferous in their opposition, but although Ayub backed down on the issue of Pakistan's name which had not been titled an Islamic republic in the 1962 constitution, he stood firm with respect to the Family Laws Ordinance which received constitutional protection. He opined that Islam was originally 'a dynamic and progressive movement ... but with the passage of time, the Muslims at large sought to concentrate more on the dogmatic aspects of Islam ... those who looked forward to progress and advancement came to be regarded as disbelievers and those who looked backward were considered devout Muslims. It is a great injustice to both life and religion', Ayub continued, 'to impose on twentieth century man the condition that he must go back several centuries in order to prove his bona fide as a true Muslim' (Khan, 1961, pp. 110–11). Throughout the remainder of his career, Ayub made little attempt to hide his detestation of the *mullahs*. He declared that they were as 'covetous of wealth and power as any politician and did not stop short of any mischief' (Syed, 1982, p. 106).

The Land Reforms regulation of 7 February 1959 was the first serious attempt at land reform in the landlord-dominated West Pakistan, despite Mian Iftikhar-ud-Din's earlier promptings. The regime's publicists hailed it as a radical measure. The high ceiling (500 acres of irrigated land, 1,000 acres unirrigated) together with intra-family transfers severely restricted the amount of land which was resumed. Moreover, there were numerous irregularities concerning the resumption of land. Local officials cancelled sales to tenants and landlords still charged rent on land that tenants had purchased! Part of the resumed land was to be sold directly to its cultivating tenants, the remainder was to be disposed of in public auction. In either case, the new owners were to pay back to the government an annual amount at a fixed rate of interest.

The importance that Ayub attached to economic development can be seen in the fact that, in an echo of Nehru's approach, he assumed the chairmanship of the Planning Commission in 1961 and elevated the post of his deputy to central cabinet rank. This nationalisation of planning, however, reduced the representation of Bengali views as it did away with the East Pakistani Planning Board which had previously formulated plans for the eastern wing. Ironically, Ayub saw economic development achieving both the aim of modernisation and of aiding east–west national integration.

In order to reduce east–west economic disparities, East Pakistan was given a greater share in central taxes. In comparison with the 1947–58 period, there was also a significant increase in public-sector developmental expenditure. This had little impact as it was the private sector dominated by West Pakistani entrepreneurs, many of whom were *mohajirs*, that provided the motor for Pakistan's significant economic achievements during the so-called 'Golden Decade' of development during the Ayub era.

The emphasis on a private-sector-led development stood in stark contrast to India's approach. It reflected the preferences of the United States, Japan and West Germany which were Pakistan's major aid givers and whose economic largesse was crucial to the aim of bringing about rapid industrialisation. It was also in keeping with the ideology of the World Bank which provided loans for the PICIC and IDBP. Moreover, the Planning Commission, which played a key role in coordinating the state's import substitution and export promotion policies, was assisted by the Development Advisory Service of Harvard University. In a real sense, therefore, Pakistan was a laboratory for modernisation theory's prescription for a 'take-off' into sustained economic growth through massive infusions of capital directed to industry by government and the establishment of a cultural, political and economic environment conducive to the releasing of entrepreneurial abilities.

The Pakistan economy made rapid strides during the Ayub era. Large-scale manufacturing grew at almost 17 per cent each year and economic growth rates averaged 5.5 per cent annually. This achievement outstripped the Indian performance. Ayub's strategy of channelling resources to an entrepreneurial elite, however, increased still further the inequalities in Pakistani society. In a staggering concentration of capital, a private entrepreneurial class emerged, comprising Gujarati-speaking Khojas and Memons leavened with a sprinkling of Punjabi Chiniotis, which controlled two-thirds of all industrial assets, and around three-quarters of insurance company assets and bank assets. This class hardly required co-opting, dependent as it was on the government for credits, permits and licences. Nevertheless, it became increasingly linked with the military, bureaucratic and landlord elites through strategic marriages.

While a small elite reaped the advantages of the rapid economic growth, the bulk of the population had to bear the burden of rising prices. Moreover, rapid urbanisation added to the misery as housing, health and transport services lagged hopelessly behind. Despite the high levels of growth, maldistribution of wealth meant that the absolute number of impoverished people rose from 8.65 to 9.33 million between 1963 and 1968. The disenchantment increased as the economy slowed down in the wake of the decline of foreign investment following the 1965 war with India. Drought also hit the agricultural sector which despite the industrial development still accounted for just under half of the total GNP in the mid-1960s.

Ayub, freed from the political constraints of his predecessors, had hoped to achieve an economic breakthrough in the development decade. By emphasising growth at the expense of income distribution, the existing inequalities in Pakistani society had been exacerbated. The regime was to reap the whirlwind of both growing social tensions and regional conflicts as the imbalances increased between the eastern and western wings. For all its endeavours and achievements, Pakistan's first experiment with untrammelled military-bureaucratic rule hampered rather than hastened the nation-building process.

Populism and nation building: the Zulfiqar Ali Bhutto era 1971–1977

The mounting opposition to the Ayub regime was orchestrated in West Pakistan by his former protégé, Zulfiqar Ali Bhutto (1928–79). Western-educated, the scion of a leading Sindhi landholding family, Bhutto increasingly distanced himself from Ayub after the unpopular conclusion to the 1965 Indo-Pakistan War. He eventually quit his post as Foreign Minister and in November 1967 founded the Pakistan People's Party. Bhutto's vague references to 'Islamic socialism' were grounded by such party ideologues as Hanif Ramay in the concept of Islamic *musawaat* (egalitarianism/socialism).

Bhutto's populism was designed to unite all classes and parties within the country. According to the foundation document of the PPP, the people were unwilling to 'tolerate the present conditions much longer'. The party had been formed to 'discharge the responsibility' of establishing a 'new system based on justice and attached to the interests of the toiling millions'. The campaigns against Ayub eventually resulted in his handing over power on 25 March 1969 to Yahya Khan (1917–80), a hard-drinking soldier who had risen from his humble background as the son of a police superintendent to the rank of commander-in-chief.

The PPP swept to power in West Pakistan in the country's first national elections in 1970. Its inability to share power with the Awami League, which as the mouthpiece of Bengali nationalism had won all but a handful of seats in the eastern wing, formed the background to the launching of the disastrous military action known as Operation Searchlight on 25 March 1971. The resultant breakup of Pakistan provided Bhutto with a window of opportunity for civilian rule. The army had been discredited as news of its brutalities in East Pakistan leaked out. Moreover, its humilating surrender at Dhaka to the Indian forces dealt a major blow to its cultivated aura of invincibility.

Bhutto embarked on a series of land and labour reforms and the nationalisation of industries and banks which had parallels with Mrs Gandhi's populism. The 1972 land reform was certainly more radical than Ayub's, but experienced similar problems of implementation. At the beginning of the year, Bhutto had also introduced the nationalisation of over 30 large firms in ten basic industries. Far more controversial and ultimately damaging to his support base amongst small-scale Punjabi entrepreneurs was his nationalisation of the vegetable oil (ghee) industry in August 1973. In foreign affairs Bhutto launched Pakistan into the Islamic and third-world orbits breaking with the more traditional pro-Western stance. New departures included the decision to leave the Commonwealth (30 January 1972) and the SEATO security pact (8 November 1972). Bhutto also attempted to reform the bureaucracy and the army to nullify their influence. Bureaucratic reforms which introduced lateral entry into the elite civil service of Pakistan served only to politicise the administrative services, while Bhutto's use of the army to contain tribal insurgency in Balochistan from 1973 onwards re-established its political influence. The problems in Balochistan were symptoms of Bhutto's growing authoritarianism. This formed the background to the eventual coup which brought Zia-ul-Haq to power on 5 July 1977. Ironically he had only been promoted to the post of the chief of army staff over the heads of more senior officers some three years earlier because of what was seen as his apolitical attitude.

Populist reforms made Bhutto enemies but were not sufficiently radical to transform power relations. Bhutto's half-hearted commitment to socialism and to the abolition of feudalism has been cited as a key factor in his failure to bring about the new Pakistan of which he spoke. Far more important was his inability to institutionalise his authority by restructuring the PPP itself. When in power its incipient right–left ideological tensions and factional rivalries came to the surface. Opportunist landlords flocked to its band-wagon and replaced loyal party workers. Patronage counted for more than organisational structures. Like the Muslim League earlier, it proved unable to assist in the nation-building enterprise in a similar manner to the Congress in neighbouring India.

Populism thus ultimately raised expectations which could not be met by an increasingly authoritarian regime. Nevertheless, Bhutto still retained support amongst the lower classes especially in Sind. The furore raised by his alleged 'rigging' of the March 1977 elections provided an opportunity for those who had suffered from his nationalisation programme and disliked both his authoritarianism and attitude to Islam to take to the streets in the Pakistan National Alliance. The increase in investment from the Middle East, the export of labour to the region and the reduction at a stroke in 1971 of the non-Muslim minority from 14 to 3 per cent of the population (when Bangladesh broke away) all encouraged pressures for Islamisation. They were only to be given full rein, however, by the agent of Bhutto's downfall, Zia, who came from a puritanical Deobandi Islamic background.

Zia-ul-Haq: depoliticisation and Islamisation, 1977–1988

Zia came to power in the coup code-named Operation Fairplay. It was by no means certain from the outset, however, that he would dominate Pakistan's political life. Zia in fact promised to hold elections as early as October 1977. Their delay, Bhutto's trial and his eventual execution on 4 April 1979 after a flimsy conspiracy-to-murder trial marked a sea change in Zia's attitude to power. Increasing both in confidence and in authoritarian sentiment, he justified his position as the overseer of Pakistan's Islamic destiny. Some writers link Islamisation policies with Zia's personal piety, others regard his programme as a cynical manoeuvre to secure a 'cover' for an illegitimate and oppressive regime. In August 1983 the advisory Council of Islamic Ideology pronounced that a presidential form of government was the 'nearest to Islam'. It was later to rule that political parties were non-Islamic. Whatever its motivation, it is clear that Zia saw Islamisation as holding the key to Pakistan's three-decade-long search for stability and national unity. The state-sponsored Islamisation process ironically achieved almost the opposite effects. Today Pakistan is suffering its bitter fruits of sectarian division and violence. The latter has intensified in the wake of the flood of arms into the country as a by-product of the Afghan War. So why was Islam no more successful than Bhutto's populism or Ayub's modernisation in establishing national unity?

The answer lies in terms both of the nature of Pakistani Islam and of the programme of Islamisation itself. Although Zia may have wished to make it so, Islamic expression in Pakistan was not monochrome. The puritanical approach of his Deobandi sect coexisted with the colourful and vibrant life of the *sufi* shrines which marked the tombs of the saints who had played a leading role in the spread of Islam into the region. At the shrines, music and even ecstatic dance were not frowned upon as religious expression. The state's legalistic imposition of Islam and the humanist traditions of sufism were to come into conflict. Some of the custodians of the shrines and the saints' descendants were members of the Barelvi movement which had fought a bitter battle with the Deobandis and had formed their own political party (Jamiat-ul-Ulema-i-Pakistan) to rival the Deobandi party Jamiat-ul-Ulema-i-Islam. Disputes over the department dealing with endowments to religious shrines led to a major confrontation between Deobandis and Barelvis at the Badshahi Mosque in Lahore on 21 May 1984. In Sind, the home province of the martyred former Prime Minister Bhutto, sufism had always been an integral component of regional cultural identity. Significantly the *pirs* of Sind played a leading role in the agitation by the Movement for the Restoration of Democracy (MRD) in August and September 1983. Fifty thousand disciples of the Makhdum of Hala successfully blocked the national highway on one occasion. The strong sense of Sindhi identity which fuelled the MRD struggle can be glimpsed in such poems as *Love for Homeland* by Niaz Hamayooni.

In addition to Deobandi–Barelvi divisions, Pakistani Islam was divided on Sunni–Shia lines. The Shias formed a significant minority which inevitably questioned an Islamisation process that favoured Sunni interpretation in legal matters. While Zia talked of raising laws in accordance with Islam, the moot point remained whose Islam and what Islam should be implemented by the state. Lack of sensitivity to Shia interpretations undermined the Islamisation process, especially as it coincided with heightened Shia sensitivities following the Shia-sponsored Iranian Revolution. An important catalyst for Sunni–Shia tension was provided by an ordinance introduced in 1979 with respect to alms (the Zakat Ordinance). The giving of alms was an Islamic duty, but Shias objected both to its being made compulsory and that the money raised would go to Sunni charitable activities. When Shias were eventually exempted, Sunni extremists became increasingly hostile. Some even began to talk of Shias as non-Muslims. In addition to differences over *zakat*, Shia jurisprudence parts company with the Sunni over such matters as marriage and divorce (especially temporary marriage), inheritance and wills and the imposition of *hadd* (Islamic) punishments. Islamic jurisprudence became politicised with the foundation of the movement for the establishment of Shia *fiqh* (law) (Tehrik-e-Niaz-e-Fiqh-e-Jafaria). Sunni–Shia riots, which had always occurred at the flashpoint in the religious calendar of the Muharram festival, intensified and extremists from both communities began to arm themselves.

Islamisation was resisted by members of local law associations, political and human-rights activists, journalists and by educated elite women who banded together in 1982 to form the Women's Action Forum. Human-rights activists were concerned about the impact of Islamisation on non-Muslims. They were not only marginalised from the mainstream by the introduction of separate electorates, but were increasingly vulnerable to charges under the blasphemy ordinance. Some lawyers regarded the induction of the *'ulama* in May 1981 as judges for the first time in Pakistan's history as a retrograde step. Educated women objected not only to attempts to enforce Islamic dress codes and discourage women from active participation in the labour force, but also to 'discriminatory' Islamisation measures. The Law of Evidence, for example, enacted by Presidential Ordinance in October 1984, laid down the principle that the evidence of two women was only equal to that of one man. The Hudood ordinances which were designed to introduce Islamic punishments laid down in the Quran and Sunnah were controversially based on the Law of Evidence for sexual crimes. This was either self-confession or the witness of four *salah* (upright) males. For men in rape cases self-confession was verbal; for women, however, it could include pregnancy or medical examination. Women who had been raped could thus be punished by flogging for adultery (*zina*) while their assailants went unconvicted. The Hudood ordinances were regarded by its opponents as typical of much of the Zia Islamisation process in that Islam was being reduced to a system of punishments. Little attention was being given to its implementation with respect to social justice.

Islamisation not only introduced sectarianism and aroused the ire of 'secularised' elites, it also failed to diminish ethnic awareness. Indeed it could be argued that the legacy of Zia's regime, both by holding the 1985 'partyless' elections and in his alleged divide-and-rule strategy in Sind through encouragement of the *mohajir*–Sindhi split, was a further ethnicisation of Pakistan politics. This was also encouraged by the centralisation of his regime and the claim that martial law was resulting in a 'Punjabisation' of Pakistan. Not all regions or social groups in Punjab benefited from martial law, but the perception of 'Punjabisation' was to be another of the negative legacies of the Zia era.

In 1985 the Sind–Balochistan–Pushtoon Front under the leadership of Mumtaz Bhutto came together to advocate a confederation of Pakistan. Sindhi nationalists went a step further than confederalism and demanded total independence. Mir Ghaus Bakhsh Bizenjo, the Baloch leader of the Pakistan National Party, argued less radically for a 'loose' federation reflecting the existence of the four nationalities in Pakistan. Cultural pluralism and the rich inheritance of South Asian Islam itself could not be forced into the straitjacket of a self-proclaimed ideological state. In the words of Bizenjo, 'You can occupy, suppress but not create a nationality.'

Democratisation and ungovernability: Pakistan 1988–1999

Zia's death in a plane crash on 17 August 1988 remains a mystery. Various theories have been given concerning its causes and which groups within the region may have sought to sabotage the ill-fated C-130 aircraft. Whatever its circumstances, the crash paved the way for the restoration of democracy. Following elections, Zulfiqar Ali Bhutto's daughter Benazir (1953–) became the first female leader of a Muslim state. The more relaxed atmosphere saw an end to unconvincing attempts to depict Jinnah as an Islamist wanting to establish an Islamic state. But as Syyed Vali Reza Nasr, for example, has maintained, the Zia era left a legacy of the 'gradual sacralization of the national political discourse'. Thus when the Shariat Act was piloted through the National Assembly in May 1991 by Benazir's successor, Nawaz Sharif, Pakistan's first industrialist Prime Minister (1949–), hailed its passage as 'historic', going on to declare that the 'the objective of the creation of Pakistan had been realised'. Benazir Bhutto's much remarked-upon wearing of a *dupatta* (scarf) draped across her head can be seen as another concession to the Islamisation process. Neither of her governments (1988–90, 1993–96) removed the legislation introduced during the Zia era which prejudiced women's interests like, for example, the Law of Evidence or the Hudood ordinances.

Nevertheless, the post-1988 Bhutto administrations sought to portray the image of Pakistan as a moderate Islamic democracy which was open for business and willing to assist the West in the struggle against drugs and terrorism. A new cultural basis for Pakistani identity which rebuffed Islamist thinking emerged from the deliberations of a National Commission on History and Culture chaired by the Punjabi author and PPP leader Fakhar Zaman. It attempted to demonstrate that Pakistani identity was not a modern construct, but was rooted in the soil of the Indus region. The legacy of the pre-Islamic era was openly acknowledged, something which would have been impossible in the Zia era. The basis for toleration and resistance to oppression was linked with the *sufi* imprint on the region. These themes were taken up by Aitaz Ahsan, the Interior Minister in Benazir Bhutto's first government, in his study entitled *The Indus Saga and the Making of Pakistan.*

However, the security services were simultaneously pursuing their own policy of patronising the Islamic fundamentalism of the Taliban in Afghanistan. Islamic militancy, the backwash of the Afghan War and the accompanying 'kalashnikov culture' saw mounting sectarian violence in both Karachi and the Jhang district of the Punjab. Armed conflict between Sunnis and Shias in the remote Kurram Valley claimed 100 lives in September 1996. Islamic militancy in Pakistan was paraded before an international audience through the celebrated Salamat Masih and Rehmat Masih blasphemy trial. Its notoriety intensified when another of the accused Christians, Manzoor Masih, was gunned down in Lahore on 5 April 1994 immediately after a trial appearance. The vocal opposition of the *mullahs* prevented limited reforms of the 'blasphemy law' despite its exploitation to settle grudges or to cow upwardly mobile members of minority communities.

The governments of Nawaz Sharif (1990–3, 1997–9) slowly continued the Islamisation of the Zia era. The 1991 Shariat Act was, however, dubbed by one leading Deobandi critic who wanted a much more comprehensive measure as 'holy water in a bottle of whisky'. Sharif's commitment to economic liberalisation and to the encouragement of overseas investment was to be embarrassed by Shariat Court rulings that the taking of interest (*riba*) was repugnant to Islam. Nawaz Sharif demonstrated more affinity with the heady brew of populism and authoritarianism of Zulfiqar Ali Bhutto than his daughter was able to manage. He was also to share the same fate of being toppled by a military coup. In July 1992, Nawaz Sharif fixed a monthly minimum wage of Rs 1,500 for unskilled workers. The best example of Sharif's populist politics was, however, his introduction three months earlier of Yellow Cab Employment. While opponents derided the scheme to provide loans for cab purchase as gimmickry that would do little to increase jobs, the measure was undoubtedly instrumental in widening the Muslim League leader's constituency of support. By 1993 around 40,000 households had benefited from government loans which had been sanctioned for 95,000 taxis, buses, coaches and trucks. Sharif displayed a similar headline-grabbing approach in his celebrated bus diplomacy with the BJP Indian Prime Minister in February 1999. Sharif's second tenure of office was also marked, however, by increasing centralisation of power leading to further claims of Punjabisation and that he was running an elective dictatorship. Sharif successively curbed the power of the Chief Justice and the President, and ensured that a close friend of his father's was installed in the latter office. Much effort was also taken up in hounding his opponent Benazir Bhutto on corruption charges. This led to claims that he was following a one-sided accountability process. The Punjabi Prime Minister got away with prematurely retiring the chief of army staff General Jehangir Karamat in 1998, but when he attempted to repeat the process a year later, he encountered his nemesis in General Pervez Musharraf.

Aside from the ongoing economic crises, the single most important development both for Pakistan's self-identity and its international status during Sharif's second tenure in office was the May 1998 nuclear explosions. Pakistani nationalism has traditionally been largely reactive to the Hindu/Indian threat, whilst coexisting somewhat uneasily with Islam. Significantly the most quoted phrases regarding the tests at Chagai were Pakistan's 'tit-for-tat' explosions and the 'Islamic bomb'. Prime Minister Nawaz Sharif, in a televised speech, reflected the former dominant strand in the nationalist discourse when he jubilantly declared: 'We paid them back.' Islamist groups who had clamoured for this response celebrated not only their hostility to the Hindu 'other', but the fact that Pakistan's weapon capability would enable it to act as guardian of Islamic civilisation. Jinnah's claim in 1947 that Pakistan would act as a 'laboratory' of Islam had acquired vindication, although not in the form then expected. In keeping with the established nationalist discourse, opponents of the testing were dubbed 'unpatriotic' and even '*kafirs*'. Despite the introduction of a state of emergency, however, such newly formed peace groups as the Action Committee Against the Arms Race sprang into existence in Karachi.

The contested nature of Pakistani nationalism was revealed, however, not by the dissidence of individual intellectuals, but by the hostility to the tests displayed by Balochi and Sindhi nationalists. They portrayed them as serving the interests only of the Punjabi civilian and military elites. The likelihood of further budget cutbacks for human development was bitterly resented in these minority provinces which had already seen their programmes cut, while grandiose schemes survived in the Punjab powerbase of the Nawaz Sharif government. Despite its clawing ever more central power to itself, the economic sanctions arising from the tests threatened to bring an already tottering Pakistan economy to its knees.

In the event, assistance from the IMF prevented a default on Pakistan's debt early in 1999. Nawaz Sharif further attempted to bolster his power by assailing independent journalists and by reining in the growing influence of NGOs. Symptomatic of his populist approach was the celebratory marking of the first anniversary of the nuclear tests. The reality of their reactive nature was forgotten in a series of lavish television advertisements and in calling the 28th May 'Youm-e-Takbeer'('time of celebration'). Prayers were offered in mosques after the Friday congregations in thanks for the 'gift' of the bomb. Opposite the Punjab Assembly Building in Lahore Faisal Chowk was decorated with banners triumphantly acknowledging the nuclear tests, alongside a massive hoarding of Prime Minister Nawaz Sharif. The Pakistan leader flew his cabinet down to Karachi for a mass meeting at the official shrine to Pakistani nationalism – the mausoleum of Quaid-i-Azam Mohammad Ali Jinnah. Earlier, the Indians, perhaps mindful of the impact on international opinion in the wake of heightened tension in Kashmir, had more modestly celebrated the anniversary of their tests as 'Technology Day'.

The role of a new nuclear culture in Pakistani nation building was also demonstrated in the erection of monuments. A model of a Ghauri missile was set up on the way to Islamabad airport, while at Lok Virsa in Islamabad a replica of Raskoo Mountain, where Pakistan detonated its nuclear devices, was set up. A residential locality on the banks of the Rawal Lake was renamed Gulshan-e-Qadeer in honour of the 'father of the Pakistani bomb' Dr Abdul Qadeer Khan.

Institutions and nation building

The army and the bureaucracy have been the self-appointed guardians of the Pakistan state since independence. Political parties and constitutions have come and gone or been transformed, but these twin unelected institutions have remained the pillars of the state. When General Pervez Musharraf toppled Nawaz Sharif in October 1999, he used the time-worn phrases that the army would uphold the 'stability', 'unity' and 'integrity' of 'our beloved country', having intervened in a situation of institutional and economic collapse which had 'rocked the very foundation of the federation of Pakistan'.

Popular wisdom in Pakistan has dubbed the elite Civil Service of Pakistan (CSP) cadre which accounted for under 1 per cent of the entire bureaucracy the 'Sultans of Pakistan' and 'the best organised political party in Pakistan'. The CSP inherited the outlook of the colonial civil service and as such became increasingly critical of the country's chaotic political process during the first decade of independence. Well before the military and its bureaucratic allies formally sent the politicians packing in October 1958, power had slipped into their hands. By the time that the first Pakistani constitution was ratified in March 1956, the Pakistan Muslim League, the only nationwide political organisation, had disintegrated and a tradition had been established of executive dissolution of both provincial and national governments. Indeed in a judgement with subsequent wide-ranging implications, the supreme court had legitimised the action by the Governor-General Ghulam Mohammad (1895–1956), a former colonial civil servant and finance expert, to dismiss the first Constituent Assembly in October 1954.

During the Ayub period of martial law, the bureaucracy was the senior partner in the administrative process. The troops were in fact ordered back to their barracks as early as November 1958. By the end of the following year, only 53 army officers held civilian administrative positions. Ayub initially made some attempt to purge the bureaucracy of 'corrupt' elements, but the screening process initiated under martial law regulation no. 61 was only half-hearted, in part because Ayub's concern for stability limited his room for innovation. One of the leading figures of the Ayub era was the bureaucrat Altaf Gauhar who as Information Secretary was popularly held responsible for the muzzling of the press.

Bhutto was to curb the bureaucracy more successfully than the army. He castigated the former's elite cadres as representing a Brahmin and Mandarin class, 'unrivalled in its snobbery and arrogance'. Nevertheless, even after his abolition of the CSP and the introduction of a unified grade structure, the former 'Mandarins' continued to hold key positions in the Central Secretariat. Bhutto's personal control of the administrative system was nevertheless secured through the creation of special posts and the establishment of a lateral entry scheme administered not by the Federal Service Commission, but by a politicised Establishment Division. Critics claimed that this raised an 'army of stooges' who were the sycophantic appointees, relatives and hangers-on of federal ministers.

It was for this reason that Zia's purge of the bureaucracy was far more extensive than Ayub's and he ensured that its members were the junior partners in his regime. Zia inducted army officers into many civilian bureaucratic posts by means of the introduction of a military preference in the federal quota system, as well as giving them lucrative assignments in the autonomous corporations. General Fazle Raziq, for example, became the chairman of the Water and Power Development Authority. In the period 1980–85, no less than 96 army officers entered the Central Superior Services on a permanent basis, while another 115 were on contracts. Until the Sindhi landlord Muhammad Khan Junejo (1932–93) was sworn in as Zia's handpicked civilian Prime Minister on 23 March 1985, all the powerful provincial governors had been military men.

Zia so entrenched the role of the Pakistan Army that it continued to exert a considerable influence in the 11 years that elapsed between the 1988 restoration of democracy and the country's return to army rule. During this period of indirect military control, Benazir Bhutto (1990, 1996) and Nawaz Sharif (1993) were removed from office largely because they threatened the army's institutional interests. Throughout this period, the elected Prime Minister was in fact the least powerful member of the *troika*, the term given to the grouping of President, Prime Minister and chief of army staff. The army not only possessed a veto over defence allocations, but over key areas of foreign policy relating to Afghanistan and Kashmir. Indeed its intelligence wing the Inter-Services Intelligence (ISI) virtually ran its own independent policy with regard to these issues. The lack of supervision became clear in 1993 when under American pressure there was an attempt to haul in its activities. Following the sacking of the ISI chief General Javid Nasir, Nawaz Sharif discovered that an unaccounted ISI budget of around $3.3 million a month had been spent on assisting Kashmiri militants. Nuclear policy was also in the army's hands, although the quest for a Pakistan bomb had been initiated by the civilian administration of Zulfiqar Ali Bhutto.

Nawaz Sharif's second government, which was abruptly ended by the coup of 12 October 1999, had been dubbed by some commentators an 'elective dictatorship'. No civilian Prime Minister had wielded such power since Zulfiqar Ali Bhutto, as Sharif successively clipped the powers of the President, the Chief Justice of the supreme court and even ensured that the chief of army staff, General Jehangir Karamat, retired early in October 1998 and was replaced by General Musharraf, who was regarded at the time as a junior appointee. Nevertheless, it was argued, even without the wisdom of hindsight, that the more the Prime Minister empowered himself, the more he undermined the legitimacy he had acquired following his sweeping 1997 general election victory. The continuing collapse of Pakistan's institutions meant that many routine administrative tasks were handed over to the army. During the course of 1998–9, it thus found itself overseeing census operations, hunting out 'ghost schools' (schools that existed only on paper, although teachers drew their monthly salaries) in the interior of Punjab, briefly running anti-terrorism courts in Karachi and even forcing electricity consumers to pay their bills to the Water and Power Development Authority. Finally, for all Nawaz Sharif's power, the army remained an institution outside of his control. The Prime Minister's ill-advised attempt to strengthen his grip on it by replacing General Musharraf with the ISI chief, Lieutenant-General Ziauddin, who possessed close ties with his father, was a disastrous step too far.

Before examining the ways in which Zia entrenched the army's role in Pakistan politics, it is necessary to remind ourselves of the reasons for its earlier dominance. Certainly, as early as 1958, an American intelligence report assessed that the 'Pakistan Army had developed as a pressure group' and would 'continue to have priority over economic development for appropriations' irrespective of the Indian factor (Jalal, 1990, p. 238).

One key to the army's influence has been its unity and discipline. The chain of command from the chief of army staff and the powerful corps commanders has largely remained unchallenged in the post-independence era. There have been only isolated incidents in which junior officers have challenged the commanders' approach to domestic and security-related foreign policy. A radical group of young officers known as the Young Turks came into being after the ceasefire at the end of the 1947–8 Kashmir War who believed that they had been cheated of victory. A number were to be involved in the 1951 abortive military coup which has gone down in history as the Rawalpindi Conspiracy. The coup attempt was important not just because of its roots in the Kashmir conflict but because of the involvement of the senior figure, Major-General Akbar Khan, a veteran of the 1948 fighting. The last occasion that army factionalism led to a coup attempt was in September 1995. The conspirators, Major-General Zaheerul Islam Abbassi,

Brigadier Mustansar Billah, Colonel Muhammad Azad Minhas and Colonel Innayatullah Khan, along with some other junior officers, had secured weapons from the tribal areas and planned to storm a commanders' meeting on 30 September. They hoped that the liquidation of the military and political elite would pave the way for the establishment of an Islamic dictatorship in Pakistan which would secure Kashmir through *jihad*. When the news of the arrests was finally made public, Benazir Bhutto attempted to secure Western sympathy and to use the episode to further buttress her regime's image as a bastion against fundamentalist forces.

Equally important to the army's influence was the state's decision to bolster the armed forces in the aftermath of partition even though this meant diverting scarce resources from human development. The priority of building up the armed forces was spelled out by Liaquat Ali Khan in a broadcast to the nation on 8 October 1948. 'The defence of the State is our foremost consideration', declared the Pakistan Prime Minister, 'and has dominated all other governmental activities. We will not grudge any amount on the defence of our country' (cited in Ali, 1967, p. 376). Henceforth, in Ayesha Jalal's telling phrase, scarce resources were devoted to the establishment of 'a political economy of defence'. The army regarded itself and was perceived by others as the ultimate guarantor of national security. During the years 1947–50 up to 70 per cent of the national budget was allocated to defence.

The decision to prioritise defence expenditure did not of itself create a determining role for the armed forces in Pakistan's political life. But the longer-term conditions for military involvement were established, as funds were pumped into the army at the same time as political institutionalisation remained weak. In contrast with the 'Congress system', the Pakistani political process was chaotic immediately after independence, displaying a bewildering array of shifting allegiances and alliances. By 1954 the Muslim League which had founded the state was in terminal decline. Personalities counted rather than ideologies or party institutionalisation. The lack of expenditure on what would today be termed human development hampered the emergence of a civil society which might have questioned the growing influence of the army.

Despite Pakistan's skewing of its economy to meet its strategic defence requirements, it could not match unaided the resources of its Indian neighbour. This fact was recognised from the outset. Indeed, as early as October 1947, Pakistan unsuccessfully requested a two billion dollar loan from the United States. Britain lacked the financial resources to provide major assistance and also needed to appear evenhanded in its dealings with the Indians and Pakistanis. The Americans thus appeared a better bet, especially in the light of their requirement for regional Cold War allies as part of their containment policy of the Soviet Union and China. When external US military and economic assistance eventually arrived in 1954, it inevitably came with the strings attached of membership of CENTO, SEATO and the Baghdad Pact. The US–Pakistan strategic relationship was to be filled with tensions because Pakistan's concern over Communist bloc threats was secondary to its preoccupation with India.

Despite such frustrations, both sides saw sufficient gains in the relationship to persist with it. The Pakistan authorities thus eschewed ties with the Muslim world which would have commanded popular support and became increasingly locked into a dependent relationship with the United States. It provided the bureaucrats and their military allies at the centre with both the motives, i.e. the exclusion of political interference on foreign-policy issues, and increasingly the resources to tilt the balance of power away from representative parties and politicians. A full five years before Ayub's takeover of October 1958, the Governor-General, Ghulam Muhammad, had appointed a Bengali political non-entity Mohammad Ali Bogra (1901–63) as Prime Minister because of his pro-American stance.

American aid to Pakistan was cut off following the 1965 war with India. It was not to resume its 1950s' significance until the Soviet occupation of Afghanistan in December 1979. Overnight Zia was transformed in many American eyes from a pariah, because of his human-rights record and stance at the time of the burning of the US embassy in Islamabad the previous month, into a frontline ally in the struggle against the 'Evil Empire' of communism. Early in 1980 the incoming Reagan administration agreed an economic and military aid package worth $3.2 billion spread over a six-year period. The Afghan conflict undoubtedly bolstered the Zia regime because of the resources which flowed into Pakistan. Nevertheless, the leakage of weapons destined for the *mujahadin* was to result in the 'kalashnikov culture'. Henceforth militant religious groups, ethnic warriors and even common criminals possessed easy access to weaponry. The latter group were involved in the increasingly lucrative drug-dealing industry which spread its tentacles from the poppy fields of the northern tribal areas to the fishing villages of the Makran coast and the great commercial port of Karachi.

Under Zia the military, with its stocks replenished by Republican-ruled America, moved to the forefront of Pakistan's life more than ever before. The army's composition changed along with its role. It became more middle class in background and more Islamically oriented than the Sandhurst-trained force of Ayub's day. Pushtuns were inducted into the officer corps, although this remained an overwhelmingly Punjabi body. When the army was used to quell the unrest in Sind in 1983 it looked as much a colonial occupying force as it had done earlier in both East Bengal and Balochistan. This further weakened a sense of national unity in the minority provinces of Pakistan. Zia, whose family were Arains from the Jullundur district of what after partition was the Indian Punjab, surrounded himself with advisors from this background. Significantly, he picked General Arif as his vice-chief of army staff who came from East Punjab, while General Akhtar Abdur Rahman from

Jullundur commanded the powerful ISI from 1984 to 1988. Operation Fairplay, which had ended the Bhutto regime, had been executed by Zia's fellow Arain from Jullundur, Lieutenant-General Faiz Ali Chishti.

In another crucial respect the Zia era also marked a break with earlier periods. This involved the growing influence of the ISI in the conduct of covert activities. The rise of the ISI to prominence resulted from its use by the Americans as an arms conduit to the Afghan *mujahadin*. This established a field of operations for the organisation in Afghanistan which continues to this day in its support for the Taliban. The ISI shared Zia's aim of establishing a client state in Afghanistan which in the wake of the collapse of the Soviet Empire would enable links to be forged with the newly emerging Muslim states of Central Asia. Pakistan would not only secure trading advantages and access to oil but, it was anticipated, would have finally redressed the strategic balance with India.

More controversial than the ISI's involvement in Afghanistan was its role in the 'proxy' wars being fought in the Indian Punjab and Kashmir. The insurgencies in both regions were not created by Pakistan, but by the Indian state's mishandling of ethno-nationalist demands. The Zia regime was none the less well prepared to take advantage of the secessionist struggles. There was an element here of revenge for the Bangladesh breakaway. Involvement in the Kashmir *intifada* was, however, rooted in the long-standing Kashmir dispute rather than merely being opportunistic. It was to become clear that Pakistan stopped short of backing the Jammu and Kashmir Liberation Front's (JKLF) demand for the 'third option' of Kashmiri independence. As in Afghanistan, the ISI played a role in influencing the course of the struggle by favouring pro-Pakistan and Islamist militant groups with its weapons supplies at the expense of the JKLF.

Zia created the conditions for the army's continued behind-the-scenes influence following his unexpected demise by strengthening the office of President through the eighth amendment to the constitution. We have already noted how the power to dissolve the assemblies and to dismiss the elected Prime Minister hung like a sword of Damocles over Benazir Bhutto and Nawaz Sharif in the early 1990s until it was removed by the latter. From the army's viewpoint, this ended the ability to bring the politicians to heel without the necessity for a coup. Ironically, Nawaz Sharif created the circumstances in which a coup became the only method to topple him.

Conclusion

Pakistan has simultaneously displayed the characteristics of both a 'soft' and a 'hard' state. The latter is evidenced in the brutal repression of internal unrest, whether in East Bengal, Balochistan or urban Sind; the former in the collapse of institutions and state authority. By the early 1990s, whether in the opium-growing tribal areas abutting Afghanistan or in Karachi, the authority of the state seemed no longer to run. Basic administrative tasks involving taxation, school inspection and census enumeration have either been impossible to undertake or have relied on the army for their oversight. The non-existence of the state in large areas of Pakistan's life appears to be the outcome of weak legitimisation and poor institutionalisation. Why then has Pakistan not imploded, but to the contrary displayed remarkable resilience in the face of partition, civil war and mounting economic crises?

A populist explanation is that its survival is the result of the long-suffering people who have continued their daily struggles regardless of the power plays of self-interested elites. There is, of course, truth in this. We have glimpsed how self-help as much as government rehabilitation programmes enabled individuals to piece their lives together again following the trauma of partition. A modern nation state cannot, however, continue on this basis alone. Neither of the two main political groupings since independence, the Muslim League and the Pakistan People's Party, have been able to advance nation building like the Congress did in the early years of Indian independence. They remain weakly institutionalised, the victims of the personalisation of power and rent by factionalism and corruption. In the absence of strong political parties, unelected institutions have imperfectly but crucially played key roles in nation building.

The prominence of the bureaucracy and the army have perpetuated the vice-regal tradition inherited from the Raj (Talbot, 1999), privileging administration and order over the encouragement of political participation. Periodic bouts of martial law, while temporarily keeping the lid on dissent, have in the long run exacerbated resistance to what has seemed to some a remote and colonial-style state. The association of the military and to a lesser extent the bureaucracy with the Punjab has especially in the post-1971 era raised charges that there has been a Punjabisation of Pakistan.

Ironically, the unelected pillars of the state are thus a central part of the problem of Pakistan's nation-building enterprise rather than the answer to the need for unity. Regional economic disparities intensify this feeling of a state run on Punjab's behalf. The urban Punjab with the exception of Karachi is the most economically developed in the country. While the adult literacy rate in urban Punjab and Sind is just over 50 per cent, in Balochistan it is merely 17 per cent. Pakistan's national adult literacy rate is 36 per cent, although for women it is just 23 per cent. The female literacy rate in rural Balochistan stands at the shockingly low figure of 3.2 per cent. Urban Sind marginally led urban Punjab in the human development index (0.537) in the late 1990s. This figure was internationally comparable to Zambia. Rural Balochistan which has the lowest index (0.388) is, however, on a par with the former Zaire (Haq, 1997, p. 38).

Over half a century after its creation, Pakistan remains a nation in the making. It faces not only the massive human development problems of clothing, housing and feeding but, most importantly of all, the need to educate a rapidly growing population. Civil society remains fragile in relation to the state's coercive capacity. Institutional life is weak and under-developed. Finally, the role of Islam in the state and the relationship between Pakistani and more 'primordial' identities still await their resolution.

|9|

Globalisation and the nation state in the subcontinent

In this fast paced 'globalization' and 'modernization'
of the World, the marginalized communities may
remain marginalized, if they do not struggle on all
possible avenues simultaneously i.e. education, economics,
politics, technology and cultural progress ... we have been
reaching out to Sindhi people through the Internet, Newspapers
(USA/UK/Sindh/Pakistan) ... Please view these statements at
http: //www.sindhi.org/wsc.htm

World Sindhi Congress, USA Chapter, 2 August 1998

Being an Indian, it is important not only to abide by our laws
but it is also important to live as we do, to accept our culture
and respect our truths. And not only that, one must accept
that Hinduism has by far the largest following in the country.
Those who refuse to accept this have no right to live in this
country. Those who have all their lives spoken ill of Hindutva
are not going to be spared. Embrace this country in its
entirety as Hindustan. Else leave.

Bal Thackeray, *Indian Express*, 11 October 1998

The Chinnaswamy stadium in Bangalore reverberated with huge explosions as the Wills World Cup Cricket quarter final between India and Pakistan reached its climax on 9 March 1996. Through the smoke, the floodlights picked out a huge banner draped across the half-finished new stand which read 'Pakistan Ends in Bangalore – India in Lahore'. The Indian victory was greeted with rowdy celebrations in which youths on motorcycles rode up and down the MG Road chanting, 'Bharat Mata, ki jai', 'Pakistan hai hai' ('Victory to Mother India, Defeat to Pakistan'). Celebrations also went on late into the night in Bombay, Delhi and Madras. Across the border, youths in

Map 4 Major cities of the contemporary subcontinent.

Lahore chanted slogans against the luckless Pakistan captain, Wasim Akram, while PTV played mournful funereal sitar music.

On Sunday 10 June 1984, around 50,000 Sikhs joined a protest march in London which wound its way from Hyde Park to the Indian High Commission. This climaxed the local demonstrations in *gurdwaras* across Britain against the Indian Army's desecration of the Golden Temple in Amritsar a week earlier. The Indian government's official version of the events surrounding 'Operation Bluestar' in the form of videotapes were ceremonially burnt. Thousands also turned out in large demonstrations in New York and Vancouver. In the latter city, the demonstration had started at the historic Ross Street *gurdwara* and had been accompanied by chants of 'Khalistan Zindabad'.

I visited the MQM International Secretariat in North London on Wednesday 26 March 1997. The MQM election results in the recent Pakistan elections were still prominantly displayed. Altaf Hussain, wearing his trademark sunglasses although there were no external windows in the building, warmly greeted me. He had just addressed party workers in Karachi by satellite linkup. I joked with the party workers and representatives from Pakistan about their ubiquitous mobile phones whose use had been banned in Karachi by the Benazir Bhutto government because of their utilisation in the coordination of 'terrorist' activities. Altaf Hussain gave me a personal lecture on the sufferings of the *mohajir* community in Pakistan, animatedly illustrating this on a white board. While I was served a generous meal, the Quaid of the *mohajir* movement once again addressed a gathering in Karachi.

These three vignettes neatly introduce the impact of globalisation on the subcontinent which forms the focus of this chapter. The advent of satellite television and overseas diaspora communities transformed the 1996 Cricket World Cup not only into a commercial bonanza with Pepsi and Coca Cola vying to be the event's official beverage, but a showcase of assertions of national identity. Instant communications relay not only sporting, but real tragedy. The horror of the desecration of Sikhism's most sacred shrine following the army's assault on this 'terrorist centre' had been brought directly into the living rooms of Sikh families across North America and Britain. Shock turned to outrage, even amongst those who had previously disavowed the militancy of Jarnail Singh Bhindranwale, hence the processions and demonstrations from Seattle to Southall. Globalised communications have also made possible the 'remote control' leadership of Altaf Hussain. In an earlier generation he could not have remained at the forefront of a political movement while in such a distant self-imposed exile. In order to retain his influence he would perforce have returned to Karachi, no doubt to await the assassin's bullet.

As late as the mid-1980s, the term globalisation did not form part of the lexicon of social science. Within a few years, however, it has become a fashionable buzz-word for political scientists, journalists, advertisers and politicians alike. There is talk of 'global cities' (Sassen-Koob, 1990) and of a challenge to the nation state's exclusive citizenship claims as a result of the 'deterritorialisation of social identity'. Lying behind the concept of globalisation is a sense of the emergence of supra–territorial phenomena such as cyberspace, global companies, television and newspapers and of a shrinkage of time and space resulting from instantaneous communications. This is deemed to mark a qualitative break with the past. In these 'new times' globalisation is seen as the motor of history, bringing in its wake both trans-national organisation and activity, but also decentralisation and fragmentation The latter is seen as a counter-response, dubbed by Stuart Hall (1991) a 'reach for groundings'. Both the integrating and disintegrating tendencies within globalisation have been seen as posing a challenge to the sovereignty of the nation state (Williams, 1996).

Thomas Blum Hansen has made the strongest link between globalisation and the rise of Hindu nationalism. He sees Hindutva as a response to the sense of 'lack' – of Indian peripherality in a globalising world (Hansen, 1998). There are, however, many contradictory currents in the Hindutva drive to assert national strength and pride. While Shiv Sena and sections of the BJP embrace economic liberalisation in order to build national wealth, many RSS ideologues favour the self-reliant path of *swadeshi*. Consumerism, despite its appeal to a BJP-voting urban middle class, is equated with Western 'moral pollution'. Similarly there are clashes between advocates of decentralisation and of a strong unitary state. Again some RSS activists regard culture and society rather than the state as the bringer of national unity. Neo-traditionalist and modernist responses to globalisation are uneasily held together by the need for Hindu/national self-strengthening in the face of the Muslim/Pakistan 'other'.

Despite the work of such theorists as McGrew (1992), Hall and Jacques (1989), Robertson (1992) and many others, globalisation remains an ambiguous concept. Globalisation has not only been very loosely defined, but has been used as a reductionist explanation for political change and ethnic conflict in the former Soviet Union and Yugoslavia in ignorance of cultural specificities and historical continuities. Globalisation is differentiated in its impact by geography, gender and class. Moreover, it is not a process which suddenly began at the end of the twentieth century. As we have noted during the course of this work, there have been earlier communications revolutions which have impacted upon political identity in the subcontinent. Print capitalism allowed the new communal, ethnic and nationalist communities imagined by elites responding to colonial rule to be articulated to a wider audience. The railways assisted in the actualisation of supra-local senses of identity. Indianness was also encouraged by overseas migration of free and bonded labourers. In a foretaste of the Khalistan movement, Sikh settlers in the Pacific coastal region of North America sought in the Ghadr movement to export revolution to the homeland.

Finally, the impact of globalisation in India must not be overexaggerated. Economic liberalisation has proceeded slowly and the internal market remains far more important for Indian industry than the export market. The one exception is the software industry that has spung up in Bangalore as a result of liberalisation, financial incentives and the presence of a pool of trained, but by international standards cheap, personnel. This has seen the rapid emergence in India's silicon valley of trans-national corporations geared for export to the world's software markets. By the early 1990s, four of the five leading software-exporting companies were fully foreign-owned or joint ventures and three-fifths of the industry's income came from exports.

For all these reasons, the temptation should be avoided to hypothesise fissiparous tendencies in contemporary India and Pakistan in terms of a generalised globalisation impact. Instead we will focus on four specific aspects of globalisation which have influenced cultural and political development within the subcontinent. We shall turn first to the de-industrialisation of Bombay arising from economic liberalisation and the influence this has had on the rise of Shiv Sena; second, we shall trace the impact on the rise of *mohajir* ethnicity of both the global arms and drugs trails linking Pakistan to the West in the wake of the Afghan conflict and the downsizing of the state; third, we shall examine the role of the new mass media on political identity; and finally, we shall describe the role of overseas communities in the politics of homeland through the case study of the Khalistan movement.

Globalisation

From Bombay to Mumbai

Bombay has taken on some of the characteristics of a global city with a pre-eminent economic role in the national economy. As India's largest city, it jumbles together affluence, poverty, declining traditional industries and rising new ones. The city has mushroomed in size since independence, with the population rising to around 12 million people. They are the victims of overcrowding and the instability arising from successive waves of migration, including South Indians, Gujaratis and Maharashtrians from Bombay's relatively underdeveloped hinterland. During the past decade, the city has been transformed from a cosmopolitan centre to a hotbed of communalism and ethnic chauvinism.

The road from Bombay to Mumbai has been scarred with violence and intolerance. The communal clashes in the city in the wake of the 1992 demolition of the Babri Masjid were the most intense since partition. Bombay's transformation has resulted from the rise to prominence of Shiv Sena. While to Western audiences its activists are primarily known for the relatively harmless activity of digging up cricket pitches to prevent Pakistan engaging with India on their field of dreams, there is a much more sinister side to the organisation. Almost from its inception, Shiv Sena developed links with the city's criminal underworld (Gupta, 1982, p. 90). Protection rackets help fund its activities. These have been directed against 'outsiders', initially South Indians and communists, latterly Muslims who are portrayed as agents of Pakistan. Despite its 'sons of the soil' nativism and communalism, Shiv Sena is not a traditionalist movement; its vision is rather of a 'modern' Mumbai criss-crossed by flyovers, served by helicopters and even a hovercraft transport service. This 'modernity' has been dubbed by critics as 'philistine' and 'fascistic' (Hansen, 1998, p. 153), as squatters, especially the demonised 'illegal Bangladeshi' immigrants, are to be swept out of sight in the drive for a middle-class 'cleanly' aesthetic. Foreign investment is actively sought to help provide the infrastructural development required for this putative 'Asian tiger'. The city's appeal to foreign investors has of course been increased by the employer 'friendliness' of the Shiv Sena-led unions. The Shiv Sena leader Bal Thackeray's openness to global capital created tensions between Shiv Sena and its post-1989 BJP coalition partners who espoused *swadeshi* ideals. These were seen most clearly in the controversy involving the American power company Enron in 1995.

Bal Thackeray, a former political cartoonist, who founded and has dominated Shiv Sena, undoubtedly drew inspiration from Marathi history and especially the Shivaji myth. Shiv Sena functions continue to be marked by the garlanding of a bust of Shivaji. The leading role of Maharashtra in the freedom movement at the time of Tilak forms another historical influence. This is echoed in the cry that a strong Maharashtra is vital for a strong *rashtra*. Even before Shiv Sena's inception, Thackeray, in his periodical *Marmik*, was inveighing against the declining job opportunities of Maharashtrians in an increasingly competitive and dynamic labour market. Better-educated South Indian migrants were 'stealing' jobs from the sons of the soil, while strikes by communist trade unionists were simultaneously hitting the Maharashtrian-owned businesses. Shiv Sena provided an answer to the latter problem by its violent blacklegging of strikes. In many factories, leftist unions were replaced by the Bharatiya Kamgar Sena, the trade-union wing of Shiv Sena which was established in August 1968. Shiv Sena's popularity was greatly increased by its demand for 80 per cent reservation of jobs for Maharashtrians. Parallels can be seen here with the MQM's 'solution' to growing *mohajir* economic problems in Karachi.

Shiv Sena's privileging of ethnicity over class consciousness was summed up by Thackeray's comment, 'Anyone who gives bread and employment to the Maharashtrians is ours, be he Tata, Birla or any other' (cited in Gupta, 1982, p.137). This ideology was well established by the time that Bombay faced increasing economic strains and stresses resulting from the contemporary processes of de-industrialisation and downsizing of the state. 'In such a situation', the Indian journalist Arvind Das has declared, 'the by now almost classical paradigm of alienation finds increasing expression ... While people lose control over themselves in the realm of production, they also seek to assert their group identities in the localised cultural context' (Das, 1994, p. 69).

Sikata Banerjee has revealed how Shiv Sena mushroomed from its modest beginning at a rally in a North Bombay park on 19 June 1966 against the background of the city's textile industry's decline. Its death throes were accompanied by the workers' abortive attempts to save their jobs in the 1982–3 labour strike (Banerjee 1995, pp. 221–2). A quarter of a million strikers were involved in this 18-month dispute during which 75,000 employees were dismissed. Economic liberalisation meant that the millowners were faced with an uphill struggle to stay competitive because of the outmoded machinery and relatively high wages of a strongly unionised labour force. Retrenchment and relocation of units of production to

Bhiwandi and Surat decimated Bombay's manufacturing base. Shiv Sena's emphasis on the self-respect and sense of family cohesion of its activists carried great appeal in this situation of growing insecurity (Heuze 1996, pp. 216ff).

Indeed Shiv Sena provides a classic example of a movement riding to power on the back of working- and middle-class fears of a 'trend towards massification and dispossession'. Moreover, it was able to recycle funds to its supporters as a result of a growing treasure chest from business and retailers, part of which took the form of protection money. Its powers of patronage were also increased when it took control of the Bombay Municipal Corporation from the mid-1980s onwards. It was not until the 1995 elections that the Shiv Sena–BJP combine finally superseded the Congress at state level. Shiv Sena's continued appeal at a time of rapid change was trumpeted by Thackeray himself in an article in the *Indian Express* in October 1998. 'Anywhere you find a sense of insecurity among the Hindus, you will also find the Shiv Sena', he boasted. 'For the endangered and the insecure ... the Shiv Sena is the only hope. The Shiv Sena can never betray the trust reposed by the hopeless millions.'

Just like European fascist parties of the interwar period, Shiv Sena's warmth and inclusiveness was achieved first at the expense of downgrading democracy in favour of the leadership principle and second at the expense of the scapegoated 'outsider'. From the outset Thackeray held unrivalled power as the Sena Pramukh ('supreme leader of the (Shiv) Sena'). Looking back at the Shiv Sena's formation, he declared, 'I constantly maintained that those who join me should be willing to obey me as their leader. I don't believe in so-called democracies' (cited in Gupta, 1982, p. 73). On another occasion Thackeray opined, 'I look upon the *Sainiks* [activists] as my children. A family can only run when one man makes the decisions' (Gupta, 1982, p. 97). In August 1972, Thackeray admitted that he admired Hitler and also respected him as an artist (Gupta, 1982, p. 139). By the late 1990s, signs of dissent were emerging in Shiv Sena, however, because of the corrupting influence of the centralisation of power (Hansen, 1998, p. 145). There was also disquiet regarding the beginnings of a dynastic rule (*gharanashahi*) following the grooming of Thackeray's nephew, Raj, as a future leader.

Given Thackeray's former association with the Rashtriya Swayam Sevak Sangh and his attachment to the Shivaji cult, there was always an anti-Muslim element in Shiv Sena's ideology. An early Thackeray cartoon in *Marmik* portrays Bharat Mata as a fragile maiden scolding a Hindu politician protecting riotous Muslims (Gupta, 1982, p. 137). Thackeray's opposition to family planning was premised by the belief that while the 'Hindu soldiers' would decrease, the Muslim population would continue to increase. At first, the Shiv Sena's main 'other' was the South Indian outsider. A column in *Marmik* in July 1966 entitled 'My Troubles, Your Stories' was illustrated by a fierce and huge South Indian harassing a gentle and small Maharashtrian

(Gupta, 1982, p. 129). Calls for a Marathi Mumbai carried great weight, for it was Tamil 'outsiders' from South India derisively termed '*lungiwallas*' who, although only 10 per cent of the population at the time of the 1961 census, were faring far better than Maharashtrians in white-collar jobs because of their superior education and command of English. This background made them the main beneficiaries of 'post-industrial' service-sector job opportunities in Bombay.

Thackeray increasingly targeted the Muslim rather than a non-Maharashtrian or communist 'other'. Stereotypical portrayals of the Muslim community, which comprises around 15 per cent of Bombay's population, as 'lascivious' and 'dirty' were accompanied by calls for a *sundar* (beautiful) Mumbai. Such ideological borrowing was a natural progression from Shiv Sena's earlier adaptation of the RSS organisational model. In the 1991 Lok Sabha election campaign, Thackeray in fact went so far as to hail Gandhi's murderer a 'national' hero. His symptomatic willingness to say the previously 'unsayable' emerges clearly in the extract below which was penned in October 1998.

> Look at our country. Our laws, our rules. A whole list of don'ts meant only for Hindus. And who are the ones who are empowered? The Mussalmans. How long are we to tolerate this? How long are we to stand by and watch these actions in the name of religion? How long can we pretend not to see what goes on in the name of concession to the so-called minorities? ... Let us have a little laugh over our peculiar brand of secularism. The mosques blare out at us spreading the word of Allah a good five times a day. But no Hindu can dare to play cymbals or beat the prayer drums while he passes the house of Allah ... Secularism in our context ... [is] just another coinage and convenience, a piece of useful jargon. But the intent is deadly.
>
> *Indian Express* (Mumbai), 11 October 1998

It was the Shiv Sena's articulation of Hindu hostility to the disruption caused by Muslim calls to prayer which formed the background to the devastating January 1993 riots in Bombay. These were far more widespread than the Ayodhya-linked December 1992 outbreaks and resulted at the most conservative estimate in over 500 deaths. The looting and arson attacks which destroyed complete areas of Muslim shops, businesses and dwelling places were orchestrated in part by Shiv Sena activists (Massellos, 1996). However, criminal gangs and developers anxious to clear Muslim shanty dwellers from valuable plots of land also had a role in the violence (Agnes, 1996).

Shiv Sena's powerful ideological appeal has been reinforced by its ability to provide services abandoned by a shrinking state. Its Sthaniya Lok Adhikar Samiti organisation, founded in 1972 as a white-collar association, acts as a kind of labour exchange for educated unemployed Maharashtrian youths. *Saamna*, the Shiv Sena mouthpiece in Bombay, daily reports on such social-service activities in the fields of education, disability and job creation. Shiv Sena's alternative state in Bombay received important symbolic reinforcement by its management of the great Hindu festivals of Durga Puja and Shivaji Jayanti.

Kalashnikov Karachi

A parallel situation could be seen in Karachi where the MQM took over many of the state's social-service and policing activities in the late 1980s. Unlike in Bombay, however, the state in its local manifestation had declined not so much from downsizing resulting from globalisation as from persistent governability crises.

Pakistan's involvement in the dying stages of the global Cold War conflict between the United States and the Soviet Union fought out in neighbouring Afghanistan brought a bitter harvest. By the mid-1980s the country was awash with weapons and drugs. Arms seeped from the supply conduits established by the CIA and were channelled by the Pakistan military security agency (ISI) to favoured groups of Afghan *mujahadin*, notably Gulbuddin Hekmatyar's Hezb-i-Islami Afghanistan (Afghanistan Islamic Party). The traditional arms bazaars in the Frontier such as at Darra, together with new centres of production adjacent to the Afghan frontier, added to the glut of weapons by reproducing replicas of high-velocity machine guns and rifles and even of US supplied Stinger missiles. The kalashnikov culture was born, as it soon became possible for a relatively small sum of money to hire a weapon for the day on the streets of Karachi. Criminal gangs, ethnic groups and rival sectarian Muslim groups soon possessed a firepower which far surpassed that of the police and even the militarised Rangers. Rival student groups stockpiled weapons in their hostels at Karachi University campus.

Guns and drugs often went hand in hand. Afghan *mujahadin* financed their military operations with drug money, while criminal drug gangs acquired weapons in their turf wars. The traditional opium poppy fields of the tribal areas of the North-West Frontier Province dramatically increased their production in the unsettled conditions brought by the influx of three million Afghan refugees following the 1979 Soviet occupation. Heroin followed the same clandestine routes out of the country as weapons had found their way in, later to surface on the streets of Europe and North American. Pakistan's black economy thrived as some individuals well placed in the security, military and political establishment took advantage of the heroin boom. Indeed a report produced by the caretaker administration of Moin Qureshi in 1993 listed 164 former legislators as active in the drug trade (Waseem, 1992, p. 66). Government attempts at halting poppy planting met with armed resistance on one occasion in March 1986, led by a national assembly member (van Hollen, 1987, p. 150).

The impact of drug-laundered money on consumer demand in Pakistan has never been quantified. Nor, with the exception of Ugo Fabietti's work

(1996), has the impact of heroin smuggling on the local economy been studied. Fabietti has pointed out, however, that the monetisation of the economy of the coastal Makran region of Balochistan was greatly assisted by drug trafficking. Its controllers have become leading entrepreneurs in the building trades, agriculture and the fish processing industry. They have become influential distributors of local resources and have been courted by politicians. Indeed Makrani society has seen considerable social mobility resulting from the influx of black drug money and remittances from the one in ten of the population who are migrant workers. Heroin has found its way not only on to global markets, but to an emerging domestic Pakistani market. According to a UN Drug Control Programme report, Pakistan possessed 1.5 million heroin addicts by the mid-1990s, three-quarters of whom were under the age of 30. If unchecked, it was estimated that addiction would rise to two and a half million by the start of the new century. In some jails one in five inmates were already addicts.

Karachi's situation as Pakistan's major port and commercial centre meant that it was inevitably going to be a staging post in the global drug and weapons trails. The city already possessed a potentially volatile ethnic mix of populations before the advent of kalashnikovs and heroin. From the late 1960s onwards it was seen as a distant city of dreams, drawing men from their native land by its promise of wealth. 'Guddi holay holay chala' went one such song, 'luma safar Karachi da' ('drive the train slowly for the journey to Karachi is a long one'). Around a tenth of the total world Baloch population is squeezed into Pakistan's leading city, clustering mainly in the chronically congested environs of the Lyari district. Karachi's population had risen from under half a million at independence to 12 million by the mid-1990s. It has been estimated that a quarter of a million Pushtuns and Punjabis settle in Karachi annually.

Urban migration encouraged a construction boom. It also, however, placed tremendous pressure on the infrastructure and created pollution and environmental degradation. The citizens of Karachi by the early 1990s were daily generating 35,000 tonnes of waste. Three hundred million gallons of untreated sewage was being daily discharged by the Lyari and Malir rivers into the sea. The former green belt of Malir housed the country's largest pesticide dump and was being turned into a desert as a result of illegal sand mining in the river bed to supply the construction industry. Karachi's ethnic violence of the 1980s must be viewed in part against the background of the outstripping of transportation, housing and water supplies by the mushrooming population.

The Mohajir Qaumi Mahaz (MQM), which emerged in March 1984 out of the cadres of the All-Pakistan Mohajir Students Organisation (APMSO), was very much a product of Karachi's urban problems. One of its early demands was for the legalisation of *katchi abadis* (slum settlements) as a step towards providing them with better amenities. Piped water, for example, was available to less than half the homes in the unregulated slum areas at the end of the 1980s. Yet a rising proportion of the population, nine in every 20 inhabitants, lived in the *katcha abadis*. Resentment at the formal state's inability to tackle socio-economic problems or provide law and order led to the rise of the informal MQM 'secondary state'.

Criminal violence in the 'biggest Pushtun city in the world' was largely drug-related from the mid-1980s onwards. The presence of large numbers of Pushtuns either from the traditional poppy fields of the tribal areas, or from the new producing areas of wartorn Afghanistan interfaced with the rising global demand for heroin. Karachi increasingly suffered from the presence of drug mafias and the growing social problem of addiction. This both precipitated the increasing tension between *mohajirs* and Pushtuns and operated under its cover. Further factors in the emergence of a 'new ethnicity' *mohajir* political identity were the socio-economic changes of the Zia era in Karachi. These saw an acceleration of Punjabi migration and of an increasing Punjabi role in the expanding bureaucracy at the expense of the *mohajirs* at the elite level.

Simultaneously, Pushtuns increased their stranglehold on the city's transport, labouring and construction industries. Baloch settlers also formed another important component of the labouring force. *Mohajirs* found themselves squeezed out of employment and were angered by the ostentatious display of 'new money' which accompanied the flood of guns and heroin from the areas adjacent to the Afghan war zone. Significantly, the MQM initially allied itself with the native Sindhis against the Pushtun/Afghan, Baloch and Punjabi 'outsiders'. It was also by no means coincidental that the first major ethnic riot in April 1985 followed the death of a *mohajir* schoolgirl, Bushra Zaidi, under the wheels of a Pushtun-driven mini-bus. The violence spread to large areas of the city, especially to Orangi where Pushtuns and Biharis engaged in a series of ethnic attacks. Days of curfew ensued in selected districts of Karachi.

The partyless elections of 1985 further encouraged ethnic loyalties. The political responses to this situation were seen in the *mohajirs'* claims that they should be recognised as a fifth 'nationality' and in the formation of the Punjabi–Pushtun Ittehad (Union) in March 1987. One significant episode in the escalation of ethnic violence was clearly linked to the drug mafias. The bulldozing of the largely Pushtun/Afghan-inhabited north Karachi slum area of Sohrab Goth in December 1986 by the army and police in search of illegal arms and drugs precipitated retaliatory ethnic attacks on poorer *mohajir* localities elsewhere in the city. A more cynical interpretation would see this not just as motivated by the need for *badal* (revenge) but an attempt by 'drug traffickers and land developers ... to get the law enforcing agencies off their back by initiating an ethnic riot' (Malik, 1995, p. 61). The use of machine guns certainly suggested that this was no spontaneous riot. Equally sinister was the careful targeting of non-Pushtun businesses and homes for arson in scenes reminiscent of the 1984 Delhi riots.

The weak state power demonstrated at the time of the 1986 unrest encouraged the rise of the MQM. Its political breakthrough in the 1987 local government elections in both Karachi and Hyderabad impacted, however, on its relations with the Sindhi community which had previously been cooperative. Indeed the foundational Charter of Resolutions had talked of *mohajirs* and Sindhis as 'real' Sindhis and sought to limit the franchise and the ability to buy property to them. By 1988, however, Pushtun–*mohajir* violence was being replaced by a pattern of Sindhi–*mohajir* conflict which was to intensify with the restoration of democracy following Zia's mysterious death in the air crash of 17 August 1988. By the mid-1990s *mohajir* audiences were chanting 'Sindh mein hoga kaise guzara, adha hamara adha tumhara' ('How can we co-exist in Sindh? half is ours, half yours') (*Newsline*, 28 March 1994, p. 27).

We have already seen earlier in this work how, from the partition era onwards, Sindhis had resented the influx of *mohajirs* and their control of Karachi and Hyderabad's economic life. For their part *mohajirs* regarded themselves as victimised by the quota system for federal employment and access to educational institutions which had been introduced in 1973 and favoured rural Sindhi representation. Alongside these long-term influences, three more immediate factors lay behind the Sindhi–*mohajir* violence which increasingly imperilled national solidarity: first, the MQM's flexing of its muscles as it sought to dominate the local political scene and thereby secure national leverage; second, the increasing nationalist and anti-*mohajir* outlook in Sindhi politics as seen in the rise of Dr Qadir Magsi's Jiye Sindh Progressive Party; third, the spread of Sindhi-*mohajir* civil disorder from Hyderabad to Karachi. Settlement patterns had always encouraged a much more direct competition for resources between the communities in Hyderabad. The tension finally spilled over in the violence of 30 September 1988, which in its turn prompted the *mohajir* backlash in Karachi.

New media and political identity

Globalisation theory distinguishes between what may be termed the 'old media' of terrestrial television, radio and cinema and the 'new media' of satellite television, video- and audio-cassettes, mobile phones, fax and personal computers from which one can surf the cyberspace of the internet and download information. In their archetypal representations, the old media are depicted as centralised, state-run and associated with homogenisation. The new media are conversely regarded as decentralised, 'emancipatory' and pluralist. Their emergence is portrayed as both mirroring and contributing to the decline of the nation state whose interests were formerly served by the old media. How does this theory accord with the realities of the subcontinent?

We have seen in earlier chapters how state-controlled television and to a lesser extent the cinema have been used in India and Pakistan to forward the nation-building enterprise. The monopolistic state-run 'old-media' Indian and Pakistani television services with their homogenising tendencies in respect of content and language do appear to display some of the character-istics of the theoretical schemata of such writers as Enzensberger (1970). The situation with respect to the cinema is more complex, as it was never directly under state control. Nevertheless, its ability to strengthen regional identities in the subcontinent has been partly mitigated by state censorship. The declining radicalism of Tamil releases is linked with this. *Parasakthi*, for example, was banned for a time by the authorities. As in the former Soviet Union, creative writers could, of course, circumvent censorship to a certain extent by subtle allusions and the use of historical drama. A number of Tamil films, however, were so badly mangled by the censor that they automatically became box-office flops. The state's gatekeepers cannot easily censor the contents of home pages on the web or destroy the messages and documents despatched by e-mail. However, access to the information superhighway is limited in South Asia because of the cost of high-technology computers and modems. By 1998 only 0.3 per cent of India's urban population could be reached through the internet. Diaspora communities and students living abroad have nevertheless used the web to engage in sometimes vicious polemical discourses of identity politics.

The new media of cassette tapes and videos have proved equally difficult to police. Moreover, unlike computers they are plentiful and cheap, as would be illustrated by a visit to Delhi's crowded electronics retail centre at Lajpatrai Market across from Shah Jehan's imposing Red Fort. By the end of the 1980s, around two and a half million cassette players were being sold annually, along with $21 million worth of recorded music.

A decade later, the new media of cable television had also made its mark. According to an Indian readership survey of 1998 around 13 million urban households and five million rural homes had access to cable television. The cable revolution facilitated the proliferation of private channels from the beginning of the 1990s. Doordarshan found that it had to compete with the trans-national channels such as Rupert Murdoch's Star TV along with private Indian channels like Zee TV. Concerns about an 'invasion from the skies' were reduced when, for commercial reasons, the foreign-owned satellite channels began to indigenise their output. This resulted not only in such cultural curiosities as a Hindi-speaking Pamela Anderson in *Baywatch*, but in the emergence of the hybrid 'Hinglish' language medium. Recent scholarship has revealed that the 'localising' of trans-national satellite programming has resulted in more 'modern' representations of Indianness than that provided by the 'staid' Doordarshan, but this imagery is equally stereotypical and stylised (Butcher, 1999, pp. 165–99). At the other end of the spectrum from MTV and Channel (V) are the broadcasts made by local cable operators. A recent study of neighbourhood broadcasting in South Delhi has revealed the importance of religious events for live telecasts. According to one resident, by allowing 70 days of *jagrans* (night long festivals) to be broadcast, modern technology had led 'more people [to] become religious'. At the same time the character of the temple celebrations had been altered by the broadcast. '*Jagrans* have become commercial, the scale of the event grows every year to reflect the ego of the organiser. Sometimes, I feel I am watching a movie – the lights, the filmi music' (Mishra, 1999, pp. 269–70).

The impact of the cassette revolution

The cassette revolution provides yet another fascinating example of the subcontinent's tradition and modernity syndrome. This is epitomised by Gulshan Arora, the Richard Branson of the Indian recording industry. He turned a hobby in cassettes into the major T-Series business enterprise manufacturing 25 million cassettes annually by 1991, in addition to making and selling pre-recorded cassettes, producing feature films and exporting televisions and cassette recorders. Arora attributes his success, however, not to his business acumen, but to the blessings he receives from a goddess, Vaishno Devi, whose shrine is situated in Jammu. He has constructed temples to her, given generously to charities in her name and produced cassettes of devotional music (Manuel, 1993, p. 68).

While traditionalists have been affronted by the setting of Hindu hymns of devotion (*bhajans*) to film tunes and disco beats, they have proved immensely popular. They are not only played in homes but in temple *jagrans*. Sikh devotional music (*shabd gurbani* and *shabd kirtan*) has also been widely recorded, while the Muslim *qawwali* music recorded by the late Pakistani singer Nusrat Fateh Ali Khan was marketed commercially to an international audience. Regional devotional music has also shared in the cassette boom. It had been previously marginalised both by radio broadcasting and the highly centralised Indian recording industry dominated by GCI (Gramophone Company of India), a subsidiary of HMV and later EMI. Indeed nine-tenths of its output had been devoted to Hindi film songs. By the mid-1980s, however, GCI's musical market share had been reduced to under 15 per cent by large newcomers such as T-Series, Venus Records and Tapes and a host of small music producers. Film music now accounted for only 40 per cent of the market sales.

Modernisation rather than hastening homogenisation encouraged religious 'little traditions', as independent cassette producers marketed regional devotional music. Typical of the latter were the folk music tapes in the Agra district Braj dialect of Hindi in devotion to the local goddess Kaila Devi (Manuel, 1993, p. 213). The *languria* Braj devotional songs have been accompanied by the secular *rasiya* cassette genre. Many of these folk songs, like those in other emerging regional secular genres are ribald *masaledar* (spicy) works. Their bawdy content is indicated by such titles in collections in the Bhojpuri (Varanasi district) Hindi dialect as *Bastard Banana*, *Nine Inch Banana* and *Bhojpuri Eggplant*. Indeed a purist critique of the cassette culture is that it has objectified women and commodified religion. Some of the lewdest tapes are to be found amongst the Punjabi truck drivers' music, '*Driveran di Mauj*' (drivers' entertainment), a genre that did not exist prior to the cassette phenomenon (Manuel, 1993, pp. 173–4). In Europe and North America, Punjabi music is of course best known in its hybrid *bhangra* form. In contrast, the songs of Bhupen Hazarika are virtually unknown outside the subcontinent. His music, which contains a strong Assamese nationalist strain with its identification of the Assam homeland with the Mother, received a much wider audience following the audio-cassette boom (Baruah, 1997, pp. 502ff).

In previous chapters we have noted how from the time of the *swadeshi* movement onwards, folk music and drama was used for propaganda purposes. In post-independence India, the CPM in Bengal has continued this tradition. Touring theatre groups have also been employed by the state to popularise sterilisation as a family-planning technique. Audio-cassette tapes have increased the possibilities for the dissemination of political messages either through song or the spoken word in a semi-literate society. Ayatollah Khomeini, the inspiration of the revolution against the Shah of Iran, was a pioneer in their use in this respect. Within India, Sant Jarnail Singh Bhindranwale was the first to make use of the electronic pulpit. Bhindranwale became head of the orthodox Damdami Taksal 'seminary' at Chowk Mehta near Amritsar in 1977. The following year he had risen to prominence following clashes with the heterodox Nirankari sect whose leader Baba Gurbachan Singh claimed to be a living deity. Bhindranwale went on to challenge the Akali Dal 'moderate' leadership through support from the All-India Sikh Students' Federation which had been revived by Amrik Singh, the son of Jarnail Singh's predecessor as head of the Damdami Taksal. Bhindranwale also secured support from the lower-class Jat peasantry of the Punjab's Manjha region.

Although he was publicy ambivalent towards the Khalistan demand, which had been supported by a splinter group of the Akali Dal since 1981, it was clear that Bhindranwale espoused the need to achieve a sovereign authority for the Khalsa. Through his taped sermons Jarnail Singh Bhindranwale was able to reach a much larger audience than had previously been possible even in the peripatetic Sant tradition of travelling the countryside in order to give readings of Sikh sacred texts. Indeed part at least of Bhindranwale's charismatic authority rested on his use of the new cassette medium. Even when he was holed up in the Akal Takht (the shrine representing the temporal power of God) in the Golden Temple complex surrounded by the Indian Army, he was able, through taped sermons, to provide an alternative source of authority to the state. At his daily congregations he also dispensed justice, issued statements on religious and political issues and granted interviews to foreign newspaper and television journalists. Bhindranwale died along with his 2,000 companions, many of whom were ordinary pilgrims, in the blaze of publicity in which he had lived. As we have seen, televised reports of the Indian Army action at the Golden Temple shocked the world Sikh community to the core.

Audio-cassettes enabled the *dhadi* (eulogist) tradition to extend its impact beyond the confines of its customary performance centres. *Dhadi* musicians recorded their commemorations of the Sikh struggle against the state and the Indian authorities were unable to censor them. General Labh Singh of the Khalistan Commando Force was honoured in a number of recordings following his death in July 1988. Around 6,000 cassettes were initially distributed in England and the songs were sung in many *gurdwaras* (Pettigrew, 1991/2, p. 85). Jarnail Singh Bhindranwale and his companions in the Golden Temple in June 1984 were, as might be expected, the most frequent subjects of the *vars* and *gits* (people's songs) of the *dhadi* musicians. The extract from a cassette tape reproduced below provides the flavour of such recordings. In the traditional *dhadi* style the song is preceded by a spoken introduction.

Introduction
Out of the martyr's sacrifice is the power and dignity of a nation born.
The blood of these heroes constitutes the soul of the nation. I, Kamal,
say that a nation needs to smear its forehead with the ashes of such
martyrs. Their sacrifice sweetens the life of the nation. By their
martyrdom they breathe new life into the nation.

Musical interlude

Come let's bow down to the martyrs,
those who for the sake of the nation have died.

Musical interlude

Come let us bow down to the martyrs,
those who for the sake of the nation have died.

Musical interlude

Those who for the sake of the nation have died,
such as the great Sant Jarnail Singh Bhindranwale:
How great he was!
Who put this nation on a new path.

Musical interlude

He gave a vital message to a nation

that was on the point of forgetting itself,
and awakened the nation by sacrificing himself.

Musical interlude

He awoke its spirit.
Wonderful were Amrik Singh and our brother, General Shubeg
Singh,
who carried out their obligations to the *Panth*.

Pettigrew (1991/92, pp. 108–9)

The Sangh Parivar has also made extensive use of audio-cassettes in the popularisation of Hindutva. These became increasingly inflammatory in the wake of the first unsuccessful attempt by *kar sevaks* to demolish the Ayodhya Mosque in October 1989. Such tapes as 'Mandir ka nirman karo' ('Build the Temple') were widely available, despite government bans. This professionally produced cassette included songs performed by the film vocalist Narender Chanchal. Typical of their lyrics was the following:

> The time has come, wake up, young men and go to Lucknow
> You must vow to build Ram's temple
> The conches sound, Ram's forces are standing ready for battle
> Gandiv (Arjuna's bow) is twanging, his conch calls
> Whoever joins with the wicked, smash their dreams
> Turn the political dice and blast their policies
> Advance in the battlefield of politics and hit hard
> To compare Ram with the wicked is beyond disrepect
> Destroying his temple is the limit of madness
> Don't play their farcical game of acting in a courtroom
> Liberate the janmabhoomi of the jewel of the house of Raghukul
> If they don't heed with words, whip out your swords ...
> Face our enemies with courage
> Now isn't the time for contemplation.

Manuel (1993, pp. 252–3)

A number of the 'banned' tapes included speeches by the militant female activists Uma Bharati and Sadhvi Rithambara who were subsequently to become BJP parliamentary candidates. The extroverted Bharati in her saffron robes and short hair cut was perhaps inevitably dubbed by the press the sexy *sanyasin* (religious celibate). Rithambara, who like Bharati comes from a rural low-caste background, was noted for the passionate rage of her speeches which on a number of occasions had instigated riots (Basu, 1993, p. 27). Their coarse and violent speeches at one level trangress traditional gender roles; at another they are sanctioned, as women can have licence to speak from emotion rather than reason. Both women also derive their influence from the fact that they are celibate, which is accompanied by notions of spirituality and power in Hindu thought. At the same time, however, they can play the iconic role of the Hindu wife and mother chiding dutiful sons and mocking errant husbands into political activism. Their value to the Sangh Parivar lay also in their frequent allusions of Muslim rape of Hindu women, through which the BJP symbolised the general victimisation of the Hindu community. 'Hindus wake up', Bharati rages on the cassette *Jai Shri Ram* ('Hail Ram'), 'they've looted you and you stayed silent; they sacked your temples and raped your mothers and daughters, and you kept quiet. What reward did you get for your equanimity?' (Manuel, 1993, p. 253).

Even more sinister than cassettes containing such vitriolic speeches were those designed with no other purpose in view than to promote violence. When tapes containing sounds of gunfire, blood-curdling screams and violent slogans were blared at night from cars in already tense Agra neighbourhoods in October 1989 they actually incited riots. At the other end of the spectrum of the uses of cassettes are those produced by Jagori, the Delhi women's rights organisation. These have included not only songs about gender-related issues such as dowry extortion and *purdah* set to well-known folk and film tunes, but also calls to transcend religious bigotry:

> God has become divided in temples, mosques and churches ...
> The Hindu says the temple is his abode
> The Muslim says Allah is his faith
> Both fight, and in fighting die
> What oppression and violence they wreak over one another!
> Whose goal is this, whose scheme?
>
> Manuel (1993, p. 240)

Similar sentiments were expressed in the Westernised pop style of the Goan singer Remo Fernandes in his track 'SOS India', which opened with the lines: 'religious madness catching hold of the nation, Politicians' gladness, their manipulation, children's sadness, They cannot understand why mother hates, why father kills, Killing in the name of love, killing in the name of God' (Manuel, 1993, p. 192).

Religion, lies and videotape

The market for video-cassette entertainment in India is much smaller than that for audio-cassette tapes, but nevertheless it has grown rapidly in recent times. A 1991 National Council of Applied Economics research poll, for example, revealed that low-income housholds with an annual income of up to 25,000 rupees accounted for a third of all the video-cassette recorders sold in India (Farmer, 1996, p. 112). It is therefore not surprising that videos have been increasingly used as a tool of mass mobilisation. The Congress-I first exploited this new media in the 1985 elections with its compilation of speeches given by the late Indira Gandhi. The BJP, however, has made the most sophisticated use of video-cassette technology. Shortly after the October 1989 temple campaign, the BJP issued videos purporting to reveal the police brutality against the *kar sevaks* at Ayodhya. In the 1991 elections, the BJP deployed 108 specially built 'video *raths*' (chariots) each equipped with 300-inch screens to tour constituencies. Promotional videos were also distributed to local branches of the party. These included speeches by party leaders and films of crowds massed at election rallies, interspersed with clips of Hindu deities culled from film and television productions.

The BJP propaganda was also piped to those affluent enough to have access to cable television. Elderly voters and women who were unlikely to attend party gatherings formed the target audience. Final evidence of the BJP's mastery of the new technology was afforded by the launching of a satellite television channel. This was the brainchild of the BJP Upper House member J. K. Jain who had provided the technical backing for the video *raths*. Jain has estimated that tens of thousands of copies were made of his 1990 Ayodhya video, *Pranh Jha Hu Vachanu Na Jaye* ('We Can Give Up Our Lives, But We Cannot Break Our Vows'). The satellite network acronym (JAIN, Joint American Indian Network) testifies not only to the role of Jain studios, but to the ties between wealthy North American non-resident Indians and the BJP.

Independent film producers unattached to the BJP have also turned to the video to put across their version of cultural nationalism. The most notable example was the Bombay-based Bharat Bala Production Company's 'Bande Mataram' project which marked the fiftieth anniversary of Indian independence. The freedom movement's anthem was given a pop beat and was accomapnied by evocative video images culminating in the nation assembling under the Indian flag. Commercial advertising clips for such companies as Bajaj (scooters) and BPL (electronics) have deployed similar patriotic images. Significantly, the 'Bande Mataram' project's producer declared that, 'nation building is the *basic brand* that is required today, India *needs* that' (Brosius, 1999, p. 109).

The internet, Hindutva, communal and ethnic reassertion

The internet with its sites and newsgroup discussion fora has provided another means of communicating the Hindutva message to the diaspora. In the words of one web watcher it is especially important in generating a sense of identity for participants who 'sell their souls to corporate capitalism all day and in the evenings hook up to community networks to get news from "home"'. Hindutva pages first appeared on the world wide web in 1993 starting with the key hub of the Global Hindu Electronic Network (GHEN). Since then the RSS, VHP and BJP have all developed their own sites.

Bharat Mata is a recurring visual image. The home page of the BJP website in India (www.bjp.org), for example, displays on its home page Bharat Mata placed in front of a map of India, accompanied by the salutation 'Bande Mataram'. The VHP Hindu net sites include Bharat Mata images alongside pictures of temple volunteers who were shot dead during the 1990 struggle at the Babri Masjid. The Hindu Vivek Kendra acts as an important information resource on the net with one of its tasks being the refutation of Western academic criticisms of Hindutva. Donations by credit card can be made to *ashrams* and other charitable causes at the Hindu Heritage Foundation site, an operation of the VHP. Some of the material on the net is relatively uncontroversial like, for example, the biographies of great Hindus at the Hindu Universe site. But that contained on the web page Satyameva Jayati ('Truth alone triumphs') is virulently anti-Muslim. Articles on Islam which can be visited there include such titles as the 'Wonderous Treatment of Women in Islam' and 'The X-rated Paradise of Islam'. Such material follows on the polemic against Islam waged by such nineteenth-century Hindu activists as Lekh Ram. One particularly interesting site relates to the claim that the Taj Mahal has been built on the site of a Shiva temple. It must thus be 'liberated' as the Babri Mosque was at Ayodhya. The flavour of the piece can be gauged from the extracts below.

> By now you all know through my previous articles, the irrefutable facts and deductive logic that Islam is evil at its very foundation. It is not a religion, but a means to legalize rape, murder, loot and destruction. These *dacoits* [criminals] have looted and raped many countries, but no country can tell a bloodier tale of Muslim oppression than India! The Muslim *dacoits* started their rule over India in 712 AD with the invasion of Mohamed Qasem and looking at the present situation of our country, it still continues on today! … Aurangzeb himself destroyed over 10,000 Hindu temples … some of the larger temples were converted into mosques or other Islamic structures … Ram Janbhoomi (at Ayodhya) and Krishna Temple (at Mathura) are just two examples. Many others exist.

> The most evident of such structures is Taj Mahal – a structure supposedly devoted to carnal love by the 'great' Moghal King Shah Jahan to his favourite wife Mumtaz Mahal. Please keep in mind that this is the same Shah Jahan who had a harem of 5,000 women and the same Shah Jahan who had an incestuous relationship with his daughter justifying it by saying *'a gardener has every right to taste the fruit he has planted.'* Is such a person … capable of imagining such a wondrous structure as the Taj Mahal let alone be the architect of it?

> The Taj Mahal is as much an Islamic structure as is mathematics a Muslim discovery! The famous historian Shri P. N. Oak has proven that the Taj Mahal is actually *Tejo Mahalaya,* a Shiv Temple Palace. His work was published in 1965 in the book, *Taj Mahal. The True Story.* However we have not heard much about it because it was banned by the corrupt and power crazed Congress government of Bharat who did not want it to alienate their precious vote bank – the Muslims … There is a similar story behind *every* Islamic structure in Bharat. They are all converted Hindu structures.[1]

---

[1]   A link to the Satyameva Jayati web page can be found at the South Asia Citizens' Web: http://www.mnet.fr/aiindex

The Orientalist discourse on Muslim licentiousness is thus alive and well on the web. The author goes on to provide the URL (unique resource locator) of Oak's home page, along with the address of a publisher in Houston who can supply the book. History, as we have constantly noted in this book, is crucial to the Hindutva ideology. It is not surprising, therefore, that there are numerous chat rooms and fora on the Hindu net to discuss such topics as 'Aryan Invasion Theory', 'India's Golden Ages' and 'India Under Islamic Rule'. One Hindutva site (www.hindunet.org/hindu–history) has a section of history through comic books and can be linked to another site which contains slides of the freedom struggle. Online magazines that are sympathetic to the Hindutva enterprise such as *India Star* (www.indiastar.com) feature extensive reviews of such writers as Sita Ram Goel and Ram Swarup, which in the words of one writer to its editor, challenge the 'political correctness of official Indian history'.

The BJP–VHP effective propaganda use of technological innovations reveals the powerful blending of tradition and modernity in the Hindutva cause. Parallels can of course be found with nineteenth-century religious activists' deployment of the new print culture, while claiming to uphold 'tradition'. Indeed, from this period onwards, reformulation and innovation under the cover of tradition have been at the heart of the construction of a pan-Indian Hindu community. The demonisation of the Muslim 'other' has also been a constant.

At the other end of the political spectrum, the Jammu and Kashmir Liberation Front (JKLF) has made extensive use of the information super-highway. The JKLF, which has lobbied for and engaged in armed struggle for the 'third option' of an independent Kashmir, was founded in Birmingham on 29 May 1977. The UK Zone with its 20 branches remains one of the three zonal groupings which make up the JKLF organisation. (The others are the Azad Kashmir Gilgit-Baltistan Zone and the Indian-occupied Jammu Kashmir Zone.) There are also individual branches in the Middle East, Europe and Australasia. On 3 October 1980 the New York branch disrupted the UN General Assembly meeting by causing a commotion in the visitors' gallery. Up-to-date news of the independence struggle is posted on its home pages on the Kashmir net. The JKLF also produces an internet magazine, the *Voice of Kashmir*, which provides 'facts' about Kashmir and comments on leading events.

Another site provides a full-length biography of Maqbool Ahmad Butt, a pioneer of the armed struggle in Jammu and Kashmir who was hanged in New Delhi on 11 February 1984. The Indian Deputy High Commissioner in Birmingham, Ravindra Mahatre, had been kidnapped a week earlier in an abortive attempt to secure Butt's release. The JKLF continues to lobby via the net and other media for the release of the two students Abdul Qayyum Raja and Mohammed Riaz who were convicted in 1984 'by circumstantial evidence' of the diplomat's kidnapping and subsequent death. Intriguingly, the JKLF shares another web page with the Sri Lankan Tamil Eelam separatists (www.wavefront.com/~homelands/india.html).

The new media and Pakistan

Within Pakistan, successive regimes have strictly censored the old news media. This has not of course prevented recourse to the BBC World Service. Nevertheless, the globalisation of communications with the advent of satellite television has created an unprecedented situation. The mushrooming of satellite dishes in such working-class areas of Karachi as Lyari, Lasbela and Karimabad has revealed that Star Television is not just a luxury for the rich. The copying of Western technology and the piping by cable to an entire tenement the pictures received by a single dish has spread access even to those on low incomes. This threatens not only the state's control over political and intellectual outlooks, but Pakistani social mores. Indeed, members of the *'ulama* have inveighed against the beaming in of 'cultural pollution' and the 'sexual anarchy' which it was encouraging.

Unsurprisingly Pakistanis have linked themselves up to the information superhighway more slowly. By the middle of 1995 the total number of networkers was estimated at little over 3,000. But the problems for domestic censorship arising from cyberspace were already apparent with the posting of the MQM news bulletin on the net. This regularly updated releases from Nadeem Nusrat at the North London MQM International Secretariat. Indeed, as we have already noted, without modern technology, Altaf Hussain could not have directed MQM operations in Karachi from his London exile. In July 1995, in an attempt to curb 'terrorism', the Bhutto administration took the controversial step of suspending the entire cellular telephone network and pager system in Karachi and Hyderabad.

Aside from MQM, its erstwhile rival for the urban vote in Sind, the Islamist Jamaat-i-Islami, has made the most effective use of the new technology of audio-cassettes. Pasban, which had commenced life in 1990 as its youth wing, soon shed the conservative image of its parent organisation to campaign on such social injustices as rape. Its rallies employed video screenings, music and laser light shows to attract a youthful audience. Such 'vulgar' displays dismayed the Jamaat leadership and caused the split that followed the 1993 elections. Pasban retained the media spotlight by successfully organising Imran Khan's fund-raising campaign for the Shaukat Khanum Memorial Cancer Hospital in memory of his mother. It played a key role in its culminating event, the celebrated Awami show celebration in Lahore's Fortress Stadium on 28 December 1994. Later, however, Pasban shifted its ties to the PPP government.

Trans-national Asian communities and the politics of homeland

The roots of the large overseas South Asian communities in the United Kingdom (1.4 million at the time of the 1991 census) lie in the movements of peoples during the colonial era (Tinker, 1974) and the postwar labour shortage. Despite the presence of pioneering communities on the Pacific coast of North America at the beginning of this century, large-scale migration to America and Canada followed the British tightening of immigration restrictions at the beginning of the 1960s. During the 20 years from 1961, for example, the South Asian community of Canada increased from less than 7,000 to around 600,000. Five thousand new Sikh settlers from the Punjab alone were arriving each year.

Globalisation with its mass air travel and instantaneous communications has intensified the cultural, economic and political exchanges between these diaspora communities and their homelands. Family remittances from overseas have played important although largely undocumented roles in the economies of Indian Punjab (Thandi, 1994) and Azad Kashmir (Ballard, 1983). In addition to family members, charities, schools and hospitals have all benefited from remittances. It is especially interesting in the light of his later rallying of diaspora support for the Khalistan demand that Dr Jagjit Singh Chohan, when Punjab Finance Minister in 1968, made an early bid for overseas help for back home. He formulated a scheme whereby tractors could be sent to Punjab farmers by their British relatives without customs duty. Everyone gained in this global exchange as the bulk of the 3,000 tractors that were sent had been built by Massey Ferguson whose head-quarters were in Coventry, a Midlands city with a large Sikh population, many of whom were employed in the car factories. Remittances could also, of course, support cultural concerns. Sikhs in the Midlands provided funds for the restoration of Sikh shrines abandoned in Pakistan following the partition of the Punjab. Remittances also paid for the establishment of the Ghadr heroes' memorial in Jullundur. The 'crossover' musical style of *bhangra* (Bauman, 1990), initially popularised by the British Asian band Alaap, has been carried back to Punjab by such exponents as Gurdas Maan, while chic Bombay fashions are paraded on the streets of London, Toronto and New York.

The tradition of overseas communities' involvement in the politics of their Indian homeland dates to the Ghadr movement during the First World War. A small number of Canadian Sikhs took part in the Jaito Morcha during the *gurdwara* reform movement. The communications revolution and increasing wealth of sections of the diaspora communities has, however, intensified this trend. Satellite television, the internet and a burgeoning South Asian press in North America and Europe, epitomised by such publications as *Jang* and *Des*

Pardes, supplements the information about 'home' arising from personal family communications and frequent visits for marriages and to see ageing parents. Muslim *pirs* and *'ulama* and Sikh *sants* frequently visit their overseas followers and have built mosques and *gurdwaras*. The issues of subcontinental politics are further kept alive by the overseas branches of political parties and the activities of socio-religious movements such as the Arya Samaj and VHP. The psychology of expatriate support for the Hindutva and Khalistan movements has been laid bare by the Anglo-Indian writer Shashi Tharoor:

> The attitude of the expatriate to his homeland is that of a faithless lover who blames the woman he has spurned for not having sufficiently merited his fidelity. That is why the support of extremism is doubly gratifying. It appeases the expatriate's sense of guilt at not being involved in his homeland, and it vindicates his decision to abandon it. (If the homeland did not have the faults he detests, he tells himself, he would not have had to leave it.)[2]

Identification with subcontinental community and political developments is further encouraged by the sense of pride and recognition these bring to those alienated from the host society as a result of racism (Goulbourne, 1991). Ironically, British South Asian support for 'fundamentalist' religious-based identities within the subcontinent may have been encouraged by the post-colonial anti-racism pluralist discourse of multiculturalism. While fostering the notion of Britain as a multiracial society, this has constructed Asians through state funding and patronage as religiously monolithic communities with their self-appointed spokesmen. This reproduces the colonial state's understanding of Indian community, although in all other respects the legacy of Empire is disavowed by liberals working in the multicultural industry.

Diaspora communities have, of course, their own interests and concerns both in national politics and in such 'community' interests as education and state intrusion on their cultural autonomy. These have been seen, for example, in the dress code turban campaigns, whether with respect to the Wolverhampton Public Transport Authority in the 1960s or the Royal Canadian Mounted Police in the 1990s. British Muslims have campaigned for grant-maintained status for Islamic schools, while British Hindus struggled in the 1990s to prevent the closure of the Watford (Bhakti Vedanta Manor) Temple. Nevertheless, interest in the subcontinent's politics has remained high, as was evidenced by L. K. Advani's fund-raising visit to Britain during the summer of 1995 in advance of the Indian general elections. Mainstream Indian and Pakistani nationalism has drawn sustenance from overseas communities: for example, from the Indian Overseas Congress during the emergency period (1975–77). In recent years, however, the greatest impact has been made by supporters of those in conflict with the

2 Shashi Tharoor, 'Growing Up Extreme: On the Peculiarly Vicious Fanaticism of Expatriates', http: //www.mnet.fr/aiindex/tharoor.htm (South Asia Citizens' Web)

post-colonial settlement. Sindhi, Kashmiri and Sikh separatists have all been active in this way, as have supporters of the BJP and MQM. They have lobbied legislatures in Britain and North America, arraigned national governments for human-rights abuses and demonstrated against visiting national leaders. They have also used the new media to popularise their chosen cause and have raised funds for political and other forms of struggle in the homeland. Activists from minority communities engaged in conflict with the state have joined in public protests, like the time of the fiftieth anniversary of Indian independence and earlier, in May 1994, when the then Prime Minister Rao visited the United States. Within the UK there were protests in Leicester, London and Birmingham in August 1997. The following extract from a study by a British Sikh activist typifies the attitudes of such protestors to the Indian state.

> It is abundantly clear for all to realize that the India of today is a superficial state imposed from above by the transfer of power from the British Raj and ... is an unnatural outcome ... Several nationalities of India in their territorial units, which like Khalistan should be able to form their own sovereign states of Maharashtra, Tamil Nadu, Assam, Sikkim, Nagaland, Mizoland, Kerala, Jammu and Kashmir and come together in a new economic union as the European Economic Union with full freedom for self-development in unity and mutual regard for each other.
>
> Sihra (1985, p. 10)

Key organisations in the Kashmiri and Sikh separatist struggle of the 1980s were founded overseas. Tensions between supporters of the status quo and its opponents have led to violent clashes. In June 1986, for example, in a telling illustration of the impact of globalisation, Indian consulate officials in Lahore were beaten up by Sikhs on a visit from Canada. There have been a few instances of murder or attempted murder, like, for example, that in Luton of Sohan Singh Liddar, president of the Indian Overseas Congress late in 1985, and the case involving the Deputy High Commissioner to which we have already referred. The fallout from such incidents and the alleged conspiracy to murder Rajiv Gandhi when he visited the UK in September 1984 intensified Indian claims that the British government was 'soft' on terrorism. Its displeasure was made clear by the cancellation of the £65 million Westland helicoptors deal. JKLF publications claim that the arrest of its chairman Amanullah Khan on explosives charges and his subsequent deportation to Pakistan in December 1986, despite acquittal, resulted from this Indian pressure. The British government eventually agreed to an extradition treaty with India in 1992 (Siddharth, 1992). This followed the conclusion five years earlier of an Indo-Canada extradition treaty. The Canadian government had increasingly viewed support for the Khalistan movement as illegitimate in the backlash arising from the alleged involvement of Sikh militants in the Air India disaster off the Irish coast on 23 June 1985.

The greater freedom to operate overseas along with increased awareness of homeland politics partly explains the mushrooming of separatist organisations in Britain and North America. Another factor has been the composition of South Asian diaspora communities. In Britain, for example, around two-thirds of the South Asian community comprises settlers from the troubled Punjab region of India and Azad Kashmir in Pakistan whose population is committed to the ongoing struggle in the neighbouring Indian state of Jammu and Kashmir. In addition, there is a large Punjabi Sikh community settled in the United States and Canada. Indeed three-quarters of the estimated one million Sikhs living overseas are concentrated in Britain and North America. The 1984 White Paper published by the Indian government on the Punjab agitation blamed this almost entirely on the Pakistani 'external hand' and these overseas communities whose activities took up a sixth of the report.

Size is not, of course, everything. Well-educated and affluent activists from the much smaller *mohajir* communities in both Britain and America have made their presence known in the MQM's struggle with the Pakistani state. The small Sindhi and Azad Kashmiri populations in Britain have also been highly active in the World Sindhi Congress and the JKLF. The internet has helped link the scattered Hindu professionals in North America in the common Hindutva cause. The best-documented and most important involvement of an overseas community in the politics of homeland, however, remains that of the Sikhs and the Khalistan struggle in which Dr Gurmeet Singh Aulakh of the Council of Khalistan has acted as an especially effective lobbyist on Capitol Hill (Tatla, 1999). It is to this case study that we shall turn in the remainder of this chapter.

The Sikh diaspora and the politics of homeland

The self-proclaimed political party of Sikh identity, the Akali Dal, established its organisations amongst overseas communities first in Britain (1968) and then in North America (1976). The newly launched Akali Dals were from the outset closely linked with the Punjab parent organisation whose leaders made frequent visits. The Akali Dals competed for support with old-established organisations such as the leftist Indian Workers Association in Britain and the traditionalist Khalsa Diwan Society (Canada). In a mirror image of developments within the homeland, the overseas Akali Dal secured greatest support from the Jat Sikhs, with Sikhs from scheduled castes supporting caste-based (Bahujan Samaj Party) or leftist organisations such as the Communist Party of India. It was later from amongst the Jat Sikhs that the strongest diaspora support emerged for separatist demands. The overseas Akali Dal organisations focused on issues of Sikh identity, in particular the vexed issues of Sikhs' freedom to wear turbans in certain occupations (for example, as bus conductors) and to carry the *kirpan* (ceremonial sword). Leftist parties amongst the diaspora were more concerned with such issues as immigration controls.

The importance for the homeland of trans-national Sikh politics first became apparent in 1971 when the Akali Dal dissident Dr Jagjit Singh Chohan arrived in Britain. In public demonstrations at Hyde Park in London and in Birmingham he shouted Khalistan slogans and unfurled a Khalistan flag. The following month, on 12 October, he placed an advertisement in the *New York Times* which claimed that the Congress had betrayed its promises to the Sikhs at the time of partition.

> In 1947 it was agreed that the Sikhs shall have an area in which they will have complete freedom to shape their lives according to their beliefs. On the basis of the assurances received, the Sikhs agreed to throw in their lot with India, hoping for the fulfilment of their dream of an independent, sovereign Sikh homeland, the Punjab.
>
> cited in Cohen (1997, p. 112)

In a parallel development in Canada, a 'Republic of Khalistan' office was established which issued passports and currency. Although not quite a voice crying in the wilderness, Dr Chohan and his supporters received little sympathy from the diaspora until the growing crisis in the Punjab in the early 1980s. Its circumstances will be examined in detail in the next chapter. Suffice it to say here that a number of *gurdwaras* in Canada and Britain passed resolutions in support of the Akali Dal's Punjab autonomy campaign (Dharam Yudh Morcha) launched in September 1981 and sent weekly donations to the Akali leaders in Amritsar. The campaign made no mention of independence or of Khalistan. Nor, for that matter, did Sant Jarnail Singh Bhindranwale whose preaching at this time was gaining increasing support amongst disaffected Sikh youth.

Attitudes within the diaspora were transformed by the actions of the Indian Army in Operation Bluestar. In the polarisation of opinion which followed, existing Sikh organisations including the Akali Dal were swept aside by the rise of such new groupings as the World Sikh Organisation (WSO), the Khalistan Council (UK-based), the Council of Khalistan (North America-based), the Babbar Khalsa and the International Sikh Youth Federation (ISYF). The WSO was formed on 28 July 1984 following a meeting in Madison Square Gardens in New York. Within three years, its North American membership was estimated at 16,000. The bi-lingual weekly *World Sikh News* sought to popularise its aim of an independent Sikh homeland which was to be achieved 'by peaceful means'. Within Canada, the WSO was to become increasingly embroiled in factionalised struggles for control of *gurdwaras*, which dissipated its energies.

The Khalistan Council and the Council of Khalistan similarly emphasised peaceful struggle as the means to acquire a Sikh homeland. The latter organisation emerged following Dr Aulakh's split from the WSO and established its headquarters in Washington as befitted its lobbying role. As a result of its activities, the human-rights record of the Indian government received greater international scrutiny than ever before. Funding was received from *gurdwaras* both in America and Western Europe. The Khalistan Council was formed under Dr Chohan's leadership during a tumultuous Sikh rally at Southall, West London, three weeks after Operation Bluestar. Since that time, despite factional and ideological splits, it has consistently argued for Sikh sovereignty in rallies at *gurdwaras*, through the monthly *Khalistan News* and in a short-lived 'Voice of the Sikhs' radio broadcasting venture.

The Babbar Khalsa and the ISYF have adopted a more radical and less secular stance. Both organisations have been linked with militant groups active in armed struggle in Punjab. They have also allegedly been responsible for acts of international terrorism such as the bombing of the Air India plane. The Babbar Khalsa both in the Punjab and in Britain and North America is a staunch upholder of Sikh orthodoxy. Along with its fundamentalist stance have gone calls for revenge against the 'Hindu imperialists' in its monthly publication (1987–94) *Wangar*. In North America it is based in Vancouver and the British headquarters are in Birmingham where Gurmej Singh has headed a government-in-exile. Funds raised overseas have been sent back to Punjab to aid the Khalistan struggle and to provide for its 'martyrs'.

The Babbar Khalsa has been embroiled in acrimonious struggles with the ISYF for control of British *gurdwaras*. The elections to their controlling committees witnessed violent struggles in such places as Coventry in the mid-1980s. Control of the *gurdwaras*, as well as bringing prestige, provided access to patronage and a ready-made propaganda platform. Despite being the largest Sikh organisation in Canada, within a year or two of its foundation in 1984 with some 20,000 members, the ISYF was unable to wrest control of the prestigious Ross Street *gurdwara* in Vancouver from the WSO's grasp. The ISYF has been closely linked with the Bhindranwale family. Its British branch spawned the Sikh Human Rights group based in Southall. The organisation has suffered a number of divisions, most notably in 1988 when its leading figure Jasbir Singh Rode, following his release from prison, abandoned the goal of independence for autonomy within India.

Aside from the cases of Canadian and British Sikhs who have been arrested in India for 'terrorist' actions and the claims of the security services, it is difficult to gauge the direct involvement of the diaspora organisations in the 'homeland' struggle. Their role is much clearer, however, with respect to lobbying and the propaganda war. The global Sikh community has ensured that human-rights issues in Punjab have been closely scrutinised. It has also joined the 'ethnic theatre' of lobbyists at Capitol Hill and the Dag Hammarskjold Plaza outside the UN in New York. The Council of Khalistan, albeit briefly, gained membership of the UNPO in 1993. However successfully counter-insurgency and the return to the 'normalcy' of 'transactional' politics may be managed by the Indian state in Punjab, sections of the global

Sikh diaspora now remain wedded to the ideal of a separate and sovereign Khalistan.

Conclusion

This chapter has emphasised four aspects of globalisation that have influenced the politics of identity in the Indian subcontinent, namely: the impact of economic liberalisation with particular reference to the rise of Shiv Sena; closer and more intensive economic interaction and flows of both legal and illegal goods which is most dramatically illustrated by Karachi's kalshnikov culture; the communications revolution which has limited the ability of the state to censor the media and has encouraged regional cultures; and, finally, the growth of global South Asian communities involved in the politics of homeland as a result of international migration.

Interesting parallels can perhaps be drawn between elite assertion of communal and ethnic identity in late nineteenth-century colonial India arising from a situation of socio-economic instability and the print explosion and ethnic and religious reassertion at the mass level in a contemporary subcontinent undergoing the impact of globalisation. Globalisation's challenges to the Nehruvian vision of India has been summed up by Sunil Khilani in the compelling symbolism of Bombay and Bangalore. Bombay has been stalked by de-industrialisation and the accompanying rise of Shiv Sena. Bangalore has experienced the rapid growth of its silicon valley born of the multinational arrivals Hewlett-Packard, Agfa and IBM. The glistening shopping malls of Fifth Avenue and the Barton Centre where one can forget one is in India have followed. Both Bombay and Bangalore, despite their contrasts, 'manifest an exhaustion of the nationalist imagination', Khilani maintains.

> They have spawned ideas of India at sharp variance with Nehru's. To an adherent of the Shiv Sena in Bombay, defining oneself as Maharashtrian, or Hindu, seems to deliver more direct benefits: Indianness has become an instrumental choice, a less advantageous identity. Likewise, to the young MBA or software expert in Bangalore, India is merely one stopping place in a global employment market.
>
> Khilani (1997, pp. 148–9)

10

Ethno-nationalism, insurgency and secessionism in India and Pakistan

What is being forgotten is the historical inevitability
of the collapse of India and the creation of more
than twenty nation states in the subcontinent. This
will release tremendous energy of the people now
bottled up by the reactionary colonial Indian system.

World Sikh News, 18 February 1994

The Nation with all its paraphernalia of power and
property, its flags and pious hymns, its blasphemous
prayers ... and the literary mock thunders of its patriotic
bragging, cannot hide the fact that the Nation is the
greatest evil for the Nation.

Tagore (1917, p. 29)

Since the end of the 1960s, the Indian and Pakistani nation states have experienced violent ethnic and ethno-religious movements. Insurgencies have
not been limited to the last three decades or to the four case studies which are
analysed here. But the intensity of these struggles which together claimed the
lives of hundreds of thousands of militants, members of the security forces
and ordinary citizens, raises important questions concerning the competing
claims of national, communal and ethnic identities.

Given the subcontinental state's accumulation of coercive capacity
(Sathyamurthy, 1997, pp. 249–51), it seems more important to understand
the causes of insurgency than the reasons for its failure. We shall turn first,
however, to the subcontinent's only successful post-independence secessionist movement, the breakaway of East Pakistan and the emergence of
Bangladesh as a sovereign state in 1971.

Bengali nationalism and the breakup of Pakistan

A number of writers have seen the 'geographical absurdity' of the separation of the western and eastern wings of Pakistan and the existence of a strongly defined Bengali collective consciousness as together ensuring the inevitable emergence of Bangladesh. The reality was far less clear-cut. The Indian state's co-option of an equally strong Tamil consciousness reveals that pluralism does not of itself doom federal political arrangements. Moreover, the Pakistan state itself has co-opted Pushtun nationalists, thereby, at least for the moment, killing off the Pakhtunistan demand. The crucial difference, however, was that a Pushtun elite could take its place as junior partners in the Punjabi-dominated establishment. The Bengalis threatened to overwhelm this with their own agenda, which conflicted with the interests of the army, bureaucracy and their landlord allies. A united Pakistan could have survived, but it would have been a very different state from that conceived by the West Pakistan powerholders.

There are a number of key landmarks on the road to the breakup of Pakistan: namely, the 1952 language riots in Dhaka which provided the first martyrs for the Bengali separatist cause; the dismissal in May 1954 by the Governor-General Ghulam Muhammad of the popularly elected United Front government, which in the provincial elections three months earlier had dealt a humiliating blow to the Muslim League; the introduction of martial law throughout Pakistan in October 1958 which marginalised the Bengali voice in the West Pakistan military-dominated regime; the inability of the Pakistan People's Party under military encouragement to share power with the Awami League following the first national elections in 1970; and, finally, the fateful decision to launch a military crackdown in East Pakistan on 25 March 1971.

Common to these events was Bengali marginalisation and the centre's refusal to accord legitimacy to Bengali demands. These were at best dismissed as inspired by misguided provincialism; at worst they were seen as evidence of an Indian fifth column in Dhaka. The constant questioning of Bengali loyalties served only to encourage disenchantment and claims that East Pakistan was being internally colonised both economically and politically. By the close of the Ayub era, Pakistan's unity was gravely imperilled.

The Bengali language movement and the 1952 riots

Just as the Urdu–Hindi dispute shaped the course of North Indian Muslim politics in the colonial era, so Bengali's status influenced the initial trajectory of Pakistani politics. In both instances, struggle for political power was expressed in linguistic terms.

Urdu became the state-sponsored language of Pakistan, despite the fact that Bengali was the mother tongue of over half the population, and within

East Pakistan itself only around 1 per cent of the populace regarded Urdu as their first language. From March until September 1948 students led a widespread popular movement in favour of Bengali. Among those arrested at this time was the future leader of Bangladesh, Sheikh Mujibar Rahman. The language movement re-emerged in East Bengal early in 1952 following the publication of the interim report on the constitution which declared Urdu as the national language. The government's tactless handling of the language issue intensified the protests. The death of four student demonstrators in clashes with the police at the Dhaka University campus on 21 February marked an important milestone on the Muslim League's road to ruin within the province. It was far easier for the police to destroy the memorial (Shahid Minar) erected to the martyrs than it was for the government either in Karachi or Dhaka to quell growing Bengali cultural and political self-assertion. This was heightened every year on 21 February which was celebrated as a day of mourning and protest known as *shahid dibas* or Martyrs' Day.

The United Front and the demise of the Muslim League

The language issue coincided with a growing feeling that West Pakistan was colonially exploiting East Bengal. The economic disparity between the two wings intensified during the 1950s as industrial production and infrastructural development in West Pakistan outpaced that in the east. Manufacturing output grew at an annual rate of 21 per cent in East Pakistan during the period 1949/50 to 1954/55 compared with 34 per cent in West Pakistan. This was explained by the effects of placing the federal capital in the western wing, the dynamism brought to its economy by migrant entrepreneurs and the greater foreign capital investment in West Pakistan. But far more obvious to Bengali critics were the disparities in the governmental loans and grants between East and West Pakistan. The greatest criticism was reserved for the transfer of resources from east to west through the diversion of foreign exchange earnings from jute, the main East Pakistani export, into the western wing's coffers for the import of industrial raw materials.

From 1951 onwards the Awami League orchestrated Bengali protests. It delivered its attacks on the federal government through the columns of *Insaf*, the party newspaper. The February 1952 disturbances greatly boosted its appeal. It further pressured the government by cooperating with other opposition forces including the octogenarian Fazlul Huq's Krishak Sramik Party. Huq's reputation and still formidable oratorical skills propelled him to the forefront of the opposition Jukta Front which was formed to contest the 1954 provincial elections, although his party lacked the institutional strength of Suhrawardy's Awami League. In what was to become an increasingly common feature of Pakistani politics, the Front consisted of a broad church of ideologically disparate parties, some of which were little more than one-man bands united only by their opposition to a common foe – in this instance the Muslim League.

The Front campaigned on a 21-point manifesto that called for a regional autonomy, which left only defence, foreign affairs and currency to the centre. While this foreshadowed future separatism, the manifesto also looked back to the earlier language movement with its emphasis on the need to recognise Bengali as a national language and the demands to make 21 February an official memorial day (point 18) and to erect a memorial to its martyrs (point 17). Support from non-elite groups was sought by including calls for 'fair' agricultural prices and for a removal of income disparities between the high- and low-paid salariat. Such demands were extremely popular in a climate of inflation and distress resulting from the collapse of the Korean War boom. Finally, by demanding the nationalisation of the jute industry, the Front struck at the leading symbol of East Bengal's 'colonial' status.

The Muslim League's identification with the distant centre of power in West Pakistan resulted in its rout. It captured just ten seats in an assembly of 309; the United Front, which had polled 65.6 per cent of the vote, had secured 223. The electors had rejected the contemporary manifestation of the Muslim League, but were voting in many respects for the future of East Bengal as envisaged by the Lahore Resolution. The Karachi powerholders' intransigence, however, drove the Bengalis further down the path of complete separation.

Huq's government was summarily dismissed following charges of pro-communist and pro-Indian leanings. The howls of protest were partly stilled because of the undeniable deterioration in the law-and-order situation during its brief tenure. This climaxed in the riots at the Adamjee jute mills which claimed 400 victims and were only suppressed by the army's intervention. The question of whether *agents provocateurs* were behind the labour disturbances remains unresolved. The dismissal of the United Front government radicalised the Awami League's 21-point programme into the six-point programme. This called for the establishment of full provincial autonomy in East Pakistan on the basis of the Lahore Resolution. Fiscal autonomy which had not been included in the original 21 points was now added, with the provision that the eastern wing should raise its own taxes, mint its own currency and operate its own separate foreign exchange account. The centre was limited to responsibility for defence and foreign affairs. Significantly with regard to defence, the 21 points' call for the moving of the Pakistan naval headquarters to the eastern wing was beefed up in 1966 with the demand for a separate militia or paramilitary force.

The Ayub era and Bengali alienation

Pakistan's first martial law regime exacerbated the Bengali political elite's alienation with disastrous consequences for national integration. Many

Bengali politicians regarded the October 1958 coup as a pre-emptive strike by the West Pakistan establishment fearful that national elections would bring to power a Bengali-dominated government committed to land reform and *rapprochement* with India. Whatever the truth in this reading of events, the stifling of democracy disadvantaged the eastern wing.

Bengalis were underrepresented in both the army and the bureaucracy, which now called the shots. In the numerous commissions of inquiry that were instituted, in such varied fields as land reform, franchise and constitutional recommendations and the press, Bengalis accounted for just 75 of the 280 members. None of Ayub's key aides were Bengalis. He thus 'had no one around him to advise him adequately or intelligently'. In a classic case of too little too late, the recruitment system was changed to redress the imbalance, so that ten of the 16 probationers for entry to the central secretariat in 1968 were drawn from the eastern wing. By this stage the unrest was mounting in both wings of the country which was to force Ayub to hand over the reins of power to Yahya Khan.

The 1970 elections and their aftermath

Yahya allowed Pakistan's first national elections to take place in December 1970. Nearly a quarter of a century had passed since independence and a whole generation had grown up without the opportunity to choose the national government. The lengthy electioneering had hardened attitudes towards the centre in East Pakistan. Further alienation had been caused by its mishandling of the terrible tragedy of the November 1970 cyclone which claimed an estimated one million lives in East Bengal. Mujib denounced Islamabad for its slow response to the emergency. The West Pakistani elite condemned him for attempting to exploit a national disaster for personal political gain.

The Awami League contested the polls on the six-point programme and in opposition to the western wing's treatment of East Bengal as a 'colony'. It held out the prospect of a *sonar* (golden) Bengal, if the autonomy programme was implemented. Increasingly the candidates of the West Pakistan-based parties such as the Jamaat-i-Islami (JI) and the three Muslim Leagues were likened by the Awami League to Mir Jafar who had traitorously assisted the East India Company's ascendancy in Bengal in 1756. Two people were killed during a JI meeting and rallies of other parties were broken up by crowds chanting *Joy Bangla* ('Victory to Bengal').

The West Pakistan-based PPP did not contest East Pakistan constituencies and the Awami League ran just seven candidates in the western wing. This strategy enabled both parties to maximise their influence in their major centres of support, but was to create problems after the elections. The Awami League's hopes of gaining a foothold in West Pakistan through an alliance with Wali Khan's Frontier- and Balochistan-based National Awami Party had been dashed when their negotiations broke down in late September.

The results revealed the Awami League's total eclipse of its rivals in East Pakistan. It secured complete control of the Provincial Assembly. Out of the 162 seats allotted for East Pakistan in the National Assembly, it won 160 and secured three-quarters of the total votes polled in the eastern wing. Although it failed to win a single seat in the four provinces of West Pakistan, its landslide victory ensured a majority in the National Assembly.

The Pakistan People's Party formed the second major party. Contrary to official expectations, it had beaten off the challenge of the religious parties to capture 81 of the 138 West Pakistan seats. The former had depicted the election as being a contest between Islam and socialism evidenced in such slogans as 'Socialism kufr hai. Muslim millat ek ho' ('Socialism is heresy. Let the Muslim people remain one'). But these backfired as they confirmed in the mind of the voter the PPP's projection of itself as the only party concerned with relieving the poverty of the masses. This was summed up in the ringing PPP cry of *Roti, Kapra, Makan* ('Food, Clothing and Shelter'). Most PPP victories (62) had been secured in the Punjab; all but one of the remainder were seats in Bhutto's native Sind.

The outcome exposed the long-standing political cleavages between East and West Pakistan. The Bengalis had responded to years of political marginalisation by propelling to national power a party which threatened the established economic and political interests of the West Pakistan-dominated civil–military establishment. National stability now rested on the complex negotiations between Bhutto, Mujib and Yahya Khan. The Pakistan President had confidently expected a much stronger showing from the religious parties and the Muslim League which would have produced a regionally less polarised result.

The emergence of Bangladesh

The circumstances surrounding the descent to civil war continue to evoke bitter controversy. An increasingly drink-befuddled Yahya and an opportunist and arrogant Bhutto have been cited by some writers as the causes of the tragedy. Conspiracy theories attach responsibility to Indira Gandhi who is portrayed as plotting and scheming Pakistan's division assisted by the 'fifth column' of the Awami League. In the absence of available records, a definitive account of this period has still not been written.

Three points, however, clearly emerge from the polemical discourse: first, the distrust which surrounded the negotiations following the elections was rooted not just in personal animosities and ambitions but in the earlier treatment of Bengali aspirations and in the zero sum game approach to Pakistani politics. Second, responsibility must rest with Yahya Khan for ordering the fatal military crackdown of 25 March. Again this reflected a long-held belief that the aspirations of regional groups within Pakistan were illegitimate and should be met by repression rather than by political negotiation and bargaining. Finally, it is clear that the Indian military intervention ensured the success of the Bengalis' secessionist struggle after 25 March.

By late afternoon on 23 March, the army command had recommended to Yahya that military action was now essential to suppress the Awami League rebellion. The crackdown code-named 'Operation Searchlight' which sealed the fate of national unity was launched at midnight on 25 March. Yahya later justified it by citing the threats to non-Bengali Muslims, the murders committed by the Awami League and its insults to the army, the Pakistan flag and the Quaid-e-Azam.

Hundreds of students were killed in the army assault on the Iqbal and Jaganath halls of residence in Dhaka University. 'Two days later bodies still smouldered in burnt out rooms, others were scattered outside, more floated in a nearby lake' (Choudhury, 1974 p. 185). These massacres, together with the firing on the headquarters of the police and East Pakistan Rifles, provoked the 'mutiny' of the East Bengal regiment under Major Ziaur Rahman. The Pakistan Army initially encountered little resistance as it 'cleared' the urban areas of rebels throughout the whole of the eastern wing. The flood of four million refugees across the border precipitated the Indian military intervention on behalf of the *mukhti bahini* (freedom fighters).

This influx was judged as 'unacceptable', not only because of its volume but because its destination was to 'the politically volatile' north-eastern hill states of Tripura and Meghalaya and to West Bengal, the scene of struggle with Maoist revolutionary Naxalites (Franda, 1971). Support for the Bangladeshi 'freedom fighters' was thus motivated as much by the desire to 'quarantine' and control them as by a long-held desire to undo the partition. Nevertheless, the Indian decision to 'go to war was deliberate, not taken under duress, or with a sense that immediate action was needed to stave off disaster' (Sisson and Rose, 1990, p. 278).

Pakistan lost half its navy, a third of its army and a quarter of its air force during the course of the two-week conflict. General Manekshaw, the Indian chief of army staff rejected pleas for a ceasefire which would have enabled the Pakistan Army to be repatriated to the western wing complete with its weapons. Under intense diplomatic pressure from America, Yahya agreed to accept the Indian ceasefire terms. The Pakistani commander General Niazi unconditionally surrendered on 16 December along with his 93,000 troops who had been surrounded at Dhaka. While Mujib returned in triumph to Bangladesh after his incarceration, the West Pakistan military establishment faced the humiliation of seeing an important section of its forces languishing as Indian prisoners-of-war.

The foregoing narrative emphasises that Bangladesh's emergence was not inevitable. The Pakistan state had not fallen apart because of Bengali primordialism or Indian machinations. The responsibility lay primarily in Islamabad. Chauvinism had compounded folly in the failure to co-opt Bengali demands.

The challenge of *mohajir* nationalism to the post-1971 Pakistan state

The rise since the mid-1980s of a *mohajir* political identity and nationalism in the urban centres of Sind has posed the greatest challenge to Pakistan's national unity since the breakaway of Bangladesh. The state's resort to force, including extra-judicial killings, rather than to political accommodation, carried disquieting echoes of the earlier conflict in East Pakistan. Equally resonant was the refusal to accept the MQM's demands as legitimate amidst claims that its leaders were in the pay of India.

The restoration of democracy in Pakistan in 1988 following Zia's demise ushered in a new phase in the Karachi crisis. This took the form of a mini-insurgency in which armed MQM militants battled the security forces and their MQM(H) proxies. The state justified its repression by claiming that the MQM threatened secession with its plans for a Jinnahpur based on Karachi. While there was no immediate prospect of a further breakup of Pakistan because of the MQM struggle, the disturbances in the country's major commercial and industrial centre contributed to the deepening foreign exchange and internal budget deficit crises of the 1990s.

Three key factors had lain behind the Karachi crisis: first, the weak attachment to consensus and accommodation in the Pakistani political culture; second, the kalashnikov culture bequeathed by the Afghan War; and, finally, the military and the intelligence agencies retained a strong influence despite the restoration of democracy in 1988. On key occasions they appear to have acted independently of the Prime Minister. Claims have often surfaced in the Pakistani media that it was in their institutional self-interest to keep the Karachi situation on the boil.

The crisis stemmed from the failure of the Karachi Accord between the PPP government of Benazir Bhutto and the MQM. The latter's success both in the 1988 Sind provincial elections and in the national elections had demonstrated the replacement of an Islamic orientation (seen in support for the JI) by an ethnic *mohajir* political identity amongst the Urdu-speaking voters of Karachi and Hyderabad. The PPP's precarious hold on power at the federal level (it had captured 92 out of 207 seats) gave the MQM with its 13 representatives considerable political leverage. The result was the Karachi Declaration signed between the MQM and PPP on 2 December. Both signatories dubbed it 'a charter of peace, love and rights' designed to 'reunite the rural and urban populations of Sind as the destiny of Pakistan rests on a united and unstratified society'. The student origins of the MQM were reflected in the fact that 10 out of 59 points concerned educational matters. Points 32 and 47 addressed the long-standing grievance of job quotas and domicile certificates. Significantly, the document omitted the demand for *mohajirs* to be recognised as a nationality.

The speed with which the accord unravelled questions its signatories' motivations. Had the MQM merely been buying time and signed the accord to secure the release of its activists? Did the PPP really intend to risk alienating its Sindhi supporters by acquiescing to *mohajir* economic and political demands? The MQM's public explanation for the growing rift concerned non-implementation of the innocuous-sounding point 34 that: 'Those Pakistanis living abroad by choice or compulsion will have all the privileges accorded to citizens of Pakistan.' What lay behind this was the demand for the repatriation of the quarter of a million or more Urdu-speaking Biharis who since the 1971 war had eked out a refugee 'stateless' existence in camps in Bangladesh. Their fate had long become a central element of MQM rhetoric and community identity. Sindhi politicians resolutely opposed their migration to Pakistan as it would further diminish the Sindhi majority in their 'homeland' province. Hawks within the Sind PPP organisation limited Benazir Bhutto's room for manoeuvre in meeting MQM demands.

Early March 1989 witnessed unexplained shooting incidents in Karachi. On the tenth of the month a pedestrian was killed and scores injured following shooting from speeding cars in the Gulshan-i-Iqbal, Quaidabad and Nazimabad *mohajir* localities of the city. The following week similar attacks by masked men led to ten deaths in the Malir and Khokrapar colonies. Altaf Hussain in a speech at Landi on Pakistan Day (23 March) maintained that the killings were designed to spark off riots. He also claimed that conspiracies were being hatched against the MQM 'by elements who feared that MQM might unite all oppressed classes in the country and challenge their system of exploitation'.

MQM speakers joined Nawaz Sharif's opposition party in condemning the deteriorating law-and-order situation in Karachi during an adjournment motion in the National Assembly. On 3 May, the three MQM ministers, Mohammed Juwaid Akhtar (Health), Syed Altaf Hussain Kazmi (Local Government) and Shamsul Arfeen (Public Health) resigned from the Sind cabinet. In a conciliatory gesture, the federal government reversed its decision to cut the urban quota of places (i.e. those which would be filled by *mohajirs*) in Dawood Engineering College admissions. This did not prevent the MQM from observing a 'black day' of protests on 26 May. Although this passed off peacefully, the following weeks were marked by an upturn in violence which included a shoot-out at Karachi University on 8 July between PSF (People's Students Federation) and APMSO student supporters which left three dead. After an incident on 14 July in which gunmen had sprayed bullets on two roadside MQM hide-collection camps, 17 MQM members of the Provincial Assembly publicly expressed their grave concern at the 'wave of terror'. To PPP outrage they also revealed that Altaf Hussain had spoken to the Pakistan President Ghulam Ishaq Khan (1915-) and sought his intervention in Sind affairs.

Despite these warning signs, the PPP was shocked when Altaf Hussain appeared at a joint press conference with Nawaz Sharif the day after the opposition had tabled a no-confidence motion. The defection of the MQM members threatened the Bhutto government's majority. According to some reports, President Ghulam Ishaq Khan had been instrumental in the MQM move which followed a new 17-point accord with the faction of the Muslim League loyal to Narwaz Sharif in which the repatriation of Biharis figured prominently. During the tension-filled week that followed the tabling of the motion both the government and the opposition sequestered their supporters in an endeavour to prevent defections. In the event the government carried the day by 12 votes, but the democratic process had been badly damaged by charges and counter-charges of political harassment and attempts to buy votes.

During the months that followed, the MQM was at the forefront of the anti-Bhutto movement. The Combined Opposition parties' rally in the grounds of the Quaid-e-Azam's mausoleum in Karachi on 26 January 1990 was a personal triumph for Altaf Hussain and displayed to the full the MQM leader's charisma and oratorical skills. It was undoubtedly the largest political gathering in Pakistan's history. Just under a fortnight later the dark side of the MQM's mass mobilisation strategy was seen when a call for a peaceful strike unleashed a day of violence which left 57 dead, a number of whom were innocent victims caught in the crossfire between police and 'unknown persons'. Ishaq Khan reportedly 'summoned' the PPP federal Interior Minister Aitzaz Ahsan to explain the gravely deteriorating situation in the country's commercial capital.

In protest at the 'killing of *mohajirs*' Altaf began a hunger campaign on Sunday 8 April 1990. By the following Thursday the panel of doctors who had examined him for an hour had come to the conclusion that his life was in danger. However, it was only after an appeal by a number of top Combined Opposition party leaders who had come to Karachi that the MQM leader broke his fast. He was receiving medical treatment for kidney problems at the Princess Grace Hospital in London when the tide of violence reached its peak.

The crisis in urban Sind climaxed in Hyderabad with the Pucca Qila incident of 27 May 1990. This episode, which has been likened by *mohajir* leaders to the notorious 1919 Jallianwala Bagh massacre, remains shrouded in controversy. The Pucca Qila area in the centre of Hyderabad was a *mohajir* locality. On the day of the massacre a Sindhi police party entered it to recover suspected illegal arms. They opened fire, allegedly killing over 40 people and wounding many more. The police version of events is that the firing was in retaliation to sniping, the MQM's that it was indiscriminate. Many of the victims were women and children. The former, in the MQM account, had been carrying copies of the Quran over their heads and were pleading for the police to stop the massacre. Whatever the truth of the matter, the event and the wave of violence that followed in Karachi including the Qayyum bus massacre of 31 May was cited by President Ghulam Ishaq Khan as part of his justification for the dismissal of the first Bhutto government.

The fact that Nawaz Sharif's assumption of power following the 'rigged' 1990 elections did not end the Karachi crisis owed much to the independent activities of the security services and the army in Sind. Laying aside conspiracy theses that this was Nawaz Sharif's 'payback' for his independent Gulf War policy (Talbot, 1999) and his differences with the President in 1993 over the choice of army chief, it is clear that the so-called 'democratisation' of Pakistan in 1988 had only been partial and that the unelected institutions of the state continued to wield great influence. Ultimately, the situation in Sind was to be used to manoeuvre Nawaz Sharif out of office like his predecessor. The limits of the Prime Minister's power were clearly emphasised by the lack of consultation over the decision to launch the army 'crackdown' in Sind in May 1992. This had originally been expected to be directed against the 2,000 or so criminal bandits (*dacoits*) who were terrorising the interior of the province. Instead the might of the army was directed against the MQM. The action was justified in terms of the deteriorating law-and-order situation in the city and by the discovery of alleged MQM torture cells (*khels*). It intensified the bloody rivalry between the mainstream MQM(A) and the breakaway MQM(H).

Altaf Hussain claimed that only criminals had been expelled from MQM, and that the security services co-opted them to weaken the organisation following its decision to transform itself into a Pakistan-wide movement of the *gharibon* 'downtrodden' (to be known as the Muttaheda Qaumi movement). An alternative reading is that this transformation generated genuine opposition within the organisation led by a 'gang of three' which included a MQM provincial minister Badar Iqbal and the MQM's joint secretaries Aamir Khan and Afaq Ahmed. They were expelled and fled to the United States. The purge included other zonal leaders including Rashid Ahmad and Mujtaba Khan and the whole of the Zone 'A' committee which represented Landhi, Korangi, Malir and Shah Faisal Colony. The dissensions were accompanied by Altaf Hussain's retreat to a hospital bed in the Abbasi Shaheed Hospital and by violence and boycotts against such newpapers and journals as *Dawn*, *Takbeer*, *Herald* and *Newsline* which had reported on the MQM's internal divisions. On 22 March, in an unprecedented step, the Karachi edition of *Dawn*, the paper founded by Jinnah, was suspended following threats against its journalists, distributors and hawkers.

The deployment of over 60,000 troops in the city shocked the MQM. The entire central committee and its MNAs (legislators) were forced into hiding. The military's uncovering of arms caches and *khels* dealt the organisation a major propaganda blow, although MQM(A) has constantly claimed that they did not exist prior to the army operation and were used by MQM(H) 'hoodlums' to terrorise workers into changing sides. With the support of the army and the intelligence services, the MQM(H) group ('genuine' group) re-established itself in June 1992 in large areas of the city. What was left of the MQM was headed by Azim Tariq, although all crucial decisions remained in the hands of Altaf Hussain who had taken up a self-imposed exile in London on 27 January 1992.

The election of a second Bhutto government in 1993 following the dramatic events surrounding Nawaz Sharif's dismissal by the President (Talbot, 1999) ushered in a new stage of conflict. This crippled the economy and raised the spectre of *mohajir* secessionism. The catalyst was provided by the withdrawal of the army from Karachi. Thereafter the MQM(A) fought a 'mini-insurgency' against the state and its MQM(H) proxies. In a parallel to the situation in the Indian Punjab, counter-insurgency policies, including extra-judicial killings, curbed militancy, but did not solve the underlying political problems. Many ordinary *mohajirs* who were caught in the crossfire were alienated from the state.

The army's hasty retreat from a futile two-year operation in the city early in December 1994 led to a spiral in the violence. In its first two weeks alone there were over 100 deaths. The government blamed the MQM(A). The latter, supported in many instances by independent human-rights organisations, declared that state terrorism was directed against it and that its workers were being unlawfully detained, tortured and extra-judicially killed. Much of the mayhem resulted from the clashes between the rival MQM(A) and MQM(H) factions in such localities as Shah Faisal Colony, Korangi, Landhi and Pak Colony. Sectarian violence further contributed to the death toll. There were also claims of Indian involvement and of conflict arising from rivalries between Pakistani intelligence agencies.

There was little respite for Karachi during the opening months of 1995. In February a fresh wave of sectarian violence saw attacks on mosques. Twenty-five people were killed by unknown assailants in two incidents on 25 February alone. The next month, world attention was directed to the city following the killing in broad daylight on 8 March of two US consular officials when their van was ambushed by unidentified armed gunmen on one of Karachi's busiest roads, Shahrah-e-Faisal. The ensuing security crackdown reduced the April tally of violent deaths to just 21. This was, however, only the lull before the storm. Violence erupted on 18 May with a day-long pitched battle between the security forces and the MQM(A) militants in the *mohajir* locality of North Nazimabad. During the week that followed there were repeated clashes in which more than 70 people were killed. The authority of the government collapsed in large areas of central, eastern and western Karachi.

Rocket launchers were fired at the Pakistan Television station and Liaqatabad police station, cars carrying government number-plates were attacked and police and Rangers' armoured cars were ambushed. The MQM(A) held the upper hand in what amounted to an insurgency until the end of June. From then onwards concerted action by the security forces, involving extra-judicial means, made inroads into the militant strongholds of Orangi, Korangi and Gulbahar. On 2 August, for example, Farooq Dada and four other MQM(A) workers were killed in what the police called an 'encounter' near Karachi's Quaid-e-Azam International Airport, although family members claimed they had been earlier arrested from their homes.

The May–June MQM campaign against government officials and the security forces and the latter's sense of operating in 'foreign' territory were dangerously reminiscent of events in East Bengal in 1970–71. Another chilling reminder was the parading on national television of alleged MQM(A) terrorists who confessed to their crimes. The almost total alien-ation of the *mohajir* population from both the provincial government of Chief Minister Abdullah Shah and the federal authorities was rooted in the excesses of law-and-order enforcement during 'Operation Cleanup'.

Male residents of whole neighbourhoods were rounded up, stripped to the waist and blindfolded before being carted away by the security forces. Bribes were often demanded before they were returned to their relatives. Such heavy-handed actions bred a sense of militancy amongst *mohajir* youth. Their alienation was compounded by the *mohajir* community's lack of a political voice in the administration of the city following the Sind government's refusal to call elections for local bodies. An almost unbridgeable chasm in fact existed between the political interests of the rural Sindhis and the urban *mohajirs*. This stood at the heart of the failure to achieve a dialogue between the PPP and the MQM(A). Yet this was essential to remove the wider threat Karachi's violence posed to Pakistan's economic life and its national unity. There was a domestic capital flight to the Punjab, while foreign investment dried up in the wake of the violence in the country's leading commercial centre. During the first three months of 1995 alone 102 billion rupees of market capitalisation were wiped off the Karachi Stock Exchange.

Karachi's violence continued unabated during the second half of 1995. The body count between late August and early November alone stood at 500. These deaths, however, marked the onset of relative normality rather than a fresh spiral of violence. The new atmosphere was most evident during the following spring, at the time of Ramadan and the Sixth Cricket World Cup fixtures which were held in the city shortly afterwards.

Just as in the Indian state of Punjab, counter-insurgency measures had eliminated the 'terrorist' threat. Eleven police 'encounters' took place in January alone, resulting in the death of 23 MQM activists or sympathisers (*The Herald*, Karachi, February 1996, p. 74). Such leading 'terrorists' as Naeem Sharri and Fahim Commando died in what appeared to be 'fake' encounters with the police, who along with the Rangers seemed to have been given a free hand in dealing with the militants. Extra-judicial killings, however, not only claimed their innocent victims, but further encouraged the brutalisation of Pakistani society. In the absence of a meaningful political dialogue, the root of the disorder remained unchecked. Indeed by the middle of 1998 violence was once again mounting in a depressing repetition of the mayhem of three years before, despite the presence of the MQM(A) in a coalition Muslim League government. The army was once again called on, this time in Nawaz Sharif's controversial scheme to run anti-terrorist courts.

Sikh ethno-nationalism and the Punjab crisis

The Indian state faced its greatest post-independence crisis as a result of the emergence in the 1980s of a militant Sikh ethno-nationalism in the Punjab. Its leading figure Sant Jarnail Singh Bhindranwale deployed the traditional vocabulary of *dharam yudh* (holy war) and of martyrdom. Significantly, he fought his final battle against the Indian state from the Akal Takht (the shrine in the Golden Temple complex representing the temporal power of God) while playing out his campaign before the international media.

Bhindranwale never called for Khalistan. His message was always couched in terms of the need for Sikh moral reform and renewal. The Akali Dal's parallel campaign was even more unequivocally about a call for greater autonomy within the Indian Union rather than for secession from it. Moreover, many of the autonomist demands had existed since the 1974 Anandpur Sahib Resolution. Four sets of questions thus confront the historian seeking to understand the Punjab crisis. First, why did Sikh demands for autonomy resurface in the early 1980s? Second, why were these portrayed at the time as evidence of secessionism? Third, what were the circumstances in which calls for autonomy toppled over into the vociferous nationalist demand for Khalistan? Fourth, why was the Indian state able to counter this?

The background to the Dharam Yudh Morcha

In 1981 the Akali Dal launched what it termed a righteous struggle (Dharam Yudh Morcha) against the Indian central government. Volunteers courted arrest in acts of civil disobedience reminiscent of the *gurdwara* reform movement. Despite the holy war terminology of the struggle, the protests focused on the largely secular issues raised by the Anandpur Sahib Resolution such as a reversal of the assignment of reserved powers between the centre and the states. Economic issues relating to farm product prices and water distribution also figured prominently in the campaign, as did the issue of changing Chandigarh's status as joint capital of Punjab and Haryana.

The Akali Dal's autonomy movement is explicable in terms of three historically contingent factors aside from the Sikhs' long-established notions of distinctive group consciouness and the fear of absorption into a hegemonic Hindu culture (Mahmood, 1989, pp. 326–40). These were: first, the social and economic impacts of the Green Revolution; second, the political role and strategies of the Akali Dal; and, third, what might be dubbed the Indira Gandhi factor.

The Impact of the Green Revolution

The Punjab became the centre of the Green Revolution in wheat production in the mid-1960s. This was based on a package of high-yielding varieties of cereals, chemical fertilisers, insecticides and controlled water supply made possible by the proliferation of tubewells following rural electrification. The state's agricultural performance was crucial to the national foodgrains plan with the region producing a third of India's wheat supplies. The impact of the Green Revolution was so great that by the time of the 1981 census, the Punjab ranked first in terms of per capita state domestic product. Its per capita income of Rs 2,768 was way above the Indian average of Rs 1,571 and was only remotely approached by that of Haryana and Maharashtra.

The 'wheat–whisky' culture (Deb, 1977) associated with the new prosperity disquieted the religiously orthodox and formed the background to Bhindranwale's rise to prominence as a puritanical religious reformer. Importantly, the new agricultural wealth was unevenly distributed across both regions and social groups. Significantly Bhindranwale secured his greatest support from the Manjha region which because of its less developed infrastructure did not fully join in the agricultural bonanza. Poor farmers even in the more favoured Malwa region, however, did not benefit as they were unable to afford the expensive inputs. The landless were left even further behind. One reading of the Akali Dal's more activist stance in the early 1980s sees it as an attempt to substitute communal solidarity for emerging class conflict (Singh, 1984, p. 43).

Intensified agricultural production encouraged a harvest-time influx of Hindu landless labourers from the eastern UP and Bihar. According to one scholar (Wallace, 1986, pp. 363–77), this threatened the Sikhs' hard-won majority status in their Punjab homeland and thereby encouraged a more communalist political outlook. The Punjabi Sikhs undoubtedly perceived themselves as an insecure majority community, not just because of Hindu immigration but because large numbers of Sikh youths were migrating to Delhi, Bombay and parts of UP in search of urban sources of employment. There were few openings in Punjab as its industrial growth had not matched its agricultural development. The bulk of the Punjab's industrial supplies and processed food products were imported from other states. Similarly, a region that accounted for 17 per cent of India's cotton growing possessed only 0.6 per cent of the textile industry's looms and 1.3 per cent of the spindles. The Punjab also produced only about a third of its fertiliser consumption and the capacity for tractor and trailer production lagged far behind demand.

A number of writers blamed this situation on the centre's deliberate policies. Analyses pointed to the relatively low level of public-sector investment in Punjab with transfers going to the poorer states. Added to this criticism of industrial strategy was a litany of complaints concerning pricing policy regarding such inputs as fertilisers and seeds. Furthermore, low procurement prices were denying the farmers their deserved profits. The Anandpur Sahib Resolution can thus be understood as representing an alternative developmentalist approach to the interventionist model favoured by the central government in New Delhi.

Two other impacts of the Green Revolution have been linked with the growing Sikh militancy. First, the proliferation of higher educational opportunities without jobs resulted in educated youth unemployment. Those who did not migrate provided Bhindranwale's core of support in the All-India Sikh Students' Federation (Telford, 1982, pp. 969–87). A parallel can be seen here with the role of disaffected *mohajir* youths in the MQM's development. Second, such writers as Robin Jeffrey have highlighted the fact that the Punjab's modernisation resulted in an explosion of 'print capitalism'. The rivalry between the Sikh Gurmukhi press and the Hindi press contributed to, as well as reflected, the polarising situation by exchanging 'half-truths and blatant lies' and by reopening 'old scars and wounds' (Jeffrey, 1986, p. 85).

The political role and strategies of the Akali Dal

The struggle for Punjabi autonomy needs to be understood in terms of two characteristics of the Akalis' political role and strategy. The first was the Akali Dal's claim as the supreme political representative of the Sikh community. This perception dated to the *gurdwara* reform movement and its relationship with the SGPC. It persisted although many Sikhs voted for the alternative Congress and Communist parties. The rise of Bhindranwale raised fears that the Akali Dal would be outflanked in terms of its moral leadership. Bhindranwale's growing charismatic authority was increased by his carrying a steel arrow in his hand at all times just as the Tenth Guru Gobind Singh had done. It was also rumoured that the *baaz* (holy falcon) associated with the Tenth Guru had been seen hovering over him. In such circumstances, the SGPC and the Akali Dal were pushed into ever more radical stances to avoid being sidelined.

Second, the Punjabi autonomy campaign must be understood in terms of the Akali Dal's alternating strategy of agitation and legislative politics. It had resorted to civil disobedience at the beginning of the 1960s in the struggle for a Punjabi-speaking state. Following the creation of the state in 1966, the Akalis had turned to legislative politics and formed a number of short-lived coalition ministries with non-Congress parties. The Anandpur Sahib Resolution was passed during a period of Akali opposition. But it was put on the back burner with the return of the Akalis to office in 1977. Significantly, it only moved up the political agenda again following Indira Gandhi's toppling of this government following her 'second coming' to power in New Delhi in 1980.

The Indira Gandhi factor

Indira Gandhi's role in the emerging crisis in the 1980s is contentious, but is regarded as central by a number of scholars. She is credited with patronising Bhindranwale while smarting from her 1977 election catastrophe. This was part of a divide-and-rule strategy designed to embarrass the Akali moderates both in the Punjab and national Janata coalition governments. When she was restored to power in New Delhi in 1980, Mrs Gandhi's political style became noted for its personalisation and centralisation of power. James Manor has maintained that the new centralised Congress was unable to emulate its Nehruvian predecessor in being the major instrument for conflict management in India (Manor, 1983, pp. 725–34). Certainly one consequence of the personalisation of power and 'de-institutionalisation' of the Congress was that disputes which might once have been resolved locally became national issues.

The Akali coalition ministry in the Punjab was dismissed along with other state governments in Andhra Pradesh, West Bengal, Jammu and Kashmir that would not toe Mrs Gandhi's line. In one sense, therefore, the Punjab crisis formed part of a wider crisis in centre–state relations in the early 1980s (Leaf, 1985, pp. 475–98). The situation became more volatile in the Punjab because religious identities became intertwined with demands for political autonomy. The Akali campaign drew on a rich repertoire of Sikh cultural symbols in its resistance to the *zulm* (oppression) of the central authorities.

It undoubtedly suited Mrs Gandhi's purposes to emphasise the religious element in the Punjab autonomist movement. This was designed to deflect Hindu support from the newly founded BJP. By first building up the Sikh threat and then taking tough action against it, the wily Indian Prime Minister sought to undercut her Hindutva opponents. This explains the failed attempts at conciliation and the otherwise perplexing police harassment of Sikhs entering Delhi at the time of the November 1982 Asian Games which undermined the Akali Dal's negotiations with Mrs Gandhi. Certainly the final round of discussions which preceded the army action in June 1984 have been described by one participant as a 'charade' (P. Singh, 1994).

Mrs Gandhi's portrayal of the autonomy demands as religiously motivated only just stopped short of dubbing them secessionist. The press had a field day in drawing parallels between Bhindranwale and the Ayatollah Khomeini. The hyping of the Sikh threat was assisted by two further developments. The first was the passing of a resolution in favour of Khalistan by the World Sikh Convention in March 1981. The Convention had in fact only been sponsored by a breakaway faction of the Akali Dal. The second was the merging of the Akali Dal's autonomist struggle with Bhindranwale's agitation over the arrest of his right-hand man, Amrik Singh, the president of the All-India Sikh Federation, some of whose members were charged with the murder of opponents and criminal activities including bank robberies. The Akali Dal leader Sant Harchand Singh Longowal (1932–85) who directed the Akali Dharam Yudh Morcha declared that Bhindranwale 'is our *danda* [stick] with which to beat the government' (Gill, 1997, p. 85).

Not in order to make any claim about sovereign authority, but in order to avoid arrest, Bhindranwale took refuge in the sanctuary of the Golden Temple at Amritsar. He initially stayed in the Guru Nanak Rest House. Eventually Gurcharan Singh Tohra, the president of the Temple Management Committee, allowed him to move to the Akal Takht. This decision followed a fight between Bhindranwale's henchmen and those of Longowal within the hostel complex.

Operation Bluestar and the Khalistan movement

The Indian Army action against the Golden Temple was officially justified by the need to maintain national integrity in the face of a secessionist movement supported by overseas Sikhs and a 'foreign hand'. In reality, the Khalistan movement only gained support both amongst the diaspora and in Punjab because of the outrage created by the army operation. Part of the anger and shock arose from the fact that many of the victims of the three-day pitched battle at Sikhism's holiest site were not 'terrorists' but pilgrims caught in the crossfire. Their bodies, along with Bhindranwale's and Amrik Singh's, were hurriedly and unceremoniously disposed of.

Initial shock gave way to anger when the extent of the 'sacrilege' and *ghallughara* (massacre) became apparent. Television pictures graphically revealed the shell damage to the Akal Takht and other sacred buildings including the Harimandir – the holiest building in the Sikh faith. The sense that this was a deliberate attempt to humiliate the community was intensified by the news that the Sikh Reference Library, which housed historic religious documents including letters written by the Gurus, had been deliberately destroyed (Kaur, 1991). For many Sikhs loyalty to their community superseded that to the state. This was immediately symbolised by the mutiny among the Sikh 18th and 19th Regiments and the return of honours and the resignation of

Sikh MPs (Kaur, 1990). In the longer term Sikh militancy intensified. A prominent victim was Sant Harchand Singh Longowal who was assassinated almost before the ink had dried on his accord with Rajiv Gandhi in July 1985. Militancy also claimed the moderate Akali Dal government of Surjit Singh Barnala which was installed in 1985 but dismissed two years later. Five years of President's Rule followed.

A Khalistan resolution was passed by the Sarbat Khalsa at the Golden Temple on 26 January 1986. The tradition of an assembly of the whole community of the pure meeting to decide matters concerning the Khalsa dated from the early eighteenth century. The occasion of the Sarbat Khalsa was thus a significant event in securing sanction for the Khalistan struggle, although many of those present who were elected to the Panthic Committee which was to act as a cabinet committee of the Khalistan government were either members of Bhindranwale's Damdami Taksal Seminary, or of the AISSF or the Bhindrawale Akali Dal (J) faction.

Diaspora Sikhs boosted the support within Punjab for the Khalistan demand. The Panthic Committee, for example, was recognised by both the World Sikh Organisation and the International Sikh Youth Federation. The Indian authorities responded by launching a second assault on the Golden Temple complex on 30 April 1986. Operation Black Thunder was carried out by special anti-terrorist forces. Unlike the earlier Bluestar operation, it passed off smoothly as there was no return of fire and there were no militants in the area at the time of the assault (Sharma, 1996, pp. 122ff). The final assault on the Golden Temple complex, Operation Black Thunder II took place in May 1988. Again there was little loss of life or damage to the sacred buildings. The humiliating surrender of nearly 200 militants at the conclusion of the operation by the National Security Guard forces severely damaged the Khalistan cause.

The Sikh militant movement and disturbances

Operation Black Thunder II occurred against a background of mounting violence in the Punjab. Just under 2,000 persons were killed in 1988 in comparison with just 63 in 1985 (Sharma, 1996, p. 208). By 1990 the figure had risen to a peak of 2,841. The victims included security personnel, militants killed in police encounters and Hindus who had become targets of ethnic cleansing. As a result of the violence some Hindus moved from the rural areas to the relative safety of Amritsar. Despite highly publicised mass killings of Hindus like, for example, the Haryana Roadways Bus incident of 6 July 1987, 80 per cent of all victims during the period 1986–92 were Sikhs. The number of militants killed in encounters with the security forces rose from 78 in 1986 to 700 in 1990. This was the prelude to the security actions of 1991–2 which eliminated most of the 'hardcore' militants. During the months that followed the September 1992 Operation Night Dominance, there was a much trumpeted return to 'normalcy' in the Punjab.

Profile of the militant organisations and their members

The main militant organisations included the Khalistan Commando Force (KCF), the Khalistan Liberation Force (KLF), the Bhindranwale Tiger Force of Khalistan (BTFK) and the Babbar Khalsa. In addition to these armed groups, militant activities were carried out by the various wings of the AISSF. Only the Babbar Khalsa pre-dated Operation Bluestar. It was the most united and ideologically cohesive of the militant groupings. Like the Khalistan Liberation Force it acted independently of the Damdami Taksal and the Panthic Committee. The latter too became increasingly factionalised during the course of the struggle. Even in their heyday, the militant groups were small organisations, although they claimed to have mass support in their struggle for a separate Sikh homeland. The largest group, the Khalistan Commando Force, numbered just 140 members in 1987, (Sharma, 1996, p. 169). The maximum strength of the Babbar Khalsa at the same period never exceeded 65. These tiny bands failed to coordinate their activities. Indeed there was increasing polarisation between the militant organisations.

Most militants were Jat Sikh youths in the 18–25 age range. Jats had been traditionally attracted by the Khalsa martial values of courage and martyrdom. Most of the militants had received some schooling, but as they came from poorer families they had few employment prospects. They were enticed by the lure of criminally acquired wealth. Idealism and personal loyalty to the militant commanders also motivated them. A militant's life expectancy was no more than three to four years. Despite the high attrition rate, youths continued to volunteer, often because of the security forces' activities. These included extortion rackets, harassment of the relatives of militants, disappearances and secret detentions. There were numerous extra-judicial killings in fake encounters, especially after the director-general of the Punjab police, Julio Ribeiro, introduced a 'bullet for bullet' policy in 1986.

Counter-insurgency

The Indian state waged war on its citizens in the Punjab from 1987 onwards. By the beginning of 1993 when the militant threat had been eliminated, there were 15,000 troops, and 40,000 paramilitaries including the Border Security Force backing up the 60,000-strong Punjab police force in the 'fight against terrorism' (Thandi, 1996, p. 162). Army trucks and lorries were visible everywhere and sandbagged special police outposts had been set up in around 700 'terrorist' affected villages. Despite the myth of the Punjab police's role in curbing the militants, a myth recently burnished in K. P. S. Gill's autobiography, troops from outside Punjab had played a key role in eliminating the militants. Nine divisions had been deployed at the time of Operation Rashak II. The army had also played a key role in the decisive Operation Night Dominance. At the most conservative estimate, 20,000 people died during the Punjab insurgency; the real figure may be nearer 40,000.

Militants, the police and the army alike perpetrated murder, rape and torture (Human Rights Watch, 1991). The security forces' 'terrorism' took place in the context of the discretionary powers afforded by the Armed Forces Special Powers Act and the Terrorist Affected Areas (Special Courts) Ordinance. The notorious Terrorist and Disruptive Activities (Prevention) Act (TADA) of 1985 enabled preventive detention on a large scale. By 1990, 10,000 TADA cases had been registered. The elimination of the leaders of the KCF, KLF and BTFK in 1991–2 coincided with over 41,000 rewards being given to Punjab policeman (Jaijee, 1995). The successful 'pacification' of the Punjab nevertheless depended upon the militants' factional divisions and the infiltration of their organisations.

Factionalism and the personalisation of power were reflections of the traditionally individualistic Sikh Jat society. Personal enmities hindered coordination and prevented the emergence of a single leader accepted by all the organisations. The death or capture of the tall poppies threw groups into disarray. The KLF, for example, received a major blow in October 1987 with the elimination of its chief Avtar Singh Brahma. His successor, Gurjant Singh Budh Singhwala, met a similar fate in August 1992, as did the Babbar Khalsa leader Sukhdev Singh Babbar.

The militant organisations were relatively easy to infiltrate. They could then be undermined either by setting them against each other or by encouraging criminal activities which alienated the local population. It appears that the police even created undercover militant groups with this express objective (Pettigrew, 1996, pp. 142ff). Certainly the oppressive atmosphere arising from state repression and the criminal activities of some militants undermined their solidarity with ordinary Sikhs. Part of the security forces' successes in 1992–3 resulted from villagers turning in the guerrilla leaders.

Their popularity had also diminished because of the overbearing behaviour of the parallel governments which militants ran in some areas. Khalistan Khalsa Panchayats enforced Panthic dress codes by forbidding women to wear cosmetics or *bindis*, and men to visit the barber. They also attempted to ban cigarette smoking in public places and to replace all Hindi signboards with Punjabi ones. Trucks were attacked in the Ludhiana district in March 1991 because they did not have Punjabi number plates. A shopkeeper was killed in the Patiala district as part of the anti-tobacco drive. The ban on singing the Indian national anthem in schools was also widely implemented. Video shops and beauty parlours were closed in the drive for 'purity'. Their owners resentfully complied out of fear rather than sympathy with the militants' cause.

State repression in 1992 was accompanied by a return of the political process. The Punjab elections, however, took place against a backdrop of the deployment of a quarter of a million army, police and paramilitary personnel. There was a turnout of just under 25 per cent. The Congress-I led by Beant Singh duly took office after capturing 87 out of 117 seats. Although the anti-terrorist drive continued at first and Beant Singh was to fall victim to the assassin's bomb on 2 September 1995, the return to 'normalcy' persisted. The Akali Dal once again confined itself to the loaves and fishes of patronage politics, returning to power in coalition with the BJP after the 1997 elections. In the words of one astute commentator, however, the coercive power of the Indian state had 'hardly' exorcised 'the ghost of Sikh ethno-nationalism'. Contradictions would continue to exist between it and India's 'ethnic democracy' in the absence of a political settlement which seriously considered consociational options for ethnic management (G. Singh, 1996, pp. 132–3).

The insurgency in Kashmir

The Indo-Pakistan Kashmir dispute entered a new phase in December 1989 with the spontaneous eruption of a violent secessionist struggle in the Vale of Kashmir. The insurgency which transformed the fabled happy valley into a valley of death brought India and Pakistan to the brink of a nuclear conflict in May 1990 (Hersh, 1993). The flareup in fighting in the Kargil region in the summer of 1999 undermined the hoped-for breakthrough in Indo-Pakistan relations following the bus diplomacy and Lahore Declaration earlier in February that year.

The scale of the Kashmir disorder was such that by the mid-1990s an estimated 400,000 security services personnel had been deployed, a quarter of a million Hindus had fled to Delhi and beyond, and there had been 15,000 casualties including militants, civilians and service men. Some observers maintained that the Kashmir uprising represented an even greater challenge to the Indian state than the Punjab crisis (Ganguly, 1997).

The uprising shocked the Indian authorities. It conflicted with official stereotypes of Kashmiri Muslim 'docility' and of an adherence to a composite secularised *Kashmiriyat* identity (Punjabi, 1992, p. 137). Certainly at the time of the 1965 Pakistani infiltration of forces into the valley in the abortive Operation Gibraltar there had been little popular support for insurgency. What then had happened during the ensuing two and a half decades to transform the isolated efforts of a handful of militant groups into a general *intifida* against the Indian state?

Kashmir: happy valley

At the time of the 1983 state elections Kashmir appeared contented. The tourist industry was booming and the state wore a permanent holiday air. The Kashmiri population benefited from a massive increase in both rural electrification and educational provision. During the preceding decade the literacy rate had grown by over 40 per cent and the spread of state-run schools and colleges had been accompanied by a mushrooming of Islamic *madari* (colleges). Prosperity marginalised those political groupings who were still pressing for the redemption of Nehru's distant promise to hold a plebiscite to ascertain the state's constitutional future. Even the death in September 1982 of Sheikh Abdullah, the dominant political figure for the past half century and personification of *Kashmiriyat,* had not apparently disrupted the state's serene progress. His son, the young English-educated doctor Farooq Abdullah, had succeeded him both as head of the ruling National Conference and as Chief Minister.

Farooq's frequent motorcycle rides around Srinagar symbolised the relaxed atmosphere. While his father's struggles during the 1940s had dubbed him with the epithet of the 'Lion of Kashmir', Farooq was soon termed the 'disco Chief Minister'. Jamaat-i-Islami activists who murmured disapprovingly at the proliferation of bars, video shops and beauty parlours in Srinagar were dismissed as anachronistic. Kashmir, however, was poised on the brink of Islamic revival rather than increased secularisation. Moreover, its future status was soon to be questioned more than at any time since the troubled days of 1947–8.

The Indira Gandhi factor again

The Indira Gandhi factor was to be as important in Kashmir as in Punjab. New Delhi had previously interfered in the state's affairs as was demonstrated both by Sheikh Abdullah's periods of incarceration from August 1953 onwards and a series of rigged elections. (Bazaz, 1978). Mrs Gandhi, however, for personal political gain, dangerously introduced the communal card into Kashmiri politics at a time when a new generation of Muslim Kashmiris were more politically aware then ever before.

The 1983 state elections were bitterly fought between the National Conference and Congress-I. Mrs Gandhi staked her personal prestige on the outcome by touring widely. She became increasingly hostile to Farooq Abdullah (Malhotra, 1989, p. 278), as he refused to be browbeaten into a pre-electoral arrangement with Congress-I. Moreover, he had mended fences with the prominent religious leader Mirwaiz Mohammed Farooq. The uncle of the Mirwaiz (chief preacher) Yusuf Shah had been a major opponent of the secularist approach of Sheikh Abdullah during the 1930s and 1940s.

Mirwaiz Mohammed Farooq himself had always been regarded as a pro-Pakistani figure.

The 1983 Kashmir elections were generally acknowledged as the 'freest' in its history. The National Conference captured 46 out of 75 seats, 20 more than Congress-I. The latter had played the Hindu card, especially with fears regarding a Muslim influx to Jammu if Farooq's proposed Resettlement Bill became law, as it enabled pre-1947 residents to return to the state. This short-term strategy succeeded in reducing the BJP to just two seats in the Hindu-dominated Jammu region. The cost was heightened Hindu–Muslim tension. This intensified with Mrs Gandhi's refusal to accept defeat. She sought to woo Farooq's brother-in-law, G. M. Shah, who had been a rival for the National Conference's leadership in 1982. She also launched a press campaign aimed at the Chief Minister's alleged 'disloyalty' and 'softness' on Pakistan. Farooq's visit to Muzaffarabad in Pakistani Azad Kashmir was trumpeted, although this had taken place in 1974 while he was still training as a doctor in England. Another propaganda coup was provided by the booing of the Indian team and the flying of Pakistani flags during a cricket match with the touring West Indians held in Srinagar in October 1983.

Farooq Abdullah supported the efforts of other state politicians who were building a common front against Mrs Gandhi's zealous centralisation of power. She was particularly incensed when he hosted an opposition conclave involving 59 state leaders at Srinagar in October 1983. Henceforth she was determined to topple him. When her cousin Braj Kumar Nehru displayed a reluctance to do this on tenuous grounds, he was replaced as Governor by Jagmohan Malhotra. Jagmohan subsequently played a controversial role in the slide towards insurgency. He was undoubtedly an able administrator, but lacked a responsiveness to Muslim sensitivities.

Farooq Abdullah was dismissed less than a month after the army operation in Amritsar against the Golden Temple. Events were henceforth to follow the Punjab's depressing catalogue of violence, repression and alienation of the populace. A wave of protests greeted G. M. Shah's elevation to the post of Chief Minister at the head of a breakaway National Conference faction. In the words of the journalist Tavleen Singh who was covering developments in the state, 'The clock [was] put back thirty years ... Kashmir has been reminded that no matter how much it feels it belongs to the mainstream of India, no matter how often its Chief Minister asserts that he is Indian, it will always be special, always be suspect' (Singh, 1995, p. 79).

Paradise lost

G. M. Shah's period in office became known for its corruption charges and for growing communal tension. The 'disco Chief Minister' had been replaced by the 'Gul-e-Curfew' (The Curfew Flower). Disruptions to trade and business ended the economic boom. Mounting unemployment extended the appeal of Islamist groups. Shah appeared unaware of the yawning political abyss. Rajiv Gandhi encouraged repression by extending the provisions of TADA to Kashmir rather than prodding Shah towards political accommodation. In September 1985 some 600 villages were designated as restricted areas. This measure, designed to curb Pakistani infiltration, only alienated their inhabitants who were subjected to searches by paramilitary patrols.

Terrorism and strikes were rife. Communal tensions were exacerbated by the national rise of the BJP and the emergence of the Babri Masjid dispute. Kashmiris had now lost their traditional isolation. The police opened fire on protesters in Srinagar in February 1986 following the news that the locks on the disputed building at Ayodhya had been removed. In an echo of the national dispute, the use of rooms adjoining a temple situated in the Jammu secretariat by Muslim state employees for worship sparked off a Hindu agitation. Jagmohan used the subsequent rioting and curfews as a pretext to dismiss the Shah government.

The strikes in the Muslim Vale of Kashmir were unabated. In November a chastened Farooq Abdullah returned to power in an interim National Conference–Congress coalition government. The Rajiv–Farooq accord was no more successful in encouraging political moderation than had been the ill-fated Rajiv–Longowal agreement in Punjab. Henceforth, Farooq was widely regarded as New Delhi's man. The motorbike rides around Srinagar were a distant dream as his every movement was accompanied by a phalanx of security guards in the wake of several assassination attempts. This procedure was still required in May 1996 when Farooq attended a book launch hosted on my behalf at the India International Centre in New Delhi.

By apparently throwing in its lot with the centre, the National Conference could no longer serve as a secular home for those who wanted to limit New Delhi's intervention in Kashmir. The ensuing vacuum was filled at first by the JKLF which also professed secular values. These were accompanied by a determined commitment to the so-called 'third option' of an independent Kashmir. The JKLF itself was later to be pushed to one side by Islamist groups which thrived on weapons and support from Pakistan in an echo of the Afghan situation.

Kashmiri Muslims' alienation from the Indian state intensified after the blatant rigging of the June 1987 state elections. The group of Islamist parties that had come together in the Muslim United Front (MUF) headed by the Jamaat-i-Islami had drawn enthusiastic crowds during the campaign. But the MUF won only four seats in what was widely regarded as a 'tarnished triumph' for the Congress-I–National Conference coalition which was returned with 60 seats (Ganguly, 1997, pp. 98ff). It was not surprising that the 'stolen election' was followed by mounting Muslim militancy. The government also had to cope with a BJP-inspired agitation, when it declared that it would no longer shift the winter seat of government from Srinagar to

Hindu-dominated Jammu. When it backed down on this economically motivated decision, it seemed that agitation was the best method for advancing
community interests.

The growing tension in Kashmir was matched by increasing Indo-Pakistan
hostility. New Delhi roundly blamed the Pakistanis for fighting a proxy war
in Kashmir. In addition to the periodic shelling along the line of control, both
countries engaged in a costly military conflict in the remote Siachen Glacier.
This area was north of the demarcated line of control. Sporadic fighting
continued in the area throughout 1987. Eventually the deteriorating situation in the Vale of Kashmir to the south was to threaten an all-out conflict
involving India and the newly democratised Pakistan state.

Kashmir: valley of death

The final year of Farooq Abdullah's government witnessed sporadic bomb
blasts, communal riots and strikes. The situation worsened as a minority
non-Congress government led by Vishwanath Pratap Singh took office in
New Delhi. The JKLF perpetrated many of the 'terrorist' outrages at this
time. Its activists were involved in the celebrated Rubaiya Sayeed affair.
Rubaiya Sayeed was the daughter of Mufti Mohammed Sayeed, the new
Minister for Home Affairs in the V. P. Singh government. Her kidnapping on
8 December laid bare the weaknesses of both the national and state governments. Following Rubaiya's release in exchange for five militants, Jagmohan
was reappointed Governor amidst considerable political intrigue. Shortly
afterwards, in January 1990, Farooq Abdullah threw in the towel.

Jagmohan's new 'mailed fist' strategy was symbolised by the firing on an
unarmed crowd of protestors at Gawakadal bridge in Srinagar. Over a
hundred were shot or leapt to their death in the icy waters of the Jhelum
river. Despite shoot-to-kill orders, there were numerous protests in Srinagar
itself and other towns. 'It was no longer a fight between the militants and the
security forces', the respected Indian writer Balraj Puri observed: 'it gradually assumed the form of a total insurgency of the entire population' (Puri,
1993, p. 60). From 20 January to March 1990 Srinagar was under almost
total curfew and resembled a besieged city. Foreign correspondents and
representatives of human-rights organisations were banned from the Vale of
Kashmir as New Delhi attempted damage limitation.

The Pakistani authorities were equally taken aback by the thousands who
braved the streets in Kashmir to call for independence. Anarchy across the
border not only risked a pre-emptive Indian military strike, but carried
dangerous implications for Pakistan's fragile statehood. Islamabad thus hit on
a policy of maximising Indian discomfiture on the human-rights issue while
allowing limited support for pro-Pakistan Islam-orientated militant groups.
This would ensure that India had to engage in a costly counter-insurgency

operation at the same time as limiting the likelihood of a wider Indo-Pakistan conflict. Significantly, when JKLF sympathisers attempted to cross the line of control which they refused to recognise in February 1992, the Pakistanis halted their progress to avert an international incident.

The deteriorating law and order sparked off a mass exodus of the Hindu Pandits from the valley. Jagmohan's motives in facilitating this flight by providing government transport remain controversial. The arbitrary arrests and violence which accompanied his cordon and search policy intensified the Muslims' alienation. This was completed when 50 people were killed by the security forces shooting on Mirwaiz Mohammed Farooq's funeral procession in May 1990. The Mirwaiz had been shot by unknown assailants who, it was claimed, were members of India's intelligence agencies.

Jagmohan remained unrepentant: 'unless the militants are fully wiped out', he declared, 'normalcy cannot return to the valley' (Schofield, 1996, p. 248). The attempt to reproduce the successful 'bullet for bullet' policy adopted in the Punjab suffered from the fact that Kashmir's mountainous and thickly forested terrain lent itself to guerrilla activity. Despite Pakistan's official denials, weapons flowed across this border, having originated either in the Frontier's arms' bazaars or in Afghanistan. They were channelled to militant groups such as the Harkat-ul-Ansar, Janbaz Mujahadin and the Hizb-ul-Mujahideen by both the ISI and Jamaat-i-Islami. The Indian authorities claimed by the mid-1990s to have recovered over 13,000 AK-47 and AK-56 assault rifles, 700 rocket launchers and some 16,000 grenades. Outright military victory for the security forces against such a well-armed and dispersed militant force was thus far less likely than in the Punjab.

New Delhi increasingly claimed that the Kashmiri disturbances were solely caused by the export of terrorism from 'a neighbouring country'. Official publications claimed the existence of over a hundred terrorist training camps in neighbouring Afghanistan, Pakistan-occupied Kashmir and in Pakistan. Photographs were published of captured terrorists, many of whom appeared to be non-Kashmiri and veterans of the Afghan War like, for example, Sajjad Khan, the chief commander of Harkat-ul-Ansar who had been arrested in February 1994. The Pakistan government, despite such evidence, continued to deny any interference in Kashmir. It emphasised the indigenous roots of the uprising (which were equally undeniable) and publicised the deteriorating human-rights situation in the valley.

As in Punjab, the introduction of TADA and other measures such as the Armed Forces Jammu and Kashmir Special Powers Act (September 1990) abetted the perpetration of numerous human-rights abuses. State terrorisim only encouraged greater militancy. By the mid-1990s the armed militants had risen to between five and ten thousand in number. Moreover, India's international reputation suffered immense damage from events such as the alleged gang rape of 53 Muslim women at Kunan Poshpura during a security operation conducted by the 4th Rajput Rifles in February 1991.

The 'mailed fist' strategy was replaced by more sophisticated counter-insurgency techniques when Girish Chandra Saxena, a former head of the RAW intelligence agency, became Governor in May 1990. The Rashtriya Rifles was created as an elite army unit designed to fight the militants. It operated alongside regular army units and the federal security forces – the Central Reserve Police Force and the Border Security Force. A special division of the Jammu and Kashmir police known as the Special Task Force was also established. To remedy the sympathy of the regular police for the insurgency, it comprised non-Muslim, non-Kashmiri recruits.

Drawing on the Punjab example, attempts were made to subvert and criminalise the militant groups in order to undermine their local support. State-sponsored 'renegade' militant groups included the Ikhwan-ul Muslimoon, the Taliban and the Muslim Mujahadin. The first group was led by Koko Parray, a folk singer and former JKLF militant. 'Security' operations were 'sub-contracted' to these groups by the regular security forces who also financed them. The Taliban (not to be confused with the militant Afghan Islamist group), for example, works closely with the Indian Army, the Ikhwan-ul Muslimoon with the Rashtriya Rifles and the Special Task Force. Many of the members of these state-sponsored groups were militants who had been 'turned around' either through torture (one of the favourite techniques was crushing the legs with a wooden roller) or the threatened torture of their relatives. Others were attracted by the pay on offer, or by the need to escape the factional infighting and revenge killings of the militant organisations. The growing differences between the JKLF and the Jamaat-i-Islami-supported Hizb-ul-Mujahideen (HUM) undoubtedly assisted the Indian counter-insurgency effort. HUM and JKLF militants were soon turning their guns on each other. The JKLF was bedevilled by internal splits from 1993 onwards as it was increasingly sidelined by the HUM and its Islamist allies both in the armed struggle and in the political grouping known as the Hurriyat (Freedom) Conference. The Hurriyat had brought together representatives from 30 parties early in 1993, but it was dominated by the pro-Pakistan Jamaat-i-Islami.

General Krishna Rao replaced Saxena as Governor in March 1993, but there was no letup in the operations against the militants. Signs of war-weariness amongst a populace caught in the crossfire of the security services and the militants encouraged the government of Narasimha Rao in New Delhi to contemplate the adoption of the final phase of the Punjab model, the restarting of the political process by holding elections in the state. This strategy suffered an initial setback with the destruction of the Charar-e-Sharif shrine of the fourteenth-century *sufi* saint Sheikh Nooruddin Noorani in May 1995. The conflagration which consumed one of Kashmiri Islam's holiest places climaxed a siege of the shrine which carried echoes of Operation Bluestar. On this occasion the insurgent leader, Mast Gul, a veteran of the Afghan War who had taken refuge in the sacred space of a reli-

gious building, lived to fight another day. The Indian authorities blamed the
fire on the Harkat-ul-Ansar militants, but the sacrilege sparked off another
round of protests. This did not prevent the security forces' action against the
even more sacred Hazratbal shrine in Srinagar (the shrine was the repository
of the Moh-i-Muqaddas, a strand of hair from the beard of the Prophet
Muhammad) the following March.

Elections for the Lok Sabha were held in Kashmir during May–June 1996.
The high voter turnout of 40 per cent had only resulted from widespread
intimidation by the security forces who forced Kashmiri Muslims to the polls
at bayonet point. These scenes were not, however, repeated in the September
state elections which witnessed a victory for Farooq Abdullah's National
Conference, although the boycotting Hurriyat Conference dismissed this
result as a 'sham'. Farooq appeared as much New Delhi's man as after his ill-
fated accord with Rajiv Gandhi. Nevertheless, some Indian commentators
heralded the fact that Kashmir was emulating Punjab's return to normalcy.

Ethno-nationalism, conflict and the South Asian state: theoretical reflections

What light do the crises of the past three decades shed on the body of theoretical literature regarding ethnic mobilisation and violence in South Asia?
Moreover, what do they tell us about the nature of the state in the subcontinent? Certainly they reveal the inadequacy of monocausal explanations
whether these are primordialist or modernisation theory driven. For such
accounts cannot do justice to the complexities and historical contingencies
revealed in the foregoing narratives. Explanations of Kashmiri and Bengali
secessionism in terms of a preordained primordial 'captive' ethnicity fail, for
example, to shed light on the timing of the struggle against the Indian and
Pakistani states. Why did the Kashmiris not spontaneously rise up in 1965?
Why was there a 20-year gap between the language riots in Dhaka and the
achievement of Bangladesh? Similarly, why did the Akali Dal only throw its
weight behind Khalistan demands after Operation Bluestar?

Modernisation theory explanations are more satisfactory in some respects.
Rapid socio-economic transformation and the spread of literacy form the
background to all the cases of ethnic violence that we have examined.
Unemployed educated youths were at the forefront of the militancy in Punjab
and the Kashmir and Karachi insurgencies. Religious 'fundamentalism' in
both the Punjab and Kashmir emerged at least in part in response to orthodox
fears concerning the moral 'corruption' of modern-isation as seen in the
wheat–whisky culture, the video shops and beauty parlours. Modern methods
of communication including video-cassettes and audio-cassettes, and satellite
linkups in the case of the MQM, have also proved vital to the mobilisation
against the state, as has the support from diaspora communities.

Nevertheless, traditional cultural symbols have played an equally important sustaining role. Altaf Hussain's and Jarnail Singh Bhindranwale's authority was rooted in their followers' conception of them as a *pir* and *sant* respectively. Indeed Bhindranwale was even regarded as possessing some of the attributes of Guru Gobind Singh. Concepts of holy war and martyrdom have inspired successive waves of Sikh and Muslim militants to wage an unequal struggle against the Indian state. Mosques and *gurdwaras* have not simply been refuges for 'terrorists', but symbols of a sovereign community beyond the moral authority of the modern nation state.

Instrumentalist and rational choice approaches to ethnic mobilisation and violence fail to capture this 'inwardness' of a struggle which for many of its participants takes on aspects of a cosmic struggle for moral authority. There is something far deeper here than a decision to utilise religious symbols for mobilisation purposes, or turning to ethno-religious channels of dissent in preference to 'secular' alternatives. Explanations of the Kashmiri and Punjabi insurgencies that link them primarily with the de-institutionalisation and centralisation of power by Mrs Gandhi similarly underplay the significance of ethno-religious sentiment. The weakness in such accounts is summed up in the fact that the 1980s' crisis in centre–state relations had much more serious repercussions in the Punjab and Kashmir than in, for example, Karnataka or Andhra Pradesh.

A careful historical account of the insurgencies reveals in fact that there are elements of truth in primordialist, state-centric and modernisation theory explanations. Core ethnic and religious cultural symbols and values have played a part in mobilisation and violence, but these have been activated and indeed articulated in the context of the changes brought by modernisation. Mobilisation along ethno-religious lines did not, however, inevitably lead to insurgency and secessionism. In all the cases we have considered it was the failure of the state to manage and accommodate demands from minority groups that drove them to shift from demands for cultural and political autonomy to seek territorial sovereignty.

Two other points concerning the South Asian state emerge from our narrative. First, distinctions between 'authoritarian' Pakistan and 'democratic' India have been previously overdrawn. Both states have displayed no mercy towards what they have deemed to be 'secessionist' movements, even when repression has been counterproductive in radicalising domestic opposition and arousing international condemnation of such human-rights abuses as the widespread use of torture, extra-judicial killings and gang rape. Second, both states have steadily increased their coercive capacity, while at the same time losing their ability to accommodate pluralism.

The contemporary South Asian state's panoply of legal powers and deployment of armed force against internal dissent far exceeds anything its colonial predecessor possessed. Counter-insurgency techniques have been increasingly perfected. The underlying causes of the alienation of significant numbers of citizens have not, however, been addressed. In the absence of social justice, a decentralisation of authority and the replacement of a political culture of confrontation with one based on accommodation, it seems unlikely that circumstances for future armed resistance will disappear. Nevertheless, in the immediate future, the increasing coercive powers of the post-colonial South Asian state appear likely to compensate for its declining legitimacy.

Conclusion

Indian nationalism was spurred only in part by the grievances of the professional and propertied classes. It was similarly only in part derived from Western notions of liberalism and self-determination. Sacrifice as well as self-interest stimulated its advance. A crucial element in the sense of patriotism was the belief in India as a holy motherland whose sons were called to the duty of freeing her from a repressive foreign rule. This image was complemented by the possibility of the restoration of the golden past. This myth, which owed much to Western Orientalist speculation, however, divided Muslims from Hindus, as did the cultural symbolism of an indigenising nationalist movement.

Muslims turned to separatism not just because of the blandishments of the colonial state or in the race for patronage and profit. A sense of history and past glory again played an important role. The contrast between contemporary decline and former greatness was as strong for Muslims as for Hindus. Orientalist writings also played a part in their communalising of the past. While the creation of Pakistan was not inevitable, from the turn of the twentieth century onwards significant Muslim elites were uncomfortable about the cultural as well as the economic consequences of future Hindu rule.

Indigenous ideas, symbols and memories were thus crucial in the articulation of nationalism. Furthermore, these were not, as Hobsbawm indicates, any kind of symbols quarried from the treasure house of the past at the whim of elites in the 'invention' of tradition. They were powerful precisely because they 'resonated' with the populace to whom they were addressed.

The ideas inspiring Indian nationalism and Muslim separatism could be articulated to a wider audience than ever before because of the communications revolution brought by the colonial state. It was not by chance that many politicians were journalists or owned papers. The burgeoning press also encouraged the strengthening of ethnic and linguistic allegiances which nestled alongside nationalist sentiment. The leaderships of both Congress and the Muslim League sought to accommodate these 'parochial' identities which lay barely submerged beneath the freedom movement. The protean nature of nationalist struggle does not fit in easily with either the cut and dried approach to identity portrayed by primordialism or with the 'diffusionist' understanding of modernisation theory. The nationalist struggles also blended 'tradition' with 'modernity' in their utilisation of spectacle, drama, poetry and song to reach out to a largely non-literate society. Discursive networks played a role, but they by no means monopolised communication, as Benedict Anderson would have us believe.

Independence changed the rules of the game in enabling the nationalist elites to control the machinery of the state. This was now to be deployed in the nation-building process. The distortions arising from partition, alongside the need to balance economic reform with the entrenched power of elite groups, impacted from the outset on these processes. They were to be most successful when the nationalist elites sought to accommodate the pluralisms of society rather than to use the state apparatus to enforce centralisation.

Ethnic and communal resurgence have coincided with globalisation. This has unleashed a second communications revolution which has sharpened community identities. It has also intensified the problems of state legitimacy already reduced by developmentalist failures and mounting problems of corruption and ungovernability. The idealism of the nationalist struggle has been replaced by cynicism, opportunism and national and community identities based increasingly on hatred of 'the other'. The subcontinental state has become fearful of its citizens. Its coercive capacity alone has been enhanced.

Political identities have not only been formed in unyielding resistance to a hostile state, whether in the form of Indian nationalism during the Raj, or Sikh and Sindhi nationalism in the contemporary subcontinent. They have also been structured by the opportunities provided by state patronage. Muslim political identity in colonial India and contemporary caste-based movements have alike been nurtured by an administrative framework, whether of separate electorates or affirmative action. Such identities based around language, religion and caste are Janus-faced, inclusive when facing inwards and exclusive when directed outwards.

Just as identities have been constantly renegotiated, so history has been rewritten, even the history of the recent past. Thus the Islamising regime of Zia-ul-Haq ignored the ambivalence of many of the *'ulama* to the Pakistan demand and moved them to its forefront. Jinnah was implausibly portrayed as seeking to establish an Islamic state. The AIADMK leader Jayaram Jalalyitha, whose support was crucial for the emergence of the BJP Vajpayee-led coalition government following the 1998 elections, and was to prove its eventual nemesis, has conveniently erased the anti-Brahmin characteristics of the self-respect movement of the 1930s. BJP state governments in Madhya Pradesh and Uttar Pradesh have replaced 'secular' textbooks with Hindutva propaganda. The BJP–RSS combination has made serious attempts to 'saffronise' historical writing and research. It established, for example, a rival professional body to the prestigious Indian History Congress entitled the Indian Society for History and Culture. The advent of the Vajpayee government provided an opportunity for the reconstitution of the Indian Council for Historical Research to include a majority of historians who concurred with the Sangh Parivar's stance on the Ramjanmabhoomi issue that Ram was born at the site of the Babri Mosque and that this was constructed after demolishing the Shri Ramjanmabhoomi Temple. A government order changed the objective of the Council from providing a 'rational' to giving a 'national' interpretation of history.

The blatant re-writing of history for political purposes is not of course unique to the subcontinent, but it has taken on immense importance in both India and Pakistan because constructions of the past are vital to contemporary ethnic, communal and national ideologies. A peculiar fascination with history unites such otherwise diametrically opposed groups as the Pakistan establishment, the MQM and the Sangh Parivar. Within Indian society there is of course a well-established tradition of manipulating historical 'facts' for community gain. Caste groups who are seeking to match rising economic status with ritual ranking employ genealogists to uncover, for example, a Rajput heritage.

It is important to note not only the variety of uses to which historical discourses have been put, but the sharp divide between those based on caste and religious community and official imaginings of the past. Only the latter, whether in India (pre-1998) or Pakistan, view nationhood as being completed by the freedom struggle. Islamists and Hindu nationalists see the drive to establish an Islamic state or a Hindu *rashtra* as part of the unfinished business of independence. Caste and ethnic-based historical discourses also point to the incompleteness of the nation-building enterprise, this time in terms of its failure to achieve social justice and its exclusion of marginalised groups. In some instances such historical understandings totally deny the legitimacy of the post-colonial state.

This work has revealed some of the parallels between the contemporary Hindutva movement based on fears of disunity and the moves towards Hindu political community around the turn of the twentieth century. Similarly, contemporary debates about Sikh identity following the crisis years of the 1980s are paralleled by those a century earlier as the community experienced the uncertainties of the transitional colonial era. Indeed, the leading scholar G. N. Barrier has gone so far as to see the partisan traffic in ideas about identity emanating from some 1,500 Sikh websites at the beginning of 1999 as replicating the earlier tract warfare of the Singh Sabha era (Barrier, 1999, p. 23).

Five decades after independence a national Indian and Pakistani 'imagined community' coexists both with localised communities based on ethnicity and language and with essentialised religious identities. Each possesses its collective memories and channels of communication. Taken to extremes this latter tendency can threaten genocide and ethnic cleansing within the successor states to the Raj and allout military conflict between them.

Sabre rattling and internal repression have gone hand in hand. Neither response holds out any prospect for long-term stability in a subcontinent which contains the world's largest numbers of illiterate adults (around 400 million), over a third of its poor (around 500 million people survive with an income of less than one US dollar a day) and in which, according to 1993 figures, 293 million were without access to safe drinking water.

In the realm of economics the 'crisis' of the state in the subcontinent can only be solved by emphasising social equity and human development over capital accumulation and expenditure on a senseless arms race. The systemic political crisis with its symptoms of mounting violence and corruption within both India and Pakistan calls for the privileging of accommodation and public service over confrontation and self-aggrandisement.

Turning to the 'poetics' of identity around which much of this work has focused, the challenge is whose 'imagined' community will prevail in the twenty-first century. The secular nationalist discourse 'invented' by the founding fathers of India and Pakistan still holds out the tantalising possibility of developing a democratic polity, yet it is burdened by over half a century of intensifying economic and social inequality. The pseudo-traditional but in reality equally modernist imaginings of the nation by Islamists and followers of the Hindutva philosophy afford an even bleaker future of mean-spirited and socially and economically divisive governance. Although there may be a short-term bolstering of the central state buffeted by the forces of globalisation, Islamist and Hindutva attempts to 'reinvent' the nation would ultimately result in regional ethno-nationalist 'retaliation' which could move rapidly from autonomist to secessionist demands.

The subcontinent is very much two nations, but not the two nations of Muslim and Hindu imagining. Rather, as the late T. V. Sathyamurthy described it, there is the relatively economically privileged nation above, in which there is intra-elite conflict for resources in the name of caste, religion and region; and there is the nation below through which 'runs a common denominator of dispossession, disinheritance, poverty and marginalisation' (Sathyamurthy, 1996, p. 835). The growing economic, social and ecological struggles of the nation below (minorities, women, *haris* and *dalits*) may ultimately, like a 'prairie fire', spread a new 'pro-people' sense of identity which transcends existing elite styles.

Appendix: Chronology of publications in the history of modern ideas about identity in the subcontinent

1866   Foundation of the *Aligarh Institute Gazette* which was to lay the basis for Islamic modernism and Muslim separatism.

1869   Mahatma Jotirao Phule publishes his attack on Brahminism in *Priestcraft Exposed*.

1875   Swami Dayananda's combative Hindu 'fundamentalist' work *Satyarth Prakash* appears.

1877   Helena Petrovna Blavatsky sets out the credo of the Theosophical movement in *Isis Revealed*.

1879   Dadabhai Naoroji publishes *The Poverty of India* which provides an economic critique of British rule; Hali's *Musaddas* is published.

1882   *Ananda Math* containing the famous hymn 'Bande Mataram' is published by the Bengali author Bankim Chandra Chatterjee; Muhammadan Tract Society is founded in Lahore.

1883   Singh Sabha opens the Khalsa Press in Lahore.

1886   The Sikh reformist *Khalsa Akhbar* begins publication under Ditt Singh's editorship.

1892   Communal tension intensifies in Punjab following the publication of the Arya Samajist Pandit Lekh Ram's tract *A Treatise on the Waging of Holy War, or the Foundation of the Muhammadan Religion*.

1893   Sri Aurobindo publishes *Bhawani Mandir*, which becomes a source of inspiration for the extremist movement in Bengal.

1894   Bhai Vir Singh founds the Khalsa Tract Society with the aim of strengthening Sikh identity.

1897   Sikh identity is asserted in Kahn Singh Nabha's famous tract *Ham Hindu Nahin*.

1898   Bhai Vir Singh's first Punjabi novel *Sundari* is published.

1900   Sister Nivedita publishes *Kali. The Mother*, which feeds into Bengali extremism.

1902	Stereotypes of Mughal 'depravity' are provided with additional encouragement by the publication of Kisorilal Goswami's Hindi novel *Tara*.
1909	V. D. Savarkar provides a nationalist interpretation of the events of 1857 in *The Indian War of Independence*. Gandhi's political philosophy sketched out in *Hind Swaraj* in Gujarati.
1910	*Hind Swaraj* published in English.
1910–12	Pan-Islamic sentiments are expressed in *Hamdard*, *Zamindar*, *al-Hilal* and *Comrade* which are all founded during this period.
1913	Annie Besant publishes *Wake Up India*.
1916	Publication of *Young India* by Lala Lajpat Rai.
1917	The anti-Brahmin movement in South India is boosted by the launching of the *Dravidian* and *Justice*.
1922	Publication of Syed Ameer Ali's influential modernist text *The Spirit of Islam*.
1923	V. D. Savarkar publishes the Hindu nationalist text *Hindutva: Who is a Hindu?*
1923–5	Master Tara Singh forcefully argues the Akali case during the *gurdwara* reform movement in the daily newspapers *Akali* and *Akali te Pardesi*.
1926	The belief that Punjabi Hindus were a 'dying race' which paved the way for the construction of a modern Hindu identity based on confrontation with the Muslim 'other' is set forth by Swami Shraddhananda in *Hindu Sangathan. The Saviour of a Dying Race*.
1927	Publication of *An Autobiography, or The Story of my Experiments With Truth* by M. K. Gandhi who brings the new credo of non-violence to the nationalist struggle.
1928	The monthly journal the *Pukhtun* is launched by Abdul Ghaffar Khan to articulate the philosophy of Pukhtun nationalism.
1933	The name Pakistan is coined in Rahmat Ali's work written while studying at Cambridge, *Now or Never. Are We to Perish or Live for Ever?*
1934	Muhammad Iqbal's important modernist work *The Reconstruction of Religious Thought in Islam* is published.
1936	Publication of *An Autobiography* by Jawaharlal Nehru.
1939	A major RSS tract is published by its president, Madhav Sadashiv Golwalkar, entitled *We, or Our Nationhood Defined*.
1942	The Jamaat-i-Islami founder Syed Abul Ala Maudoodi publishes *Tehreek-e-Azadi-e-Hind aur Musalman* in which he opposes the secular nationalism of the Muslim League.
1944	The emergence of Pakistan as an ideological state argued by K. Durrani in *The Meaning of Pakistan*.
1946	Nehru's influential work *The Discovery of India* written while he was in prison is reprinted; publication by Swarup Singh of *The Sikhs Demand their Homeland*.

1952	Hasan Hafizur Rahman publishes *Ekushe February* to commemorate the student martyrs of the Bengali language movement.
1961	Volume 1 appears in the official nationalist history of the Indian freedom movement edited by R. C. Majumdar.
1962–3	Official nationalist interpretation of Pakistan's emergence reflected in such works as: I. H. Qureshi, *The Muslim Community of the Indo-Pakistan Subcontinent* and H. Malik, *Moslem Nationalism in India and Pakistan*.
1966	Sheikh Mujibur Rahman publishes *Six Points: Our Demand for Survival*.
1966	Golwalkar publishes *Bunch of Thoughts*.
1969	Pakhtun nationalist Abdul Ghaffar Khan publishes *My Life and Struggle: Autobiography of Badshah Khan*.
1971	The West Pakistan regime gives its own account of the crisis in the eastern wing in *White Paper on the Crisis of East Pakistan*.
1972	G. M. Syed, the standard-bearer of Sindhi nationalism, publishes *Sindhi Culture*.
1981	Re-examination of the freedom movement and Jinnah's role in the light of Zia's contemporary Islamisation process by K. Hydri in *Millat ka Pasban*; first issue of the monthly *Babbar Khalsa* by the US-based National Council of Khalistan.
1984–5	*Khalistan News*, *Awaz-e-Quam*, *Wangar*, and *Sikh Pariwar* begin publication in the UK and *World Sikh News* and *The Sword* in North America in the post-1984 diaspora support for a Sikh homeland.
1987	VHP publishes extensive attacks on secularism and in support of the liberation of the Ramjanmabhoomi.
1988	M. Verma argues for Hindu self-assertion and polemically attacks secularism in widely circulated article *Angry Hindu! Yes, Why Not?*
1990	G. M. Syed publishes *Sindhu Desh: A Study of its Separate Identity through the Ages*.

Bibliography

Agarwal, P. (1995), 'Sarvakar, Surat and Draupadi: Legitimising Rape as a Political Weapon', in T. Sarkar and U. Butalia (eds), *Women and the Hindu Right. A Collection of Essays* (New Delhi), pp. 29–58.

Agnes, F. (1996), 'Behrampada: The Busti that did not Yield', in J. McGuire, P. Reeves and H. Brasted (eds), *Politics of Violence. From Ayodhya to Behrampada* (New Delhi), pp. 49–71.

Ahmad, E. (1998), 'Pakistan: Following India into the Pit', in E. Ahmad et al., *Testing the Limits. The India-Pakistan Nuclear Gambit* (Amsterdam and Washington), pp. 26–34.

Ahmad, I. (ed.) (1973), *Caste and Social Stratification Among Muslims* (Delhi).

Ahmad, M. S. (1988), *The All-India Muslim League: From the Late Nineteenth Century to 1919* (Bahawalpur).

Ahmed, A. S. (1989), 'Identity and Ideology in Pakistan: An Interview', *Third World Quarterly* (October), pp. 54–69.

Ahmed, A. S. (1992), 'Bombay Films: The Cinema as Metaphor for Indian Society and Politics', *Modern Asian Studies* 26, 2 (May), pp. 289–320.

Ahmed, A. S. (1997), *Jinnah, Pakistan and Islamic Identity. The Search for Saladin* (London).

Ahmed, Imtiaz (1984), 'Political Economy of Communalism in Contemporary India', *Economic and Political Weekly* 19, 24, pp. 903–6.

Ahmed, Ishtiaq (1996), *State, Nation and Ethnicity in Contemporary South Asia* (London).

Ahsan, A. (1996), *The Indus Saga and the Making of Pakistan* (Karachi).

Aiyar, S. (1995), '"August Anarchy": The Partition Massacres in Punjab, 1947', *South Asia* 18, special issue, pp. 13–36.

Alam, M. (1986), *The Crisis of Empire in Mughal North India: Awadh and the Punjab 1707–1748* (Delhi).

Ali, Chaudhri Muhammad (1967), *The Emergence of Pakistan* (New York).

Ali, I. (1996), 'Sikh Settlers in the Western Punjab During British Rule', in P. Singh and S. S. Thandi (eds), *Globalisation and the Region. Explorations in Punjabi Identity* (Coventry), pp. 139–53.

Ali, S. Mahmud (1993), *The Fearful State; Power, People and Internal Wars in South Asia* (London).

Amnesty International (1989), *India: Some Recent Reports of Disappearances* (London).

Amnesty International (1991), *India: Human Rights Violations in Punjab: Use and Abuse of the Law* (London).

Amnesty International (1992), *India: Torture, Rape and Deaths in Custody* (London).

Amnesty International (1993), *India: An Unnatural Fate: Disappearance and Impunity in the Indian States of Jammu and Kashmir and Punjab* (London).

Anderson, B. (1983), *Imagined Communities. Reflections on the Origin and Spread of Nationalism* (London).

Ansari, S. (1992), *The Sufis of Sind* (Cambridge).

Appadurai, A. (1993), 'Number in Colonial Imagination', in C. Breckenridge and P. van der Veer (eds), pp. 314–39.

Austin, D. (1994), *Democracy and Violence in India and Sri Lanka* (London).

Austin, G. (1966), *The Indian Constitution* (Oxford).

Aziz, K. K. (1993), *The Pakistani Historian. Pride and Prejudice in the Writing of History* (Lahore).

Bakshi, B. (1984). 'Changing Dimensions of Communalism', *Economic and Political Weekly* 19, nos 51 and 52.

Ballard, R. (1983), 'The Context and Consequences of Migration: Jullundur and Mirpur Compared', *New Community* 11, 1/2 (Autumn/Winter), pp. 117–36.

Bandyopadhyaya, J. (1976), 'Nehru and Non-Alignment', in B. R. Nanda (ed.), pp. 170–84.

Banerjee, S. (1995), 'Hindu Nationalism and Construction of Woman: The Shiv Sena Organises Women in Bombay', in T. Sarkar and U. Butalia (eds), *Women and the Hindu Right. A Collection of Essays* (New Delhi), pp. 216–33.

Barrier, G. N. (1999), 'Controversy Among Sikhs in North America: The Implications of Conflicting Views of Tradition and Power for Scholarly Discourse' (unpublished paper given to the International Conference on Sikh and Punjab Studies, Coventry University, 1–2 May).

Baruah, S. (1994), '"Ethnic" Conflict as State–Society Struggle: The Poetics and Politics of Assamese Micro-Nationalism', *Modern Asian Studies* 28, 3, pp. 649–71.

Baruah, S. (1997), 'Politics of Subnationalism: Society versus State in Assam', in P. Chatterjee (ed.), pp. 496–521.

Basu, A. (1984), 'Gujarati Women's Response to Gandhi 1920–1942', *Samya Shakti* 1, 2, pp. 6–16.

Basu, A. (1993), 'Feminism Inverted: The Real Women and Gendered Imagery of Hindu Nationalism', *Bulletin of Concerned Asian Scholars* 25, 4, pp. 24–37.

Baumann, G. (1990), 'The Re-Invention of Bhangra: Social Change and Aesthetic Shifts in Punjabi Music in Britain', *The World of Music: Journal of the International Institute for Comparative Music Studies and Documentation* 32, pp. 81–97.

Bayly, C. A. (1985), 'The Pre-History of "Communalism"? Religious Conflict in India 1700–1860', *Modern Asian Studies* 19, 1, pp. 177–203.

Bayly, C. A. (1993), 'Knowing the Country: Empire and Information in India', *Modern Asian Studies* 27, 1, pp. 3–43.

Bazaz, P. N. (1978), *Democracy Through Intimidation and Terror* (New Delhi).

Beals, A. R. (1980), *Gopalpur. A South Indian Village* (n.p.).

Besant, A. (1915), *How India Wrought for Freedom: The Story of the National Congress Told from Official Records* (Adyar).

Beteille, A. (1997), 'Caste and Political Group Formation in Tamilnad', in S. Kaviraj (ed.), pp. 71–94.

Bose, S. K. (1974), *Surendranath Banerjea* (New Delhi).

Brass, P. (1974), *Language, Religion and Politics in North India* (Cambridge).

Brass, P. (1979), 'Elite Groups, Symbol Manipulation, and Ethnic Identity Among the Muslims of South Asia', in D. Taylor and M. Yapp (eds), *Political Identity in South Asia* (London), pp. 35–77.

Brass, P. (1984), 'National Power and Local Politics in India: A Twenty-Year Perspective', *Modern Asian Studies* 18, 1, pp. 89–118.

Brass, P. (1991), *Ethnicity and Nationalism: Theory and Comparison* (New Delhi).

Brass, P. and Franda, M. (eds) (1973), *Radical Politics in South Asia* (Cambridge, Mass.).

Breckenridge, C. and van der Veer, P. (eds) (1993), *Orientalism and the Postcolonial Predicament. Perspectives On South Asia* (Philadelphia).

Broomfield, J. (1968), *Elite Conflict in a Plural Society* (Berkeley).

Brosius, C. (1999), 'Is This the Real Thing? Packaging Cultural Nationalism', in C. Brosius and M. Butcher (eds), pp. 99–139.

Brosius, C. and Butcher, M. (1999), *Image Journeys. Audio-Visual Media and Cultural Change in India* (New Delhi).

Brotel, J.-Z. (1998), 'The BJP in Uttar Pradesh: From Hindutva to Consensual Politics', in T. B. Hansen and C. Jaffrelot (eds), *The BJP and the Compulsions of Politics in India* (Delhi), pp. 72–101.

Brown, J. (1989), *Gandhi. Prisoner of Hope* (Yale).

Brown, J. (1995), *Modern India. The Origins of an Asian Democracy*, 2nd edn (Oxford).

Brown, J. (1999), *Nehru* (London).

Butalia, Urvashi (1995), 'Muslims and Hindus, Men and Women. Communal Stereotypes and the Partition of India', in T. Sarkar and U. Butalia (eds), *Women and the Hindu Right. A Collection of Essays* (New Delhi), pp. 58–82.

Butalia, Urvashi (1998), *The Other Side of Silence. Voices from the Partition of India* (New Delhi).

Butcher, M. (1999), 'Parallel Texts: The Body and Television in India', in C. Brosius and M. Butcher (eds), pp. 165–99.

Cashman, R. I. (1975), *The Myth of the Lokamanya. Tilak and Mass Politics in Maharashtra* (Berkeley).

Census of India Reports (1881, 1911) (Calcutta).

Chakrabarty, D. (1996), 'Modernity and Ethnicity in India', in J. McGuire, P. Reeves and H. Brasted (eds), *Politics of Violence. From Ayodhya to Behrampada* (New Delhi), pp. 207–19.

Chakravarty, S. S. (1993), *National Identity in Indian Popular Cinema 1947–1987* (Austin).

Chandra, Bipin (1971), *Modern India* (New Delhi).

Chandra, Bipin (1989), *India's Struggle for Independence* (New Delhi).

Chatterjee. P. (1986), *Nationalist Thought and the Colonial World. A Derivative Discourse?* (London).

Chatterjee. P. (1989), 'The Nationalist Resolution of the Women's Question' in K. Sangari and S. Vaid (eds), *Recasting Women. Essays in Colonial History* (Delhi).

Chatterjee. P. (1993), *The Nation and Its Fragments. Colonial and Postcolonial Histories* (Princeton).

Chatterjee. P. (ed) (1997), *State and Politics in India* (Delhi).

Chatterji, J. (1994), *Bengal Divided. Hindu Communalism and Partition 1932–47* (Cambridge).

Chaudhri, S. B. (1965), *Theories of the Indian Mutiny* (Calcutta).

Choudhury, G. W. (1974), *The Last Days of a United Pakistan* (London).

Chowdhury, I. (1998), *The Frail Hero and Virile History. Gender and the Politics of Culture in Colonial Punjab* (Delhi).

Cohen, R. (1997), *Global Diasporas. An Introduction* (London).

Cohen, S. P. (1984), *The Pakistan Army* (Berkeley).

Collins, L. and Lapierre, D. (1975), *Freedom at Midnight* (London).

Copland, I. (1997), *The Princes of India in the Endgame of Empire 1917–1947* (Cambridge).

Copley, A. (1997), *Religions in Conflict. Ideology, Cultural Contact and Conversion in Late Colonial India* (Delhi).

Dadabhai, N. (1878), *The Poverty of India* (London).

Dalmia, H. (1996), *The Nationalization of Hindu Traditions. Bharatendu Harischandra and Nineteenth Century Banaras* (New Delhi).

Das, A. N. (1994), *India Invented. A Nation-in-the-Making* (New Delhi).

Das Gupta, C. (1991), *The Painted Face: Studies in India's Popular Cinema* (New Delhi).

Datta, N. (1997), 'Arya Samaj and the Making of Jat Identity', *Studies in History* 13, 1 n.s., pp. 97–119.

Deb, D. C. (1977), *Liquor in a Green Revolution Setting* (Delhi).

Deutsch, K. (1966), *Nationalism and Social Communication: An Enquiry into the Foundations of Nationalism* (Cambridge, Mass.).

Dewey, C. (1991), *The Settlement Literature of the Greater Punjab* (New Delhi).

Dhanagare, D. N. (1986), *Peasant Movements in India 1920–1950* (Delhi).

Dirks, N. B. (1987), *The Hollow Crown. Ethnohistory of an Indian Kingdom* (Cambridge).

Dirks, N. B. (1992), 'Castes of Mind', *Representations* 37 (Winter), pp. 56–78.

Duggal, K. S. (1989), *Ranjit Singh – A Secular Sikh Sovereign* (New Delhi).

Dumont, L. (1972), *Homo Hierarchicus: The Caste System and its Imperatives* (London).

Durrani, K. (1944), *The Meaning of Pakistan* (Lahore).

Dayananda, Swami (1975), *Light of Truth* (trans. C. Bharadwaja) (Sarvadeshik Arya Pratinidhi Sabha).

Embree, A. (1990), *Utopias in Conflict* (Berkeley).

Engineer, A. A. (ed.) (1991), *Communal Riots in Post-Independence India* (London).

Enzensberger, H. M. (1970) 'Constituents of a Theory of the Media', *New Left Review* 64, pp. 13–36.

Epstein, S. (1982), 'District Officers in Decline: The Erosion of British Authority in the Bombay Countryside 1919–1947', *Modern Asian Studies* 16, 3, pp. 493–518.

Fabietti, U. (1996), 'Equality versus Hierarchy: Conceptualising Change in Southern Balochistan', in P. Titus (ed.) *Marginality and Modernity. Ethnicity and Change in Post-Colonial Balochistan* (Karachi), pp. 3–28.

Farmer, V. L. (1996), 'Mass Media: Images, Mobilization and Communalism', in D. Ludden (ed.) pp. 98–115.

Forbes, G. (1996), *Women in Modern India* (Cambridge).

Fox, R. (1985), *Lions of the Punjab: Culture in the Making* (Berkeley).

Franda, M. F. (1971), *Radical Politics in West Bengal* (Cambridge).

Freitag, S. (1980), 'Sacred Symbol as Mobilizing Ideology: The North Indian Search for a "Hindu" Community', *Comparative Studies in Society and History* 22, pp. 597–625.

Freitag, S. (1989), *Collective Action and Community. Public Arenas and the Emergence of Communalism in North India* (Berkeley).

Gallagher, J., Johnson, G. and Seal, A. (eds) (1973), *Locality, Province and Nation. Essays on Indian Politics 1870–1940* (Cambridge).

Gandhi, M. K. (1957), *Selections from Gandhi* (ed. N. K. Bose), (Ahmedabad).

Ganguly, S. (1996), 'Explaining the Kashmir Insurgency: Political Mobilization and Institutional Decay', *International Security* 21, 2 (Fall), pp. 76–108.

Ganguly, S. (1997), *The Crisis in Kashmir. Portents of War. Hopes of Peace* (Cambridge).

Gazdar, M. (1997), *Pakistan Cinema. 1947–1997* (Karachi).

Geetha, V. and Jayanthi, T. V. (1995), 'Women, Hindutva and the Politics of Caste in Tamil Nadu', in T. Sarkar and U. Butalia (eds), *Women and the Hindu Right. A Collection of Essays* (New Delhi), pp. 245–70.

Ghosh, G. (1998), '"God is a Refugee". Nationalism, Morality and History in the 1947 Partition of India'. in G. Ghosh (ed.), *Partition, Unification, Nation: Imagined Moral Communities in Modernity*, special issue of *Social Analysis* 42, 1, pp. 33–63.

Giani, B. S. (ed.) (1994), *Planned Attack on the Adi Sri Guru Granth Sahib; Academics or Blasphemy* (Chandigarh).

Gill, K. P. S. (1997), *Punjab. The Knights of Falsehood* (New Delhi).

Gilmartin, D. (1988), *Empire and Islam. Punjab and the Making of Pakistan* (Berkeley).

Golwalkar, M. S. (1939), *We, or Our Nationhood Defined* (Nagpur).

Golwalkar, M. S. (1996), *Bunch of Thoughts* (Bangalore).

Gopalankutty, K. (1983), 'The Integration of Anti-Landlord Movements with the Movement Against Imperialism – The Case of Malabar 1935–39', in B. Chandra (ed.), *The Indian Left. Critical Appraisals* (New Delhi), pp. 201–15.

Gordon, L. A. (1974), *Bengal: The Nationalist Movement. 1876–1940* (New York).

Goulborne, H. (1991), *Ethnicity and Nationalism in Post – Imperial Britain* (Cambridge).

Grant, E. A. (1912), *Census of India 1911* (Introduction Iii), (Calcutta).

Grewal, J. S. (1990) *The Sikhs of the Punjab* (Cambridge).

Grover, R. (1999), 'Ties that Double Bind: The Visibility of the Timber Contractors in Colonial North India', *International Journal of Punjab Studies* 6, 1 (January-June), pp. 33–55.

Grover, V. (ed.) (1992), *Raja Rammohan Roy. Political Thinkers of Modern India* (Delhi).

Grover, V. (ed.) (1993), *Swami Vivekananda. Political Thinkers of Modern India* (Delhi).

Guha, R. (ed.) (1989), *Subaltern Studies*, vol. 6 (Delhi).

Gupta, D. (1982), *Nativism in a Metropolis: The Shiv Sena in Bombay* (New Delhi).

Hall, S. (1991), 'The Local and the Global: Globalization and Ethnicity', in A. D. King (ed.), *Culture, Globalization and the World System: Contemporary Conditions for the Representation of Identity* (London). pp. 19–39.

Hall, S. and Jacques, M. (eds) (1989), *New Times: The Changing Face of Politics in the 1990s* (London).

Hansen, K. (1992), *Grounds for Play. The Nautanki Theatre of North India* (Berkeley).

Hansen, T. B. (1998), 'The Ethics of Hindutva and the Spirit of Capitalism', in T. B. Hansen and C. Jaffrelot (eds), *The BJP and the Compulsions of Politics in India* (New Delhi), pp. 291–315.

Hansen, T. B. (1999), *The Saffron Wave. Democracy and Hindu Nationalism in Modern India* (Princeton, N.J.).

Haq, Mahbub ul (1997), *Human Development in South Asia 1997* (Karachi).

Hardgrave, R. L. (1969), *The Nadars of Tamilnad: The Political Culture of a Community in Change* (Berkeley).

Hardgrave, R. L. (1979), *Essays in the Political Sociology of South India* (New Delhi).

Hardgrave, R. L. (1980), *India. Government and Politics in a Developing Nation* (New York).

Hardy, P. (1972), *The Muslims of British India* (Cambridge).

Harun-or-Rashid (1987), *The Foreshadowing of Bangladesh: Bengal Muslim League and Muslim League Politics, 1936–1947* (Dhakar).

Hasan, M. (ed.) (1981), *Communal and Pan-Islamic Trends in Colonial India* (New Delhi).

Hasan, M. (1996), 'The Myth of Unity: Colonial and National Narratives', in D. Ludden (ed.), pp. 185–206.

Hasan, M. (1997), *Legacy of a Divided Nation. India's Muslims since Independence* (Delhi).

Hasan, Z. (1996), 'Communal Mobilization and Changing Majority in Uttar Pradesh', in D. Ludden (ed.), pp. 81–97.

Hasan-Askari, R. (1988), *The Military and Politics in Pakistan 1947–86* (Delhi).

Hersch, S. (1993), article in *New Yorker*, 29 March.

Heuze, G. (1996), 'Cultural Populism: The Appeal of Shiv Sena', in S. Patel and A. Thorner (eds), pp. 213–48.

Hewitt, V. (1995), *Reclaiming the Past? The Search for Political and Cultural Unity in Contemporary Jammu and Kashmir* (London).

Hill, J. L. (ed.) (1991), *The Congress and Indian Nationalism* (London).

Hobsbawn, E. and Ranger, T. (eds) (1983), *The Invention of Tradition* (Cambridge).

van Hollen, E. (1987), 'Pakistan in 1986. Trials of Transition', *Asian Survey* 27, 2 (February), pp. 143–55.

Hooker, R. (1998), 'The Theme of Partition in Yashpal's Novel *Jhuta Sac* (A False Truth)', *International Journal of Punjab Studies* 5, 1 (Jan–June), pp. 87–99.

Human Rights Watch (1991), *Punjab in Crisis: Human Rights in India* (New York).

Human Rights Watch (1998), *India. India's Secret Army in Kashmir. New Patterns of Abuse Emerge in the Conflict* (New York).

Hutchins, F. G. (1973), *India's Revolution. Gandhi and the Quit India Movement* (Cambridge, Mass.).

Ikram, S. M. (1977), *Modern Muslim India and the Birth of Pakistan (1850–1951)* (Lahore).

Irschick, E. F. (1969), *Politics and Social Conflict in South India. The Non-Brahmin Movement and Tamil Separatism 1916–1929* (Berkeley).

Islam, R. (1976), 'The Religious Factor in the Pakistan Movement', *Proceedings of the First Congress on the History and Culture of Pakistan,* vol. 3 (Islamabad).

Israel, M. (ed.) (1991), *Nehru and the Twentieth Century* (Toronto).

Jaffrelot, C. (1995), 'The Genesis and Development of Hindu Nationalism in the Punjab: from Arya Samaj to Hindu Sabha (1875–1910)' in I. Talbot (ed.), *Indo-British Review* special issue of *Modern Punjab Studies* 21, 1, pp. 3–41.

Jaffrelot, C. (1996), *The Hindu Nationalist Movement and Indian Politics 1925 to the 1990s* (London).

Jaijee, I. S. (1995), *Politics of Genocide* (Chandigarh).

Jalal, A. (1985), *The Sole Spokesman. Jinnah, the Muslim League and the Demand for Pakistan* (Cambridge).

Jalal, A. (1990), *The State of Martial Law. The Origins of Pakistan's Political Economy of Defence* (Cambridge).

Jalal, A. (1991), 'The Convenience of Subservience: Women and the State in Pakistan', in D. Kandiyoti, *Women, Islam and the State* (Basingstoke), pp. 77–115.

Jalal, A. (1995a), 'Conjuring Pakistan: History as Official Imagining', *International Journal of Middle East Studies* 27, pp. 73–89.

Jalal, A. (1995b), *Democracy and Authoritarianism in South Asia. A Comparative and Historical Perspective* (Cambridge).

Jalandhry, S. (1984), *Sant Bhindranwale* (Jalandhar).

Jansson, E. (1981), *India, Pakistan or Pakhtunistan? The Nationalist Movements in the North-West Frontier Province, 1937–47* (Uppsala).

Jayawardena, K. (1995), *The White Woman's Other Burden. Western Women and South Asia During British Rule* (New York and London).

Jeffrey, R. (1986), *What's Happening to India: Punjab Ethnic Conflict, Mrs Gandhi's Death and the Test for Federalism,* 1st edn. (London).

Johnson, G. (1973), *Provincial Politics and Indian Nationalism: Bombay and the Indian National Congress 1880–1915* (Cambridge).

Johnson-Campbell, A. (1951), *Mission with Mountbatten* (London).

Jones, K. W. (1989), *Socio-Religious Reform Movements in British India* (Cambridge).

Kakar, S. (1996), *The Colours of Violence; Cultural Identities, Religion and Conflict* (Chicago).

Kandiyoti, D. (1998), 'Identity and its Discontents: Women and the Nation', *Women Living Under Muslim Laws,* dossier 20 (January) pp.7–24.

Kaur, Harminder (1990), *Bluestar Over Amritsar* (New Delhi).

Kaur, Madanjit (1991), *Co-existence in Pluralistic Society: Punjab Issues and Prospects* (Amritsar).

Kaviraj, S. (1992), 'The Imaginary Institution of India', in P. Chatterjee and G. Pandey (eds), *Subaltern Studies* vol. 7: *Writings on South Asian History and Society* (Delhi) pp. 1–40.

Kaviraj, S. (1995), *The Unhappy Consciousness. Bankimchandra Chattopadhyay and the Formation of Nationalist Discourse in India* (Delhi).

Kaviraj, S. (ed.) (1997), *Politics in India* (Delhi).

Khan, M. A. (1961), *Speeches and Statements*, vol. 1 (Karachi).

Khan, N. et al. (1994), *Locating the Self: Perspectives on Women and Multiple Identities* (Lahore).

Khilani, S. (1997), *The Idea of India* (London).

Kishwar, M. (1985), 'Gandhi on Women', *Economic and Political Weekly*, 5 October, pp. 1691–1702.

Kohli, A. (1997), 'Crisis of Governability', in S. Kaviraj (ed.), pp. 383–97.

Kopf, D. (1969), *British Orientalism and the Bengal Renaissance. The Dynamics of Indian Modernization 1773–1835* (Berkeley).

Kothari, R. (1964), 'The Congress "System" in India', *Asian Survey* 4, pp. 1161–73.

Krishan, Y. (1983), 'Mountbatten and the Partition of India', *History* 68, pp. 22–38.

Krishna, G. (1971), 'The Development of the Indian National Congress as a Mass Organization, 1918–1923' in T. R. Metcalf, *Modern India. An Interpretive Anthology* (London), pp. 257–73.

Krishna, L. R. (1977), *Panjabi Sufi Poets. AD 1460–1940* (Karachi).

Kundu, A. (1998), *Militarism in India. The Army and Civil Society in Consensus* (London).

Lall, K. B. (1976), 'Nehru and International Economic Cooperation', in B. R. Nanda (ed.), pp. 185ff.

Leaf, M. (1985), 'The Punjab Crisis', *Asian Survey* 25, 5, pp. 475–98.

Lelyveld, D. (1978), *Aligarh's First Generation* (Princeton).

Leopold, J. (1970), 'The Aryan Theory of Race', *Indian Economic and Social History Review* 7, pp. 271–97.

Low, D. A. (1991), 'The Forgotten Bania: Merchant Communities and the Indian National Congress', in D. A. Low (ed.), *Eclipse of Empire* (Cambridge), pp. 101–19.

Ludden, D. (1993), 'Orientalist Empiricism: Transformation of Colonial Knowledge', in C. Breckenridge and P. van der Veer (eds), pp. 250–79.

Ludden, D. (ed.) (1996), *Contesting the Nation. Religion, Community and the Politics of Democracy in India* (Philadelphia).

Lutgendorf, P. (1990), 'Ramayan. The Video', *The Drama Review* 4, 2, pp. 127–76.

Mahmood, C. K. (1989), 'Sikh Rebellion and the Hindu Concept of Order', *Asian Survey* 29, 3, pp. 326–40.

Major, A. J. (1995), '"The Chief Sufferers": Abduction of Women During the Partition of the Punjab', special issue of *South Asia* 18, pp. 57–72.

Malhotra, I. (1989), *Indira Gandhi* (London).

Malik, H. (1963), *Moslem Nationalism in India and Pakistan* (Washington).

Malik, H. (1970), 'Sir Sayyid Ahmad Khan's Contribution to the Development of Muslim Nationalism in India', *Modern Asian Studies* 4, 2, pp. 129–47.

Malik, I. H. (1995), 'Ethno-Nationalism in Pakistan: A Commentary on Muhajir Qaumi Mahaz (MQM) in Sindh', *South Asia* 18, 2, pp. 49–72.

Malik, I. H. (1997), *State and Civil Society in Pakistan. Politics of Authority, Ideology and Ethnicity* (London).

Manor, J. (1983), 'Anomie in Indian Politics', *Economic and Political Weekly* 18, 19, pp. 725–34.

Manuel, P. (1993), *Cassette Culture: Popular Music and Technology in North India* (Chicago).

Manuel, P. (1996), 'Music, the Media and Communal Relations in North India, Past and Present', in D. Ludden (ed.), pp. 119–40.

Marenco, E. K. (1974), *The Transformation of Sikh Society* (Portland).

Marqusee, M. (1996), *War Minus the Shooting. A Journey through South Asia during Cricket's World Cup* (London).

Marriott, M. (ed.) (1955), *Village India* (Chicago).

Marwah, O. (1977), 'North-Eastern India: New Delhi Confronts the Insurgents', *Orbis* (summer), pp. 353–73.

Masselos, J. (1996), 'The Bombay Riots of January 1993: The Politics of Urban Conflagration', in J. McGuire, P. Reeves, and H. Brasted (eds), *Politics of Violence. From Ayodhya to Behrampada* (New Delhi), pp. 111–27.

Mathur, K. (1992), 'The State and the Use of Coercive Power in India', *Asian Survey* 32, 4 (April), pp. 337–49.

Mayo, K. (1927), *Mother India* (New York).

McCully, B. T. (1935), 'Origins of Indian Nationalism according to Native Writers', *Journal of Modern History* 7, pp. 295–314.

McGrew, T. (1992), 'A Global Society', in S. Hall, D. Held and T. McGrew (eds), *Modernity and Its Futures* (Cambridge), pp. 61–116.

McLeod, W. H. (1980), *Early Sikh Tradition: A Study of the Janam-sakhis* (Oxford).

McLeod, W. H. (1989), *Who is a Sikh? The Problem of Sikh Identity* (New Delhi).

Mehrotra, S. R. (1971), *The Emergence of the Indian National Congress* (Delhi).

Mendelsohn, O. and Vicziany, M. (1998), *The Untouchables. Subordination, Poverty and the State in Modern India* (Cambridge).

Metcalf, B. D. (1982), *Islamic Revival in British India: Deoband, 1860–1900* (Princeton).

Minault, G. (1982), *The Khilafat Movement. Religious Symbolism and Political Mobilization in India* (New York).

Mishra, S. (1999), 'Dish is Life: Cable Operators and the Neighbourhood', in C. Brosius and M. Butcher (eds), pp. 261–79.

Mitra, S. (1995), 'Rational Politics of Cultural Nationalism: Sub-National Movements in South Asia', *British Journal of Political Science* 25, pp. 57–78.

Moon, P. (1964), *Divide and Quit* (London).

Moore, R. J. (1983) *Escape from Empire: The Attlee Government and the Indian Problem* (Oxford).

Nanda, B. R. (ed.) (1976), *Indian Foreign Policy: The Nehru Years* (New Delhi).

Nanda, B. R. (1977), *Gokhale: The Indian Moderates and the British Raj* (Princeton).

Nandy, A. (1983), *The Intimate Enemy. Loss and Recovery of Self under Colonialism* (Delhi).

Nasr, S. V. R. (1992), 'Democracy and the Crisis of Governability in Pakistan', *Asian Survey* 32, 6 (June), pp. 521–37.

Nehru, J. (1946), *The Discovery of India* (Calcutta).

Niazi, Z. (1997), 'Towards A Free Press', in V. Schofield (ed.), *Old Roads. New Highways. Fifty Years of Pakistan* (Oxford), pp. 174–99.

Noorani, A. G. (1984), 'Civil Liberties: The Terrorist Ordinance', *Economic and Political Weekly* (August) pp. 1188–9.

Oberoi, H. (1994), *The Construction of Religious Boundaries. Culture, Identity and Diversity in the Sikh Tradition* (Chicago).

O'Hanlon, R. (1985), *Caste, Conflict and Ideology: Mahatama Jotirao Phule and Low-Caste Protest in Nineteenth Century Western India* (Cambridge).

O'Hanlon, R. (1993), 'Historical Approaches to Communalism: Perspectives from Western India', in P. Robb (ed.), pp. 247–66.

O'Hanlon, R. and Washbrook, D. (1992), 'After Orientalism: Culture, Criticism and Politics in the Third World', *Comparative Studies in Society and History* 34 (June), pp. 141–67.

Ohm, B. (1999), 'Doordarshan: Representing the Nation's State', in C. Brosius and M. Butcher (eds), pp. 69–99.

Overstreet, G. and Windmiller, M. (1959), *Communism in India* (Berkeley).

Pal, Rajwinder Singh (1995), 'The Forging of the "New" Arya Woman: The Arya Samaj and Female Education in Colonial Jallandhar', in I. Talbot (ed.) *Indo-British Review. A Journal of History*, special issue of *Modern Punjab Studies* 21, 1 (August), pp. 41–59.

Pandey, G. (1989), 'The Colonial Construction of "Communalism": British Writings on Banaras in the Nineteenth Century', in R. Guha (ed.), *Subaltern Studies*, vol. 6 (Delhi).

Pandey, G. (ed.) (1993), *Hindus and Others. The Question of Identity in India Today* (New Delhi).

Pandey, G. (1997), 'Communalism as Construction', in S. Kaviraj (ed.) pp. 305–18.

Pandian, M. S. S. (1997), 'Culture and Subaltern Consciousness: An Aspect of the MGR Phenomenon', in P. Chatterjee (ed.), pp. 367–90.

Patel, S. and Thorner, A. (eds) (1996), *Bombay. Metaphor for Modern India* (Bombay).

Pettigrew, J. (1975), *Robber Noblemen: The Political System of Sikh Jats* (London).

Pettigrew, J. (1991/2), 'Songs of the Sikh Resistance Movement', *Asian Music* 23, 1 (Fall/Winter), pp. 85–118.

Pettigrew, J. (1996), 'The State and Local Groupings in the Sikh Rural Areas, Post–1984', in G. Singh and I. Talbot (eds), *Punjabi Identity: Continuity and Change* (New Delhi), pp. 139–59.

Phadnis, U. (1989), *Ethnicity and Nation-Building in South Asia* (New Delhi).

Philips, C. H. (ed.) (1961), *Historians of India, Pakistan and Ceylon* (London).

Phule, J. G. (1981), *Sarvajanik Satyadhrma Pustak* (Poona).

Potter, D. C. (1973), 'Manpower Shortage and the End of Colonialism: The Case of the Indian Civil Service', *Modern Asian Studies* 7, 1 (January), pp. 47–73.

Prior, K. (1990), 'The British Administration of Hinduism in North India 1780–1900', Ph.D. thesis, Cambridge University.

Punjabi, R. (1992), 'Kashmir: The Bruised Identity', in R. G. C. Thomas (ed.), *Perspectives on Kashmir: The Roots of Conflict in South Asia* (Boulder), pp. 131–52.

Puri, B. (1993), *Kashmir: Towards Insurgency* (New Delhi).

Qureshi, I. H. (1962), *The Muslim Community of the Indo-Pakistan Subcontinent* (The Hague).

Qureshi, I. H. (1965), *The Struggle For Pakistan* (Karachi).

Rahman, S. (1946), *Why Pakistan?* (Calcutta).

Rakisits, C. G. P. (1988), 'Centre–Province Relations in Pakistan under President Zia: The Government's and the Opposition's Approach', *Pacific Affairs* 61, 1 (Spring), pp. 78–97.

Ray, R. K. (1984), *Social Conflict and Political Unrest in Bengal 1875–1927* (Delhi).

Raychaudhri, T (1979), 'Indian Nationalism as Animal Politics', *Historical Journal* 22, 3, pp. 747–63.

Richter, W. L. (1979), 'The Political Dynamics of Islamic Resurgence in Pakistan', *Asian Survey* 19, 6 (June), pp. 547–57.

Rittenburg, S. A. (1977), 'The Independence Movement in India's North-West Frontier Province 1901–1947', Ph.D. thesis, Columbia University.

Rittenberg, S. A. (1988), *Ethnicity, Nationalism and Pakhtuns: The Independence Movement in India's North-West Frontier Province, 1901–1947* (Durham, N.C.).

Robb, P. (ed.) (1993), *Society and Ideology. Essays in South Asian History* (Delhi).

Roberts, A. (1994), *Eminent Churchillians* (London).

Robertson, R. (1992), *Globalization: Social Theory and Global Culture* (London).

Robinson, F. (1975), *Separatism Among Indian Muslims. The Politics of the United Provinces' Muslims 1860–1923* (Delhi).

Robinson, F. (1979), 'Islam and Muslim Separatism', in D. Taylor and M. Yapp, *Political Identity in South Asia* (London), pp. 78–112.

Robinson, M. (1988), 'Religion, Class and Faction. The Politics of Communalism in Twentieth Century Punjab', D.Phil, thesis, Sussex University.

Rocher, R. (1993), 'British Orientalism in the Eighteenth Century: The Dialectics of Knowledge and Government', in C. Breckenridge and P. van der Veer (eds), pp. 215–50.

Rothermund, D. (1993), *An Economic History of India. From Pre-Colonial Times to 1991*, 2nd edn (London).

Roy, M. N. (1971), *India in Transition* (Bombay).

Roy, P. (1998), *Indian Traffic. Identities in Question in Colonial and Postcolonial India* (Berkeley).

Roy, R. K. (1984), *Social Conflict and Political Unrest in Bengal 1875–1927* (Delhi).

Rudolph, S. H. (1971), 'The New Courage. An Essay on Gandhi's Psychology', in T. R. Metcalf (ed.), *Modern India. An Interpretive Anthology* (London), pp. 240–57.

Russell, R. (1992), *The Pursuit of Urdu Literature. A Select History* (London).

Said, E. (1978), *Orientalism* (New York).

Saiyid, D. (1998), *Muslim Women of the British Punjab. From Seclusion to Politics* (Basingstoke).

Samad, Y. (1995), *A Nation in Turmoil. Nationalism and Ethnicity in Pakistan, 1937–1958* (New Delhi).

Sarkar, S. (1973), *The Swadeshi Movement in Bengal 1903–1908* (New Delhi).

Sarkar, S. (1985), *Modern India 1885–1947* (New Delhi).

Sarkar, T. (1992), 'The Hindu Wife and the Hindu Nation: Domesticity and Nationalism in Nineteenth Century Bengal', *Studies in History* 8, 2, n.s., pp. 213–35.

Sarkar, T. (1995), 'Heroic Women, Mother Goddesses: Family and Organisation in Hindutva Politics', in T. Sarkar and U. Butalia (eds), *Women and the Hindu Right. A Collection of Essays* (New Delhi), pp. 181–216.

Sarkar, T. (1996), 'Imagining Hindurastra: The Hindu and the Muslim in Bankim Chandra's Writings', in D. Ludden (ed.), pp. 162–84.

Sassen-Koob, S. (1990), *The Global City* (Princeton).

Sathyamurthy, T. V. (1996), 'Centralised State Power and Decentralised Politics. Case of India', *Economic and Political Weekly* (March 30), pp. 835–43.

Sathyamurthy, T. V. (1997), 'Impact of Centre–State Relations on Indian Politics: An Interpretative Reckoning 1947–1987', in P. Chatterjee (ed.), pp. 232–71.

Sayeed, K. B. (1984), 'Pakistan in 1983: Internal Strains More Serious Than External Problems', *Asian Survey* 24, 2 (February), pp. 219–28.

Schofield, V. (1996), *Kashmir in the Crossfire* (London).

Seal, A. (1968), *The Emergence of Indian Nationalism: Competition and Collaboration in the Late Nineteenth Century* (Cambridge).

Sen, K. M. (1981), *Hinduism* (Harmondsworth).

Seshu, G. (1999), 'Media and Kargil: Information Blitz with Dummy Missiles', *Economic and Political Weekly*, 9 October.

Shaikh, F. (1989), *Community and Consensus in Islam. Muslim Representation in Colonial India, 1860–1947* (Cambridge).

Sharma, D. P. (1996), *The Punjab Story. Decade of Turmoil* (New Delhi).

Sharma, U. M. (1970), 'The Problem of Village Hinduism: "Fragmentation" and Integration', *Contributions to Indian Sociology* 10 (December), pp. 1–22.

Siddharth, V. (1922), 'New Indo-British Extradition Treaty: What is the Purpose?' *Economic and Political Weekly* (21 November), pp. 2531–2.'

Sihra, K. S. (1985), *The Sikh Commonwealth* (London).

Singh, B. L. (1965) *Autobiography*, ed. G. Singh (Calcutta).

Singh, Gopal (1984), 'Socio-Economic Bases of the Punjab Crisis', *Economic and Political Weekly* 19, 1, p. 43.

Singh, Gurharpal (1994), *Communism in Punjab* (Delhi).

Singh, Gurharpal (1996), *Re-examining the Punjab Problem*, in G. Singh and I. Talbot (eds), *Punjabi Identity. Continuity and Change* (New Delhi), pp. 115–39.

Singh, Gurharpal (1997), 'Understanding Political Corruption in Contemporary Indian Politics', in P. Heywood (ed.), *Political Corruption*, special issue of *Political Studies* 45, 3, pp. 626–38.

Singh, P. (1994), *Of Demons and Dreams: An Indian Memoir* (London).

Singh, Tavleen (1995), *Kashmir: A Tragedy of Errors* (New Delhi).

Singh, T. (1994), *Ernest Trumpp and W. H. McLeod as Scholars of Sikh History, Culture and Religion* (Chandigarh).

Sisson, R. and Rose, L. (1990), *War and Secession: Pakistan, India and the Creation of Bangladesh* (Berkeley).

Smith, A. (1997), 'The "Golden Age" and National Renewal', in G. Hosking and G. Schopflin (eds), *Myths and Nationhood* (London), pp. 36–60.

Smith, A. (1998), *Nationalism and Modernism* (London).

Srinivas, M. N. (1952), *Religion and Society Among the Coorgs* (Oxford).

Srinivas, M. N. (1978), *Caste in Modern India* (London).

Stern, R. W. (1993), *Changing India. Bourgeois Revolution on the Subcontinent* (Cambridge).

Stocking, G. W. (ed.) (1991), *Colonial Situations: Essays in the Contextualization of Ethnographic Knowledge* (Madison).

Sufi, G. M. (1946), *Commonsense on Pakistan* (Bombay).

Suntharalingam, R. (1983), *Indian Nationalism. An Historical Analysis* (New Delhi).

Syed, A. H. (1982), *Pakistan, Islam, Politics and National Solidarity* (New York).

Tagore, R. (1917), 'Nationalism in the West', in *Nationalism* (London).

Talbot, I. (1984), 'Mountbatten and the Partition of India: A Rejoinder', *History* 69, pp. 30ff.

Talbot, I. (1988a), *Provincial Politics and the Pakistan Movement. The Growth of the Muslim League in North-West and North-East India 1937–47* (Karachi).

Talbot, I. (1988b), *Punjab and the Raj 1849–1947* (New Delhi).

Talbot, I. (1996a), *Freedom's Cry. The Popular Dimension in the Pakistan Movement and Partition Experience in North-West India* (Karachi).

Talbot, I. (1996b), *Khizr Tiwana, the Punjab Unionist Party and the Partition of India* (London).

Talbot, I. (1999), *Pakistan. A Modern History* (London).

Tatla, D. S. (1999), *The Sikh Diaspora. The Search for Statehood* (London).

Telford, H. (1982), 'The Political Economy of Punjab: Creating Space for Sikh Militancy', *Asian Survey* 32, 11 (November), pp. 969–87.

Thandi, S. (1994), 'Strengthening Capitalist Agriculture: The Impact of Overseas Remittances in Rural Central Punjab in the 1970s', *International Journal of Punjab Studies* 1, 2 (July–December), pp. 239–71.

Thandi, S. (1996), 'Counterinsurgency and Political Violence in Punjab, 1980–94', in G. Singh and I. Talbot (eds), *Punjabi Identity: Continuity and Change* (New Delhi), pp. 159–87.

Thapur, R. (1989), 'Imagined Religious Communities? Ancient History and the Modern Search for a Hindu Identity', *Modern Asian Studies* 23, 2 (May), pp. 209–31.

Tinker, H. (1974), *A New System of Slavery. The Export of Indian Labour Overseas, 1830–1920* (Oxford).

Tiwana, Umar Hayat Khan (1929), *The Man and his Word* (Lahore).

Tomlinson, B. R. (1979), *The Political Economy of the Raj 1914–1947. The Economics of Decolonisation in India* (London).

Tripathi, A. (1967), *The Extremist Challenge* (Bombay).

Tully, M. (1991), *No Full Stops in India* (London).

Tuteja, L. K. (1997), *Hindu Consciousness, Communalism and the Congress in Pre-Partition Punjab*, Presidential Address Section III: Modern Indian History. Indian History Congress, 58th Session, Bangalore, November.

Upadhyaya, P. C. (1992), 'The Politics of Indian Secularism', *Modern Asian Studies* 26, 4, pp. 815–53.

van der Veer, P. (1988), *Gods on Earth: The Management of Religious Experience and Identity in a North India Pilgrimage Centre* (London).

van der Veer, P. (1992), 'Ayodhya and Somnath: Eternal Shrines, Contested Histories', *Social Research* 59, 1 (Spring), pp. 85–109.

Vohra, Ranbir (1997), *The Making of India. A Historical Survey* (New York).

Wagle, N. K. (1991), 'Govindrav Babaji Joshi Goes to Madras: A "Diary" of the Third Indian National Congress' in J. L. Hill (ed.), *The Congress and Indian Nationalism* (London), pp. 114-33.

Wallace, P. (1986), 'The Sikhs as a "Minority" in a Sikh Majority State in India', *Asian Survey* 26, 3 (March), pp. 363–77

Waseem, M. (1994), *The 1993 Elections in Pakistan* (Lahore).

Waseem, M. (1996), 'Ethnic Conflict in Pakistan: The Case of MQM', *The Pakistan Development Review* 35, 4, part II (Winter) pp. 617–29.

Williams, M. (1996), 'Rethinking Sovereignty', in E. Kofman and G. Youngs (eds), *Globalization: Theory and Practice* (London), pp. 109–23.

Wolpert, S.A. (1962), *Tilak and Gokhale* (Berkeley).

Wolpert, S. (1993), *A New History of India*, 4th edition (New York).

Zaheer, H. (1995), *The Separation of East Pakistan. The Rise and Realization of Bengali Nationalism* (Karachi).

Index

Index